Operations Management
Principles and Practice

Anne Tomes and *Mike Hayes*

Prentice Hall
New York   London   Toronto   Sydney   Tokyo   Singapore

First published 1993 by
Prentice Hall International (UK) Ltd
Campus 400, Maylands Avenue
Hemel Hempstead
Hertfordshire, HP2 7EZ
A division of
Simon & Schuster International Group

Typeset in 10 on 12 pt Plantin
by MHL Typesetting Ltd, Coventry

Printed and bound in Great Britain by
Redwood Books, Trowbridge, Wiltshire

Library of Congress Cataloging-in-Publication Data

Tomes, Anne.
   Operations management : principles and practice / by Anne Tomes
and Mike Hayes.
     p.   cm.
   Includes bibliographical references and index.
   ISBN 0-13-639063-3 (pbk.)
   1. Production management. I. Hayes, Mike. II. Title.
   TS155. T56 1993
   658.5—dc20
                               92-28861
                                CIP

British Library Cataloguing in Publication Data

A catalogue record for this book is available
from the British Library

ISBN 0 13 639063 3 (pbk)

2 3 4 5 97 96 95 94 93

Contents

3 Machines — the process and the cost · 39

4 People — motivation and organization · 60

7 The quality revolution   132

8 Forecasting — from predictions to plans   164

Preface

This book has been written for people new to the subject of operations management. We start by involving the reader in observation, investigation and experiment, to build up a solid foundation of knowledge closely associated with the driving objectives of the operations manager. Gradually, we introduce the reader to techniques which can handle the situations observed in practice. Finally, we give guidance on how all these techniques can be co-ordinated and orchestrated to achieve an organization's grand strategy. In general, our approach is to enable the reader to overcome the many mental blocks thrown up by a subject which is challenging and calls for a wide range of skills.

The changing syllabus and techniques of operations management

Operations management (OM) is a young subject with a continually changing agenda. Some topics which previously appeared to provide a backbone to the subject are now rarely used in business, even if they live on in textbooks. Contrarily, a fashionable technique may be oversold by consultants, taken up too eagerly by practitioners, and dwindle into insignificance all in the course of three or four years. Understandably, with such a rapidly evolving subject matter there are fierce disputes between advocates of rival systems. We think it right that the reader should be exposed to the major controversies. For this reason, we have taken a very challenging approach. However, though challenging, we have tried to maintain a positive rather than a critical approach.

We are all in favour of a problem being tackled by parallel methods even if some of these methods overrule our personal preference.

Problem solving

In operations management, there is no escape from complexity, imperfect information and mess-management. From the moment they enter business, new employees have to juggle with many products, customers, materials, routes, processes and time periods. In our experience, it is not much help to them if they have spent too much of their time being educated in very simple, artificial exercises. They want to be able to cope with complexity quickly and this is what our book provides. In our exercises, we suggest simple ways in which large messy problems can be untangled, understood and laid out. Then we recommend quick and dirty heuristic techniques for finding any answer. We find that if people start their learning in this way, it stimulates their confidence and maintains their interest: practice with these rough-and-ready techniques arouses their curiosity and provides an excellent foundation for anyone who, at a later stage, needs to know more about optimization.

Technology transfer and the scope of OM

Our examples and exercises cover a broad range of applications: manufacturing, retail, transport, leisure, services, military, non-profits and administration. These functions, though diverse, share similar problems: for example, in how the staff communicate with each other, in how they cope with an uncertain future, or in how they provide a quality service. Our approach to OM emphasizes the transferability of management technology not only across organizations but across cultures and nations as well.

References

This book encourages people to learn by first-hand experience. However, this experience needs to be compared, revised or reinforced by reading about other people's observations. There is a rich source of such material in case-books and case studies on operations management. We have made a careful selection from these sources, choosing and ordering certain case studies so that people can progress from easy to more difficult problems.

Acknowledgements

We need to thank everyone who has helped to accumulate our databank of material; we cannot thank each person individually as they number several hundred. Throughout the book we have relied heavily on local businesspeople who have given access to their organizations. Not all of them wish to be identified, but we thank them nonetheless. Also, due to the efforts of our students we were able to gather a varied and high-quality picture of operations management: this was much more extensive than anything that we could have assembled by ourselves.

We would like to acknowledge some particular people whose work we have heavily relied upon. From business: Austin-Rover, Deltacam, Ian Turner of Chatsworth Estates, Andy Tapley of Rotary Electric, A. Grant and D. Whittles from the NHS, S. Hellewell of SYT, P. Wilson of Pine Furniture, Lesley Davis and Mike Hancock of British Coal, Bryan Upton of Westall Richardson, Chris Whitehead of Mowlem, Hamish Hamilton of Buffalo Mountain Equipment, Akimasa Kurimoto of Yamazaki, the Institute of Logistics and Distribution Management, and Mike Pupius of the GPO. We would also like to thank those students who have allowed us to quote extensively from their reports: Ailsa Falconer, Catherine Vickers, Beverley Ashworth, Nicola

Claydon, Simon Fanshawe, Julie Grandison, Paul Rawding, Jamie Bewick, David Foster, Steve Matthews, Paul Fraser, David Boorman, Helen Russell, Helen Hidle and Muhtar Hassan.

We would also like to acknowledge the intellectual contribution of one or two of our ex-students of whom we have lost track. If Ron Skuse, Neil Hynd or John M. Brown read this, we would be delighted to hear from you. Although you took your masters degrees at Sheffield many years ago, each of you had important ideas that are still relevant today and are reflected in different chapters of this book. Indeed, we would like to hear from any of our ex-students who have contributed to our understanding of operations management and have an abiding interest in the subject.

The typing and word processing of this book has fallen entirely on the shoulders of Sharon Rose. Sharon is, in fact, very close to being a joint author as we have relied on her judgement and grammatical knowledge in sorting out messy first drafts and advising us on how to present our material in an intelligible manner.

Lastly, we would like to thank members of our respective families for their forbearance whilst we have beavered away at this work. Our elder children were all at a critical stage in their scholastic careers whilst we were writing this book. They were models of tolerance and understanding when they had every reason for believing that they were the ones under the greatest academic pressure. One of the authors has two small daughters who thought the whole subject was boring, but that is understandable. We were also fortunate in having spouses who have a national reputation in their different professions and who are well versed in management skills. Their advice has helped us to sharpen up our communication skills and to keep the subject matter relevant.

Chapter 1

The operations manager

Operations management (OM) is a relatively new business discipline. It was not until the 1980s that it became a common subject on business school syllabuses. OM grew because it was realized that many, very different organizations were experiencing similar business problems; these organizations spanned manufacturing, retail, transport, leisure, services, the military, non-profit making organizations and administrative sectors. OM is a good example of exploiting the transfer of management technology. For example:

- If you mastered the art of supplying soldiers with ammunition, your skills could also be used to supply supermarkets with fresh vegetables.
- If you could timetable all the actors and support staff needed for a TV film, you would have a good understanding of the problems involved in planning schedules in magistrates' courts.

There are many examples which we will give, throughout the book, where a skill, thought to be unique to one profession or application, is in fact transferable to a completely different situation. In each situation, however, there will be a different and significant human element. Thus, although the principles and basic skills are transferable, one cannot ignore this vital human element and we must modify our approach to each situation.

This modification of the basic approach is of particular relevance when we consider the transfer of business skills across countries and cultures. A major concern of operations managers, and this book, is how successfully Japanese business techniques can be modified and transferred to Western cultures. This issue crops up at many points and by the end of the book we will have covered several insights into this problem. Thus, although there is a commonality in the problems faced by diverse business organizations, and basic skills which can be transferred from one to another, we recognize that excellence in OM is not just a matter of focusing on just one glamour country such as Japan or just one glamour industry such as telecommunications and simplistically copying the techniques used to achieve success in those particular situations.

Effective operations managers draw from the experience of many countries, organizations and professions, modifying the approaches and techniques used to reach a tailor-made solution for their own situation. Throughout the book, therefore, we use case studies to illustrate a wide range of OM situations and this first chapter is no exception. To give a feel for the scope of operations management we introduce the book with interviews we conducted with successful operations managers from five diverse organizations. The accompanying exercises point the way to themes which we deal with in detail in subsequent chapters.

1.1 Case study 1 — the farm

1.1.1 *Background situation to the farm*

Our farm is part of a large country estate in the north of England. As well as the farm, the estate consists of a stately home, its gardens and woodlands. The whole area is a popular tourist attraction with a policy of easy public access long before the National Parks came into being.

The farm covers 5200 acres. Like most farms, its area has changed over the years. Forty years ago some of the land had to be sold off to meet death duties. In the 1960s it expanded as it took over some small farms which were finding the going tough. Consequently (and again like many farms) buildings and access roads are not always ideally situated; nor do we manage a compact area — the dairy unit is an isolated patch of rich pastureland cut off from the rest of the estate.

The farm itself is entirely devoted to livestock (i.e. no arable crops are grown). The types of animal kept are tailored to the nature of the terrain which varies from high, exposed moorland, much of it above one thousand feet, to parkland designed by Capability Brown in a wide, sheltered river valley. The nature of the farm's animal stock is also affected by the other operating units on the estate: many of the animals have to be able to co-exist with members of the public; or the animals must not interfere with the work of gamekeepers or forestry (and vice versa).

This thumb-nail picture of our farm suggests that we are subject to certain special constraints. Most noticeably, we are an area of outstanding beauty, attracting tourists from all over the world. More than other farms, our operations must preserve the beauty of the landscape; but, just like other farms, we have to show that we are a commercially viable unit. Moreover, just like other farms, we are greatly affected by government and EC agricultural policy.

In Europe, there is over-capacity in the dairy industry and the EC introduced regulations to cut back milk output. It was difficult to devise a fair way of securing this cutback. Some farms, just building up their herds, were faced with making drastic reductions. We had an established herd, and our quota, as calculated by the EC didn't come out too badly. All our output goes to the Milk Marketing Board. You don't have to sell milk via this channel, but if you do sell direct to the public you need to set up your own bottling plant and distribution network. We wouldn't do that. It isn't worth the bother. We have taken up another use for milk — turning it into cream and yoghourt and selling it in our farm shop.

Apart from environmental, commercial and government constraints, we also work within a few extra self-imposed constraints. Partly, these arise from the different interests and organizations that make up our estate: we move our stock out of the way for horse trials or the RAC rally, and we also restrict our farming activities for private hunting, shooting and fishing parties organized by the estate's owner. Also, being in the public eye, and with beautiful landscape to maintain, there is an instinctive motivation for all of us at the farm to go for quality, both in what the public sees of our animals, land and buildings, and in how we tackle jobs. This is helped because we, as managers, have a lifetime commitment to our workers, and vice versa. We couldn't have generated this commitment if we had operated a hire-and-fire policy via casual labour. Before taking on a new full-time person we have often had contacts with them for quite a time previously; and when they join us, it is for life, with a free house and a non-contributory pension scheme, among other fringe benefits.

1.1.2 *Planning and decision-making at the farm*

I have mentioned how we are an entirely livestock farm partly because of the soil and climate, but also for historic, landscaping and social reasons. With livestock you have to make strategic decisions about which particular animals are most suitable for you. Then you have to make secondary decisions, about which are the most suitable breed for any animal type, how many you are going to have, and what type of replacement cycle you are going to stick to. From this information you can work out roughly the services, fodder and grassland necessary to support them.

In our case, the major strategic decision (after taking account of the EC milk quota) is influenced by matching animals to our terrain. Sheep for moorland; deer, sheep and beef cattle on the parkland; dairy cows and bulls on rich pastureland separated from the rest of the estate. The exact tally is:

        180 milking cows
        120 'followers' (younger cows which will mature into milk-cows)
         16 pedigree bulls
        230 beef cattle
       4500 breeding ewes (of a tough Swaledale variety for those out on the moorland)
        370 red and fallow deer

We need to have farm staff both for duties directly involved with the animals (milking, sheep-dipping) and for support services such as foddering and silaging. In our case, we employ the following full-time workers:

        2 herdsmen — they have the dairy herd under their close care and know every
          milk cow individually
        3 shepherds
        4 workers who carry out a variety of general farm duties. There is also myself (the

farm manager), my assistant manager and the secretary, who also muck in with any work at busy times.

By its nature, all farming involves a lot of peaks and troughs of work over the seasons. We partly overcome this by working from dawn to dusk at busy times (such as hay-making) and taking our holidays at slack times (such as the winter); but that is not the entire answer. We will also employ some part-timers, but these are usually students or locals whom we know well. We also use subcontractors for special jobs, where it is not worth our while getting expensive machinery that would only be used for a few days a year — hedging and lime-spreading are examples.

I like to have a 'keep it simple' approach to planning. For example, seven of our workers each have their own tractor which is replaced once every seven years. This is seen as fair, and the worker will also look after the tractor as if it were his own car. Notice, we couldn't have this quality attitude if we allocated tractors randomly or if we hired and fired frequently.

I like to have a similar rotational system of replacement and renewal for buildings and other items of machinery, not just for reasons of efficiency but to stimulate motivation, team-work, and good housekeeping.

Although I was brought up in a town, I love my job and wouldn't change it for any other. Having said that, I am not blind to all the other happenings in the world. Like most other industries, we have to watch out for foreign competition, over-capacity, new technology and government interference. Consumer tastes change too: I've noticed the greater popularity of our venison as people look for leaner meat. Really, although we pay our way from our livestock sales, I see other farms like ourselves branching out into all sorts of other activities. We led the way with a very successful farm shop, but this could be extended to another retail outlet like a garden centre, or other leisure uses for the farm such as clay-pigeon shoots, BMX or golf courses. On the whole, though, I'm happy to run a business to which people from all over the world are happy to come and admire.

▼   **Exercise**

(a) What are the threats which could decimate one of the farm's main lines of business and force them to diversify?

(b) We list below ten new business activities which some people thought this particular farm might like to consider. Some of these suggestions are plain crazy, others open up genuine opportunities. Choose the two best activities which you think the farm should consider seriously. Choose also the two worst, which you think the farm should dismiss out of hand. Compare your choices with those of other people tackling this exercise and be prepared to justify your position. From the facts you are given about this particular farm, have you any very different suggestions that you think they should explore?

▷

    (i)   Centre to cater for all types of shooting
   (ii)   Caravan park
  (iii)   Giant adventure themepark
  (iv)   Intensive deer farming
   (v)   Intensive horticulture with greenhouses/market garden
  (vi)   Golf centre, courses, driving range and retail outlet
 (vii)   Mountain biking/trail biking centre
(viii)   Tree nursery to supply exotic shrubs and seedlings to garden centres
  (ix)   Wildlife park and zoo
▲   (x)   Cemetery and crematorium

1.2 Case study 2 — engineering firm

I am the managing director and principal shareholder of a small Sheffield engineering company (twenty-seven workers). Traditionally, we produce aluminium gravity diecast valves for the shotblast market. We also manufacture rollers of all types — from large ones that you see in steel rolling mills to the much smaller ones found in, for example, photocopying machines. However, we are not set up to make things via a production line. Rather, we are part of a network of Sheffield companies that provide an engineering service; and there will be an ebb and flow of business subcontracted between these companies depending on who has too much or too little work. For rollers, we make batches of 50−1000, but much of the remaining batches will be smaller than that — typically under 10 items.

Competition for business is very intense at the moment. Everyone offers to deliver pronto. More and more companies have followed us in getting BS5750 accreditation [a recognized quality standard: see Chapter 7]. As for competition on the prices quoted, there is a recognized industry formula for deriving prices from labour, materials, machinery, etc. inputs. If you go above or below what the formula suggests by too much, a customer would be suspicious. Apart from delivery, quality and price, how else can we win business? In our case, we have built up a reputation with our customers for reliability, honesty, and providing a complete service through to the product being delivered, installed and tested. In order to emphasize these customer-service elements, a lot of my time is spent on customer contact. A final way in which we can gain a competitive advantage arises from changing foreign exchange rates. In general, there has been a long-term trend for the Deutschmark to rise in value, compared with the pound. This means we can offer very competitive prices for replacement parts going to steel mills that were originally put down by German companies. For example, there are German-built rolling mills in a number of countries where it is possible to win substantial business.

Really, this highlighted a critical decision I had to take as general manager when devising a long-term marketing strategy. Should I focus my energies on strengthening

Figure 1.1   Replacement parts for a rolling mill — wear strips and plates.

sales through the local network of subcontractors, or should I go for the tougher option? Go for the export market, with higher potential returns but with higher initial costs greater risks and complications? I went for the export market and it worked, but, among other reasons, only because I could trust my staff to run the business during my long absences abroad — that is the advantage of having a family firm with a family atmosphere. I've been careful to cultivate this aspect for several reasons. I've built up a core of long serving skilled workers by offering them stability of employment — but this means refusing some business if I think it is a surge that will not be maintained. I'd rather do this than operate a hire-and-fire policy. For some of my workers, there are temptations to move to local competitors offering more overtime at higher rates, but I don't like setting up an employment system that cannot or shouldn't last in the long run. This means that the workers I have kept are stable, loyal and with a pride in their job. Often we produce too good a job in terms of finish and specification. But I'm happy to go over the top on quality as it keeps both our customers and workers happy.

So far as shopfloor organization is concerned, we've got a 'keep it simple' approach — no fancy computer control systems. We use route cards to follow our work through the shop (as we have to for BS5750). We refer to the route cards both to help with stock-control decisions, and to work out manufacturing times when tendering for new jobs. We have weekly meetings to determine production flow — what and how much we'll make, when we'll make it, and when it will be ready for the customer. For getting raw materials we have a call-off schedule for heavily used standard items — that is we place orders four times a year but get goods delivered on a monthly basis. A call-off schedule involves making advanced commitments but enables us to get a better deal. For other materials we make ad hoc decisions at monthly production meetings.

Our manufacturing system has to be tailored to the special nature of our major products. Even a 'standard' product like a steel roller in fact has a myriad of variations. For that reason it is unwise to 'make for stock' and hope for a sale later. We prefer for an order to be confirmed before going ahead with a definite production plan. We might buy some basic raw material in anticipation of business, but we won't process it until a definite customer has been lined up for it.

Because we have organized ourselves in this way we are not really set up for long, regular runs of a standard product. If we were to go down this path we would be employing advanced, specialized CNC machines and an assembly-line type labour force involved in more repetitive tasks. I don't want to run that sort of operation, and have to accept that I can't compete with firms set up to make standard products. Strangely enough, this means having to be very cautious when some parts of our business become too successful. Look at our experience of supplying replacement photocopier rollers. When photocopiers were a new product we did very well out of supplying spare parts and were ahead of the competition in doing so. But I was always looking over my shoulder knowing that one day, someone, probably in the Far East would set up a vast factory specifically to make replacement rollers and nothing else. That has now happened — a large Taiwanese competitor has undercut us and we have had to move out of that business.

It was for the same reason that I moved out of other areas where we were doing (temporarily) very well; this was equipment for sampling and testing molten steel. In the older days when steel was melted in open-hearth furnaces, the testing process was very slow: a small ladle would draw off some molten steel which was rushed off to a laboratory but results weren't available for thirty or forty minutes. You can't have this sort of delay with electric arc furnaces where melt-to-melt times are one hour, so a new, cheap, disposable sampling device was developed in the US which did the job in one-and-a-half minutes. It drew out a thin lollipop of steel which cooled immediately and could be tested quickly. This had great advantages for the furnace operators, and we developed a non-flare coating to stop the violent 'spitting' of molten steel as the tester was inserted into the ladles. We started manufacturing and selling the revised design. The major sales for the device were for temperature measurement, where more samples are taken per melt. We therefore sold out to a large temperature-sensing-devices company because I felt they had the resources to set out a proper manufacturing system for this type of product.

We do a lot of business with Saudi Arabia and companies in other parts of the world. We used to pay insurance via the ECGD scheme so that we would be covered if our customers didn't pay us. But we stopped paying insurance because it cost 4 per cent — and in Saudi Arabia's case, they had always been reliable. Then the Gulf War blew up. Our customer's rolling mill was right next to the Kuwait border. Naturally he had more important things to deal with and our payments got delayed. In addition, if the Iraqis had bombed or taken over the steel mills we would never have got our money back. In the end, everything was all right, but you can be sure that we now pay our ECGD insurance for all our export orders.

In general, business is all about risks — evaluating risks, taking some risks and avoiding risks. So far, we have avoided committing ourselves to a venture where we are stuck in a corner with no escape if things go wrong. Like most companies in this field, we start from a solid technological basis. With our equipment, workers, experience, and the Sheffield environment we provide a high-quality engineering service. But in these difficult times these factors are not sufficient in themselves to succeed or even to survive.

▼   **Exercise**

Here are some factors which may or may not have played a part in ensuring the engineering firm's survival. Rank them in order of importance and give reasons for your ranking.

1. Avoiding overtime working
2. Freedom from dominance of a big customer
3. The manager acts as his own salesman
4. Insight to appraise changing markets
5. It is a family business
6. Prudent attitude to the cash flow situation
7. Ability to innovate
8. Not locked into an inflexible production line
9. Luck
▲ 10. Anticipation of exchange rate movements

1.3 Case study 3 — department store

My job is to ensure that the several million pounds of merchandise in the shop at any one time moves through as fast as possible. In other words, we are interested in increasing turnover. But we do this always bearing in mind the philosophy behind our business. We have a trading policy which we always adhere to. First of all, we must offer excellent value, a high level of service and a wide assortment of merchandise, and we always trade with absolute honesty. For example, we don't use small-print disclaimers found on some sale goods in some stores. I think you can see that such a trading policy means that we have to be internally very efficient. The company collects a lot of statistics, and we spend quite a lot of time examining our own navels.

There is competition between the branches and each week the percentage change in sales of each is published, not just within the company, because outsiders can easily get this information as well by subscribing to our journal. So you're really kept on your toes. If you're not performing, someone wants to know why. We break down this accountability to department level. Each department manager is reviewed on the progress of his or her department during the previous year. If one department is doing badly compared with a similar department in a different city, I need to know why. There are sometimes good reasons. For example, a boyswear department is going to do better in a city with a younger population, where the education authority requires school uniform to be the standard, than in one with an older population where the schoolwear is, shall we say, less formal. I take such things into account.

The policy of a high level of customer service extends across the board. If a customer writes a letter of complaint to me personally, then I answer personally. Incidentally, during the past year we received 138 complaints compared with 86 complimentary letters. I suppose with some 6 million customers a year that's not bad, but I would like us to do better. Having said that, I do occasionally have to take decisions in the interests of economics, which will upset a few customers. For example, I had to close the waitress-service restaurant recently. The tables were almost empty, whereas the self-service café was bulging at the seams and unacceptable queues were building up. So, to satisfy the silent majority, I have had to upset a very small minority. In fact, I have had eleven letters of complaint, the most I've ever had on one subject. But the decision had to be made. On the other hand, the number of customers served increased by five hundred in the first week. So we hope we have another five hundred happy customers to balance those who were upset.

The essence of retailing is speed. For example, our central warehouse makes deliveries to us every day and on Friday afternoons. If we don't get that stock into the shop for Saturday morning, our biggest selling day, we risk running out of stock on fast-moving items and losing sales. This is where we try to get the lead on our other branches. If we don't move quickly enough the merchandise won't reach the selling floor until Monday or Tuesday; by then we should have sold a lot of last week's delivery and be re-ordering. So we get a fast turnover and also first call on the merchandise in Central Warehouse.

Stocking policy is a critical area in retailing. Broadly speaking, we know that about 20 per cent of our assortments (or lines) generate 80 per cent of our sales. So we work very hard to ensure we can keep that top 20 per cent continuously available and keep as much of the remaining 80 per cent in stock as seems reasonable. This keeps our stock levels down whilst satisfying the majority of our customers. Naturally, we can always get other items for a customer should we happen to be out of stock. We can ask another branch, for example, to send something over quickly, or we can put in an order quickly to the Central Warehouse.

Another important area of my work is looking at the customer flow through the shop. It is important for customers to be able to move around comfortably, without being jostled, when they are making for a particular department. But we would like to encourage them to look at other items on the way, and to make another purchase in addition to the one for which they came into the shop. For example, we used to have a 15 ft-wide straight walkway from the main entrance to the escalator. This meant that customers frequently didn't consider walking around the floor, but made straight for the escalators. So we shortened this walkway and introduced a Y-shaped walkway configuration. It is still possible to go straight ahead, but now the invitation is there to walk around the ground floor. Sales have improved since.

Another retailing headache is scheduling staff lunch breaks. At the busiest time in the day, one-third of our staff are on lunch break. We use part-timers who work over this three-hour period but I don't think we have got the complete solution. I don't think anyone has, unless overlapping shifts are used and that would be costly.

We are interested in providing a good service, so we look at the queue lengths at the tills. We won't tolerate queues of more than four customers if we can possibly help it. To provide a no-queue situation we would need an uneconomic number of cash registers which would use up merchandising space and require many more staff. So our costs would go up, and prices would follow. We have got to keep a balance. The main thing is to make sure all the tills we have available are in operation when needed, and departmental managers are expected to ensure this happens.

Retailing is highly competitive and we have to give the customers what they want in terms of value and service. There is no room for compromise. But most of all we have to do it quickly!

▼ **Exercise**

Assume the answers to this exercise are directed towards the type of department store that we have just described.

(a) Suppose you were a customer of this department store, and that you had chosen an item and brought it to the checkout. Fill in the queue-ranges below to show what size of queue would provoke a different response from you.

A queue over this range . . .   *would provoke this response from you*

		I would wait quite happily
		I would wait, but feel aggrieved
		I certainly wouldn't wait if I was in a hurry
		I certainly wouldn't wait under any circumstances

(b) Suppose you were a sales assistant of this department store. Sometimes you have to tell a customer that you haven't any in stock when he or she asks for an item. Some of these customers will go elsewhere depending on the type of item and how long you say they will have to wait. Fill in the table below showing your own estimates of the percentage of business that will be lost for the particular circumstances.

The time you say that customer will have to wait

	2 days	1 week	2 weeks
Ghetto blaster	_____	_____	_____
Expensive perfume	_____	_____	_____
Wallpaper	_____	_____	_____

(c) Suppose you were a department store manager considering four schemes to motivate staff performance. In your opinion, which of these four schemes is

▷

the best and which the worst? If there are two or more schemes which are good, can they be operated simultaneously, or would one interfere with another?

1. Give successful departments prime sites in the store, more space and more stock.
2. Operate a league table comparing the performance of each department within the store. Each month hold a well-publicized award ceremony where a silver cup and 'We're the Tops' T-shirts are given to the department that has improved the most.
3. 'Promote' staff in successful departments by putting them in charge of unsuccessful departments.
4. Let it be known that substantial monetary bonuses will be given to staff in successful departments but avoid invidious comparisons by keeping the exact size of individual bonuses confidential.

▲

1.4 Case study 4 — public-sector bus operator

In a nutshell, we are in the business of selling movement for reward. The function of operations in the transport business is quite specific: we are there to deliver the service specification. In other words, if we promise that there will be a bus leaving point A at 8.15 and arriving at point B at 8.30, then it's our job to ensure that that happens. With unlimited resources, of course, this job would not be too difficult. If we had plenty of spare buses and crews at different locations waiting to be called on whenever we needed them, many of our problems would disappear. But whether we are operating British Airways, or a fleet of supertankers, the key to an efficient and successful operation is to make sure that the capacity on offer mirrors the demand.

Too much supply incurs costs; too little supply leads to irate customers and a breakdown in the service which makes costs rise. So when we get estimates of demand, we have to match our capacity to that. Generally, if I were to give one rule of thumb, what we need to do is minimize 'light running'. In other words, minimize the mileage our buses travel with no passengers between routes or back to the garage. We leave day-to-day scheduling in the hands of the garages with minimal central guidance. The minute-by-minute operation is in the hands of inspectors and the foreman.

To give you some idea of the size of the operation, we run 1000 buses, 360 days of the year, 7 days a week, 20 hours a day. So I must delegate. As it is, I find that I often work one day at the weekend, and a few hours each evening, but I enjoy it. This extra work has really come about by massive changes in the provision of local bus services. Now the situation is settling down, and we are beginning to be able to concentrate on operating an efficient service in the new environment. I had better try to explain. The bus industry in the UK has now become deregulated. In other words, operators can run a bus service on any route as long as they give 42 days' notice of their intentions and have a valid operators' licence. So there is competition back in the bus industry. This hasn't been known since the 1930s, when road-service licensing regulations were first brought in to protect the public from competing cowboy bus operators who were not maintaining adequate safety standards. Deregulation has inevitably had a radical effect on our thinking. In addition, the metropolitan counties were abolished. This caused massive organizational changes. Not only this, but many councils were then rate-capped. This meant operators found that subsidies disappeared and we were forced to put up fares, in some cases by up to 250 per cent, to meet the operating costs.

All these factors coming within months of each other threw the operation of local bus services into turmoil. As far as the public was concerned, however, the only thing they could see was a massive fare increase for the same service. In fact, the public's response was much less hostile than many operators feared. The public knew very well that a cheap-fares policy was heavily subsidised, costing millions of pounds per year, and accepted, usually with resignation, the inevitable.

Our philosophy has therefore changed, but I don't think my management style has. I still think communication is the key factor both up and down the organization. The new structure has cut out many levels of hierarchy in the organization, and that means that we can get a decision acted upon much more quickly. As I said earlier, I believe in delegation. We have six large and two small garages which are each allocated routes, and the garage itself is responsible for those routes. The staff must schedule the vehicles and crew to meet the frequency requirements of those routes. They must ensure that they keep up a good vehicle-maintenance programme.

Obviously, we at head office monitor what's going on, and not only through our statistics. I am certain that the only way to manage is to go to the place where the work is done. People who work on the routes know the wheezes. They know how to squeeze that extra minute out of a schedule.

Since deregulation, bus drivers see other operators' buses on their routes. They know that competition exists and we are finding that they are becoming increasingly motivated to improve the service they offer. The motivation is less in evidence with the maintenance workers in the garages. I am sure this is because the underneath of a deregulated bus is just the same as that of a regulated bus. The change is not so apparent to them.

We still have to improve productivity. We have too many spare vehicles and too big a workforce. We pay the maintenance workers a flat rate as long as they reach a productivity standard of 75–80 per cent. The drivers also get paid a flat rate, no matter which day of the week they work, as long as they also achieve a productivity standard of 80 per cent. In their case this is simply wheel hours divided by percentage attendance hours. For the engineers it is a bit more complicated. We use a computerized efficiency scheme based on standard times.

The scheduling of bus services is complex. You need to know not only the times taken for a bus to travel between each point on the service route when loaded, but also the time it takes for buses travelling empty between routes. When empty, buses can cut across the city, off the service routes, so we have to consider low bridges, and

Figure 1.2 A maintenance engineer calling up details of the history of a bus on the computerized system.

'access-only' roads all over the city to minimize this light running time, because this is costing us money and bringing in no revenue. So we use two matrices: a 'loaded' and a 'light' matrix to record this information. We need yet another matrix to cover things like the time it takes for a driver to walk between the canteen and the bus stations, and the time it takes him to sign on and off.

Rostering of bus crews is a major task too. This is carried out differently at different garages. In particular, the degree of union involvement varies. In the past, tentative rosters were produced, and then the union was consulted before the schedules were finally fixed. Agreed schedules are posted for ten days before they come into operation. This enables the crews to plan their family life and activities around their working hours.

Such scheduling problems cried out for computerization and for the past year we have been introducing a system. It took our schedulers one working month just to put all the data onto the computer. Obviously we have had teething troubles, like any other company introducing computerization, but we are finally winning. However, we need to get more flexibility into the system. A hand scheduler can bend the rules if he is one minute out. A computer can't.

We have had problems. We have had big changes. Our philosophy has had to change. We are learning about marketing our services. We are running a business now, not a public service. This has caused us to try even harder on the operations side, but our operations aim is still the same — to deliver the service specification efficiently.

▼   **Exercise**

A bus company has to meet the needs of very different customers, for example:

> Pensioners
> Commuters
> Students
> Mothers with young children

A difficult problem for bus companies is that service characteristics which appeal to one type of customer are not always relevant or best for another. This becomes clearer if we spell out the major service characteristics:

1. Fares charged
2. Comfort of buses
3. Frequency of service
4. Ability to keep to timetable
5. Speed
6. Safety
7. Route taken
8. Number of bus stops

It is not possible for a bus company to satisfy everyone. For one thing, it hasn't unlimited money, and for another, it sometimes has to trade one characteristic against another, for example speed against safety.

Take just one of the eight service characteristics: for example, number of bus stops. You could please the pensioners group by inserting more bus stops, shortening their walk to and from buses. If you did so, you would annoy another group (e.g. commuters) who just want to get from the suburbs to the town centre quickly. Look in turn at each of the remaining service characteristics. Identity the trade-offs that have to be considered because
▲   different passenger groups have different needs.

▼   **Contact exercise**

Contact an operations manager and ask about his or her job, the problems encountered and the skills needed to overcome them. With reference to the operations manager's organization, try to cover as many of the following points as possible in a half-hour interview:

▷

What product(s) or service(s) does it provide?

Who are its customers?

Who are its main rivals?

What is the history of its development?

How does the operations manager's function fit into the total framework of his/her business?

To whom is he or she accountable?

What are his or her main duties?

What is his or her management philosophy?

What are the stresses and strains of his or her job?

Advice on who to contact:

1. Don't choose someone whose duties are entirely routine (e.g. assembly-line workers).
2. Don't choose very important decision-makers where their operational decisions will be engulfed by their strategic policy and diplomatic roles (e.g. company director, MP).

Here are some examples:

Acceptable	*Undesirable*
Police duty sergeant	Beat policeman
Hall manager	Hall warden
Builder	Labourer
Petrol station manager	Forecourt attendant
Pub manager	Barmaid
Solicitor's clerk	Solicitor
Services officer	General/Private
Matron	Nurse/surgeon
Warehouse manager	Fork-lift driver
Chef	Waiter

▲

We now give a case study about a very busy operational manager. Read it through and answer the questions that follow the case.

1.5 Case study 5 — Harry Britton of NBD

Richard Lake is a young trainee analyst with Systematics Ltd, management consultants. He has been commissioned to investigate the despatch and transport arrangements of a Yorkshire-based food wholesaler, NBD Ltd. Management's prime objective is to install a computer-based system which will give better service than at present, and which will need less clerical assistance to operate it.

NBD operates from a large warehouse within easy reach of the M1 and M62. It receives supplies direct from manufacturers and importers. It delivers goods to discount stores, supermarkets and small wholesalers within a radius of approximately 100 miles, using its own fleet of forty 24-ton lorries. Competition from other wholesalers is intense and profitability can be achieved only by maintaining a high turnover and by always being in stock for any item that is required. NBD's survival has hinged on its ability to process any order received before noon on one day and to deliver it during working hours on the next. The number of its customers and the volume of its business has steadily increased, necessitating extensions to the warehouse, to the size of its transport fleet and to the range of stocks that it carries.

The ordering of goods coming into NBD is the responsibility of the purchasing department. This is run by Keith Jarvis, an ambitious young man with a business studies degree. He previously worked for Systematics Ltd as a junior consultant. He had been a member of a team that had been called in to investigate whether NBD could halve its purchasing staff. Keith showed how this could be done by installing a computerized ordering system. The directors of NBD were so impressed by his enthusiasm that they offered him the position of purchasing manager where he could put his ideas into practice. This he has done most successfully. NBD now has a day-to-day record of every item in stock and a computerized system of reordering. This is backed up by a vigorous campaign whereby Jarvis and his staff make repeated checks and phone calls to ensure that all suppliers deliver on the date required. Jarvis is not a popular man, but there is no doubt that he gets things done.

In contrast, the sending of goods from NBD's warehouse is organized completely differently. The work is done by the despatch department, run by Harry Britton and his two assistants, Doreen Watkins and Ray Price. Harry Britton is 55 years old and has worked at NBD for 30 years. He has no formal qualifications, having left school at 16. In his early days with NBD he was a delivery driver, then after a period of ill-health a fork lift truck operator. During a period of staff shortages he worked overtime as a despatch clerk and showed such facility for this work that he was hired permanently in this role. For the past fifteen years he has been despatch manager. His major function is to see that all lorries are loaded correctly and that each driver knows exactly where to go. This enables all lorries to get away from the warehouse early in the morning every day of the working week, Monday to Friday.

Harry lives next to the warehouse and arrives for work at 5.30 am every morning. He prepares and hands out journey schedules to the drivers who clock in and depart between 6.00 and 7.00 am. The lorries have been loaded by night-shift workers who use data provided by Harry and his two assistants at the end of the previous day. After the last lorry has departed, Harry goes home for a quick breakfast. He returns at 8.00 am. Ray Price arrives at this time and Doreen Watkins arrives an hour later, after she has dropped her children off at school. Up to 11.00 am they are always alert for incoming telephone calls from drivers who might have run into trouble: a breakdown, a traffic hold-up or bad weather. When such situations arise they have to make instantaneous and tricky decisions on rerouting or possibly sending out reserve transport to meet requirements.

From 11.00 am to 3.00 pm there is a relatively slack period when Harry and his assistants can start work on allocating loads for the next day. After 3.00 pm things get a bit hectic. At this time the accounts department passes on customers' orders received that morning and which must be delivered by the next day. This amounts to about 40 per cent of total goods to be despatched. Detailed instructions must be prepared for the night shift on how to load the lorries, and journey schedules must be prepared for the lorry drivers, each of whom will be visiting between two and eight customers, perhaps at widely-spaced and awkward-to-find locations. In addition, Harry is clocking out drivers who have finished their day's deliveries, collecting delivery notes and informing the maintenance department if any vehicle needs attending to. Doreen Watkins has to stop work at 5.00 pm; Ray Price works overtime for two or three nights a week until 7.00 pm; Harry is always willing to stay on later, often until 8.00 pm.

Harry's constitution has been weakened by the long hours and mental strain of his work. He has high blood pressure, is overweight and coughs a lot. But he never misses a day's work and loves his job. If anything happens to him, NBD will be extremely vulnerable, but so far they have been unable to find a satisfactory solution. Three years ago the company invested £30,000 in computer software which theoretically should have been able to provide an automatic and optimal schedule of route allocations and delivery loads. In spite of determined attempts to implement the system, the project had to be abandoned. Jarvis, the purchasing manager and one of the leading proponents of computerization, argued that the failure was a result of sabotage by the despatch department and the lorry drivers. Others were not so sure. There is no doubt that when it comes to assessing traffic conditions Harry has a masterful 'ear to the ground' which is far superior to the computer's mode of operation. Also he knows the likes and dislikes of every driver for different sorts of route and can allocate work accordingly. The drivers greatly appreciate his skill and there has not been the slightest trouble with the TGWU since Harry has been despatch manager.

It is noticeable that when Harry is on holiday, even though he arranged this to coincide with a quiet time of year, the despatch system all but breaks down. Tim Miller, who is a most efficient assistance maintenance manager and knows the drivers well, acts as temporary replacement for Harry. He brings in a clerk from the purchasing department to help the two regular assistants. Even with this extra help they have to work until 9 or 10 at night to get the schedule done. Also, no one has Harry's skill in handling the morning's traffic emergencies. During Harry's holidays the drivers tolerate this chaos because they know it is only temporary.

It is obvious that Harry is a rare sort of person and any assistant must have like characteristics. He must provide instructions so that the lorries can be loaded efficiently by the night shift. Each lorry must contain a package of orders to different customers and in delivering these orders each driver must be given a fair day's work. The driver must be advised on the best route to deliver his orders. If the driver runs into unexpected difficulties someone must be able to help him complete his deliveries. It is difficult to find people with the ability to make these complicated decisions speedily, efficiently and over a long working day. Of Harry's present assistants, Mrs Watkins is certainly the best; but she has three school-age children under twelve and cannot work overtime. Ray Price, aged twenty, was attracted into the job by the good pay, over 50 per cent more than he could earn elsewhere. But he is getting fed up with the amount of overtime he has to do. Harry has had four such assistants in the past five years, all of whom left because of the strain of the work.

Ever since the unsuccessful attempts to computerize the despatch department's work, Harry has been suspicious of change and rather evasive in explaining to outsiders how his 'system' works.

▼   **Initial exercise in diagnostics**

Read the case and immediately after give your gut reaction to the statements below, using the following scheme:

ˏ   I agree with this statement
X   I disagree with this statement
?   I am unsure

Thirty-four opinions about the Harry Britton case:

1. It is a waste of Harry's skills to do routine jobs.
2. It is the routine that Harry loves.
3. Something should have been done before.
4. Who is Harry's boss? I must find out.
5. When we set out all the alternatives, don't forget the no-change option.
6. Deal with emergency orders separately.
7. It is the accounts department which really needs sorting out.
8. Computerize just the loading not the routing.
9. Computerize just the routing not the loading.
10. Drivers are capable of doing some of Harry's routine tasks.
11. Drivers ought to do some of Harry's tasks.
12. Drivers would like to do some of Harry's tasks.
13. Drivers could do some of Harry's routine tasks.
14. Introduce shiftwork into the despatch department.
15. Give Price more money and more responsibility.
16. Get Harry to a doctor.
17. Get Harry to a psychiatrist.
18. Find out how similar firms manage.
19. Bring Miller over to work in despatch.
20. Hive off a lot of despatch's work to other departments.
21. Generous early retirement offer and consultant status for Harry.
22. Secretly, Harry likes all the fuss that is being made over him.
23. Mrs Watkins is a square peg in a round hole.
24. Give Harry a stake in the firm.
25. Run a computer-based system parallel to Harry's.
26. Get more office staff for Harry.
27. Jarvis would sort the whole thing out if you gave him a try.
28. NBD doesn't really need such high delivery standards.
29. Get a better system going quickly whatever the cost.

▷

30. You're kidding. We've been asked to carry out a cost-cutting exercise.
31. How much time will any reorganization take? I need to know.
32. Find out who is going to try to stop any reorganization, apart from Harry.
33. It is important to do things in the right order.
34. But first find out the right things to do.

▲ Having answered these questions it is constructive to compare your answers with someone else's and to argue about the differences. As for the 'right' answers to these questions, this is really the subject of the rest of the book.

1.5.1 *General issues which the Harry Britton case raises*

(1) *Adjusting the nature of a job to changed circumstances.* Having given a worker tasks and a title, it can be quite hard to shake off its traditional connotations at a later date. We may still think of butcher, baker and candlestick-maker even if they are deep-freeze salesman, sandwich-bar assistant and lampshade manufacturer. All workers must be prepared to adapt to technical innovation, whether it affects their job directly or indirectly, e.g. postman to electronic mail, lathe operators to CNC machines, solicitors to computerized conveyancing. And Harry Britton must come to terms with the computer revolution. It helps if NBD shows that it is committed to using computers to *assist* Harry not to *replace* him.

(2) *Identifying the beer-truck syndrome.* The term 'beer-truck syndrome' comes from Gene Woolsey who describes a certain type of employee. 'If this person (and there is at least one in every absolutely crucial part of your business) should step off a curb and be struck by a speeding beer-truck, you have no backup who can do what he does. Further, as he does such a good job, the biggies of the corporation don't even know he is there and have even less understanding of his importance.' For example:

- The only man who knows the layout of the old sewers under the town hall. (Suppose his sport is hang-gliding).
- The part-time woman who is the only remaining member of the team of brilliant eggheads who run your idiosyncratic computerized stock-control system. (Suppose her husband has just been offered a job in Australia.)
- The draughtsman who knows that your most important customer is always a bit slapdash about filling in full details on the specification sheet; who has a marvellous memory for what the customer really wants, and who is always available if a machinist is not quite clear what should be done. (Suppose he's working up to his last heart attack.)

All of these jobs need identifying and an understudy trained — *before* nemesis.

(3) *Overriding the 'indispensable workaholic'.* Like the beer-truck syndrome, this concerns a 'key link' in the organization, but there are differences:

- He is not necessarily competent.
- He has made himself *appear* indispensable, and much of his time is spent in maintaining that illusion.

(4) *Common threads to OM situations.* Logistics, calculating alternatives, communication between specialists, resource constraints, time constraints, and objectives are common threads to OM situations. One other feature makes life difficult for the student/reader, operations managers tend to be very busy and have a low profile, hence they can be quite difficult to observe in action. One feature of this book is our efforts to get the reader to break through and communicate with operations managers.

1.6 Recommended reading

The intelligent, non-technical reader can get a good grasp of the scope of operations management by a selective reading of the *Financial Times*'s daily 'Management' page, and the monthly business journals *Management Today* and the *Harvard Business Review*. Two good, simple introductory cases on the scope of operations management can be found in Voss *et al. Operations Management in the Service Industries and the Public Sector* (Wiley, 1985). In particular the 'Blood' and 'Morrell's Meat Ltd' cases, though short, are comprehensive, clear and thought-provoking for an introductory 'Scope' class-exercise. More extensive case material introducing operations management can be found in pages 1–236 ('Plant and service tours') of R. Schmenner's *Production/Operations Management: Concepts and Situations*, 4th edn (Macmillan, 1990). This book gives precedence to experience and observation as a foundation for operations management: a philosophy that we strongly share.

Chapter 2

The product and the consumer

2.1 Introduction

Question How should a product be defined?

Answer: There isn't *one* correct definition. A product is a sum of many attributes. This has important consequences for how a product is designed, manufactured, and distributed. We look at two products: water and muesli.

What is water? In the eyes of a scientist, the answer to 'What is water?' is H_2O, but in the eyes of someone who markets water it is something far more complex. This person has to consider the special attributes his very diverse consumers are looking for in water:

- *Domestic customers* need water for drinking, washing, cleaning and flushing lavatories, plus secondary, outdoor uses such as a hose in the garden or washing the car.
- *Farmers and market gardeners* need it for watering crops.
- *Manufacturing companies* need water for cooling, steam generation, and the treatment of materials, as in paper-making, or as an ingredient, as in brewing.

Each of these three major customers expects very different things from the water supplied to them, and this causes headaches to the companies supplying them.

- *Purity.* All water delivered through the mains must be chlorinated and purified for drinking (and usually fluoridated too). Yet nearly all of this pure water is used for much lower-grade purposes. There is a conflict between how different consumers regard purity: hard water may be excellent for drinking, but causes scaling, clogging up industrial pipes and boilers.
- *Continuity.* If its water source is cut off, a brewery, steel works, or power station is brought to an immediate halt. Contrariwise, farm crops can

survive moderate droughts, although farmers like to water crops in hot weather to improve yields. Domestic consumers can survive for two or three days with a breach in supplies, but if this happened regularly the populace would regard the situation as intolerable.

• *Cost.* All large industrial consumers have their supplies metered and are charged according to volume used. Metering of domestic supplies is still uncommon, which means that during droughts water companies have to appeal for self-restraint and impose hosepipe bans.

So, the water companies have to meet the needs of their different customers by balancing the elements of purity, continuity and cost. If we take purity to be an indication of *quality* and continuity an essential aspect of *delivery*, then we are left with the classic trade-off amongst quality, delivery and cost, which is a common feature of all operations management problems.

Take another example, a packaged breakfast cereal such as a sweetened muesli. Is it:

A mixture of fruit, cereals and nuts (producer's definition)?
An instant breakfast (customer utility)?
A path to health and fitness (customer dream)?
A source of income to dentists (third-party interest)?

All customers do not seek the same 'benefits' from a product, or at least do not attach the same importance to each benefit. Thus different brands are produced which satisfy different customers' needs.

Consider the reasons that toothpaste might be bought by one particular type of consumer (say a mother of children).

Primary reasons:

It prevents tooth decay.
It clears plaque.

Secondary reasons:

It has an acceptable taste to children.
It can be squeezed properly from the tube.

Now consider the reasons for a different type of consumer (say a teenager) buying toothpaste.

Primary reasons:

It guarantees fresh breath.
It makes teeth appear ultra-bright.

Secondary reasons:

It prevents tooth decay.
It has a low retail price.

The above analyses are the province of market research, which classifies customers according to the different benefits that each group seeks from a product, and quantifies the values put on these benefits.

2.2 Variation or standardization?

A product development team needs to consider a variety of options at the design stage:

1. Product formulae variations (e.g. ingredients in instant soups).
2. Product shapes (e.g. cylindrical, square or cone-shaped litter bins).
3. Product packaging (e.g. bottles, cans or paper cartons for soft drinks).
4. Product styling (e.g. when designing a new car).

These options, whilst providing the customer with added value, incur extra production and distribution costs. However, the business takes up these options voluntarily in the expectation of greater profit. Other variations will be unavoidable. A clothes shop might be expected to provide a service for all people, from children to outsize persons. The task is made a little easier by the use of standard sizes for shoes, dresses, shirts and trousers. Nevertheless, the retailer and wholesaler have to hold high stocks of finished goods to enable them to provide a service to the customer with immediate delivery from stock. This has made largely obsolescent the make-to-order system of buying clothes, with a delay of up to six weeks in delivery. Note that the older make-to-order system forced the manufacturer/wholesaler to hold high stocks of raw materials such as cloth, and inhibited the adoption of mass production.

Apart from clothing, standardization is common in many other products, e.g. standard weights for tinned foods, and octane ratings for petrol. Not all standardization originates directly from consumer wishes. The government imposes safety standards for seat belts and electrical plugs, and health standards for the lead content of petrol.

In addition, the European Commission tries to impose its own standards across countries, although this has had a mixed reception from the manufacturers and consumers involved. For example, resistance from Germany to allowing inferior beer from other countries in Europe to be sold in Germany, and the resistance of both British consumers and producers to the replacement of their traditional sausage made from offal and scraps by the higher-grade European equivalent. In general, legislation varies from nation to nation throughout Europe with respect to the attributes that a product is allowed to have. It seems as if local political and environmental reasons overrule the European Commission's attempts at harmonization.

2.3 The impact of new technology

New technology is changing the product design and development process. Computer-aided design (CAD) is being used extensively in many types of operation. What is CAD?

CAD systems enable you to design a product on a computer-terminal screen. The computer stores the design and then lets you manipulate it. Most CAD systems now show you a three-dimensional image of your design and allow you to look at this image from any angle you like. This gives a much more complete picture of the product than does a representation on a draughtsman's drawing board.

Not only this. If, for example, you were designing an aircraft wing, you can simulate on the screen the effect of vibration or stress at any point. Any changes suggested by the simulation can be incorporated into the design via the CAD screen. You can, therefore, test and update designs on the computer, without the need for physical models at each stage. This saves both time and money. The Ford Motor Company claims that the average engineer can produce three times as much work in a given period at a CAD workstation than at a draughting table. CAD systems also produce the blueprints for manufacture of the physical product, and can generate cutting paths for machining. Software is now available to convert the output from such a system into machine-tool control language and produce a magnetic or paper tape which can then be used directly to control the machine tool.

One such package, DUCT by Deltacam, produces coloured, very detailed representations on a VDU screen. Some idea of their quality can be assessed by looking at the black-and-white reproductions in Figures 2.1, 2.2 and 2.3. You can see the apparent solidity of the loudspeaker case in Figure 2.1 and make judgements on its aesthetic appeal, even though the product has not yet been produced, even in model form.

But CAD is not just a useful tool for manufacturers. Transport, retail and service organizations can benefit. British Coal's transport systems have been simulated graphically at a computer terminal and their package HAULSTAR is described in Chapter 5. The operation of a burger bar can be designed by CAD and interactive simulation techniques. Simulations showing staff and customer movements with different kitchen and counter layouts are carried out to achieve an effective working system. Customer-flow patterns around a retail store can be simulated and, via CAD, the pattern and spacing of aisles adjusted.

All these CAD applications demonstrate how technology can help in product design and development. Time and money can be saved, but the final test of the product design is always its acceptance by the customer.

2.4 Consumer-driven product development

When a business consultant is approached by a new client, what are the first words that the new client says? In our experience, by far the commonest opening request is: 'I've just developed this marvellous product. All I need now is for you to get me the customers for it.' This is *not* the right way to succeed. You must have intimate contact with your customers *before* and *during* product development. The right way to go about development is exemplified by Westall Richardson, a Sheffield cutlery

Figure 2.1 Loudspeaker case — finished prototype.

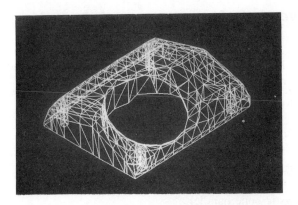

Figure 2.2 Loudspeaker case — finite element mesh.

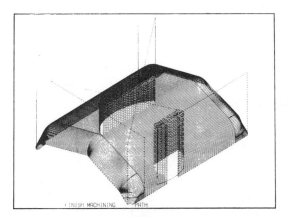

Figure 2.3 Loudspeaker case — cutter path.

manufacturer who has consistently expanded whilst the UK cutlery industry has drastically declined.

In the early 1980s, out of a workforce of 250, 10 people worked full-time on the development of new products. In addition, prototypes were always being passed around the desks of top management for their comments. As customers were always given a hotline to top management there was a bridge between customers and developers. At that time, Westall Richardson noticed that customers expressed interest in obtaining knives that never needed sharpening. Whilst developing such a knife they carried out fundamental research on optimum cutting angles. These researches indicated that the cutting edge could be increased by 50 per cent by using a waved configuration along the sharp side of the knife. Any customer resistance to such an unusual shape was overcome by the 25-year guarantee that came with the knife. By such a combination of desirable characteristics in the product and attention to the consumer, Westall Richardson has emerged as the largest producer of knife blades in Europe.

2.4.1 *Attribute analysis*

Take a single item like a kitchen knife for cutting vegetables. Even for so simple a product, these are the variables that a good manufacturer would consider when trying to meet the needs of consumers:

Degree of sharpness
Serrated edge
Length of blade
Angle of blade
Bendability of blade
Rustproof?
Feel (wood/plastic/bone handle)
Length of handle
Thickness of handle
Moulded to hand
Balance of knife
Compactness for a drawer
Point at end

▼   **Classroom exercise**

In a small group, can you brainstorm for five minutes to find a similar set of variables to those listed above for:

A pen
A cup
A pencil sharpener
A toothbrush
▲   A towel

2.4.2 *New product development and the consumer*

▼   **Contact exercise — the mobile phone revolution**

Your task is to interview a user of a mobile phone and to ask about the
operating problems and any other difficulties he or she has experienced with
service agreements and charges. Bear this in mind as you read this next
▲   section about recent developments in this field.

Within the space of five years, mobile phones have become a common feature of
industrial and commercial life. Previously found only in military and emergency services,
they became a yuppie toy in the 1980s. Now, they are considered an essential accessory
for many salespeople, delivery people, service engineers, and indeed for any mobile
worker who needs to keep in contact with headquarters.

First generation equipment — pagers

Pagers first became popular in hospitals. A little clip-on unit was carried by a doctor.
If it bleeped, it was a request for him or her to contact some central point urgently.
Now, a wider commercial market is being opened up as big companies offer paging
systems that operate over the whole country, not just a narrow area such as a hospital.
Pagers have the disadvantage that they do not allow the receiver to call back the central
point or even to say that the message has been received. Nevertheless, pagers are cheap
and have now been developed to send words, not just a bleep.

Second generation equipment — short distance cordless phone extensions

Cordless portable phones allow a home user to transmit and receive messages from
a home installation so long as it is within about one hundred metres of a base. This
idea has been extended a little by *teleporting*, whereby anybody within a hundred metres
of certain public receivers can use a cordless phone. However, that still leaves large
areas of the country outside the range of teleporting receivers. Also, as only outgoing
messages can be sent, teleporting needs to be combined with paging — a clumsy
arrangement.

Third generation equipment — local radio networks

The country is covered with short wave radio transmitters, each with its own cell, or
area within which its messages can be picked up from mobile phones. If a transmitter
is very busy it has to reduce the area that it covers so that it will not be overloaded
with the calls it has to handle. In London a cell's radius may be less than a half mile.
With such a small area of operation it quite often happens that a mobile phone user
moves between cells during a telephone conversation. There is supposed to be an

automatic switching device when this happens, but it does not always work when the lines are crowded.

Fourth generation equipment — national radio network

Band III, the frequency on which the old black and white television services were broadcast, is now no longer needed by viewers, so it has been made available to commercial mobile radio users. A user pays a fixed monthly charge, so that it has attractions for a heavy user. Individual calls are, however, limited to 30 seconds duration.

Currently, Personal Communications Network (PCN) (1992), a new national radio network, is being installed that will overcome the poor quality, overcrowding and patchy coverage of the cellular system. Cellular network companies have been excluded from operating the PCN so that there is unlikely to be an interface between the two systems and consumers will have to buy new equipment.

Fifth generation equipment — satellite and international systems

In Japan, a communication system relayed by satellite gives blanket high quality coverage for the whole country and has additional features such as being able to pinpoint the receiver's position to within fifty metres. This has obvious commercial and security advantages which will render all existing systems obsolete. Similar satellite systems are proposed from the USA and Europe.

▼ Further exercises in new product development

With mobile phones, the benefits were difficult to measure but nevertheless are *perceived* as being big enough for the phones to have become standard items of commercial equipment. However, consumers have also suffered: in their eagerness to obtain mobile phones they have not done their homework on the performance and reliability of equipment, nor on the respectability of the suppliers. With all new developments you need to have a dispassionate, scientific approach to balance enthusiasm (hype) against cynicism. Below, details are given of certain new products to see if you can assess their viability. In the advertisements you would expect these products' strengths to feature prominently. Can you also identify any hidden weaknesses? What positive recommendation would you make to a manufacturer to overcome what you perceive to be a hidden weakness?

1. *Vacuum clean your pet*
   Battery operated, mini vacuum cleaner, quick, almost silent, removes loose hair, fleas and their eggs. Price: dog version £19.95, cat version £14.95.

2. *Aqua pad flotation bed*
   Much lighter than a conventional waterbed, you fill the base of the mattress with water to the depth of 1″–2″. Above this base are layers of

▷

foam, polyester and heat-reflecting fibre. Prices: 3′ × 6′3″, £199; 4′6″ × 6′3″, £259; 5′ × 6′6″, £299; 6′ × 6′6″, £329.

3. *Home karaoke player*
   Twin cassette, high speed dubbing, continuous play, dual microphone jacks, echo feature, mixing facilities, two microphones plus a backing tape of hit pop songs. Also functions as a radio/cassette player. Price £119.

4. *Portable car alarm system*
   Needs no installation, has no wires. It possesses a 110 dB siren, so loud and penetrating that a thief will not be able to stand the volume within the car. It works via a microsensor that detects the smallest change in air pressure inside a car. Ideal for cars, caravans, boats, hotel rooms. Price £44.95.

5. *Instant oxygen*
   Aerosol type can with face-mask gives you instant oxygen any time you feel fatigued. (Not intended as a medical or life-saving device.) Price £9.95.

6. *Insect poison extractor*
   Placed immediately over a bite or sting, this small vacuum pump sucks out the poison. Price £7.95.

2.5 Value analysis and new product development

In the public mind, new products are thought to spring into life after an inventor has a sudden brainwave. In fact, nearly all innovation is a long, hard grind of little improvements and modifications grafted onto existing products. This process has been formalized under a technique known as *value analysis*.

2.5.1 *Classic principles of value analysis*

Value analysis is a method of taking a fresh look at the design of an existing product. Its origins go back to the Second World War. During that period H.L. Erlicher, Purchasing Officer for General Electric Company (USA) observed that:

1. A shortage of non-ferrous metals forced designers and production planners to search for temporary substitute materials.
2. When things returned to normal, people were surprised to find that the supposed 'second-best substitutes' were cheaper and of better quality than the original material, *and had been all along*.

These observations inspired another GEC employee, L.D. Miles, to see if the resourcefulness evident in wartime could be maintained during peacetime. From 1947 to 1951 Miles headed a value analysis section of GEC. Its success led to the adoption of value analysis by GEC's suppliers, customers and competitors. The US Department of Defense was so impressed by the improvements achieved by value analysis companies that it became a strongly recommended business technique for defence suppliers. Below are some major features of early value analysis.

(1) *Moving towards the consumer's viewpoint.* Value analysis was an early attempt to give product development some customer orientation. It introduced the concepts of 'use' and 'esteem' as separate functions of the product. On the other hand, value analysis has often been incorrectly pigeon-holed as a 'cost reduction exercise'. This cannot be right. If customers do not want your product, you are not going to rescue the situation by reducing costs. The greater impact of marketing on business operations has led to scientific analysis of what the consumer looks for in a product. This approach was discussed briefly in the introduction to this chapter.

(2) *Listing and classifying.* Miles took great care in defining exhaustive lists and classifications of components, processes and ways of doing things. This was to ensure that no alternative was overlooked. Unfortunately, this has often been interpreted as an exercise internal to the organization (e.g. checking on tolerances, waste, standardization of parts, stocking and manufacturing procedures). It is better to make more exhaustive, external investigations (e.g. listing and classifying all suppliers and contacts, and finding out what your rivals are up to and, most important of all, to make exhaustive lists of consumer aspects, as we illustrated with the kitchen knife).

The Japanese emphasize this aspect by saying that performance has priority over specification.

(3) *Snappy assessment of functions and generation of alternatives.* This states, in simple English, what every component contributes to the final product. Preferably this is done in two words, though we feel there is no need to make a fetish of this. Also, it should record the primary rather than the secondary function. Thus paint prolongs the life of a car rather than looks good. Other examples from a car could be:

headrest — ameliorates whiplash injury
choke — helps cold-starts
jack — enables DIY wheel-change
car stereo — entertains driver

Next, a full list of alternatives is sought for every part. Here, the value of the snappy functions becomes apparent: if you focus on them, it is easier to think of sometimes quite revolutionary alternatives. No alternative should be excluded, and every alternative should have a rough estimate of cost and other major characteristics attached. After an elementary cost or break-even analysis, a choice between alternatives is made.

(4) *Removing the road-blocks to creativity.* Everyone desires a certain level of stability in their life. But it is easy for this to degenerate into the 'locked-in' behaviour of tradition and ritual. In such circumstances new ideas can be actively suppressed. Value analysts try to identify road-blocks to a solution, in both their own and their colleagues' behaviour. These road-blocks may be:

(a) *Perceptual.* For example, rejecting a worthwhile invention that 'defies commonsense'. To understand why aircraft can fly requires the mind to leap to an understanding of wing configuration, airspeed and pressure differences.

(b) *Emotional.* For example, the tendency, a few years ago, for the West to dismiss Japan's economic resurgence because they were stereotyped as imitators and producers of shoddy goods.

(c) *Habitual.* Resistance is often strongest from a skilled operator of an existing method; for example, a professional pianist would not be too enthusiastic about music synthesizers. Companies with long experience in a product area become set in their ideas; for example, the game Monopoly was rejected by several games producers because it took longer to play the game than other successful products. This was assumed to be unacceptable to consumers.

(d) *Cultural.* Human social groups, religions, nations or professions are extremely stubborn when suggestions are made to 'improve' their supposedly inefficient practices. They need these practices to preserve their identity.

(e) *Embarrassment.* The originator of value analysis, L.D. Miles, greatly stressed this feature, though subsequent exponents have rather ignored it. Miles thought that value analysts did not like to appear foolish when approaching experts. Also, many value analysts fear rebuffs and this inhibits them from contacting strangers to ask a favour. Finally, experts themselves feel embarrassed if they are put in a probing situation where their own ignorance might be revealed.

(f) *Hierarchical.* In a large, traditional organization it is common for a pecking order or caste system to develop. It is hard for those at the bottom to find a listener for their ideas. For example, not many junior doctors would dare to contradict their senior consultant.

(g) *Situational.* You would expect that cuts in research funding, inadequate buildings, skimpy laboratory equipment and shortage of staff would inhibit creativity. But so perverse is human nature that there is much anecdotal evidence that creativity is stimulated by hardship. For example, in Banting and Best's book in which they tell about the discovery of insulin, we find that the researchers:

> had been given bench space in room 221, a kind of anteroom between a corridor and one of the main laboratories. Part of it was used as a storeroom for supplies and old instruments ... They worked in heat and dirt and unbelievable stench.

Some managers argue that it is only when people really have their backs to the wall that they are galvanized into productivity. In Japan, creating purposefully 'impossible?' assignments has been formalized as the *haiui no jin* (backs to the water) approach.

2.5.2 *From value analysis to implementation*

Ideas by themselves are worth nothing: they only have value when put into practice (i.e. are implemented). Therefore, once a new product is designed, every other aspect of operations management must be brought into play before success can be achieved. These other aspects are shown in Figure 2.4. In essence, this diagram summarizes issues developed in the rest of this book. So, in general, successful product development has a co-ordinated and balanced attack via all the different activities shown in the figure. Unsuccessful product development focuses on some activities and neglects others in the cycle. Product development, more than any other area of business confirms the adage, 'A chain is only as strong as its weakest link'.

2.5.2.1 Comment on the product development cycle

It might seem that the long sequence of arrows and boxes in Figure 2.4 could hold back development, especially if people are waiting for work to be done in a previous section before they spring into life. But we would argue that imposing this structure can save a lot of time on:

1. Unnecessary development work on a product that is later found to be unmarketable.
2. Late alterations in the design of a product causing panic alteration everywhere else in the system, from the shopfloor to the sales brochures.

This structure works best in an organization where multi-tasking and flexible assignments are the norm. For example, a design engineer will follow his or her idea through and turn into a production engineer, and a different production engineer will take his or her place in the design team. Increasing this flexibility to include sales engineers ensures that everyone involved in product development has an appreciation of the whole spectrum of activities from the market-place to manufacturing capabilities. This flexibility, a key element of *simultaneous engineering*, has been extended in some Japanese organizations so that, for example, top marketing and production managers swap functions.

2.5.3 *Case study in value analysis and implementation*

2.5.3.1 The revolution in outdoor clothing

In the past fifty years there have been dramatic changes in the design of clothing for extreme weather conditions. Previously we relied on thick furs or leather, or many layers of thick woollen garments, or heavy impermeable oilskins. Now, a combination of synthetic materials can provide you with a lightweight jacket that, even worn alone without undergarments, can keep you comfortable on Mount Everest, round Cape Horn, or at the South Pole.

▼ **Class exercise**

For your small group, arrange to bring together the variety of clothes that you use for outdoor wear. Choose just one market where you think that your group has special expertise. For example, choose one of:

Canoeing
Cycling
Climbing
Skiing
Mountain walking
Fell-running/orienteering
Yachting
Windsurfing

Below is a list of attributes that should be considered when purchasing clothing for these activities. This list is not complete, you might like to add others.

1. Heat insulation
2. Waterproofing
3. Sweat removal
4. Feel/texture
5. Appearance
6. Durability
7. Washability
8. Drying time
9. Cost

Your task is to adjudge the relative importance of these attributes, then, set the level of performance required when you combine the attributes to propose what, in your view, would be an ideal product (or combination of products if the sportsperson has to wear several layers of garments).

Next, look at the variety of materials which are currently available and see how far they contribute to the ideal product that your group has in mind.

Now, consider all the problems that you envisage you would face if you wished to design, manufacture and market your ideal product. Use the
▲   product development and assessment cycle as a guide for your work.

Comments on this exercise from someone who has designed, made and sold outdoor clothing

'I have successfully launched a range of outdoor clothing based on some pretty revolutionary ideas.

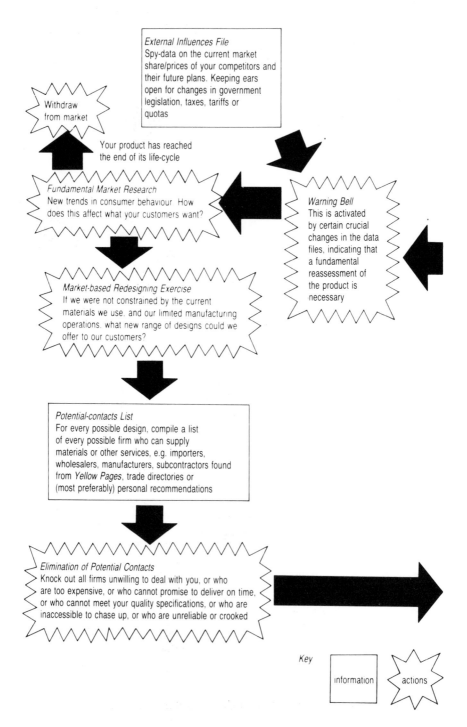

External Influences File
Spy-data on the current market
share/prices of your competitors and
their future plans. Keeping ears
open for changes in government
legislation, taxes, tariffs or
quotas

Withdraw
from market

Your product has reached
the end of its life-cycle

Fundamental Market Research
New trends in consumer behaviour How
does this affect what your customers want?

Warning Bell
This is activated
by certain crucial
changes in the data
files, indicating that
a fundamental
reassessment of
the product is
necessary

Market-based Redesigning Exercise
If we were not constrained by the current
materials we use, and our limited manufacturing
operations, what new range of designs could we
offer to our customers?

Potential-contacts List
For every possible design, compile a list
of every possible firm who can supply
materials or other services, e.g. importers,
wholesalers, manufacturers, subcontractors found
from Yellow Pages, trade directories or
(most preferably) personal recommendations

Elimination of Potential Contacts
Knock out all firms unwilling to deal with you, or who
are too expensive, or who cannot promise to deliver on time,
or who cannot meet your quality specifications, or who are
inaccessible to chase up, or who are unreliable or crooked

Key

information   actions

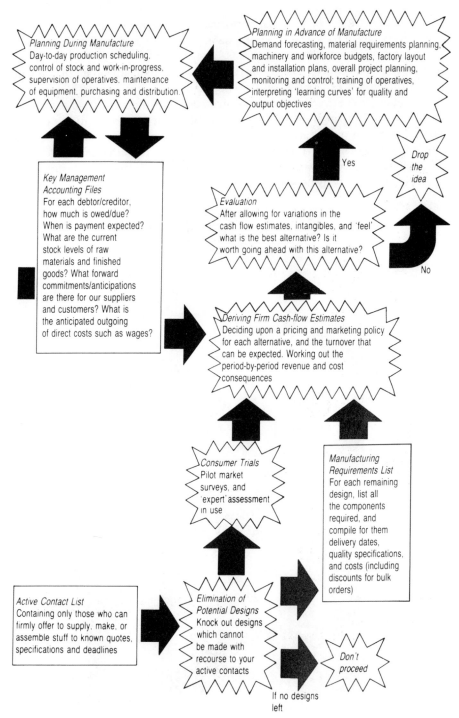

Planning During Manufacture
Day-to-day production scheduling, control of stock and work-in-progress, supervision of operatives, maintenance of equipment, purchasing and distribution.

Planning in Advance of Manufacture
Demand forecasting, material requirements planning, machinery and workforce budgets, factory layout and installation plans, overall project planning, monitoring and control; training of operatives, interpreting 'learning curves' for quality and output objectives

Key Management Accounting Files
For each debtor/creditor, how much is owed/due? When is payment expected? What are the current stock levels of raw materials and finished goods? What forward commitments/anticipations are there for our suppliers and customers? What is the anticipated outgoing of direct costs such as wages?

Drop the idea

Evaluation
After allowing for variations in the cash flow estimates, intangibles, and 'feel' what is the best alternative? Is it worth going ahead with this alternative?

Yes

No

Deriving Firm Cash-flow Estimates
Deciding upon a pricing and marketing policy for each alternative, and the turnover that can be expected. Working out the period-by-period revenue and cost consequences

Consumer Trials
Pilot market surveys, and 'expert' assessment in use

Manufacturing Requirements List
For each remaining design, list all the components required, and compile for them delivery dates, quality specifications, and costs (including discounts for bulk orders)

Active Contact List
Containing only those who can firmly offer to supply, make, or assemble stuff to known quotes, specifications and deadlines

Elimination of Potential Designs
Knock out designs which cannot be made with recourse to your active contacts

Don't proceed

If no designs left

Figure 2.4 The product development and assessment cycle.

My design priorities: I believe that performance is the principal consideration, so fashion aspects take a back seat. Even the fabrics are designed performance first, so appearance has been sacrificed.

From experience I deduced that getting rid of sweat was more important than stopping the rain getting in. My experience was that: (a) waterproofs didn't exist; (b) waterproofs which got rid of sweat at various levels of activity certainly didn't exist; (c) waterproofs which were flexible enough, and light enough not to affect mobility didn't exist; (d) the layer system was okay but somehow I could never get the balance right and was forever stopping to change. I came to associate comfort with the hot, sticky feel of superheated accumulated sweat, trapped in the layers, no matter how efficient they were supposed to be at dispersing sweat.

Figure 2.5 Mountain shirt.

Basically I was prepared to put up with the occasional soaking (which I was getting anyway) provided that: (a) the clothing was still reasonably comfortable, even saturated with cold water; (b) I could get rid of sweat as effectively as possible, and hopefully prevent that awful creeping chilling, from the small of the back outwards, which started as soon as I stopped moving, and stopped generating body heat.

Later I defined comfort as balancing insulation, ventilation, rainproofness and getting rid of sweat.

My basic product: I produced a shirt designed for climbing and running. These activities require high mobility, so it is short at the front, and finishes where your legs start to bend. I now regard this as a serious design fault for many other activities, since rain can run off the front causing discomfort and it rides-up out of a climbing harness or spray deck. Despite my reservations, it is a good general-purpose design and the best for running.

The suit consists of two layers. The outer windproof shell is made of hydropilic polymer coated fabric, windproof to 40 mph and rainproof to ½ inch per hour. The lining can be made from pile, synthetic fleece or raised polyester fabric.

The design has eight ventilation controls to balance heat output and ventilation, a spacious load-carrying hand-warmer pocket, map-pocket, and a loop on the collar for the hood. Using the ventilators, by adjusting the zips an inch at a time, you can find a balance between insulation and ventilation. Feeling cold air moving around your body takes a bit of getting used to, but doesn't necessarily mean that you are getting cold. What it teaches us is that provided the insulation is really effective, your body requires only a very light layer when active.

The shirt is comfortable when saturated with cold water, and comfortable within five minutes of immersion in icy water. Just get out and get moving. After exertion, if you skin is running with sweat, your skin will dry off within five minutes without chilling, provided that you close all the ventilators and wear the shirt next to the skin.

As a general guide the single layer will contain a comfort level from October to April (sometimes even in August) for nearly all outdoor activities. A second layer (jacket) may be needed for less active pursuits for the most severe winter weather, but watch out for overheating.

In the early days I had a lot of trouble getting my ideas across: in 1986, the first eleven companies I approached rejected me. In spite of these rejections, I persevered, knocking on the doors of climbing shops, taking stands at trade fairs and advertising extensively in outdoor pursuit magazines. I got my product produced finally and it was adopted by Himalayan and Arctic explorers. They came back extolling the virtues of my product. I thought I had it made. But I just couldn't break into the 'weekend sportsman' market. Finally, after many years I've made it, but it has been a long, hard, frustrating struggle.'

▼ **Quick exercise**

▲ Why do you think the inventor had so much trouble getting his product accepted in the wider market place?

2.6 Recommended reading

Cases

The whole emphasis of this chapter has been that operations management must be driven by marketing considerations. Excellent introductory cases that reinforce this point are 'Spanline Engineering' and 'Traidcraft Ltd' in Geoff Easton's *Learning from Case Studies* (Prentice Hall, 1982). This book has the additional advantage of providing someone new to case analysis with a careful guide on diagnosis and consultancy skills. A revealing case about a company with a chaotic marketing−OM approach is 'Speedcraft' in T.A.J. Nicholson's *Managing Manufacturing Operations* (Macmillan, 1978). See Voss *et al.*, *Operations Management in the Service Industries and Public Sector*, (Wiley, 1985) 'Malaba Beach Hotel' for a good service example of product development.

For a more complicated case, overlapping with major strategic problems, but which ties in with the latter part of this chapter see 'New Balance Athletics Shoes USA' in W.E. Sasser, *Cases in Operations Management: Strategy and Structure* (Irwin, 1982).

Specialist texts

Gruenwald, G., *New Product Development* (NTC Business Books, 1985). Easy to read, informative, US hardback.

Jewkes, J. *et al.*, *The Sources of Invention*, 2nd edn (Macmillan, 1969). Fascinating sets of cases and comments on twentieth-century inventions and what got them off the ground.

Miles, L.D., *Techniques of Value Analysis and Engineering* (McGraw-Hill, 1961). Persuasive, informative book by value analysis' founder.

Shigeo Shingo, *Key Strategies for Plant Improvement* (Nikkon Kogyo Shimbun Ltd, 1987, pp. 86−106). Shows how strongly Miles's value analysis approach has influenced the Japanese.

Chapter 3

Machines — the process and the cost

3.1 Introduction

In operations management we are principally concerned with processes: the conversion of inputs into outputs. This applies whether we are talking about manufacturing or service industries. Take a manufacturing example, we may have several inputs:

Labour — operating, maintenance and supervision
Materials — at many stages from raw (iron ore) to finished (iron screw)
Power and utilities — electricity, gases, coal, oil, steam, water, air
Capital items — permanent casings, replaceable mechanisms, control equipment
Support equipment — e.g. fans, tools and loaders

These inputs may be producing several outputs:

Product and materials — embracing semi-finished to consumer products, including by-products
Pollutants — e.g. noise, effluent, heat, dust, smoke, poisons and other health hazards

Machines are the hub of the manufacturing conversion process; they are also vital in service contexts. Take a look at p. 117 and you'll see the important role they play in service industries.

A recommended initial approach to understanding a machine might be:

1. Firstly, ignore the internal workings of a machine.
2. Identify all the inputs and outputs.
3. Identify where all the inputs come from and where all the outputs go to.
4. Summarize your information in a diagram.

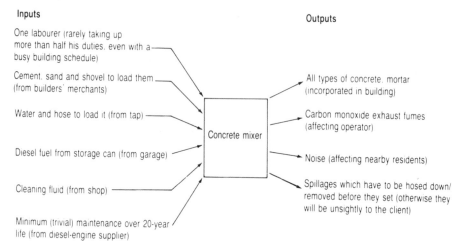

Figure 3.1 The basic inputs and outputs of a concrete mixer.

▼ **Classroom exercise** (*5 minutes*)

   (a) Choose one of the following: a typewriter or a drink-dispensing machine.

   (b) Draw all the inputs to and the outputs from that machine.

▲ **(c)** Say where every input has come from, and where every output is going to.

3.2 Throughput

3.2.1 *Introduction*

So far we have treated the machine as a 'black box'. Inputs enter and, after some mysterious *transformation*, outputs emerge. What types of transformation could be involved? Here are some examples: breaking up (cement-plant), binding (brick-plant), mixing (bread), cutting (lawn-moving), reshaping (drop forging), transporting (vehicles), power generation (turbine) or chemical conversion (polyethylene production). In most of these cases you find the method of measuring inputs is different from that of measuring outputs.

Should inputs or outputs be used as the true measure of the machine's efficiency? Is there some internal measure that can be used? This is often a tricky problem. In particular, beware of the term *capacity*, which indicates a theoretical maximum at one point of time. *Throughput* is a far more relevant economic concept: it defines a reasonable volume which can be held over a period of time.

3.2.2 *Reasons that a machine might not reach maximum throughput*

1. *To comply with safety regulations.* For example, to avoid a machine overheating, or to avoid excessive vibrations which might cause an accident, or to avoid danger to the operative.
2. *During warm-up and run-down periods.* For example, the acceleration and deceleration period of a train. Certain chemical processors (e.g. a catalytic cracking plant) may take a day or so starting from cold before they are ticking over and handling maximum volume. Likewise, nuclear reactors cannot be suddenly halted but must pass through a protracted closing-down process.
3. *Resetting a machine to make a different product.* For example, in injection moulding it might take several hours to remove one mould from a machine and install a new mould, together with jigs and support apparatus.
4. *Removing a product from the machine.* This applies to dangerous or delicate products, or where many jigs and fixtures to the product have to be removed (e.g. removing a patient after a surgical or dental operation).
5. *When a machine is slowed or stopped to replenish material.* For example, when a printer or photocopier has to be reloaded with paper although a print run has not been completed.
6. *To carry out a routine inspection and possible replacement of parts.* For example, a car undergoing its MOT test.
7. *Accidents and unexpected breakdowns.* With aeroplanes and other machines where human safety may be endangered, this applies not only to the immediate loss of any plane that crashes but to the possible grounding of all similar machines while safety checks are made.
8. *A shortage of inputs.* For example, difficulty in recruiting operatives for evening and night shifts and shortage caused by stockpiling and speculation in precious metals.
9. *Potential output in excess of demand.* For example, the spread of narrow-strip razor blades has made uneconomical many of the rolling mills making the special steel strip for this purpose.
10. *Changing environmental constraints.* For example, the weather's effect on the performance of harvesting machines.
11. *System interruptions affecting the machine.* If a machine is part of a complex system of machines then the throughput of another machine might be affected by reasons 1–10. For instance, all sorts of machines in a steel plant might suffer from the malfunctioning of an overhead crane.

3.2.3 *Example — hydraulic coil press*

Rotary Electrical, Sheffield, makes DC coils for large electric motors. At one stage in their manufacture, the coils are placed in a press so that the insulating material surrounding the copper can be fully set.

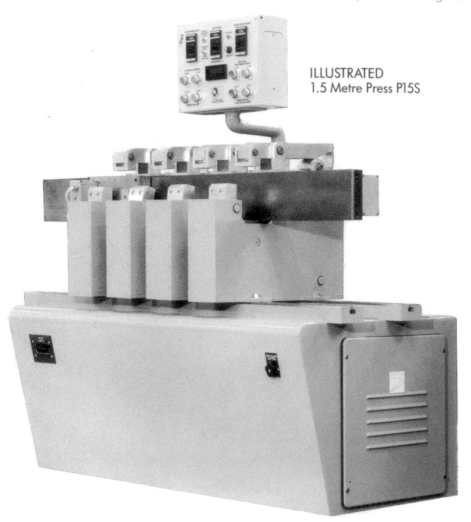

ILLUSTRATED
1.5 Metre Press P15S

Figure 3.2 Electrical coil press.

Transformation process. The insulator-covered sets of copper coil are placed between the preheated rams of the hot press and the press heads then close. The heat, approximately 153°C, and pressure, a maximum of 750 psi, causes the thermo-setting resins to flow. The coil is then transferred to the cool press, which is run at room temperature, to reset and cool the shellac insulator.

Inputs and outputs. The inputs and outputs to the press are shown in Figure 3.3.

Throughput. Only one coil can be placed in each press, each process taking 2–3 minutes. Therefore the constant attention of an operator is required. The speed of the operation is not sensitive to the skill of the operator, and, with the job rotation implemented by the department, can be conducted by any member. Time is needed

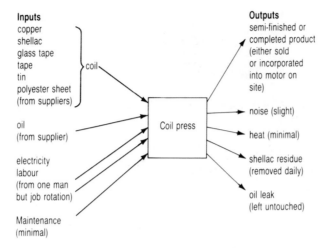

Inputs
copper
shellac
glass tape
tape } coil
tin
polyester sheet
(from suppliers)

oil
(from supplier)

electricity
labour
(from one man
but job rotation)

Maintenance
(minimal)

Coil press

Outputs
semi-finished or
completed product
(either sold
or incorporated
into motor on
site)

noise (slight)

heat (minimal)

shellac residue
(removed daily)

oil leak
(left untouched)

Figure 3.3 The inputs and outputs of the coil press.

to replace each coil in the press and to adjust controls, and delays may occur due to previous processes. The machine is not liable to overheat or slow down as a result of over-use. A feasible number of coils pressed in a 7½ hour day is 60–70.

Reasons that the machine may not reach maximum throughput:

1. Coil press is one of the final stages and will therefore be susceptible to slack periods attributable to delays in the previous processes or due to testing.
2. It takes approximately 20 minutes for the coil press to reach 155°C, which could be a cause of lost labour time. However, the supervisor usually arrives early to switch the press on, so that the machine is warmed up by the time the operators arrive.
3. A longer warming-up period is required in colder weather, and it is also more difficult to maintain the required temperature.
4. The hot press does not stay at the optimum temperature of 155°C due to air passing through the rams as they are being constantly opened. However, the machine functions sufficiently well at 153°C, the average room temperature.
5. Time is required for adjusting controls and replenishing materials.
6. As the coil-making department is quite small and uses job rotation in its functioning, throughput may be reduced if the press operator spends time helping someone else.
7. Shellac residue is cleaned off the bars every day. However, this requires only a few minutes.

However:

1. No time is lost in checking the machine or by intensive cleaning as this is not necessary.
2. No accidents or breakdowns have ever occurred.
3. Employees are generally willing to work overtime if necessary.

4. As the machine is easy to operate, no time is lost if one operator is absent due to illness or vacation.

▼   **Classroom exercise** *(10 minutes)*

(a) Choose one of the following: a train, a bus, a fish-and-chip frier, a cash-till or a lawnmower.

(b) How does it convert its inputs to outputs?

▲ **(c)** What could stop you getting maximum throughput?

3.3 The impact of new technology on machine operations

Previously, machine improvements were restricted to mechanization. Now they are associated with information processing. For example, automatic identification systems are revolutionizing the retail trade. Bar codes are now put on to almost all grocery packages. An automatic scanner reads the bar code which identifies the produce and the price, and this information is transmitted to an electronic till which automatically adds up the grocery bill as the goods are passed over the scanner. This reduces delays at checkouts as cashiers no longer have to find out prices for products which have not been manually price-labelled. There are other advantages. Customers receive an itemized bill with product-names as well as prices, making checking easier. More importantly, stores can reduce staff levels since goods do not need stick-on labels before going onto the shelves, and price changes can be made at the push of one button.

Advances in computer software, along with improvements in manufacturing equipment, have led to the development of automatically-controlled machines. Early, numerically controlled (NC) machines were controlled by instructions fed into the machines on paper tape. Instructions to move, drill and cut were coded and the machine tool automatically performed the required operation communicated to it via the paper tape. Information to change tools, such as drill-bit sizes, were also coded in this way. Now technology has advanced further and microcomputers can control machines. These machines are known as CNC (computer numerical control) machines. Automatic control means that one operator can tend several machines simultaneously. This has radically changed whole manufacturing systems.

Beyond CNC we are now witnessing a further stage in automation: the installation of industrial robots. Industrial robots have two main components:

1. A manipulator — like a human arm — to perform work.
2. A control system to provide instructions to the manipulator.

Two such robots working on the Austin Rover 800 series assembly line are shown in Figures 3.4 and 3.5.

Figure 3.4 Robot welding of door assembly.

Figure 3.5 Windscreen fitment by robot.

A robot can be taught to perform sequences of motions and even to make logical decisions. For example, a robot with a scanner can be taught to look at a component and, on the basis of whether it finds a flaw in, for example, a weld, decide whether to accept or reject the component. The manipulator on the robot can then put the 'accepts' into one pile and the 'rejects' into another. (See Chapter 7 for an evaluation of such behaviour.)

3.4 The economic evaluation of a machine

3.4.1 *Introduction to the evaluation analysis*

Why do you need to know what a machine earns?

1. Because it might be losing you money.
2. Because you might be considering purchasing a machine and you need to explore alternatives.

Figures given to you by others, even by experts, can be misleading. For example, *a salesperson* selling you a machine might quote performance figures which can be achieved only under artificially ideal conditions (e.g. when quoting to you the miles per gallon of a car or the response time of a computer software system).

An operator, asked to provide management with estimates of his or her machine's performance, is tempted to make them a little pessimistic. Not so pessimistic that the machine's worth (and possibly the operator's job) is questioned, but pessimistic enough for the operator to be able to earn a bonus if management set a target based on this estimate.

A financial accountant will have to use depreciation rates at variance with how the machine is actually declining in value because he has an obligation to tax authorities and to group headquarters, to apply fairly consistent rates over a broad band of machines. Consider, for example, jet aircraft. Singapore Airlines depreciates 80 per cent of the value of their planes over ten years. In contrast, Guinness Peat Aviation depreciates 85 per cent of the value of their planes over twenty-five years. There is a colossal difference in an airline company's profits and operating policy according to whether they take the Singapore or Guinness guidelines. (See the capacity planning section of Chapter 11 for a fuller explanation.)

More frequently, *a management accountant* may allocate all factory expenses between machines in a pretty arbitrary fashion. This is well illustrated in the following example. The written analysis hints at some interesting valuation problems, but these are obscured by the table of allocated costs (Table 3.1) which should not be used to make any decision about the machine, be it an operating or replacement decision.

3.4.1.1 Example — analysis of a clingfilm winder

The machine produces rolls of clingfilm in four different lengths: 5 m, 14 m, 30 m and 60 m. The numbers of rolls the machine can produce per hour for each length are 640, 480, 330 and 200 respectively. Down-time is caused by the operator changing the parent roll and resetting for length, by electrical or mechanical failure, by lack

Table 3.1 Annual manufacturing cost
allocated to the clingfilm winder (£)

Direct wages	22,800
Management salaries	6,500
Maintenance wages	8,800
Repairs and renewals	4,800
Property repairs	1,000
Heating	4,800
Light and power	3,700
Rates, insurance, machine hire	2,300
Depreciation	2,300

of materials or by lack of operators. This does not normally affect output as there are three other machines and two shifts of operators who will keep the machines running from 8 a.m. to 9.30 p.m. if necessary, to meet the company's forecasted demand.

Inputs necessary to keep the machine working, apart from an operator, are film tubes, cartons, shrink wrap, cases, labels and pallets. Miscellaneous items are sellotape and glue. The machine runs on electricity and compressed air. Some waste is produced which is taken into account when the company prices the product.

The policy of the company is to allocate *manufacturing costs* according to the proportion of total factory machine hours that each machine runs, as shown in Table 3.1.

These annual allocated costs total £58,300. Dividing this total by the 9000 hours per annum that the machine runs, gives a *running cost* of £6.48 per hour. This running cost is then one of several elements used to work out how a product should be priced. They are: (running costs per hour × number of hours run) + (cost of material inputs including 3% that goes to waste) + (head office and sales *overheads*) + 5% profit margin. Thus we have a rule-of-thumb method to help determine a cost-plus pricing policy. But this method is not particularly accurate in telling us about a machine's efficiency: this should be done via the more detailed analysis explained next.

3.4.2 *Costs*

3.4.2.1 Proportional costs

You can make correct decisions about a machine only if you know how costs vary with throughput. In particular, operating labour, raw materials, utilities and repair costs are often assumed to be *proportional costs*.

(1) Variable labour costs. Is it easy to match the expense of operating labour with throughput? Take an example. In the manufacture of cutlery there are machines which are fed with 'blanks' (half-finished items) by an operative. He reaches into a tub of blanks by his side, picks one out, inserts it into the machine, positions it correctly and then presses a treadle with his foot. The machine then automatically processes

and ejects the blank. This cycle of operations takes 3–5 seconds depending on how easy it is to reach into the tub and how skilled the operator is at positioning the blank correctly. If a straight piece-rate was paid, for example about £2 per 400 blanks, operating labour would be an easy variable cost to calculate. However, even in this simple situation it is quite rare to be paid a sole piece-rate without also being given an attendance allowance, an allowance for unavoidable machine or system down-time and a share of a group bonus. Also, such items as national insurance contributions are a cost attributable to operating labour.

For more complex machines, operating labour's relationship to throughput is correspondingly more difficult to define. The volume of throughput might be affected by the varying skill needed to make different products on the same machine. In such circumstances there might be a different rate fixed for each job. In other circumstances the operative might be paid by the hour, or paid overtime, making the connection between throughput and labour cost more difficult to unravel.

(2) *Variable material costs.* Surely the cost of materials and throughput are connected? For example, surely it is reasonable to assume that, if you are working at (say) 70 per cent of a previous throughput, you will incur 70 per cent of the previous material cost? This simple (and seemingly obvious) proportion rule is surprisingly difficult to verify for the following reasons:

(a) Some material prices change quickly, e.g. the international price of copper or tin might double or halve within three months.
(b) Some machines process materials of significantly different values at different times, e.g. a woodworker's lathe may use rare hardwoods or cheap softwoods, or an electricity-generating station may switch from coal to oil and back again).
(c) Sometimes the input of materials into a machine is impossible to record (e.g. coal into a coal-cutter), can be only approximately measured (e.g. the metering of a pipeline liquid), or is only measured when it is added to a stockpile fronting a machine (e.g. sand unloaded onto a building site is not measured when put into cement mixers).

(3) *Variable utility costs.* Is there a simple relationship between utility costs and a machine's throughput? For example, if you know the number of hours per year that a conveyor belt has run, is there a simple multiplying factor to tell you the conveyor belt's electricity cost? It is not that easy. There might be an easy formula to tell you the units of electricity (kWh) that have been consumed. But to transfer units consumed to costs, you have to allow for peak period surcharges, night-time or bulk-purchase discounts and increased costs if standby generation has had to be used.

(4) *Variable repair and maintenance costs.* Direct repair and maintenance costs increase with age and usage. Indirectly, there is a hidden cost of lost revenue when a machine is frequently out of service. Also, for older machines there are the delays caused by spare parts being unavailable, and the inability to meet the highest quality specifications.

3.4.2.2 Fixed costs

Fixed costs are insensitive to changes in a machine's throughput. If they have occurred in the past and are not going to recur again they are *sunk costs* and we can ignore them. The remaining fixed costs fall within the following classifications.

(1) Some costs are fixed for each order received, regardless of how many items are requested by the order. For example, there is a *set-up cost* involving skilled labour and special materials to make a printing plate, a plastics mould or a clothing pattern.

(2) Some *annual fixed costs* are independent of either the number of orders to be processed or the throughput. For example, the annual licence fee of a vehicle falls into this category. Some fixed costs are included in the general overheads of a firm even though they could be assigned to a particular machine. For example, an insurance cover note often specifies the premium for each item of equipment. Rent cannot be allocated quite so precisely, but space taken up by the machine is often a reasonable guide. Sometimes, crowded offices retain obsolescent machines for occasional use. Because they have been 'fully depreciated', some managers regard retaining them as involving no cost, which is misguided if the office space could be used for something else.

(3) Extra fixed costs which need to be examined when considering the replacement of a machine. These include:

(a) The current purchase price of the new machine (the previous purchase price may be irrelevant because of inflation, obsolescence, technical progress, trade wars by the equipment suppliers or foreign-exchange movements if it is purchased from abroad).
(b) The trade-in or scrap value of your existing machine, including the value of parts which you cannibalize for use on other machines in your organization (this is an important factor for recovered space satellites).
(c) Installation costs for the new machine.
(d) Commissioning costs, teething troubles and the running-in expense whilst bringing a product up to the required standard.
(e) Demolition and removal charges on the old machine (including the disruption to production and delays in the service to your customers that may result).
(f) Subsidies and tax allowance including both immediate and future allowable claims.

3.4.2.3 Indirect costs

The two main types of indirect cost are passed-on costs and intangible costs.

(1) *Passed-on costs* are those cost increases (or savings) in other parts of the system which arise when a new machine is introduced. For example, a new word processor might not only make a typewriter redundant, it might also replace printing and typesetting machines, and filing cabinets.

Conversely, some new machines which save operating labour may require more machinery elsewhere in the system. Consider a bank's introduction of an advanced on-line computing system which constantly handles money transfers. This can eliminate some of the paperwork and labour associated with the old cheque-clearing system, but the new system must guard against machine errors, electricity failures and sophisticated frauds. Some banks have solved this problem by installing a parallel system which duplicates the work of the first but, just to be safe, uses a different manufacturer's hardware, a different source of electricity and a completely independent team of programmers.

Finally, a new, 'more efficient' machine might require higher stock levels to service it, or might be unable to work at a low level of capacity. Compare, for example, nuclear power stations (which can supply only base-load electricity) with gas turbine generators (which can provide the more valuable electricity during peak demand).

(2) *Intangible costs* include costs which, though not easily measured in monetary terms, involve a significant social cost. For example:

* Pollution — smoke, river waste, tips
* Accidents — from traffic or dangerous cutting machines
* Long-term health costs — e.g. those affecting X-ray machine operators, garage mechanics, miners, brewery workers and tar sprayers

3.4.2.4 Example of machine evaluation — annual costs of a photocopier

Fixed costs (p.a.)
  Rental charge $= £900$

Variable costs (p.a.)

				£
Leasing cost	0.9 p/copy	× 180,000 copies	=	1620
Labour cost	£4.50/hour	× 450 hours	=	2025
Paper cost	£5.90/1000	× 180,000	=	1062
Ink cost	£69/cartridge	× 45 cartridges	=	3105
Electricity	7.5p/kWh × 500 W	× 450 hours	=	17
				7829

Explanation of these costs
Knowledge of the number of copies produced per annum is insufficient to calculate the annual labour cost. If just one copy of a master is taken, total time is 18 seconds, made up of:

Lifting lid, placing master	8 sec
Running time	4 sec
Removing master and copy	6 sec

For multiple copies, only the running time increases (4 seconds per copy). A sample of one morning's work gave the following breakdown for 336 copies.

Number of copies	1	2	3	4	5	'10'	'20'	'30'	'50'
Frequency	50	15	8	3	2	7	3	1	1
Time per job (sec)	18	22	26	30	34	54	94	134	214

This totals 43 minutes work per morning, which, when supplemented with paper loading and dealing with copies stuck in the machine, gives approximately 50 minutes' work. Fifty minutes' work per morning for 336 copies gives approximately 450 hours per annum for 180,000 copies.

These 450 hours were charged at a secretary's gross labour cost of £4.50 per hour. The photocopier was used by higher-wage employees in the organization but it would be wrong to use these higher wages when working out the labour costs associated with the photocopier as it is up to the organization to use its labour effectively.

3.4.3 *Revenues*

Revenues from a product sold direct to a customer

The easiest revenues to estimate are those charged at a flat rate for a single product, invoiced directly to a customer (for example, a car wash, or a coin-operated washing machine). Complications arise when the following have to be taken into account:

1. *Discounts* for bulk orders. This is common in industries with a relatively high set-up cost.
2. *Surcharges* for adding extra features to a standard model. This is common in consumer durables, especially new vehicles, and in the provision of services (e.g. hairdressing and dental treatment).
3. A significant number of *offcuts, seconds, rejects* or *imperfects* produced. This is found, for example, in the clothing and pottery industries. Initially, these items might have been sold off on an ad hoc basis, but sometimes it becomes a permanent marketing ploy to have such goods available, and a machine's profitability suffers because it is devoting more of its throughput to goods with a low profit margin. Although a particular machine's profits may fall by having to make seconds, the machine's owners might benefit (because, for example, there might be a much faster turnover of the inferior goods which reduces distribution and stocking costs).

Connected to the inferior-goods phenomenon is the *by-products* situation. For example, in an oil refinery, gas oil has the sulphur removed from it to make it a less pungent product. The principal purpose of the extraction process is to produce pure gas oil. It is only incidental that a by-product, sulphur, emerges, bringing in a small revenue.

An extension of the by-product situation is where you have many *joint products* made simultaneously by the same machine (e.g. a crude-oil distillation tower, an automatic loom or a continuous paper-mill). Market forces might make first one, then another product dominant (for example, the most valuable products from an oil refinery have been, at various times, paraffins, gasolines, fuel oils or petro-chemicals). When it is perceived that there has been a permanent change in the market, the refinery attempts to adjust its processing machinery to make more of the dominant product. Sometimes the market changes are so great that even the most modern and efficient processing equipment has to be closed down.

'Revenues' from a product of an intermediate machine in a series of processes

Consider a large firm such as a steelworks. Usually the value of inputs arriving at the firm and the value of outputs leaving the firm are accurately known. But within such a firm there may be a complex network of machines passing material amongst themselves. This material is known as *intermediate stock* or *work-in-progress*. How can such material be valued?

Sometimes the price of an intermediate material is known because there is an active market for it (e.g. steel bars). Sometimes you are mistaken in wanting to know the value of inputs and outputs because they will not affect the particular decision that you are worried about. If it is necessary to make an evaluation, it is best to do this only for a group of machines between inputs and outputs of known values.

Intangible benefits

Some machines — even those supplying a service direct to a final customer — produce an 'intangible' revenue, (e.g. a lift, an escalator, a traffic-light system or hospital equipment). The first step is to ask yourself whether there is any non-monetary measure of the machine's effectiveness: for a lift, the number of people using it; for traffic lights, x more cars taking y fewer minutes to traverse a road-section; for a cancer-therapy machine, x patients living y more years. When such data have been assembled, you might have a clearer picture of the social value of a machine (if social value can be measured). Some cost–benefit analysts claim that all these intangibles can be converted to money terms, but this is open to dispute.

3.4.4 Example of a student assignment on a commercial washing machine

Now that we no longer have our mothers to solve that nasty problem of 'dirty laundry', and are forced, if only for the sake of those around us, to do our own washing, we thought it might be interesting to study the godsend more commonly known as the commercial washing machine.

The machine itself:	The Maytag A23 commercial washing machine. It washes, rinses, and then spins the clothes.
The 'user' point of view:	The Maytag A23 is 99 per cent idiot-proof. All you need is a 50 pence piece, some washing powder, and a smattering of common sense. Then you put your clothes, along with your washing powder, into the machine, your 50p in the slot, and hey presto, in little over 30 minutes, your clothes are clean once again.

The only part which requires any thought is choosing the appropriate programme for your clothes, but Maytag has made even this simple. As they themselves say, you just 'dial a scientifically programmed cycle for any washable and dryable fabric, making better results and correct fabric care almost automatic'. All you have to do is decide which cycle description best fits your clothes and move the dial accordingly.

Inputs:	Dirty clothes Water Washing powder Electricity
Output:	Clean clothes
Capacity:	On average, maximum capacity is approximately 15 lb of dry clothes, although this varies depending upon the density of the fabrics. For instance, the machine easily holds 15 lb of jeans, but would have difficulties coping with 15 lb of continental quilt.
Length of transformation process/cycle:	Approximately 30–35 minutes. This varies with the length of time the machine takes to fill with water.
Maximum output:	The washing machine can be used without problems (and frequently is in places such as nursing homes) for 24 hours a day. When it is in continuous use like this, quantities of up to 25 lb of clean clothes can be produced per hour.
Life expectancy:	When used for roughly 6 hours a day, a Maytag A23 can be expected to last 12–15 years. When they finally do wear out, there are no problems with replacement — another one is simply put in its place.
Cost of installation:	A direct replacement, involving no spare parts or any other work, simply involves employing 2 men for 2–3

hours, and so costs somewhere in the region of £50–£60. The cost differs depending upon the amount of work which needs to be done; for example, a drain may need to be adapted, and this would increase the costs. Similarly, if the machine is the first one to be installed (i.e. it is not a replacement) and much work needs to be done, the installation can cost as much as £300–£400.

The cost of the Maytag A23 machine, known as the 'Rolls Royce of Top Loaders', is £1100. It is the top of the Maytag range.

Running costs:

Electricity per kWh	7.50p
Gas per therm	48.50p
Water per 220 gallons of supply including sewerage	118.27p

Cost per cycle:	
Water	14.23p
Heating water by gas	5.16p
Electricity (normal cycle)	0.72p
Total cost per cycle	20.11p

Revenues:

Revenues vary drastically from machine to machine, but a set of eight washers and driers installed in a hall of residence together raised £800. Our extensive experience of launderettes leads us to believe that of these takings, 65 per cent (i.e. £520) would probably have been from the washing machines. There are eight machines: therefore, one machine (on average) takes £65 per month. Of these takings, 25 per cent is returned to the hall to cover running costs.

Obviously the machines in this hall are profitable ones, although it is not always the case. For example, the launderette in another hall takes only £30 in a year, so the takings from halls with a good return, are used to subsidise any loss-making machines. Sometimes machines are removed completely if the loss is very great. Conversely, if the demand is exceptionally heavy, extra machines are added as required, provided that there is room for them and it is cost effective.

Spare parts:

There have been no problems with spare parts, which are still available even for 25-year-old models.

Repairs:

Any problems which are reported are dealt with either on the same day or on the next day. In certain cases repairs are left for longer than this but this is usually when machines are deliberately damaged. For example, residents at one hall blocked up the machines with cardboard 50 pence pieces, so in an attempt to teach the offenders a lesson, the repairs were left for several days.

▼   **Contact exercise**

(a) Visit a machine with which you are unfamiliar, and find out as much as you can about the inputs, outputs, throughputs, costs and revenues.

(b) Write a report which summarizes your findings. You will need to contact someone who owns or runs such a machine. Contacting these people can be a problem because:

   (i) Service engineers are elusive (they are always on the move).
   (ii) Operatives' work may be so demanding that they cannot stop and talk to you.
   (iii) Machines can be noisy, dusty, hot, dangerous and inaccessible.

▲   Our experience is that *if* you manage to get through to someone responsible for a machine they are usually delighted to tell you about it.

3.4.5 *The 'standard alternative' approach to decisions*

All decisions about a machine must be made with some imperfect information. The many reasons for this have been outlined in our review of costs and revenues above. But the problem of missing or doubtful information can be overcome if you compress decision-making to a choice between standardized alternatives. To take an obvious example, if you are comparing two cars with the same fuel efficiency, future changes in the price of petrol may be ignored. Likewise, if you are comparing two chemical extractors, so long as they handle the same input, it does not matter that there are awkward problems in valuing this input; and, if you are comparing two machines which take up the same space, you don't have to worry about the allocation of rent and rates by head office to these machines.

Therefore, to make an effective evaluation of alternatives, eliminate everything that is common to both and concentrate on the rest. The detailed breakdown of costs and revenues previously given helps you to do this. The more difficult the decisions, the more appropriate is this procedure.

▼   **Exercise**

In this exercise you will be looking at the implications of using either four big or four little buses to service a busy city route.   ▷

Basic standardized situations

Assume that:

1. You must provide a bus service on the route for 15 hours per day.
2. The route is a 12 km round trip (i.e. a 6 km journey from the suburb to the city centre and 6 km return journey).
3. Three thousand passengers a day use this route, giving a revenue of £1500 per day (3000 × 50p per journey).

Because of the difference in speed and handling capacity of different sized buses the timetabling is quite different. The operating characteristics and costs of the two alternatives are given in Table 3.2.

What would be the maximum number of passengers a bus can handle during an out-and-back route? One crude approximation is twice its capacity (if the bus is full for its journey out, and it is full with a different set of passengers for its journey in). In fact, the maximum number of passengers which could be handled could be a bit higher if you allow for people who use the bus for only a few stops.

Costs

Drivers' wages: Each bus, whether big or small, needs 2 drivers per day; one for the morning shift, and one for the afternoon shift. It is assumed that you pay the same wages to a driver, whether he is driving a big or small bus. Allowing for driver's holidays and absences, etc., it costs a bus company £65 to employ a driver for his daily shift.

Maintenance costs: These vary greatly according to the size of bus. The rule-of-thumb suggested in Croner's *Operational Costing for Transport Management* is:

Table 3.2 Operating characteristics of the two buses

	72-seater double decker	24-seater single decker
Average speed (including stops)	12 kph	18 kph
Time taken to complete a 12 km round route	60 min	40 min
Frequency of service with 4 buses	15 min	10 min
Number of out and back routes completed in a 15 hour day	15	22½
Maximum number of passengers per bus during one day	750	750
Number of passengers handled on one out-and-back trip	50	33

▷

| 72-seater | 22.5p per kilometre
(or £40.5 for the 180 kilometres it covers in a day) |
| 24-seater | 10.5p per kilometre
(or £28.35 for the 270 kilometers it covers in a day) |

Diesel fuel costs: These also vary for each size of bus:

| 72-seater | Does 2.25 km/litre; so travelling 180 km a day, it consumes 80 litres. At 24p/litre, its daily fuel cost is £19.20. |
| 24-seater | Does 4.15 km/llitre; so travelling 270 km a day, it consumes 65 litres. At 24p/litre, its daily fuel cost is £15.60. |

Tyres: Tyres need to be replaced every 3000 km.

| 72-seater | Covers 64,800 km/year, so needs 2 sets of tyres at £1,500 per set. So tyre costs are £8.22 per day. |
| 24-seater | Covers 97,200 km per year, so needs 3 sets of tyres at £480 a set. So tyre costs are £3.95 per day. |

Other operating costs: These are fairly trivial when converted to a day by day basis, these are

| 72-seater | Insurance £3.45. Road Tax £1.25. |
| 24-seater | Insurance £1.85. Road Tax £0.55. |

Capital costs

If buses are purchased, it is a bit tricky to convert the purchase price and related cash flows to a daily figure. This could be done precisely via a discounted cash flow analysis. Rather than get into an extended discussion on this technique, we suggest using a rough-and-ready calculation when making an initial stab at comparing alternatives:

	72-seater	*24-seater*
Purchase price of a new bus:	£97,750	£34,900

As we said above, it is a bit difficult to allocate this cost on a daily basis; amongst other things you need to know how many years you are going to keep the bus, and what is its disposal value when you get rid of it.

One way round this problem is to work out what is your capital loss over one year of operating the bus. The capital loss is the price that you paid for the bus at the beginning of the year, and the price you could get for it second-hand at the end of the year. This can be found from lists of used-vehicle prices. For our buses these are approximately:

▷

	72-seater	24-seater
Capital loss over a year for a new bus, or,	£11,500	£5,400
If a 4 year old bus is bought:	£ 6,000	£2,600

It is probably better to take the capital loss on four-year buses rather than to assume the heavier capital loss of a company using only new buses all the time.

Converting capital loss to an interest charge

Suppose every year the company sells its five-year-old buses and buys four-year-old buses. From the previous table, you can see that after it has sold its five-year-old 72-seater it has to find £6000 extra to purchase an equivalent four-year-old bus. If this money is borrowed from the bank at 20 per cent interest, it pays an annual interest charge of £1,200 (or £3.29 per day). For both buses, the standardized alternative can be approximated as:

	72-seater	24-seater
Daily interest charge if 4-year-old buses are used to replace 5-year-old buses:	£3.29	£1.42

(a) Comparing all the above costs and revenues, and bearing in mind hidden variations in service and traffic that might occur, what size bus would you recommend the company to use?

(b) So far we have tried to compare like with like, but at the end of the day such different machines will give different service quality. Can you identify these extra factors? Does consideration of these factors swing the balance in deciding which alternative to choose? *Hint:* Refer back to the bus operator ▲ exercise in Chapter 1.

3.5 Recommended reading

Cases

We would first recommend Quantock Plastics Ltd (B) in G. Easton, *Learning from Case Studies* (Prentice Hall, 1982). The basic information is neatly presented and the reader is guided through a model answer (with enlightening spin-offs to forecasting, capacity planning and strategy). Then we would recommend a case in R. Schmenner, *Cases in Production/Operations Management* (SRA, 1986): 'Dean's Brewery', though short, highlights some common decisions that have to be taken on materials handling equipment. For longer cases, look at 'Transcontinental' in R.C. Meier's *Cases in Production and Operations Management* (Prentice Hall, 1982) for all the administrative rituals leading up to a request for a machine purchase.

Also recommended is the 'Stoner Machinery Company' case in David A. Collier's *Service Management* (Prentice Hall, 1987). This gives an excellent comprehensive breakdown of heavy-vehicle costs as the background information for a total maintenance and repair deal being negotiated. See also Shingo, *Key Strategies for Plant Improvement* (Nikkon Kogyo Shimbun Ltd, 1987, pp. 35–85) for a whole series of mini-examples showing his intriguing lateral-thinking approach to machine improvements.

As for things that go wrong, read 'Sarpeta Paper Company' in Sasser *et al.*, *Cases in Operations Management: Strategy and Structure* (Irwin, 1982). As well as reinforcing our recommendations on analysis of a machine's performance, it gives an honest account of various managers licking their wounds after the disaster.

Chapter 4

People — motivation and organization

4.1 Objectives and corporate culture

Objectives are the broad, long-range goals that an organization's workers mutually agree to achieve. If an organization is not sure about its objectives, then there is a danger of confusion from the boardroom to the shopfloor. Thus, it is worth summarizing what these objectives usually are, and how they affect operations management.

Firstly, those with power to influence a firm's top level decisions, known as stakeholders, negotiate amongst themselves to achieve a balance between corporate objectives. For example:

The maximum dividend to distribute
Capital appreciation of shares
Dominance over competitors
Community approval
Political influence
Employee satisfaction
Growth through acquisitions

These corporate objectives drive the middle-management objectives of departmental heads and white-collar professions. For example:

Ability to meet a deadline
Maintenance of high quality output
Curbing of excessive spending

Beneath middle-management objectives are shopfloor objectives, operated by personnel department and employee's supervisors. For example:

High productivity
High skill and proficiency
Low absenteeism and labour turnover

Low rates of industrial disputes
Willingness to accept job flexibility

In effective organizations, everyone is in accord about objectives, at whatever level.

Organizations in which everyone is in accord are said to have a good corporate culture. Culture in this context refers to the noticeable way in which *all* work is done by *all* workers in an organization. For example, the strong customer-orientation at MacDonald's hamburger chain or Scandinavian Airline Services. A review of US customer-orientated firms can be found in T.J. Peters and R.H. Waterman's *In Search of Excellence* (Harper and Row Publishers Inc., 1982). Emphasis on corporate culture has been put forward as a major reason for the success of Japanese firms. When these firms set up subsidiaries in other parts of the world they lay great store on establishing a good culture. For example, when Nissan set up a new factory in Washington, County Durham, they considered 17,000 applicants before choosing 250 manufacturing staff with the special qualities they were looking for. Nissan wished to operate a system of flexible innovation. All employees were to be involved in a cycle of *planning*, *doing*, *checking* and *actioning*. Within each of these categories were subcycles. This system, more extensive than quality circles, is known as *kaizen* (continual improvement).

4.2 Management control and communications

Most large organizations have an *organization chart* which identifies every worker's boss. An example of such a chart is shown in Figure 4.1.

Identifying the span of control. For any boss on the organization chart, this is measured by the number of subordinates he has got. There is no hard-and-fast rule on the ideal number of subordinates. It varies from industry to industry and on whether there is an assembly, batch, continuous or service process. With close, one-to-one training (e.g. in dentistry), the span of control is at most two or three. With experienced workers doing routine jobs on trouble-free and simple operations, it can be 40+.

The role of cross-departmental links. Organization charts emphasize authority, command, responsibility and supervision. They are *not* meant to define other types of contact. There should be an unhindered flow of information between many departments of a firm, even if they are only remotely connected on the organization chart. For example, marketing with quality assurance, transport with packaging, progress chasers with production control, personnel with supervisors.

Communicating with colleagues. Consider boss–subordinate communications. There are distinct styles.

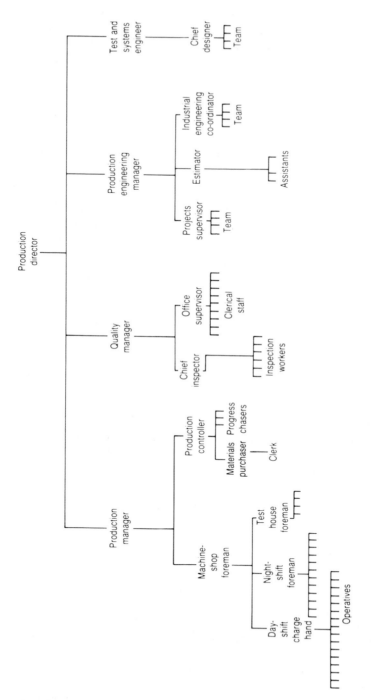

Figure 4.1 Organization chart.

	Boss to subordinate	*Subordinate replies*
(a) *Participatory*	Very interesting. What are we going to do about it?	Let us do this and this and start next week.
(b) *Delegatory*	Could you have a go at doing this yourself?	Leave it to me. I'll look after it.
(c) *Audit*	Have you done what was wanted?	Up to a point. I'll explain what I have done.
(d) *Boundary etiquette*	I gather your work is being held up by another department.	Please could you speak to someone about it.
(e) *Bureaucratic*	Our project has to go through many stages of approval.	My committee will collect detailed evidence and start work on all the necessary reports.

People who want to get things done prefer styles (a) and (b), but other styles occasionally have their advantages. For example, style (e) would be suitable for the launching of a new drug with possibly dangerous side-effects.

Communicating with outsiders. Some security-conscious firms try to minimize or formalize such contacts. This is to stop theft, bribery, the leaking of trade secrets or adverse publicity, or to stop poaching of employees. Apart from these exceptional situations, there is much to be said for encouraging outside contacts. It is an essential part of a salesperson's duty to go beyond regular customers and to make *cold contacts* with people he has never met before. Likewise a purchasing officer should actively be seeking new suppliers, especially where a firm has only one current source. Training of apprentices can often be supplemented in technical colleges. It is also useful to have access to subcontractors who can help you handle an unexpected surge in orders.

4.3 Jobs and conditions of work

Most established workers have a contract of employment. Sometimes this contract is spelt out into a more detailed job description:

1. As a reminder where the employee has a variety of duties (some done only infrequently).
2. As a means of drawing a clear boundary between who does what, where the employee's responsibilities might overlap with those of neighbouring colleagues.
3. When it is necessary to draw up detailed linkages showing communication or authority.
4. When it is used as the basis for appraising an employee's performance.

That is the good news. The bad news is that in large organizations where personnel departments have been established for some time, job descriptions can get out of hand. Fairly straightforward job descriptions may get written up exhaustively and become a confusing mixture of *responsibilities, skills, procedures, roles* and *initiatives.* Ideally, these five items should be clearly distinguished. For example, this is how you could separate some of the duties of a ship's captain.

Responsibilities:	Accepting dismissal or criminal proceedings if negligence by you or your crew endangers passengers' lives.
Skills:	Being able to steer, navigate and dock.
Procedures:	To know the procedures and documentation by which passengers and cargo are brought on board or disembarked.
Roles:	Reinforcing the perception by passengers and crew that you are in charge by the way you dress, communicate and interact socially, and by following traditions such as being the last to leave a sinking ship.
Initiatives:	To show resourcefulness in unexpected crises such as a violent storm, mechanical breakdown or a hostage incident.

4.3.1 *Job design*

Certain strenuous jobs are essential for the operation of our society, e.g. firemen, policemen, and soldiers in a battle situation.

Clearly a manager responsible for such strenuous jobs should take care in designing conditions of work. Here is a three-phase approach to this problem:

Phase 1. Take every nasty feature of a job and apply a rough unpleasantness scale.

Phase 2. Write out a rough job description, which clearly distinguishes the five features *responsibilities, skills, procedures, roles,* and *initiatives.*

Phase 3. Work out a satisfactory scheme of remuneration and fulfilment. This may not be easy.

Money alone is not sufficient compensation for the job that has to be done. One alternative is job rotation, where the dirtiest jobs are shared. Or there may be other non-monetary rewards, such as high recognition by society for firemen or policemen in the thick of activity. Or there may be early retirement and generous pensions for the most strenuous jobs. Or there may be a granting of independence and freedom from supervision. Finally, there may be a generous system of off-work allowances, longer holidays or more breaks for relaxation and recovery.

4.4 Payment systems

4.4.1 *Introduction*

All payment systems can be divided into four types:

1. Payment for the number of hours worked.
2. Payment for the number of items made.
3. A share of the profits.
4. A fixed payment for fulfilling the duties of a post.

This is a deceptively simple classification. Any firm that has formulated its wage agreement with a union will need to write out a document the length of a small book. The complications arise through a tendency to have:

1. A different wage for each craft, skill or profession.
2. A different reward for each different product made under piecework.
3. Different allowances for the many circumstances under which work takes place.

Payment systems must also be tailored to the particular operating process in question. A research laboratory functions better using profit sharing and fixed payments rather than payment by number of hours or number of items. This last type of payment would also not be suitable for a worker on a fixed-pace assembly line, but would be ideal where measurable work is required from building subcontractors. Payment for the number of hours worked would be suitable where the worker is required as much for his or her *presence* as for the *content* of what he does (as, for example, with a nightwatchman or artist's model). As most organizations have a mixture of processes, they tend to have a mixture of payment systems too.

Faced with such a complexity, are there any general guiding principles underlying payment policies? Put banally, a firm wants to give the worker an incentive to do what the firm wants that worker to do. Often, this has been crudely translated as 'How can we get the worker to maximize his output rate per hour?' More subtly, one seeks a payment system that also meets other objectives, such as high quality of finished work, low labour turnover and absenteeism, or an innovative and loyal workforce.

4.4.2 *Time-rates of payment*

When people are paid a basic *hourly* or a *day rate*, what exceptions and adjustments must be covered?

1. The *overtime rate*, according to whether it is longer working hours during the weekday, nightwork, other awkward hours during shiftwork, weekend working, or working over a statutory holiday — overtime rates traditionally appear as 1¼, 1½ or double-time mark-ups;

2. *Differentials*, to take into account the different profession, competence, experience and status of every worker in an organization.

3. *Special allowances* for: living in a certain geographic area (e.g. an isolated community, a capital city, or a war-zone); unsocial duties (e.g. a fireman handling dangerous chemicals, a policeman handling dangerous people); or doing duty outside the normal terms of contract (e.g. emergency-replacement or training others).

All of the above have to be changed every time there is a general cost-of-living increase. Such change can lead to *wage-drift*, a state of affairs where these 'extras' become a larger proportion of a worker's earnings. On the surface, wage-drift may appear fairly harmless. But in the long-run it can have a bad effect on the workforce's attitude and productivity. For example, they might surreptitiously 'go slow' during normal hours to increase work needing to be done during overtime.

Time-rate payment systems do not by themselves encourage people to work hard. So such systems have to be reinforced with close (and expensive) supervision, with disciplinary procedures to keep the bad workers on their toes, and with promotion procedures to give an incentive to the good. As well as such systems being administratively complicated, they do not permit finer, subtler elements of control of workers. Ideally, a 'reward and punishment' approach works best if it is applied in small doses, follows directly from the cause, and is an intimate matter between supervisor and worker. It is hard to get pure time-rate systems to work in this way. It is for this reason that employers sometimes supplement time-rate payments with piece-rate or bonus-rate systems.

4.4.3 *Piece-rate and variants*

In its crudest form, piece-rate rewards are directly proportional to the output a worker produces, as shown in Figure 4.2.

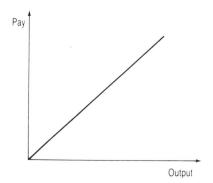

Figure 4.2 The simplest piece-rate system.

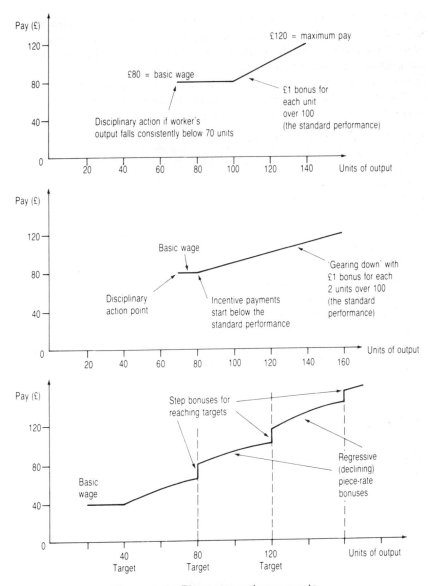

Figure 4.3 Piece rate enhancements.

The crude proportional piece-rate system is still popular with subcontractors, outworkers and commission salespeople. But most piece-rates include certain enhancements, summarized in Figure 4.3.

Stabilizing incentive schemes. If output is subject to erratic fluctuations, only partly under the influence of the worker, this can have drastic effects on a piece-worker's earnings. One way of stabilizing earnings is to arrange for them to be based on a moving average of a worker's performance (for example on his or her last three months' work). This certainly damps down extreme fluctuations, but it also creates a lag between the worker's effort and the reward received for it.

Another approach is to devise a league table of workers. The highest rates per hour are given to those 'first division' workers with the highest rate of productivity. Typically there may be eight to twelve divisions. Promotion and demotion between divisions is determined by a moving average often based over the last month's performance. Unlike in a football league, there is no fixed number of people in each division. All employees may be in the top (or bottom) division. But the rules prevent a new employee leaping from bottom to top division straight away: however good the performance, he or she can only be promoted to the division immediately above. The length of time it will take to claw all the way up to the top division is supposed to condition the worker to hard work. It is usual for a fall-off in performance to be treated a little leniently (e.g. at any review a worker may fall by no more than one, or sometimes two, divisions). This league-table procedure is a frequent feature of measured daywork piece-rate systems.

Overview of piece-rate systems. Wherever a worker's output can be easily measured, management should at least think about a piece-rate system. When doing so though, they should be aware of a whole range of possible negative effects:

1. Deterioration in quality.
2. Extra administrative costs in calculating piece-rate payments.
3. Work study having to calculate a new piece-rate each time there is an operating improvement.
4. Piece-workers hiding any improvements they make to their job in order to avoid having their rate cut.
5. Piece-workers' preference for a big queue of incoming work, encouraging high in-process stocks.
6. Discontent if a carelessly designed piece-rate system gives easy money to some.
7. Health hazards if greed encourages piece-workers to overwork.
8. Loss of job flexibility — workers will be unwilling to train others or to substitute on a job where they cannot immediately reach a high level of productivity.

4.4.4 *A fixed payment for fulfilling the duties of a job*

The rewards of many white-collar workers are fixed. For example, an MP is not — could not be — paid by hours worked, effort or contribution to profit, even if these could be measured. Managers do not claim extra payment for out-of-hours work: they work whenever required in return for greater status and job security. These are examples of 100 per cent 'payment by appointment'. Other workers may receive some of their wages in this form, such as a basic minimum wage given regardless of output or hours worked. This type of payment is also distributed via fringe benefits: company car, sports facilities, medical care, pensions, travel, fuel and clothing entitlements. These payments are distinguished by their availability to workers regardless of the effort that they put into their work. Could more blue-collar workers get paid in this fashion? This happens in Japan and may be one component in securing a committed and co-operative workforce. However, such a move must be accompanied by proper motivation and control.

4.4.5 *Bonus and profit-sharing schemes*

Pure profit-sharing schemes are found only amongst small workers' co-operatives and communes. Such organizations are run on almost family lines, the sharing of workload sometimes extending to sharing money or possessions. For larger organizations, a less intense co-ownership scheme can work well (as, for example, in the John Lewis chain of department stores). Recently, co-ownership schemes have increased in number via management buyouts. There is some risk to employees participating in a management buyout because they often have to borrow at high rates of interest to take up a share in the business.

From the employees' point of view, a less risky system is the company-wide bonus scheme. For example, the Scanlon Plan, popular in the USA, gives workers greater bonuses if they maintain high general productivity (e.g. by avoiding excessive overtime or downtime). Another successful scheme in the USA (the Lincoln Electric Plan) succeeds by a subtle mixture of individual, departmental and company bonuses.

▼   **Exercise — time rates or piece-rates for the Free Range Poultry Company?**

The Free Range Poultry Company is a family-owned meat-processing company which supplies many major retail outlets, food chains and wholesale butchers. We are concerned only with a new and expanding area of its operations — its duck sales.

The company sells 175,000 ducks per year and expects this number to increase by 25,000 per year. Currently, there is a small factory unit of 14 workers and a manager to handle the duck carcasses. The workers split up their tasks as follows.

Plucking	2 workers
Washing	5 workers
Eviscerating	3 workers
Packing	4 workers

All these workers can be fairly easily trained or replaced, but the nature of the machine system requires there to be 14 workers, no more, no less.

At present the workers are paid £3 an hour for an 8-hour day, 5-day week.

When work is slack, they still get £120 a week. If they work overtime, they get paid £4.50 an hour. Theoretically the 14 workers should be able to process 1000 ducks a day, but this only happens if the manager supervises them constantly — something which, because of his other duties, he cannot often do. Actually, only at peak season, such as preparing for Christmas sales, are more than 1000 ducks a day needed. An approximation would be to take the 250 working days during a year, and to say that for 150 working days, 500 ducks/day are processed; and for the remaining 100 days, 1000 ducks/day are processed. (When 1000 ducks per day are processed, 3 hours of overtime per worker are needed.) As demand increases yearly, it looks as though more overtime will have to be worked to meet it. Alternatively, it is known that workers are capable of much greater productivity and perhaps a different reward system would help. What would you advise? State precisely what your new rates would be, and what would be the financial, quality and supervisory consequences for Free Range Poultry?

▲

4.4.6 *Further cases on payment systems*

See Sasser *et al.*'s case study 'Fabritch Corporation and FBO Inc.' in *Cases in Operations Management: Analysis and Action* (Irwin, 1982) Fabritch is a neat, clear case with spin-offs for quality and scheduling. FBO is a horror story of how jobs and payments get over-complicated if management loses control. Read also 'The case of the unpopular pay plan' by Tom Ehrenfeld in *Harvard Business Review* (Jan/Feb 1992). This stirred up a fascinating controversy in the letters pages of the March/April issue.

4.5 Work measurement

Output is affected by varying labour, machine and material inputs. By convention, work measurement concentrates on labour input. A classic and early example is F.W. Taylor's story of his pig-iron-loading experiments in Bethlehem, Pennsylvania in 1899 (see section 4.5.6). The topic of work measurement is controversial. It influences the hiring-and-firing policy of a firm, the work practices, and the level of incentives and wages. Sometimes, especially in specialist engineering and subcontracting, the measurement of work is delegated to a foreman or rate-fixer. He negotiates with each worker the payment rate for each special job done; but this would be a laborious, haphazard arrangement in industries with a more regular pattern of work. In such industries, measurements made well in advance can be used again and again as a basis for payment, supervision and job design. These measurements are the province of the work-study personnel.

The tools of a traditional work-study officer were elementary: stopwatch and clipboard. Officers had to have an intimate knowledge of all jobs that they examined, and empathy with the workers that they observed. Also, they were valued for their experience in judging fairly the correct pace of work, allowing for workers' different abilities and different working conditions. Nowadays there is a tendency to replace, or rather enhance, the work-study officer's experience with more formal methods of analysis. This may require detailed physiological knowledge or access to a computer database. Consultants are often brought in to install a proprietary work-measurement system and to instruct work-study personnel in its operation. At the end of the day though, someone in the firm has to have an intimate knowledge of what the job of each key worker entails. If nothing else, someone has to be ready to train a replacement if a worker leaves. We explain here a four-level approach by which a work-study officer can break down and understand a job's detail.

4.5.1 *Level 1 — measurements from daily operating information*

In the day-to-day running of the workplace, certain paperwork passes amongst operatives, foremen and the production-control staff: works orders, job tickets, machine routing-and-loading instructions, material requisitions, starting and completion dates, labour usages, and inspection and delivery cards. For example, a plastic-injection-moulding unit which is run well should be able to supply a work-study officer with the following information, without necessitating extra observations on the shopfloor.

Analysis of machine downtime

Shift start-up preparations
End-of-work clearing up
Testing machine specifications
New mould installation
Old mould removal
Repair
Waiting for repair
Waiting for material
Waiting for operative
Waiting for a job

Labour information

Name of operative
Basic hours worked
Overtime hours worked
Hours assigned to each machine

Job information

Name of customer
Work order-code
Size of order
Due delivery date
Mould-preparation time
Material-loading time
Cure/press time

Even with all such information it is difficult for a work-study officer to construct the *sequence* of happenings during the day. For this purpose it is necessary to have a diary of events for the operative and each of the machines under his or her control. This information can be compressed into a resource-utilization bar chart. The charts in Figure 4.4 show the activities of an injection-moulding operative responsible for three machines: I, II and III. The shaded areas pinpoint which machine the operative is working on at any point of the day.

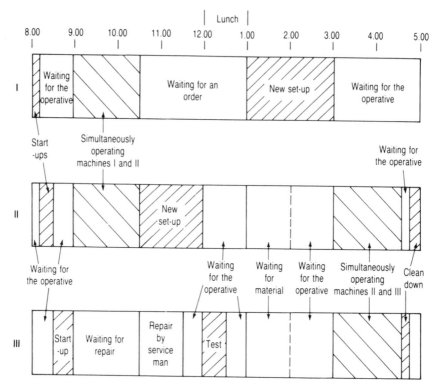

Figure 4.4 Activities of an injection-moulding operative.

Day-to-day information in this form is of great interest to the work-study officer and to production control. It helps them decide manpower planning, job structuring and productivity improvements. But at this (still broad) level of detail it is inefficient to have someone collecting records by keeping a permanent watch on the workers. During the day there are still relatively few occasions when a note has to be made that a change in activity has taken place. It is preferable if the worker involved or the foreman, rather than the work-study officer, records these data. Carrying out extra clerical duties will be a nuisance to machine operatives, and understandably their records are often not as accurate or complete as work study would like. As a general rule, you would expect better feedback from workers who feel that they are part of the decision-making process.

4.5.2 *Level 2 — cycles of work within a day*

Within a day, a worker may move repetitively between machines or jobs. Typically, such a cycle of activities could take between one and twenty minutes. This situation can be observed in a wide variety of industrial practices, particularly in the machining of metal or wood, in garment manufacture and on many assembly lines. Certain of these situations are worth analysing via a *multiple-activity chart* if the following conditions hold:

1. The worker can easily transfer his or her attention backwards and forwards between distinct machines, processes or products.
2. There are occasions when a machine runs automatically, freeing the attendant to work elsewhere for a while.

Consider the previous plastic-injection-moulding example. The operative was moving amongst three machines:

1. Loading/unloading them, or
2. Letting them work automatically on curing, or
3. Leaving the machines idle.

The products have the characteristics shown in Table 4.1. On the basis of these characteristics, the multiple-activity chart shown in Figure 4.5 was drawn up.

In day-to-day matters, it is the production control staff who make most use of multiple-activity charts. The scheduling aspect of their work is described elsewhere. The charts also provide a useful basis for certain work-study exercises:

Table 4.1 Product characteristics (time in minutes)

	Loading/ unloading	Automatic curing	Total
Product A on machine I	2	4	6
Product B on machine II	1	2	3
Product C on machine III	1	1	2

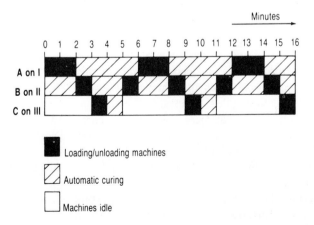

Figure 4.5 Operator's multiple—activity chart developed from product characteristics.

1. To provide information for the tackling of long-term bottleneck problems. By analysing many charts, one can discover whether it is better to research ways to cut loading/unloading times, or whether it is better to try to speed up curing times.
2. To consider the options for job structure and design. Workers might find certain switching between machines too boring or too stressful.

4.5.3 *Level 3 — job elements within a cycle*

Consider the duties of a woman responsible for clearing the tables of a canteen. Setting out from the kitchen she has this cycle of activities:

1. Push trolley from kitchen to first uncleared table.
2. Go through a *subcycle* of activities (see later) to clear that table.
3. If trolley is full, return to kitchen, otherwise
4. Push trolley to next uncleared table, and go to (2) above.

Within activity (2) is a further subcycle of activities:

1. Collect uneaten food and rubbish and put it in the trolley's bin.
2. Collect cutlery and place in trolley bins.
3. Collect cups and glasses and place on top of trolley.
4. Collect plates and stack underneath trolley.
5. Clear trays with a cloth and take to nearest stack of trays.
6. Wipe table clean.

Each of the above activities is close to what in traditional work study was known as a *job element*. In its purest form, a job element embraces everything within a uniform activity, for example:

*   Climbing a ladder of a certain height and slope.
*   Lifting a load of a certain weight to a certain height.
*   Screwing up a nut on a certain length bolt.

It is convenient to relax this definition a little to include an activity which contains a messy set of slightly variable operations but which is nevertheless quite distinct — clearing rubbish from a table is a good example of this.

The recording process also has an influence on how job elements are defined. It is useful if the observer can collect times at reasonable intervals (say between 5 and 30 seconds). One looks for a clear *breakpoint* which separates two job elements and can be used as a signal to record a time. The breakpoint may be something obvious, such as a van door being shut. But an observer might also want to use something which, although quite clear to him (e.g. an operator's regular turn of his head), nevertheless does not strictly divide two elements.

Very often, job elements are being used as the building blocks in exercises to determine people's workloads and rates of pay. Therefore a work-study officer must be aware of subtle variations in the nature of work and somehow make allowances for them. For example, the canteen worker will be affected by:

1. Object resistance — e.g. the extra power required to accelerate and brake a heavily loaded as distinct from an empty trolley.
2. Object fragility — the greater care required in collecting a high proportion of glassware.
3. Object shape — e.g. cups are easier to pick up than saucers but more difficult to stack.

Also the woman in the canteen will be affected by environmental variations outside her control, e.g:

4. Variations in efficiency of tools — e.g. jammed swivels on a trolley's wheels so that it will not run smoothly.
5. Physical blocks to efficiency — e.g. briefcases blocking passageways.
6. Physical environment — e.g. too hot, too cold, too dark.
7. Mental distractions — a loose child, dog, or wasp.

It is essential for a work-study officer to be aware of the above hindrances. They affect how he or she *rates the performance* of the person being observed. If it is judged to be slower than a normal well-motivated worker, then the *observed time* is scaled down to a *basic time*. Scaling down is a subjective issue depending entirely on the skill and experience of the work-study officer. This is aided by *tempo-rating* — observing films of workers operating at a variety of performance levels and comparing observers' assessments. Eventually, if observers do enough tempo-rating exercises, their estimates should converge.

Various allowances are added to the basic time to arrive at a final *standard time* for a job. These allowances are:

1. *Personal allowances* — e.g. refreshment or toilet breaks.
2. *Fatigue allowances* — e.g. rests after heavy lifting or a long period of concentration.
3. *Delay or contingency allowances* — e.g. where the system has broken down and there is a material, staff, machine or vehicle shortage.
4. *Interference allowance* — e.g. where there is enforced idleness even when the system is working optimally. This idleness arises from the technical nature of the process, such as waiting for a chemical mixture to settle, or for a machine to decelerate before the next job can be done.

Work study can make objective recommendations as to what these allowances should be. Often they are amended as a result of bargaining between unions and management, so actual allowances for the same job may vary from firm to firm depending on union and management bargaining power.

4.5.4 *Level 4 — micromovement within a job element*

Self-generated data. Typically, job elements at level 3 occur with a frequency of 2–20 a minute. There are situations, though, where it is desirable to make a much greater breakdown of an employee's movements, in extreme cases up to 200 per minute. This can be done by taking a film of an employee, and analysing his motions frame by frame.

For many firms, the cost of film equipment used to be regarded as prohibitive, but nowadays a quite moderate budget can obtain a cine camera and video recording equipment.

Predetermined data. An alternative to taking your own film is to call upon the experience of micromotion consultants, especially those offering variants of methods time measurement (MTM). From the analysis of enormous numbers of slow-motion films, these consultants have constructed detailed reference tables which cover pretty well every physical activity that an employee could make, permed against such things as the weight of material to be lifted, the distance over which the object moves and the outside characteristics of the object. Most micromotion systems start from a major classification of motions similar to Gilbreth's 18 'therbligs' (see next section). But within these major lines are subclassifications and within them subsubclassifications. Altogether, the MTM tables cover thousands of different situations. Even so, you have to do a lot of observation and preparatory work before you can take advantage of the MTM tables.

Consider the actions of a canteen lady from the moment she stops her trolley by an uncleared table to the moment she grasps a dirty plate two seconds later. The following list gives the *minimum* detail that you are required to assemble before starting an MTM analysis. The italicized headings on the left refer to the major classifications of motion. On the right you get an idea of the further detail that must be provided. There are shorthand codes for summarizing this detail.

Eye	*Glance* travels from trolley to table, 2.5 m, and *focuses* on a dirty plate 2.5 metres away from the eye.
Body	*Straightens from stooping* position (the stoop resulting from having pushed the trolley).
Body	*Turns* 90 degrees.
Legs	*Walk* four steps at 'obstructed' pace due to chairs in way.
Reach	At (jumbled classification) dirty plate. Left hand 0.4 m.
Grasp	Dirty plate (classed as a light, fragile, flat cylinder, 0.2 m in diameter with interference to grasp underneath).

At first sight, analysing any job in such detail seems ridiculous. And yet there are two very important applications for this technique:

1. Where the employee has to show tremendous manual dexterity to avoid a disastrous consequence (e.g. a power-plant operator, pilot or surgeon). Such work has been extensively analysed in *ergonomic laboratories.*
2. Where there is a repetitive operation using a universal machine (e.g. driving a vehicle, operating a lathe, working a sewing machine). In these cases, a costly MTM study can be justified in view of the many man-hours that a firm's employees might spend operating these machines.

4.5.5 *Therbligs*

Frank Gilbreth invented therbligs to give a comprehensive but simple classification of all the main motions of an industrial worker. For completeness, we include a few rarely used therbligs and a few recent additions.

Hand operations at a stationary workplace:

Grasp	
Release load	freeing hand from load
Position	aligning an object
Pre-position	rarely used now (see *Position* above)
Assemble	
Disassemble	
Use	handling a tool or machine
Hold	fixing material while working on it

Moving objects by hand:

Transport loaded	i.e. an arm movement
Transport empty	movement of empty hand

Mental activities:

Plan	thinking, deciding, comprehending
Search	sweep of eyes
Find	end of search
Select	choosing an item from a group
Inspect	viewing or feeling an object's quality

Delays:

Rest	recovering from fatigue
Unavoidable delay	a pause arising from the nature of the operation
Avoidable delay	a pause through idleness or inefficiency

Body movements other than head/hand/arm:

Walk	
Bend	
Sit	all pretty obvious
Stand-up	
Kneel	

▼   **Exercise**

Carry out a micromotion analysis of some simple common activity. Below are some suitable activities to investigate.

▷

Outdoors:

Fruit-picking (summer/autumn)
Snow-shovelling (winter)
Digging a vegetable patch (winter/spring)
Lawnmowing (spring/summer)
Hedgecutting (spring/summer/autumn)
Hanging out washing (spring/summer/autumn)

Indoors:

Sandwich-making
Repairing a cycle-tyre puncture
Ironing
Wiring an electrical plug
Photocopying a chapter of a book.

(a) Arrange for a variety of volunteers to try out the jobs, each for a short period of time (say two minutes each).

(b) What is the difference in technique between a skilful and a clumsy worker? Try to identify whether the skilful worker does things:

(i)   in a different sequence
(ii) with different movements
(iii) with greater speed and dexterity.

▲   For example when photocopying from a book, why does a skilled person put the book upside down and copy from the last page to the first page?

4.5.6 *Case study in work measurement — ingot-loading project at Bethlehem Steel, 1899*

The first proper scientific analysis of manual work is usually credited to Frederick Winslow Taylor. Because Taylor has had such a strong influence on the way in which work study has developed, it is enlightening to look closely at the structure of his most famous illustration.

In *Scientific Management*, Taylor devotes much space to the way in which he improved the productivity of workers whose job was to load railcars with 92-lb ingots of pig-iron. Taylor gives enough data for us to repeat his experiment. A description of the operation is deceptively simple. Piles of ingots were stacked in a field next to a railway line. Loaders were required to pick up an ingot, walk or run up an inclined plank leaning against the side of the railcar, drop the ingot in the railcar and return to repeat the operation. We are told that the average distance from lift to drop was 36 ft. From this minimal information is it possible to set up a similar work-study exercise? What equipment and arrangements are needed?

1. *The railcar.* If you do not have access to the real thing in a quiet railway siding, use any level staging, platform or bank about 3 ft above ground level.

2. *The loads to be used.* If ingots are difficult to obtain, weightlifting weights or heavy stones will do instead. Loads less than 92 lb may be used if you wish to avoid the risk of injury. More bulky, less rigid items may also be used, such as sacks of sand or cement. In an extended exercise it is interesting to consider variations in weight or bulk on the throughput rate. By a system of returning loads to the starting point (explained later) it is possible to run an experiment with only two 'ingots'.

3. *The planks.* Find two planks that can be used as ramps up to your simulated railcar. Any length of plank can be taken, although in later exercises you might like to consider the effect of steepness and 'bendability'. Place the two planks against the 'railcar floor', far enough apart so that one can be used for loading and the other for simultaneous unloading without the two handlers obstructing each other. Also, take precautions to stop the planks slipping when the handlers are running up and down them.

4. *The pig-iron handlers.* Seek volunteers a day or so in advance of the exercise. Explain that you do not want super-athletes, just people who can perform heavy manual work under a variety of instructions. Make sure that they have no illness or injury and advise them to avoid eating a heavy meal just before the exercise. You will need two handlers for each exercise that is run. It is possible that the same two volunteers will be able to perform all the exercises that you set up, although you might like to avoid a fatigue factor by using other pairs.

5. *Operating the experiment.* Place one load at a level surface just beyond the top of one of your plank-ramps. Place the other load at ground level 36 ft away at a pick-up point. Organize the experiment as follows. Whilst one person is carrying a load uphill, the other is simultaneously carrying the other load (via the other plank) back to the pick-up point. After the two handlers drop their loads, they walk back empty-handed to their starting points and repeat the cycle.

6. *Collecting information and comparing results.* Use any digital watch to record times to the nearest second. If there are several independent observers it is instructive to see how their timings compare. At its simplest, times should be taken the moment that the handler at the bottom lifts his load and the moment he lets it go at the railcar end. Initially, run the experiment for five minutes, asking the handlers to work at a pace they think could be maintained comfortably all day. Remember to point out that the uphill handler has a slightly harder task than the downhill handler. After the five-minute experiment is over, compare results amongst observers, then consider some of the following variants:

   (a) Varying the loading or unloading height from ankle to knee, waist or chest height.
   (b) Working with distances longer or shorter than 36 ft.
   (c) Working with the same distance but varying the length of the slope or the stability of the plank.

(d) Picking up from neatly stacked or jumbled ingots (requiring more than two loads).

(e) Dropping the ingots neatly stacked or higgledy-piggledy (requiring more than two loads).

(f) Working when the ground, ingot and plant are wet and slippery.

(g) Comparing a 36-ft straight run with a 36-ft path round corners.

All of these variants are crucial elements in the analysis. If you fail to find which variant has a really significant effect on the pace of work, you could come to the wrong conclusion. What starts as an elementary exercise turns out to have a remarkable number of complications. But does that justify Taylor's assertion that 'the science of handling pig-iron is so great that the man who is fit to handle pig-iron as his daily work cannot possibly understand that science'? It is worth returning to the Bethlehem experiments to see how Taylor got on.

Taylor claimed that his scientific methods of *selection*, *incentive* and *supervision* enabled him to improve the daily loading rates per man from 12½ to 47½ tons. At 92 lb an ingot, you need to load 1156 ingots to clear 47½ tons. As the handlers worked a 10-hour day (without any lunch break), they would have to shift 115 ingots an hour, or about two a minute to reach their target. In fact they would have to work a bit faster than that to allow for brief stoppages. Anyone who has duplicated Taylor's experiment will be able to confirm that over a short period of time, for the basic situation, such a rate is perfectly possible. But the rate does not seem possible with the introduction of some quite mildly adverse factors mentioned in variants (a) and (g).

Was Taylor's method a practical long-term solution? Even though America a hundred years ago was a tough, no-nonsense climate for the labouring man, it seems unlikely. One is tempted to ask why he did not use hoists for this project? (See our later discussions on attacking constraints rather than optimizing within constraints.)

▼   **Exercise**

With two colleagues, go out to a self-service petrol station. Position yourself so that you will not interfere with the running of the station but make sure that you can observe the customers' activities.

Watch a customer throughout a visit to the station, from the moment he enters the station to the moment he rejoins the road. Divide the customer's activities into about ten job elements with clear breakpoints separating them.

Get yourself organized with clipboard, pen and a watch with a second-hand. Note down when a customer reaches each breakpoint during his visit to the station. Observe between fifteen and twenty customers, then carry out a simple statistical analysis:

(a) What is the average time for a complete visit?

(b) What is the average time for each job element within this visit?

(c) Look at the distribution of times around each average that you have found.

▷

What do these distributions look like? For each job element are they packed closely to the average or widely dispersed; and are they skewed to one side of the average rather than the other?

(d) List all the reasons why some customers are better than others at filling up their cars. Are there some conditions or times of the day which would affect every customer's efficiency? Can you quantify these effects?

(e) Did the customers mind being observed? Do you think that if you had been timing a person in paid employment there would have been different ▲ reactions?

See Voss *et al*'s case study 'The Baker Street Branch' in *Operations Management in the Service Industries and The Public Sector* (Wiley, 1985) for a good case exercise on work measurement at a bank.

4.6 Teamwork and job efficiency

We are concerned here with the best way that small groups can function. For example, labouring gangs, quarrymen, forestry workers, restaurant staff, scientific researchers or a software development team. All these teams are examples of where the workers can control the pace of what they do, and also where how they get on with each other can affect productivity.

4.6.1 *Example — refuse collection*

Consider two basic ways in which refuse collection can be done:

Method A. The householder has a dustbin next to his back door. In advance of the dustcart's arrival, two men will be bringing bins from houses to the road edge. Later a dustcart with a driver and two loaders will empty the bins. Some way behind the dustcart one man will be returning the empty bins to the houses.
Method B. On the appointed collection day, the householder places his rubbish in a strong plastic sack by the roadside. As the dustcart drives along the street, three loaders pick up the plastic sacks and throw them into the cart.

How much more efficient is method B than method A?

1. *Men per dustcart.* Method A requires six men, method B four.
2. *Time to clear a given section.* Suppose in a 100-metre stretch of street there are, on average, 40 bins to pick up, grouped in twos on both sides of the road. Under method B, this stretch can be covered in 90 seconds or less (assume the dustcart moves continuously at walking pace, the three loaders slinging sacks into the cart

as it moves). Under method A, the stretch will be covered in about 450 seconds (15 seconds for the cart to move between each of the ten stopping points, and 30 seconds at a stopping point for the bins to be automatically hoisted up, emptied and lowered).

▼   **Class exercise** *(10 minutes)*

Spell out the advantages and disadvantages of methods A and B above from the point of view of (a) the dustmen, and (b) the householders.

How would you choose between A and B if you were the local authority responsible for refuse collection? Is there a third option, such as the wheelie-
▲   bin system, which is superior to both A and B?

4.7 Managing people in the overall operating context — the Lego™ experiment

The Lego experiment involves making a series of model cars. The cars should be made from Lego blocks which contain a good mix of colours. Ideally, each car should contain 20–30 pieces and you should have enough pieces to make at least 12 cars. The model in Figure 4.6 gives you an idea of the degree of complexity required. The experiment can be adapted so that it can be done by any number of participants between 7 and 12.

Setting up the experiment

First of all, build 12 or more identical cars. Set up five tables, separate from each other and spread about a large room. On each table place a 'blueprint model' which can

Figure 4.6   Model car for Lego experiments.

be inspected when people are building a new car but whose pieces are never interfered with.

Four of these tables are designated 'subassembly tables', each table being associated with one colour of lego brick. On the RED table, any assembly work must involve a red piece (i.e. either red to red, or red to another colour, or another colour to a red piece already in the model). Similar rules apply to the WHITE, BLACK and YELLOW tables, if these are the other three colours you are using.

This somewhat artificial arrangement was designed to make you think carefully about how to allocate work amongst workstations, how to improve communications and how to improve the assembly system you have set up.

The fifth table acts as a 'quality check and disassembly table', where all completed models are kept.

Allocation of manpower

Assign one person to each of the five tables. Appoint two people as transport operatives who are the only ones allowed to shift parts from one table to another. According to how many people you have available, anyone else can either double-up at a busy task or, alternatively, act as a co-ordinator, observer or umpire to see that the rules are obeyed.

Running the experiment

Firstly, using a stopwatch, see how long it takes to disassemble and reassemble one model.

At a given signal, the disassembler separates one model into its twenty or thirty parts. As he does so, the transporters take parts to the various colour assembly points. (Remember that at any table the assembler can use a part other than his special colour as long as it joins up to his colour.) As the model nears completion, the transporters will be active in shifting subassemblies between tables. Finally, a completed model should re-emerge on the disassembly table, where someone should check whether it has been made properly. Repeat the experiment half a dozen times, and note by how much the time drops for completely disassembling and assembling one model.

Extending the experiment

If you have enough parts, see what happens if six models are disassembled simultaneously and all their parts sent out to be made up again. Repeat this experiment a few times so that people can cope with the greater number of parts floating around the system.

Learning from these experiments

From your observations of work so far and similar simple extensions, you should be in a position to give tentative answers to these sorts of questions:

1. With only a single model at a time passing through the system, was there any colour table with a high percentage of idle time? If so, which two tables would you combine to get better labour utilization?
2. When six models were being made simultaneously, were there any signs of muddle, panic, material getting lost, or defective quality in the finished product?
3. Whatever number of batches were being sent through the system, what sort of improvement occurred as people became more skilled in their tasks? Do you think this improvement occurred because: (a) assemblers got more dextrous, (b) there was a better communication system between assemblers and transporters, or (c) when it was realized that one assembler was overloaded, some of his/her work was done by someone else?
4. How motivated was the group to improve its result? Were people labelled 'ham-fisted' or 'star' assemblers? Were people having trouble with their task, criticized, encouraged, or otherwise treated?
5. Who took the lead in suggestions for improvement? How adaptive were the group for trying out a new assembly system?

4.7.1 *Link-up to operations management problems in general*

Though simple, these experiments act as a useful springboard and discussion point for many management features. For example, the Lego experiments link into some important issues which are covered more fully in other chapters of the book.

1. Measuring idle operative time (Machines and Scheduling)
2. Variety control (Materials and Scheduling)
3. Good housekeeping practices (Quality)
4. Systems analysis and re-organization (Systems)
5. Batch size policy (Scheduling)
6. The Just-in-time approach (Systems and Scheduling)
7. Matching robustness to complexity (Scheduling)

The Lego experiments also throw light on some important man-management issues which are explained below.

4.7.1.1 The level of discretion allowed to the shopfloor

The Lego experiments imposed strict rules on:

1. What table can assemble what colour combinations.
2. What the final product should look like.

However, the many different ways as to *how* this could be achieved was left to workers and their supervisors to discover. So this experiment is an example of the quality circle or Japanese *kaizen* approach (improvements from the bottom up), rather than having expert industrial engineers telling the workers the best way to do the job.

4.7.1.2 Flexible assignments and multi-tasking

A common problem in British industry is that one person gets very attached to the specialist task that they do. They resist being moved to a different task, or being joined in their task by another worker. Partially this is a hangover from the British tradition of craft unions and demarcation disputes, but it also arises from greed (if a piece-rate system operates) or fear of redundancy (if the other worker is seen as a potential replacement). These bad features are lessened if, as in the Lego experiments, there is a continual chopping and changing of assignments, procedures and batch sizes. Flexibility and experimentation become an accepted feature of the workplace, accepted because they result from shopfloor discussions rather than from higher management diktat.

4.7.1.3 What to do when a learning curve gives only marginal improvements

The very first time you make a complex item all sorts of inefficiencies and delays quite naturally occur. You would expect a sharp improvement when you make the second item, and a noticeable but not so big improvement for the third (and so on). This feature is known as the learning curve, commonly observed but perhaps not always fitting into the smooth mathematical shape claimed by some authors. You should find a very noticeable learning curve for the Lego experiment, but after half an hour's practice with one method or batch, times flatten out. Rather than seek fractional improvements, this is an indication that if you want big improvements, the time has come to consider a complete revamp of the system. In other words the time has come ...

'To attack constraints rather than to optimize within them'

As a first step to attacking constraints you may wish to re-assign tasks from overworked to underemployed assemblers. How to do this is illustrated in the assembly line balancing exercise in the Technical Appendix to this chapter. At a more profound level, you may seek to *change the design* of the product or the parts as the only real way forward to greater productivity. Lastly, you may *change the assumptions underlying the operating system.*

This point is well illustrated by Japanese manufacturing methods where, rather than accepting the batch sizes suggested by Western mathematical models, they spent their energy in reducing set-up times and thus arrived at a very different manufacturing system. (Westerners had overlooked this because they took the set-up times as a fixed constraint to the problem, incapable of changing.)

4.7.1.4 Motivation, productivity and the role of observer or supervisor

Some variants of the Lego experiments can be used to test the validity of Elton Mayo's researches on women who assembled electrical components at the Hawthorne factory, USA, 1929–1931. (Nearly every management text refers to the Hawthorne experiments but few suggest ways of repeating the experiment or even looking at the dubious way the experiments were designed.) People who really want to look into Hawthorne properly should look at the references in James E. Lee's *The Gold and The Garbage of Management Theory* (Ohio University Press, 1980). At the risk of gross over-simplification of a complex research project, we would summarize Mayo's best known conclusion as follows:

> If supervisors pay more attention to good workers, [the good workers] do even better, even if this attention is accompanied by worsening conditions of work.

In an earlier book we dubbed this the *upside Hawthorne effect*, and commented that as much attention should be focused on *the downside effect*:

> If people who are doing badly are isolated and ignored, they lose interest and do worse. They are not motivated by hearing of others who are getting on like a house on fire.

We highlighted the downside effect because we often noticed in the Lego experiments that if one worker was at a table that was socially isolated from the rest, and was not getting on particularly well with his work, he or she was very likely to indulge in deviant behaviour — going slow, putting parts together wrongly, or just deriding the whole exercise. We feel that the same behaviour can apply not only to individuals but to whole teams or even factories who are told, 'Look how well we reward others who do better than you.' You can observe this effect yourself if two teams in different rooms work simultaneously on assembly. Reward the best team with some trivial prize such as a few chocolates, and arrange for all the observers to watch them closely rather than the other team. What happens?

There is also the more general issue of *why* the Hawthorne effect occurs. At least three reasons are possible:

1. *The limelight effect.* Most people slip in to an easy pace of work which only increases to maximum capacity if a spotlight is focused on them, either from a supervisor, customer or consultant. One consultant might say that he can improve workers' productivity by 25 per cent if you allow him to 'make everyone wear a white uniform', another if he 'makes everyone start and finish a half hour earlier', and/or if 'there is a meditation instead of tea-break'.

   Each of these solutions might work, for a while, but only because workers step up productivity when a consultant or anyone else is nosing around the workplace. When the pressure and spotlight is removed, productivity falls back to its old level.

2. *Emotional responses by the worker.* If a worker likes or approves of a researcher, consultant or supervisor, his reaction and performance may be very different than if he dislikes or is suspicious of someone. A good example is Frederick Taylor's ingot-loading experiments that we quoted earlier. Apart from one man (Schmidt), Taylor was hated by the remaining ingot-loaders. This is not surprising in view of Taylor's arrogant and obsessive behaviour. He even said insulting things about

his loyal servant Schmidt. It is not widely known that Taylor was soon dismissed from his post at Bethlehem Steel largely because he was too abrasive.

3. *Emotional responses: on robots and broomsticks.* The other day we were shown round a Japanese machine-tool factory in the Midlands. More than any other company in the UK it had automated every possible factory process. 'If that's the case', we asked, 'why do you use a broom to sweep up scurf from the factory floor? It is blatantly obvious that an industrial vacuum cleaner or a magnetic device would be far more efficient'.

'Ah', said the manager, 'that broom is my most valuable asset'. 'I use it regularly to show my workers that I am not too proud to work on menial tasks'.

4.8 Recommended reading

To build up people's confidence we would recommend first tackling two short cases from Schmenner, *Production/Operations Management Concepts and Situations*, 4th edn (Macmillan, 1990). These are 'Tower Manufacturing', pp. 337–338, and 'Baldridge Chain Saw', p. 340, both of which pose incentive-scheme conundrums. The cases are accompanied by an open-ended discussion. Next, we would recommend Belnap, in Meier, *Cases in Production and Operations Management* (Prentice Hall, 1982). This case includes both an introduction to the principles of motivation theory and structured questions. Next we would look at 'Midland Star Line' in Nicholson, *Managing Manufacturing Operations* (Macmillan, 1978) to investigate whether someone finds a goose that lays a golden egg, then kills it. Then, we would recommend 'Bridge Electric Ltd (B)' in C.J. Constable and C.C. New's *Operations Management* (Wiley, 1976). This case integrates payments systems, job descriptions and union negotiations. Finally, two long but enlightening cases are in Schmenner (*op. cit*) 'Knox Electronics' and 'Dayton Instrument Corporation'. We also recommend that you read F.W. Taylor's *Scientific Management* in the original rather than relying on what someone else said he said.

Technical appendix — assembly-line balancing

Simple line balancing

In Figure 4.7 each labelled box is a *job* to be done on an assembly line. The number in the box is the *job element* (in seconds) which tells you how long it takes to complete one job before passing it on down the line. The arrows show you how work is passed on from one job to the next. Several subassembly lines merge, giving one completed product (a burglar alarm) after job *x* has been done. If you have 6 workers, how should they divide the 24 jobs between them?

If each worker works 450 minutes a day, that equals 27,000 seconds per day. Multiplying by 6 for the 6 workers means you have 162,000 seconds of work available.

There are 24 jobs, and if you added up the job elements of *a*, *b*, *c*, etc. you would

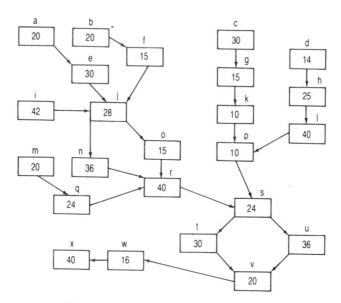

Figure 4.7 Jobs on an assembly line.

get 20 + 20 + 30, etc. — which adds up to 600 seconds to make one burglar alarm.

If you have 162,000 seconds available and it takes 600 seconds to make one burglar alarm then, if you balance your line perfectly, you should be able to make 162,000/600 = 270 burglar alarms per day.

Making 270 burglar alarms in a 450-minute working day means that one burglar alarm is being completed every 100 seconds. This figure of 100 seconds is known as the *control cycle* of the assembly line.

In elementary line balancing (like here) it is the practice to give a worker a rota of jobs, so that his or her *personal cycle* (before repetition) equals the control cycle. It is also good practice to give the worker a group of jobs that are geographically adjacent. The group of jobs assigned to one worker is known as a *workstation*.

Ideally, every worker's personal cycle should be the same. In practice, it is rarely possible to get clusters of jobs whose times all sum exactly to (say) 100 seconds. So one looks for a set of worker assignments where everyone's personal cycle is within a fairly narrow range.

▼ **Exercise**

▲ Can you assign jobs to six workers so that each worker's personal cycle lies within an acceptably narrow range, 95–104 seconds?

Time losses for job switching

Is it reasonable to expect no delay when an assembly worker switches from one job (using a certain location, posture or material) to another? Zero delay is likely only if the next job follows in a natural sequence (e.g. is next down the line on a flowchart). If this is not so, let us assume a 15-second delay.

With this new assumption you will need more than six workers to cover all 24 jobs within the 100-second control cycle. One such example is shown in Figure 4.8. This example assumes that 15 seconds are lost when switching to a job that does not flow from the previous job. Jobs are assigned to eight workers, every worker's personal cycle being less than 100.

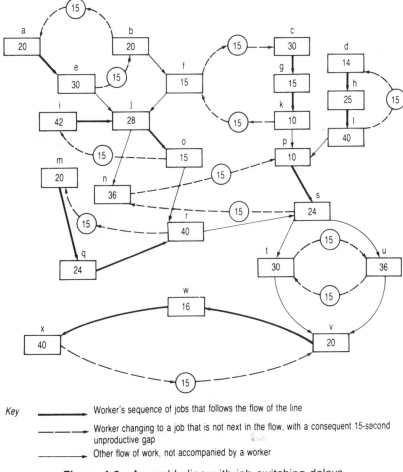

Key   ———————▶ Worker's sequence of jobs that follows the flow of the line

———————▶ Worker changing to a job that is not next in the flow, with a consequent 15-second unproductive gap

———————▶ Other flow of work, not accompanied by a worker

Figure 4.8 Assembly line with job switching delays.

▼   **Optional exercise**

▲
Suppose that the time wasted switching to an off-flow job was not 15
seconds but 5 seconds. Can you find a seven-worker solution where all
personal cycles are under 100 seconds?

High intensity assembly lines

Suppose that the assembly line that we have been using as an example was required
to make 2,700 rather than 270 burglar alarms a day. This could be achieved by
employing more workers (66 to be precise) and dropping the control cycle from 100
to 10 seconds. Now, workers are allocated to only one job or a part of one — in fact
for each 10 seconds (or part of 10 seconds) that a job takes, it receives a worker. So
job a (20 seconds) would be assigned two workers, job j (28 seconds) three workers,
and so on.

From the worker's point of view, narrowing the range of tasks makes the job more
boring and it really needs an incentive piece-work scheme to keep up productivity.
From the management point of view a high-intensity line has the potential to be more
productive mainly because time lost from job switching is avoided and only partly for
the more often quoted reason of greater dexterity through specialization. But the high-
intensity system requires greater management expertise in balancing the line and keeping
material flowing through it. See our extensive analysis of a pottery example in the
systems chapter (6.7).

Chapter 5

Materials management and logistics

5.1 Introduction

All types of operation need 'materials' in the widest sense of the word — from ores for the bulk-chemical industry to electrical components for car manufacturers; from finished products for retailers to paper for financial-service industries; from surgical instruments for health services to diesel for transport operations. Whatever the material, it has to be selected, purchased, handled, housed and utilized.

Let us start with a simple materials requirement situation and consider the implications. When you buy petrol for a car you have several decisions to make:

1. What grade (2- or 4-star) do I need to do the job? Should it be lead-free? In other words, you are asking yourself, 'What is the material specification?'
2. Where shall I purchase it? In other words, What alternatives are there? How do they compare? What benefits do they offer? Expanding the analysis of benefits: forecourt attendant service may be useful if you have your best clothes on, but irrelevant at other times. Price may be your first priority; if your fuel indicator shows empty you will worry less about price, more about the location and opening hours of the garage.
3. How will you finance the purchase — cash, credit card or company account?

The problem of how to *handle* and *house* the petrol has been solved for you by standard petrol pumps and car fuel tanks. But even then you can buy locking petrol caps to ensure security of your valuable material during storage. The effective *utilization* of your material depends on such things as the condition of your engine, the tyre pressures and good map reading to get from A to B by the most fuel-economic route. In other words, a good maintenance programme and good planning increases your petrol-utilization efficiency. You can see that, for a simple requirement like petrol, if you analyse the situation you have a whole range of factors to consider. The same factors are true of any materials requirement: what differs is the time-scale. For example, the petrol you purchase will probably last a few days. When you run low, rarely more than half an hour needs to elapse between your awareness that you are running short and the purchase and first use of the petrol. If we consider the crude-oil requirements of a major oil refinery, the time-scale is of a different order of magnitude.

5.2 Materials selection, specification and costs

In Chapter 2, we showed how a proper and exhaustive value analysis focuses on the consumer's viewpoint. At the end of that chapter, we also showed what should follow after value analysis: namely, implementation as a further step in the complete product development cycle. An early part of implementation is the comparison and selection of materials to be used, looking at things from the angle not only of the consumer but also now, from the viewpoint of the manufacturer or supplier.

5.2.1 *Case study of materials selection from the manufacturer's point of view — colemanite*

To make glass, you need three basic ingredients: boric oxide, calcium carbonate and silica.

Each of these compounds has interesting procurement problems. The most interesting is probably boric oxide, which the company can buy in two forms:

1. As an expensive semi-processed chemical, which contains a *guaranteed* 57 per cent boric oxide.
2. As a cheaper, naturally occurring volcanic substance, colemanite, which contains a *variable* amount of boric oxide, on average about 42 per cent (colemanite is boric oxide mixed with calcium, so some of the work that the glass furnace would normally do has already been done inside a volcano thousands of years ago).

The cheaper source looks the best, but there are problems. The boric oxide concentration varies. Since this source is naturally-occurring and dug out of a quarry, the boric oxide is associated with other undesirable materials, such as clay and felspar. These can be separated out by washing the ore, but this is wasteful. The difficulty really starts with the location of the ore. The only place in which colemanite is found is in a particular region of Turkey. The initial selection of ore is crude and rather like selecting good bananas in a greengrocer's. The lumps of rock from the quarry are inspected visually and those which 'look right' are accepted and sent for washing, while the rest are rejected. This selection requires skill and experience. The company requires 3000 tonnes per year of colemanite for its operation; this is equivalent to one full shipload per year. In other words, using this source, the technical manager needs to go out to Turkey once a year, choose a load which 'looks right' and ensure that he gets the selected load onto the ship for transportation to the UK.

After a two-week sea journey, the colemanite is shipped by road to be stored by a grinding company which supplies the glass company weekly with 60 tonnes of ground colemanite. As the year progresses, the boric oxide content in the weekly loads goes down due to settling of heavier materials. Therefore, when a load arrives at the factory, it has to be tested for its boric oxide content.

Obtaining boric oxide from colemanite is very high risk, and a bad batch can mean a very bad time for the company for a twelve-month period. Colemanite may contain too much sodium and thus make the melt too alkaline, or a high percentage of calcium sulphate rather than borate. Despite these problems, the company uses colemanite as its source. It does this because it has the skill to choose the right load and to utilize it effectively by adjusting furnace inputs to cope with varying percentages of boric oxide in the raw materials. At the end of the day, this gives better operating profits than taking the safe option.

This case study shows why a manufacturer needs to have clear ideas about *specifications* and *costs* in order to facilitate the materials selection policy. For example, if we are looking for a material to make an aircraft wing, we consider properties such as strength, density, resistance to sand and salt erosion, fatigue resistance and tolerance to presence of cracks. Some materials which have to meet very high use specifications can be difficult to manufacture: for instance, the exacting requirements for turbine vane materials make the manufacturing process increasingly difficult. In fact, a whole casting needs to be grown from a single crystal.

Not all materials are selected for their superior properties. Cost can be a critical factor in less exacting circumstances. Thus, stainless steel is a superior material for car exhausts but it is only used on expensive models, since car manufacturers feel that the added cost of making exhausts out of this material is not a sensible marketing move.

▼   **Exercise**

In the colemanite case study, just one material was discussed. Normally, a product is made up of several different materials and each needs to be looked at in some detail when considering specifications, costs and sourcing. Obtain a lightweight tent and consider the problems of its manufacture in terms of specifications, costs and sourcing for each of these key materials that make up the tent:

Outer fabric
Inner fabric
Groundsheet
Zips
Guy ropes
Poles
Pegs
▲   Tent and peg sacks

5.2.2 *Bills of materials and subassemblies*

As with the lightweight tent in the above exercise, nearly every finished product is a mixture of materials, parts or components. There may be thousands of types involved for a complex product such as a car, down to just a few for a simple product like a tin of baked beans. But even for a simple product, there are surprising complications. Look at a baked bean tin; you have:

> The beans themselves
> The tomato sauce they are encased in
> The tin
> The label

This is not the end of the matter. The label is made up not just of paper, but also a variety of coloured printing inks and adhesive. The tin will be a mixture of alloys coated on the outside to prevent rust and on the inside to prevent the food being contaminated. And, as for the tomato sauce, as well as tomatoes you might have water, sugar, salt, cornflour, vinegar, preservatives, spices and colouring. For an individual tin, any of these sauce components might appear trivial, but this is not the case as far as the manufacturer is concerned. He might need special containers for the tons of salt needed, or might lose thousands of pounds if one of the spices increases in price. So, in such cases, exact proportions and qualities must be known and potential variations in cost identified in advance. This is done by assembling a bill of materials where, after a breakdown of every material used, each material has attached to it a specification, a quantity needed either in its subassembly or in the full product, and its cost-history, including attendant expenses for storage, handling or treatment.

5.2.2.1 The product structure tree or Gozinto chart

Illustration — a high-performance bike

Consider how you could split up and classify the parts of a high-performance bike (either a road racing or mountain bike). At the broadest level (let us call it level 1), this could be:

> *Bike*
> > Frameset
> > Handlebars and stem
> > Saddle and seat pin
> > Front wheel
> > Rear wheel
> > Front brake assembly
> > Rear brake assembly
> > Cranks and pedals
> > Gear mechanism
> > Accessories

Within each of these categories, there will be a further level of detail. For example, take a level-2 breakdown of the gear mechanism:

> *Gear mechanism*
> > Chain
> > Chain rings

Front derailleur
Freewheel
Rear derailleur
Gear levers and cables

Or take a level-3 breakdown of the rear derailleur (if it is the Campagnolo/Shimano type)

Rear derailleur
Chain-guide components
Gear-change components

The breakdown could be continued to level 4, e.g.:

Chain-guide components
2 jockey wheels
2 halves of the derailleur cage
2 jockey wheel bolts

If every part of the bike has been classified in this way, the result is known as a product structure tree or a Gozinto chart.

▼   **Exercise**

Complete a Gozinto chart, down to at least level 3, for all items making up:

(a) A road-racing bike.

(b) A mountain bike.

▲   Compare your charts to see which parts stay the same and which are different.

Gozinto charts are a useful aid when a manufacturer wishes to work out how many original components he will need in order to assemble a collection of bikes of various models and needed for different delivery dates. Gozinto charts, then, lay the foundation for an advanced scheduling and forecasting technique (materials requirement planning, MRP) which we describe later.

5.3 Materials purchasing

5.3.1 *General overview: a purchasing manager mediates on his job*

These comments come from the purchasing manager of a large local authority.

Everyone thinks they can buy. We all go shopping for items, from light bulbs to motor cars. And so we all think we are experts. But when it comes to commercial buying, that is different. Purchasing is a profession like any other. You need specialist skills and experience. You need to know how to draw up a contract, what to look out for in any supplier, and who is reliable. You need to ensure *continuity* of supply. It is no good buying potatoes from a wholesaler who decides to have the week off when the mood takes him.

Although we are experts in *buying*, we still need to consult *users* about their exact requirements. For example, the types of pencil children of 5 use is different from those used by 16-year-old art students. It is the teachers who are the experts at knowing the exact sorts of pencils that are needed. Our job is to go off and try to get them and negotiate the best deal.

Working for a local authority, we are perhaps more open to scrutiny than some private-sector purchasers. We get offered everything from free drinks to Mediterranean holidays, but we daren't accept even a bottle of whisky at Christmas, and have to make reports on all the meals bought for us. Not only must it *be* above board, it must be *seen* to be so. Because we are accountable to councillors and ratepayers, there is a lot of red tape.

Sometimes delivery can be a problem. For example, take the heating oil delivered to our offices, schools and residential-care centres. The storage tanks at these places are of different sizes, and so are the entrances for the delivery vehicles. The oil companies provide tankers of different sizes, so we have a scheduling problem on our hands.

5.3.2 *Routine purchasing operations*

It is a prime function of purchasing to ensure that there is *no ambiguity* when an order is placed with a supplier. For the most important purchases, a legal contract will need to be drawn up. Even for the less important items, orders need to be written out clarifying:

Specifications
Quantity
Price and payment terms
Mode and date of delivery

Where there are many subtle variations in the material or goods being ordered, it helps to accompany the purchase order with:

1. A sample of the material wanted.
2. A reference number from the supplier's catalogue.
3. Reference to an industry-standard specification (e.g. a BSI number).
4. Reference to chemical or physical properties.
5. (For components) a blueprint of what is needed.

6. Reference to the treatments or processes that the material is expected to pass through before delivery.

You have to be careful about referring to 'looser' specifications such as *brand names*. For example, if you were ordering soft drinks for your chain of food stores, you would not simply ask for so many crates of Coca Cola. You would want to say which variant you needed — Diet, Old, New or Cherry Coke — and also (as the quality of water can vary around a country) from which bottling plant you would like it sent.

Furthermore, a purchase order often has to be careful in specifying the packaging and delivery mode. The material may have to come on a special pallet from a designated warehouse, with adequate protection and insurance for it en route. It may be subject to deterioration unless kept within certain temperature and humidity limits, and it may have to be collected and delivered at a specific time.

5.3.2.1 Follow-up procedures after the purchase order has been placed

1. Soon after the order has been placed, phone the supplier to confirm that the order has been received and accepted.
2. Just before the order is to be despatched, confirm with the supplier that the delivery will be as planned. For an important order with a long lead-time, it is advisable to make several regular checks on the progress of the order.
3. Arrange with whoever is to receive the incoming goods to tell you of their arrival.
4. Initiate an emergency procedure if the goods do not arrive on time. This is discussed in more detail in the 'tactical purchasing' section.

Record-keeping. If you have a comprehensive database of suppliers and materials, indexed and cross-referenced, this eases the purchasing routine. Where you need to find a new supplier, it is useful to establish a *search procedure* which even quite junior clerical staff can manage. This involves working through such sources as *Kelly's* and Kompass directories, *Yellow Pages*, Chambers of Commerce, trade associations and business libraries. If more experienced staff are to be involved in the search, it is best for them to concentrate on salespeople, users, scientists and professional contacts.

Good record-keeping can also help management to evaluate existing suppliers to avoid the worst and to direct more work to the best. Although decisions on this issue are matters of purchasing tactics and strategy, *preparing information* for these decisions is a key activity of the routine purchasing function. But one difficulty is how to take the information about a supplier, and to filter and simplify it so that it is understandable to those making tactical and strategic purchasing decisions. This has been attempted by *vendor-rating systems*.

For each existing supplier you calculate an overall rating devised from 'weights' you give to certain attributes you think important (e.g. price = 0.5, quality = 0.3, delivery = 0.2). An overall vendor rating is calculated by applying these weights to data extracted from the supplier's previous performance and summing the results. For example:

$$\text{Price rating} = 0.5 \times \frac{\text{Lowest quote}}{\text{This supplier's quote}} \quad \underset{(\text{say})}{=} 0.5 \times \frac{(£40)}{(£45)} = 0.44$$

$$\text{Quality rating} = 0.3 \times \frac{\text{Defect rate of best supplier}}{\text{Defect rate of this supplier}} = 0.3 \times \frac{(0.02)}{(0.06)} = 0.1$$

$$\text{Delivery rating} = 0.2 \times \frac{\text{Lead time of best supplier}}{\text{Lead time for this supplier}} = 0.2 \times \frac{(14 \text{ days})}{(21 \text{ days})} = 0.13$$

Total vendor rating (best possible would be 1.00)   = 0.67

A vendor-rating system should be used only as a very rough rule-of-thumb device. It can never capture the full complexity of a supply situation. This point is emphasized if you look at all the complexities of prices, quality or delivery which are covered later in this purchasing section.

One elaboration of vendor-rating systems are *credit-rating systems* found in the banking world. A good case study describing one of these is Connecticut National Bank in Collier, *Service Management* (Prentice Hall, 1987).

Supplier-vulnerability indices. A better monitoring of suppliers would be via information outside that directly associated with purchase orders:

1. Analysis of company accounts to pick out suppliers that might be having cash-flow problems.
2. A check on supplier's labour relations to see whether a strike, or overtime ban, is in the offing.
3. A check on whether there has been any management change or takeover that affects a supplier.
4. A check on whether there has been any trouble at a *supplier's supplier*, as this could work its way through to you.

All these checks involve quite a lot of clerical effort, but are well worth establishing as part of the essential routine of a good purchasing department. In general, there has been a move towards a more intimate and co-operative relationship with suppliers, both with the onset of total quality management and just-in-time (JIT) practices. These are explained later in the book.

Driven by the JIT philosophy, many purchasing officers have applied work-study methods to find ways to shrink that part of the lead-time associated with order purchasing. In this they have been helped by technical advances, so that instead of orders being placed by letter, faxes are now accepted between established business contacts. The latest development in this field, electronic data interchange (EDI), enables a customer's computer to place an order with a supplier's computer without human intervention. The full scheduling implications of this are developed in the section on ROQ/ROL scheduling in Chapter 10.

5.3.3 *Tactical purchasing*

What sorts of event can disrupt the day-to-day routine of a purchasing department? Arguments over price and discounts, late deliveries and late changes in specifications. Suppliers have to be cajoled, threatened, tempted and stimulated; in response, suppliers will try to influence the purchaser. Such activities all fall under the heading of purchasing *tactics*. As a first step, the purchasing officer must obtain some idea of how far, and when, he or she is going to get involved in personal negotiations. There is a useful rule-of-thumb which is shown in Figure 5.1.

5.3.3.1 Negotiate with whom?

Suppose that your purchasing situation falls within the bottom right-hand box in Figure 5.1 (an important deal for both you and your supplier). So you negotiate. But the first thing you must establish is the *credentials* of the person you are dealing with. Many a person has thought he has finalized a deal only to find out that it has to be approved by a higher department or committee, or even that the supplier has to confirm the position with *his* supplier before the deal can go ahead. When negotiating, it helps a purchaser (and vendor) to have these distinctions in mind.

When the purchaser approaches the supplier's sales staff, they might be constrained by:

1. Their production manager (a delivery has to fit in with *his* schedule).
2. The chief accountant (who needs to agree to any special discount).
3. The general manager (who might have a business arrangement with a firm that is a rival of yours).

It may be that these people have a direct influence on the deal that you are negotiating. Or the sales staff may say that, much as they would like to make concessions to you,

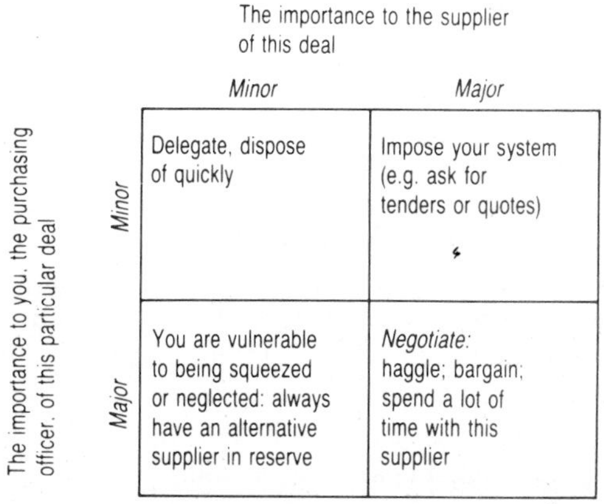

Figure 5.1 Negotiating tactics for doing deals.

people above them in the organization would veto it. (This is a useful negotiating ploy for the sales staff, whether or not it is true.)

5.3.3.2 Obtaining price discounts

These are available for nearly every purchasable commodity, especially for a business with 'clout' or influence. In particular, the fortunes of the big retailing chains have been enhanced by the discounts they obtain when purchasing. In general, discounts can be classified as follows:

1. Discounts associated with the terms of payment because you are a high-profile company with little chance of defaulting, or because you settle immediately, or within a week or month.
2. Trade discounts to franchisees, shops, wholesalers, subsidiaries or trade partners.
3. Quantity discounts for large or regular orders, for orders from single rather than multiple sources, or for large standardized packs or containers.
4. Quality discounts for a standard 'no frills, no service' product, or for 'seconds' or 'substandards' (the reverse *premium* applies where extra quality, service or guarantees are required).
5. Discounts where advance warning is given of an order, or where there is not a fierce delivery date (and the reverse premiums apply for rush orders or queue jumping).
6. Seasonal discounts (for example, getting road-salt or coal in summer, electricity at night).

5.3.3.3 Is forward buying a valid tactic?

Suppose that your raw material is subject to large price swings over the year, e.g. any food product (coffee, cocoa, sugar, grain) where supply is subject to harvest variations; or any raw material (metals, chemicals) where demand is subject to surges arising from war or over-capacity. It is tempting for a purchasing officer to play the market by ordering large immediate deliveries when the price is due to rise, and running down buffer stocks when the price is due to fall. This is only valid if the purchasing officer's information is better than the market's.

If you are speculating in coffee, do you really know more about the harvest than the trader in Brazil?

If you are speculating in copper, do you really know more about whether the US government is going to build up its stockpile than a Washington lobbyist?

In the above circumstances, the answer is rarely 'yes'. On the other hand, the purchasing officer's company may be in a unique position to know more than the market, as when Coca Cola switched from using saccharin to aspartame as a sweetener. By keeping such a move secret, they cornered the future production of aspartame and made it difficult for their rival, Pepsi Cola, to follow suit. This was a classic *tactic*. It secured a temporary one-off advantage that would not be repeated.

Apart from having superior information, firms may have other in-built advantages that open the doors to forward buying policy:

1. They may have lower-cost storage facilities.
2. Their use of a product may be growing more rapidly than that of other firms — if over-ordering occurs, stock will run down more quickly.

To summarize, then, if a firm has neither superior information nor superior facilities, forward buying is equivalent to gambling — a long-run loser. Further discussion of this issue can be found in Chapter 8.

5.3.3.4 Handling unsatisfactory supply situations

What tactics can be adopted when a supplier is not meeting promised deadlines or providing poor quality? Here are two examples.

Situation 1: crisis at Waterman's Printers. For several years you have relied upon a small printing firm, Waterman's, to supply the printed package for your product (model-aircraft assembly kits). The packaging is a key element in the marketing of your product as it outlines how the model aircraft can be constructed. The printing is in colour with much fine detail. One month ago, for the first time that you can remember, Waterman's let you down. They sent a batch of packets where so many were smudged or badly registered that you returned them asking for replacements. A new batch was promised two days later, but in fact arrived a week late. Although these were better, there were still minor imperfections and smudgings that you did not expect from a firm of Waterman's standing. You decide to visit the firm. You discover that Waterman senior is in hospital with terminal cancer and that his 20-year-old son is trying to keep the business going. He has already had to dismiss two senior employees for persistent theft. He has tried and failed to find suitable replacements. In the meantime, his remaining staff are struggling. Usually, at this time of year, you place large orders with Waterman's in anticipation of the Christmas season. What should you do now?

Situation 2: Designer Guttering. You are a Lake District builder under contract to complete a block of time-share apartments by 30 September. Your client has specified the installation of special plastic gutters, manufactured only in Austria, which do not break or clog up under heavy snowfalls. These gutters can be obtained from Designer Guttering (DG), Croydon, who are the sole importing agents. To complete the apartments, you really need to start work on installing the guttering by 1 August. To safeguard yourself against any hold-ups, you arrange with DG for your guttering to be delivered on the afternoon of Monday 1 July. They do not arrive. When you phone DG's office late on Monday afternoon, there is no answer, nor is there any reply Tuesday morning. Finally, you get through on Tuesday afternoon.

'Grasmere Contractors here. You were supposed to deliver us some gutters yesterday.'

'I'm sorry sir, there is only me in the office and I'm only a temp. I'll get them to phone you back about it.'

Nothing happens, so you phone again repeatedly on Wednesday morning. No answer. In the afternoon, you get through to a Mr Howard.

'Oh, my partner Mr Biggins is handling the matter urgently. There has been some delay. He'll phone you and explain about it.'

No phone call, and you cannot get anyone all day Thursday. On Friday, you are told that both Mr Howard and Mr Biggins are out of the office all day.

On Monday 8 July, when nothing has happened, you can only get through to the temp. Losing your temper, you say you want to know *today* when you are going to get your guttering. Later, she phones back saying that Mr Biggins has arranged a definite delivery for Monday 15 July. It does not turn up and you cannot get them on the phone. On the 16th, you can only get through to a temporary secretary. Raising merry hell, you get the home phone numbers of Mr Howard and Mr Biggins. In the evening, you finally get through to Mr Biggins who is very apologetic.

'We just had an amazing flood of orders to handle and there was this dock strike. I'll send it off tomorrow first thing. No problem.'

Next day, and the next, and the next, nothing arrives.

How to handle these situations. The above examples have different symptoms and you must apply different, suitable remedies.

Situation 1	A catastrophe due to an unforeseen act of God. (Any genuine natural disaster would count here, but not 'the computer broke down' — that is used by the incompetent as an all-purpose excuse to shelter behind.)
Remedy	Where good suppliers get into unavoidable trouble, provide help, but be careful that it is the right sort of help. In Waterman's case, for example, there would be no point in giving them more rush orders that would overload an already stressful situation. You could help Waterman's fill their vacancy, or 'lend' a member of staff to tide over a crisis.
Situation 2	Irretrievable incompetence. Usual warning signs are:

- Paperwork in a complete muddle and orders getting lost.
- Poor workmanship due to poor foremanship.
- A *recurring* shortage of staff, material or machines.
- '*Mañana* management' — continually putting off till tomorrow and breaking promises.

Remedy	*Don't* hang around. Don't try to reform the supplier. Don't bluff them with threats. Order elsewhere immediately, even if expensive. If you have a contract with the 'incompetent firm', sort out legal claims against them later.

5.3.4 *Strategic purchasing*

What weight should you give to purchasing management? This varies according to raw material value compared with all other costs. Where *value added* during processing is very large, purchasing is less significant. An extreme example would be that of the paints bought by an artist which can be a small fraction of the value of his picture. At the other extreme, it is very easy to refine, shape and stamp gold bars, whereas the purchase price of gold is phenomenal. So, in the latter case, a gold merchant must devote the bulk of his resources to forecasting gold prices and, for every deal, must haggle over the price to several decimal places.

Purchasing's importance also depends on the firm's *product mix* (i.e. the number of different lines it has on sale). A large delicatessen will have hundreds of products and much time needs to be spent on routine purchasing duties (placing, chasing and receiving orders). Contrariwise, a butcher may purchase only a few lines (pig, sheep and cattle carcasses) from one or two sources (abattoirs or wholesale freezers), so that the time on routine paperwork will be quite small.

What are the alternative ways that you can organize the purchasing function? This depends both on the weighting you give to purchasing and to the special logistic nature of your business. For example, to take two extremes, both of which are suitable for their own special situation.

1. In a Japanese car company, the purchasing department's role is influenced by the just-in-time philosophy: frequent, regular, small deliveries and long-term relationships with suppliers. Much of the clerical and tactical duties will be dealt with automatically. Instead, the purchasing staff will be involved in collaborative ventures with suppliers, helping them to improve quality standards and to design new products.
2. An independent European oil refiner, on the other hand, will be looking for irregular bulk-tanker deliveries (up to 500,000 tonnes), using the spot market to choose whatever supplier happens to be offering the best bargain. There will be a centralized, top-management decision on each purchase, the purchasing staff's vital duties being to monitor the progress of the oil delivery and to make sure that there is no hitch on the way. The purchasing staff will not have a one-to-one personal relationship with a supplier.

Further purchasing alternatives concern the *span of processes* that your firm wishes to cover. Your firm may plan *backward integration* by buying-up suppliers and this will obviously affect your attitude to them. In such circumstances, it is desirable for a larger part of a supplier's business to be routed through your firm, making it more dependent. To achieve this, special deals or discounts may need to be offered to the supplier to entice him to deal exclusively with you. Obviously, this has to be initiated by top management, even if implemented by the purchasing department. It is all part of the longer-term *make-or-buy* policy of a firm.

Alternatively, your firm may wish to concentrate its activities and cut out certain peripheral parts of its business. This can be done in two ways:

1. Using more *subcontractors*. This involves having a larger purchasing department to deal with the extra subcontracting work, checking on their credentials, supply capabilities and costings.

2.   Setting up a previous department of the company as an *arm's-length subsidiary*.
     In this case, the purchasing department will be given very strict rules, for legal
     and tax purposes, concerning the price at which materials must be bought from
     such subsidiaries.

  In conclusion, we can see that purchasing is an integral part of the weaponry a firm
needs to fulfil its grand strategy; this topic is covered in more detail in the last chapter
of this book. A good overall purchasing case study is 'Teem Aircraft Corporation' in
Meier, *Cases in Production and Operations Management* (Prentice Hall, 1982).

5.4 Materials delivery

During the 1980s, a new transport revolution began to take place; dramatic improvements and changes in freight services, quite different from what had gone before.
Previously, improvements were clearly associated with economies of scale, for example
jumbo jets, supertankers and road juggernauts. But if an industry tries to get improvements solely from economies of scale, almost inevitably it experiences disastrous over-
capacity. Now, progress is more associated with greater responsiveness, flexibility and
innovation in peripheral equipment and systems which support the central transport
operation.

5.4.1 *The old transport system and the search for economies of scale*

*Reshaping the iron ore delivery system after Steel Nationalization —
a typical example under the old approach* *

British Steel in 1965/66 had just been nationalized and so it was possible to start thinking
about optimizing the feeding of raw materials into the blast furnace. Ore was imported
from abroad, and a small ship of 25,000 dead weight tons was the size that had been
used up till then. Under a new system, this could become a large ship of 150,000 dead
weight tons, with shipping costs per ton a quarter, if not a third, less than the small-
ship costs. However, to take advantage of the cost benefits of large ships (and larger
ports to take them), capital expenditure of about £100 million was needed. It also
involved closing down some of the small ports and shipping through a few big ports.
  What were the transport consequences if there were fewer ports to supply the UK's
blast furnaces? We had to have a system which carried ore by rail over longer distances.
So, short rail hauls were replaced by longer rail hauls, but with bigger trucks having
a bottom door discharge. The stockyard in the pre-nationalization system kept a
relatively low stock level, topped up regularly with iron ore arriving from Norway in

---

Source: Sir Peter Thompson's Kearney Lecture to ILDM, 1990.

a 25,000 tonner every second or third day, With 150,000 ton lots arriving, the stockpile had to be much higher.

This move towards greater bulk carrying had all sorts of hidden disadvantages. These were overlooked by British Steel and have added to their economic difficulties in recent years. Other industries have experienced similar problems when chasing what turned out to be false economies of scale. Consider the consequences of 500,000 tonne oil supertankers:

1. *Handling*. Big ships need deeper water terminals and wider, more deeply dredged channels and canals.
2. *Shore storage*. Greater stocks of raw materials need to be held at both the loading and the unloading port, requiring the construction of more warehouses or storage tanks.
3. *Accidents*. Greater size increases the chance of certain sorts of accident. Gases that have accumulated in an empty oil tanker can blow it up. If it happens to be a berthed supertanker, it can blow up all the surrounding facilities as well (as at Bantry Bay). All bulk carriers take a long time to decelerate or change direction, thus increasing the danger of collision. Also, bulk carriers have now reached such a size that they are subject to catastrophic design failures in storm conditions.
4. *Over-capacity*. If (as in oil) there is a downturn in trade, it is more difficult to scrap or adapt a fleet of unemployed large specialist carriers.

5.4.2 *The new transport system and the container revolution*

Nowadays, there is just as much investment and attention paid to delivery but, rather than asking 'How to handle bulk?', we ask 'How to cope with variety and complexity?'

Increasing use of door-to-door delivery services has led to the decline of traditional transhipment methods such as railway marshalling yards and conventional crane docks. Location of new factories and warehouses now pays more attention to access to the motorway network, airports and container ports. The availability of a cheaper, speedier and more regular freighting system has transformed certain industries. For example, hypermarket and supermarket chains depend on a daily distribution network to underpin their operations.

A wide range of businesses have reorganized their transport system to take advantage of the standardized *container*. This has outside dimensions of 6 m × 2.4 m × 2.4 m and space inside to carry about 25 cubic metres of freight. The container (or rather the axles of the lorry that carries it) is strong enough to take up to 20 tonnes in weight. Containers can be easily transferred between road, rail and sea transport, they stack easily and protect the material from damage or theft. Cargo in a properly sealed container can be accompanied by simple documents, speeding up the work of handlers and customs men. Container ships holding between 2000 and 4000 containers in neatly boxed stacks do away with complicated storage of cargo in holds. Cranes installed on their decks can enable them to do their own loading and unloading, and to visit ports with limited handling facilities.

In the age before containers, the load was modified or broken up to conform to the transport and handling facilities (e.g. repackaged or jiggled around to fit in with the different capacities of a lorry/train/ship/crane/warehouse rack). Now, with the container unit as the universal load, the transport and handling facilities are adjusted to conform to the container (lorries, gantries or ships are designed so that their strength, performance and dimensions are tailored to the standard container).

To get a general feeling for the complexity and flexibility of the recent revolution in transport, we give two case studies of operators at the sharp end of the business.

5.4.3 *Case studies in transport management*

5.4.3.1 Case study 1 — a small haulage contractor

Notes from an interview with the owner.

The firm operating from its South Wales base is a one-man operation. It owns one vehicle, a Mercedes Benz 814 box-van, which transports furniture for a manufacturer to its wholesalers and retailers, large and small, throughout Britain.

The major constraints facing the owner are the EC restrictions on hours worked. Because his vehicle's gross weight exceeds 4.5 tonnes, he is legally required to fit a tachograph to record the speed and hours travelled, as evidence that he is driving within the legal limits. He is restricted to driving no more than 90 hours per fortnight and, within this, he must drive 9 hours a day no more than 3 times a week, or 10 hours a day no more than twice a week. In addition, he must have a 15 minute break after every 2 hours driving or, alternatively, a 45 minute break every 4 hours. He chooses to stop every 2 hours and always drives the maximum 90 hours per fortnight, travelling approximately 3100 miles.

Loading and unloading his vehicle presents him with many problems. His non-HGV licence restricts him to carrying no more than 7.5 tonnes, of which there is a maximum of 3.5 tonnes on the front axle and 4.8 tonnes on the back. He always loads to the maximum weight, carefully ensuring that the first delivery is at the back of the vehicle, through to the last delivery at the front. Aided by two workers at the loading bay, the actual loading time is usually under an hour. However, operations are frequently delayed through waiting. This may be due to waiting his turn in the queue although, often, finishing touches are being made to the furniture or the manufacturers are still awaiting parts, sometimes from abroad. It is not uncommon for him to be waiting at the loading bay from 8.00 am to 5.00 pm, and consequently losing a day's work. Similar delays are encountered at unloading bays, where invariably there are large queues. Further, he often arrives to find that the delivery has been cancelled or that it is too early. He overcomes the latter problem by finding a local carrier who will store the goods for a price and then deliver them to the customer when he is ready.

A great deal of the owner's time is spent planning, in order to save time and fuel money. Occasionally, he has just one 'drop' for which there is a set price, but he prefers the generally more profitable 'multi-drops' for which he is paid by the mile. These consist of 22–25 drops which take two days to complete, and only then does he return home. He usually undertakes two such deliveries a week, which is a tight schedule. Much thought, therefore, goes into devising the quickest route, which requires much more than the obvious geographical considerations. Most firms require him to book-in on a certain day, although some specify a particular morning or afternoon. Generally, warehouses are open from 8.00 am to 1.00 pm and 2.00 pm to 5.00 pm, except on Saturdays. However, they differ considerably, with many opening later and/or closing earlier, as well as having varying lunch hours. Also, although open, many load their own vehicles until 10.00 am forcing him to visit others first. He attempts to visit each at a time when he feels the queue there will be at its lowest. A further constraint is the traffic congestion at certain times and places. For example, he always visits London between 11.00 am and 3.00 pm and he also travels at night, arriving at his first drop at 8.00 am. Lastly, some routes must be avoided because of the 12′9″ height of his vehicle. Bridges must be over 13′ for him to travel under, which many are not on A and B roads.

He has twice been stopped, and consequently held up considerably, by the police who perform random checks to ensure that drivers are within the numerous legal limits discussed earlier. Breakdowns, most commonly in the form of a puncture, and the subsequent repair work, are another common source of delay. His travel is also frequently delayed by roadworks, particularly on motorways, and sporadic accidents which hold up traffic.

He has quite a few costs which add to his overheads. He pays £95 every 5 years for an operating licence and £130 car tax p.a., in addition to having his vehicle annually plated which is the equivalent of an MOT. His average load is worth approximately £7500, and so security is essential. He has therefore taken out a fully comprehensive insurance policy, costing £800 p.a., and a goods-in-transit policy which covers a load value of £10,000, at £150 p.a. He has also had to buy a £50 lock for his frequently unguarded vehicle and, when parking, he backs up against a wall to prevent theft. He is legally required to complete detailed inspection and maintenance forms every month, reporting and rectifying every defect. He therefore services his vehicle monthly, inspecting and adjusting or repairing where necessary.

He has invested in two cost-saving items. Prompted by the cost of overnight accommodation, he has bought a bed for the van and now can sleep as suits his work. He has also installed a telephone and, ringing numbers advertised in the monthly *Headlight* magazine, he attempts to obtain a return load, delivering any goods he can. He telephones while waiting at unloading bays, thus wasting no time, whereas previously he lost both time and money finding a telephone box. He is usually able to secure a full return load and enough money to pay for his fuel, although the load often includes returns in the shape of damaged or cancelled furniture.

5.4.3.2 Case study 2 — a large food packing and distribution firm

Notes from an interview with the chief scheduler.

The warehouse and distribution depot of this firm is situated approximately 1 mile from the packing department. It operates with a fleet of 20–30 heavy goods vehicles transporting a whole range of brand name goods to supermarkets, catering companies, hotels and boarding houses throughout the UK, with 15 per cent of these lorries carrying produce to the Continent each week. Two-thirds of the journeys made are to Tesco and Sainsbury supermarkets in England and Wales, but Scotland's stores are supplied from a central warehouse at Glasgow, to which the firm also delivers.

Since so much of their trade is focused on these two major customers, the schedulers must plan their work with priority and attention to them whenever possible. This proves difficult when both Tesco and Sainsbury require priority simultaneously: for example, when a lorry driver telephoned from Wales to say that as a result of being delayed (because of a shortage of staff to unload his cargo) at four Tesco outlets, he had used up his allocated hours and was unable to continue his journey to one of Sainsbury's larger supermarkets which, alone, accounted for over half of that day's load. The scheduler instructed the driver to return to the depot and informed the Sainsbury outlet that the goods would arrive at 8.45 the following morning. He added that the problem would have been far less serious if the fifth drop had been to another Tesco store, as they would have to accept partial responsibility for the delay.

There is then a knock-on effect of rescheduling the Sainsbury trip. The route schedule is usually worked out three days in advance. From the scheduler's experience, he schedules goods to arrive at their destinations at the 'expected' time; that is, the time that they normally arrive, although this is not usually written in the order. Any additional orders are then juggled around to find the 'best fit' in the schedule (i.e. with the minimum disruption to the usual orders). If the Sainsbury case had not been of such priority, it could have been rescheduled for as many as four or five days later, as the timetable already worked out for the next three days was nearly at full capacity. Actually, it was just fitted in as a late delivery on the following evening.

Theoretically, Tesco has no written demands of the times at which goods should arrive at their different outlets although, in practice, their supermarket managers plan to the expected arrival times: 50 per cent of Tesco stores are unconcerned over the exact time as long as the goods arrive before 3.00 pm. Familiarity with the particular requirements of each receiver assists the scheduler enormously.

This use of experience is also true for the warehouse manager, who accurately plans inventory levels according to anticipated and confirmed customer orders. By identifying each customer's preferences regarding 'sell by' dates, he can limit the transport problems caused by dissatisfied customers demanding that their goods be returned. Because of the rotation system employed in the warehouse, this rarely causes a problem, although bacon, which has the shortest 'sell by' date, has to be despatched quickly.

Product availability is another aspect of stock control which may result in transport problems. For instance, if a customer requires 18 pallets of butter and only 9 are available these must be sent, even if it means 'short loading' and making a second journey.

It is also the responsibility of the scheduler to anticipate and expedite orders based on previous demand. A single major complication to this is accounting for special offers, promotions and free samples. The two big supermarket chains, in particular, invariably have at least one brand of butter on promotion each week. The consequences of this are dynamic, with demand increasing in many cases from 4000 to 14,000 products per week.

The most recent single development which has brought about a multitude of transport problems for the company was initiated by Sainsbury's who converted all of their storage facilities into selling space, thus calling for a more reliable and efficient transport delivery system to transfer goods straight from the lorry to the shelf. Tesco has also adopted this method, which requires greater accuracy on the part of the transport department to schedule to precise arrival times. This is easier with 'direct loads' (i.e. full drops) consisting of a single product. A full load is not synonymous with a lorry full to volume capacity as there are restrictions on weight. Speed of loading is hindered by legislation requiring the weight to be distributed equally over the axles. To familiarize himself with his cargo, the driver loads his own lorry. The scheduler switches each lorry as often as possible between multi-drop and full drop routes to reduce any hostility between drivers. To facilitate scheduling, a few drivers do have regular routes and regular customers — this makes the system open to abuse as drivers may pace their work to suit themselves. However, it does have its advantages. One particular driver schedules his arrival at his final drop just as the customer is closing so that he can give him a lift home.

The pallets on which the goods are transported have created problems as drivers find that they can sell the new ones to clients and return with old ones, pocketing the profits. So far, this problem has not been satisfactorily resolved as it is impractical to monitor the movement of new pallets.

Difficulties drivers have in establishing the quickest route to their destinations have been partly resolved by the installation of CARP, a computer-based route scheduling network. But the scheduler dislikes it, claiming it has not a human's ability to interpret driver preferences. He claims that it would require a full-time operator to keep it up to date and, as no two days are ever the same, the programme would need to be constantly reset. For these reasons, it is only used as a reference base.

A further complication is the unstable nature of demand. On a weekly basis, Thursday, Friday and Saturday tend to be the period of high demand (reflecting late opening hours and weekend trade increases); on a seasonal basis, more deliveries are needed in summer to holiday resorts, particularly in Devon and Cornwall. The scheduler reckons that their current fleet of vehicles is optimal and fluctuations in demand do not warrant the purchase of any more lorries. He has overcome the seasonal problem by hiring contractors to cope with this excess demand.

Looking to the future, the scheduler perceives a further requirement from the supermarkets to add to his problems; in particular, they will demand that one type of product/brand be stacked on one pallet/set of pallets and that these be number-coded (e.g. no. 1 = butter, no. 2 = cheese, etc.). Looking on the bright side, he admits this might reduce the problem of 'black market' pallet trading! But the biggest headache is the constant interruptions from sales staff relaying late orders and cancellations; it often takes six hours to replan a morning's work as a result.

▼   **Contact exercise in transport management**

From what we have said, it is apparent that a transport scheduler has many objectives in mind in his work. For example:

1.   Rapid response to customer requests.
2.   Minimizing fuel and wages costs.
3.   Keeping within the law on loading, speed and hours worked.
4.   Giving a fair allocation of work to drivers.
5.   Arranging a fair system of priorities between customers.
6.   Deciding what parts of your business are going to be left to subcontractors.
7.   Whether your empty returning lorries should look for other people's loads to carry.

Also, his firm is subject to some very complex constraints. For example:

1.   Limited times when customers are open to receive deliveries.
2.   Limitation on the size and speed of vehicles.
3.   EC regulations on daily hours worked by drivers.
4.   Restrictions on how lorries are loaded and secured.
5.   The relatively high cost of diesel since the 1973 oil crisis.
6.   Traffic congestion, roadworks, weight and height restrictions.
7.   Random weather, accidents and security problems.

The ways in which constraints and objectives interact vary from firm to firm in a variety of ways. Check this by interviewing a transport manager of your choice. Write a detailed account of what you thought were the major diffi-culties for your particular manager. Use the previous case studies as a
▲   guideline.

A good case study in materials distribution is 'Berger Paints — Distribution' in Constable and New, *Operations Management* (Wiley, 1976). It is intriguing to combine analysis of it with the subsequent case in Constable and New, 'Berger Paints, Production Planning and Control'. Then you are in a better position to appreciate how distribution problems fit in to the overall context of customer priorities and lead times.

5.5 Storage and handling of materials

5.5.1 *Situation study — a bulk extraction problem at a coal mine*

Branching from a main 'roadway' are two 'side roads' which tunnel each side of a coal seam. Coal is excavated between the side roads as shown in Figure 5.2.
    Constraints on handling building material for 'side road' construction:

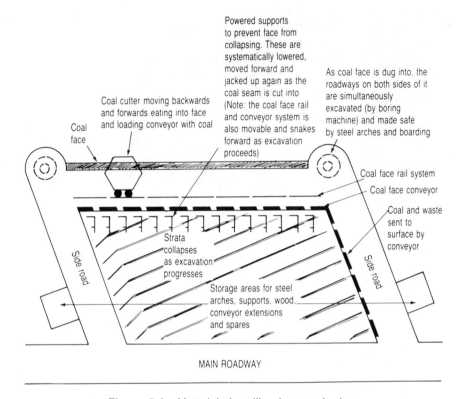

Figure 5.2 Materials handling in a coal mine.

1. The material is bulky and difficult to manoeuvre in a confined space.
2. It is difficult to avoid interference if you want to extract coal and build side roads simultaneously.
3. Operations are affected by geological uncertainties. Will the seam get shallower or thicker? Will it rise or fall? Will it be wavy or straight?
4. Communications will be imperfect because of the noise, heat and dust, and the isolation of work teams.
5. Every mine will have a unique network of roadways leading to a face. Work will take place at different levels. Roadways will be diverted to avoid or merge with roadways in neighbouring collieries. Movements in strata will cause roadways to twist and buckle.
6. One pit will have several faces operating simultaneously, all competing for supplies of materials to be delivered to them.

Consequences of the constraints:

1. From day to day there is an uneven pace of extraction, causing variable demand for building materials.

2. It is difficult to forecast how far a face will advance before being abandoned. It could be 500 m or 3000 m.
3. Dispersal of faces means that different teams of men will be responsible for passing on materials at different points in the system. Decisions will have to be made about which face is to have priority if there is a shortage of resources.

Lines on which any remedy must proceed:

1. It is not feasible to set up independent material handling systems in the same pit (i.e. it would not work to have independent arrangements for each coal face). You have to operate a global handling system for the pit covering all the constraints for every face. How should they interact? How, when and where should all material be moved? What resources are needed to achieve this?
2. Any representation must be acceptable and understandable to the men underground who are taking and implementing the handling decisions.
3. It helps if the decision-maker has alternative proposals which can be easily compared and evaluated.
4. The decision-maker must *like* the proposed approach to solving the problem. The real test comes when the planner has left. Does the decision-maker revert to old methods? Or does he update and improve the proposed method?

The Operational Research Executive Group of British Coal has developed HAULSTAR. This is a visual interactive colour simulation of material handling which is run from an IBM PC. Into the computer you input the materials requirement to achieve planned advances for all coal faces at a mine, and complete information about the network of mine roads and handling facilities. The program then generates the following information:

1. Identification of the transfer and storage points which may be potential bottlenecks.
2. Evaluation of alternative solutions, e.g. sending either individual small deliveries or bulk deliveries lasting several days to a coal face.
3. Variations and delays in material delivery caused by development work, coal extractions or the transport of men to and from the face.

For each alternative, the program visually displays or writes to file:

1. The timing and quantity of material passing through intermediate points and reaching destinations.
2. The location, movement and return of vehicles.
3. The utilization of the teams on each haulage route.

A decision-maker can observe the flow of materials simulated for any particular solution and can analyse variations quickly by changing the resources or relaxing/tightening constraints.

5.5.2 *General principles of storage and handling*

In devising handling and storage systems for a firm, there are few designer solutions which can be applied willy-nilly. A solution has to be tailor-made for each firm. There are, however, a few general considerations to be taken into account.

1. Where you must prevent a break-in (by fire, water or vermin, or theft). Here, the cost spent on securing the material, plus the insurance, is fairly easy to calculate, potential loss being limited to the total value of the material.
2. Where you must prevent the material breaking out of its containers (e.g. explosives, corrosives, poisons, radioactives). Here it is much harder to specify the money that should be spent on storage, handling and insurance. Potential damage is open-ended, possibly far in excess of the value of the material.
3. Where special consideration must be given to the movement of items. For example:

    *   fragile items requiring special packaging (eggs, glass, pottery);
    *   powdery or liquid, free-flowing materials, sloppy but easy to pump (oil, grain);
    *   heavy items (steel or concrete sections, assembled units such as generating sets). In particular, where a mixture of heavy and light items is being carried, it is desirable to arrange a *balanced load*.

In stowing or storing a mixture of items, there are many other factors apart from weight which have to be taken into account. Cotton bales can suffer rust from a ship's sides. Damp wool is liable to spontaneous combustion. Vapours from copra would taint other cargo but it cannot be ventilated. Apples exude carbon dioxide and need to be wrapped in chemically treated paper. Many common commodities have specific and unusual physical properties which have a dramatic effect on how they are stored and handled. This requires managers responsible for loading and warehousing to be fully conversant with materials technology.

This needs to be emphasized as there has been a tendency to think of inventory management as being limited to certain decisions regarding reordering and batching policies discussed in Chapter 10.

▼   **Exercise in materials storage and handling**

Compare how shelves are replenished at smaller supermarkets and the larger hypermarkets, tackling the following questions:

(a) What handling device do they use to transport the merchandise?

(b) How much interference occurs between staff and shoppers?

(c) Are goods being replaced when levels are low, or just when out of stock?

(d) Are shelves being completely filled up, or spaces left?

(e) Is the assistant doing the replenishment by zig-zagging about or following a logical route?

(f) Is the replenishment done by an individual or in pairs?

▷

(g) When an assistant has finished a load, what sort of delay is there before he or she returns with a new load?

(h) Are assistants looking for spaces on the shelves that they should fill, or are they following a predetermined system?

(i) Is old stock being moved to the front of the shelf and new stock placed behind it?

(j) Is there a significantly different replenishment system according to whether the goods fall into one of these categories: deep freeze, chill freeze, fruit and vegetables, canned food, other open shelf goods.

▲

5.6 Conclusion

What is meant by an effective overall materials management policy? One way of looking at it is to ensure that you are competent at each of the topics we have covered: selection, purchasing, delivery, handling and storage. But that is not the whole story. Effective materials utilization cannot be separated from effective labour utilization or effective machine utilization. If this is so, then the problem of materials management must be looked at in a wider context, and this is dealt with in the systems chapter (Chapter 6). Also, a careful approach to materials is a central plank of both the Just-in-Time philosophy and Total Quality Management, both of which we cover later. Therefore, this chapter on materials acts as a foundation for later, more advanced work.

And now, a cautionary tale. A company producing plastic bags was very proud of its percentage utilization of incoming material. It used high-grade plastic to produce high-quality plastic bags. Any wastage was recycled and included in the mix for lower-grade bags. Again, wastage from this process was used in the production of even-lower-grade bags, and so on. The percentage of wastage at any stage was not considered a problem since it was being recycled. The company was fooling itself. Why?

5.7 Recommended reading

Case studies and state-of-the-art reviews of materials management can be found in two monthly journals designed for members of the Institute of Logistics and Distribution Management (ILDM). These journals, *Focus* and *Distribution*, are written by and for practitioners, and the writing is clear, explains all the latest jargon and is highly relevant.

Cases referring to a specific aspect of materials management were referred to during the chapter. For an integrative case in materials management, try for a start 'Maynard Farms' in Meier, *Cases in Production and Operations Management* (Prentice Hall, 1982). A more challenging case is 'Kalen's' in Schmenner, *Cases in Production/Operations Management* (SRA, 1986). It involves designing a checkout scanning system for a new store. Other integrative cases involving materials are given at the end of the systems chapter (Chapter 6).

Chapter 6

Systems and diagnostics

6.1 Introduction

Each of the previous four chapters of this book has focused on one special part of a business: products, people, machines and materials. Now we are ready to take an overview: to look at the interaction between these separate parts. In particular, we wish to know:

How to understand and handle a complex situation.
How to simplify, translate or codify masses of detail.

Coping with complexity is a problem facing any newcomer to an operations management situation. For example, we visit a lot of heavy engineering firms in the Sheffield area. Often, on a first visit, we are given a brief factory tour before discussing business. Usually, whoever shows us round is very knowledgeable and communicative, but it is still difficult for us to grasp what is going on. For us, as for many inexperienced visitors, the environment is noisy, cramped or dangerous. And even where the workers welcome onlookers, they have not the time to explain their often-specialist jargon and procedures. This is how a typical visit seems to proceed.

Host 'Just duck under this bucket conveyor and squeeze between these stacks and you see the G-DONK, G-DONK, G-DONK which is fed by the ACKA-ACKA-ACKA-ACKA-, and on the other side is the VROOOOM-BOH-BUH-BOH-BUH-BOH-BUH-BUMP. Let's talk to Bert about what he does.'

Bert 'Analogue feed's gorra scrottle int' melt. Reckon t'grobbler circuit's flathering for 'happorth. Nowt to cletter, nowt to boot, as they say.'

This is not to downgrade the value of shopfloor visits. Any consultant or advisor should make regular visits to enhance his or her acceptability and to build up a useful picture of the organization. But such visits are best combined with a more structured investigation elsewhere: for example, in the foreman's or production manager's office. Here, there should be more time and better facilities to explore the system via special charts and diagrams.

There are many professionals whose job it is to develop an all-embracing system which reaches into every nook and cranny of the firm. But rarely can something be identified as THE SYSTEM. Rather, there is a set of parallel systems run by different professionals. For example:

Industrial Engineer	Man–machine layout and handling system
Information Technologist	Computerized information system
Management Accountant	Management control system
Purchasing	Supply-chain management system
Transport	Logistic and distribution system
Personnel	Human resource and reward system
General Management	The departmental structure

Each of the above professionals will have their view of the organization coloured, often over-magnified, by the particular system that they work with. Nevertheless, whatever the system, it should aim to meet the following general objectives:

Representation	To get a better understanding of what is happening at the moment
Operation	To help run the current business
Diagnosis	To identify potential problems
Improvement	To update the current operating system

One example of how the above four objectives can be incorporated into a particular system was given in Chapter 2 on the product development and assessment cycle. Another example was in the materials chapter (Chapter 5) where the underground handling of coal was illustrated by a simplified map. Of course, those actually running the mine will use much more detailed maps, but for those just getting to grips with a system it is best to start with pictures, maps and diagrams that are instantly recognizable.

6.2 Pictorial representations

Let us start by looking at the layout of a hospital laundry shown in Figure 6.1. This example is not too difficult to understand because we have all used similar washing machines in the home; also, the movement of the material, represented by the arrows, is easily understood. What is not shown, and what is quite a difficult management problem, is how to transfer laundry between machines by specifying precisely the people, bags and trolleys that will be needed, and where they will be positioned and moved around.

▼   **Exercise**

Have a stab at estimating the number of people and the type of handling equipment that this laundry will need to run it. Even without experience of a

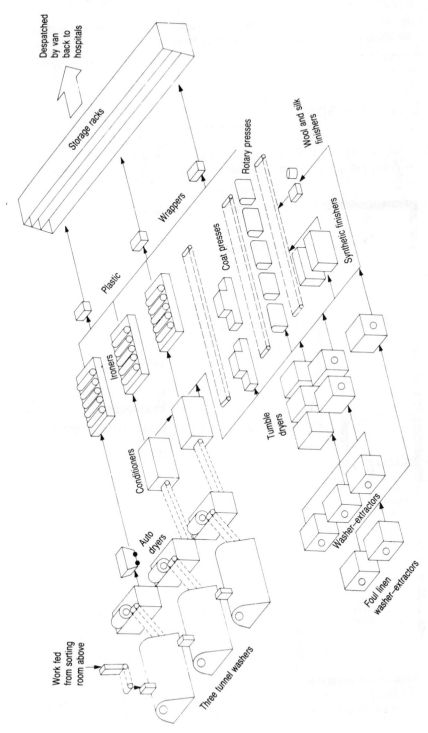

Figure 6.1 Hospital laundry system.

▲   large laundry, have a guess from your personal experience of handling
     washing and observing operations at a laundromat.

6.3 Layout maps

The hospital laundry had plenty of space and so could design a logical layout of
machines. Also, storage was neatly separated from processing. Suppose that conditions

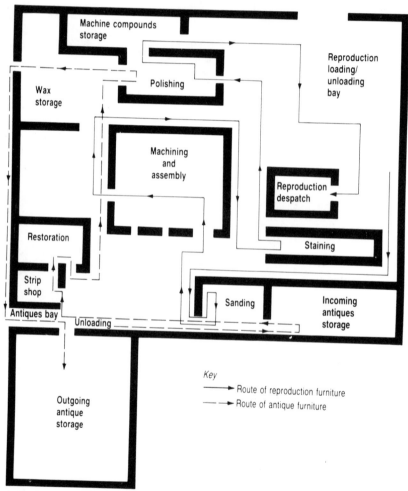

Figure 6.2   Scale diagram of the premises of a furniture renovator and manufacturer
(Paul Wilson Ltd).

are more cramped and, perhaps for historical reasons, machines are awkwardly located. Figure 6.2 shows how this could complicate the material flow.

▼ **Exercise**

Using the same area, design a layout that gives a more rational flow of materials. Try to do this without knocking down and rebuilding too many internal partitions. Of course, this exercise is made more difficult because the layout map tells you nothing about the weight, height or size of the machines, nor anything about the stacking facilities at the storage areas. But this illustrates another general point: you can't get something for nothing. If you simplify so that you can understand the whole system, you lose out on
▲ understanding some detail.

6.4 Simplifying further to a process chart

So far, our illustration bears some resemblance to what an observer would see. Often, though, it helps to depart from a geographical representation. Suppose you want to focus on the sequence of processes that a material must pass through, without worrying about how the material moves from one process to the next.

6.4.1 *A simple sequence of operations*

Consider, for example, a firm that prepares smoked salmon. Its work can be split into a chain of ten operations — a sequence of processes.

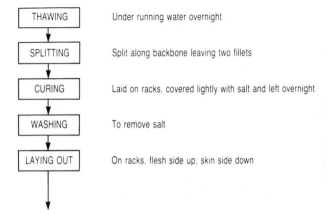

THAWING	Under running water overnight
SPLITTING	Split along backbone leaving two fillets
CURING	Laid on racks, covered lightly with salt and left overnight
WASHING	To remove salt
LAYING OUT	On racks, flesh side up, skin side down

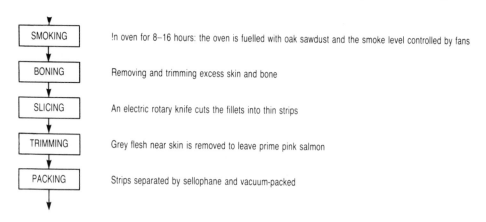

SMOKING — In oven for 8–16 hours: the oven is fuelled with oak sawdust and the smoke level controlled by fans

BONING — Removing and trimming excess skin and bone

SLICING — An electric rotary knife cuts the fillets into thin strips

TRIMMING — Grey flesh near skin is removed to leave prime pink salmon

PACKING — Strips separated by sellophane and vacuum-packed

6.4.2 *Extending process charts to incorporate materials inputs and outputs*

Usually, when you have a sequence of processes, each new process has its own special input (and possibly output) of materials. These can be represented separately in simple box and arrow diagrams. These are kept very simple on purpose: if you like, they provide the skeleton of the system. Leave clever enhancements until later. Use a box to represent a process, a machine, or a type of material. Use an arrow to show something moving between boxes. For example, this would be a bare-bones systems diagram of the brewing process.

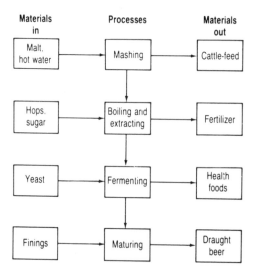

Figure 6.3 Specifying where material enters and leaves the brewing process.

▼   **Exercise**

Figure 6.3 just gives you the barest outline of what happens in brewing. Can you add the following extra information to the diagram?

(a) How much time each process takes.

(b) What quantities of materials enter and leave the system, and what revenues and costs are involved.

▲   You will need to contact someone in the brewing industry to get the answers.

6.4.3 *Extending process charts to incorporate handling equipment*

So far, we have considered only the processing and storage of material. Suppose that transport equipment is also moving, sometimes loaded, sometimes returning unloaded. Figure 6.4 shows how this can be represented.

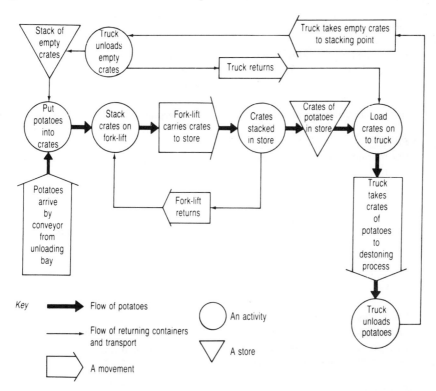

Figure 6.4   Potato handling prior to crisp manufacture.

In the manufacture of crisps, there is a central flow of activities associated with the movement of raw material — potatoes. Servicing this main flow there will be a subsidiary flow of handling equipment, sometimes running parallel, sometimes in a reverse direction to the main flow. This is illustrated in Figure 6.4 for just a small part of the system (between unloading and destoning potatoes) where, as well as potatoes, it helps to track the movement of crates, a truck and a fork-lift.

6.5 Introduction of decision points

6.5.1 *Case study — tropical and aquatic supplies*

This is the largest retailer of pet fish in a metropolitan region, selling coldwater pond fish, tropical fish, marine fish, underwater insects, anemones, plus all aquaria accessories and foods. There is an off-site warehouse which restocks the shop and which itself is supplied from London wholesalers. When a new fish arrives at the shop, the decisions that have to be made about it can be represented by a systems chart. Note, in particular, the decision box with the yes/no arrows coming out of it.

▼   **Exercise**

Is this system foolproof? Imagine that you are the manager of the firm. What factors do you think are most important for you to watch out for in view of the following special problems to be faced?

Special problems associated with the materials requirements of fish

Salts
For marine fish, the water must contain a certain density of salt, approximating the fish's natural habitat, otherwise it will ail or die.

Food
Food pellets provide all the nutrients for coldwater pond fish. For exotic fish, the diet is more complicated. A lot of the food has to be gamma irradiated and kept under very specific conditions (refrigerated to a certain temperature). The shop keeps twenty-five different food types for the marine fish alone (e.g. their 12-inch shark needs to be fed on small fish, and other live food includes shrimps, bloodworm, cockles and plankton).

Medication
More exotic fish are very prone to illness, brought on, for instance, by a tiny change in temperature. Ozone is pumped constantly through certain tanks to keep them fresh from disease.

Electricity
1.   Keeps the tanks at the necessary temperature (marine fish, 75°F; tropical

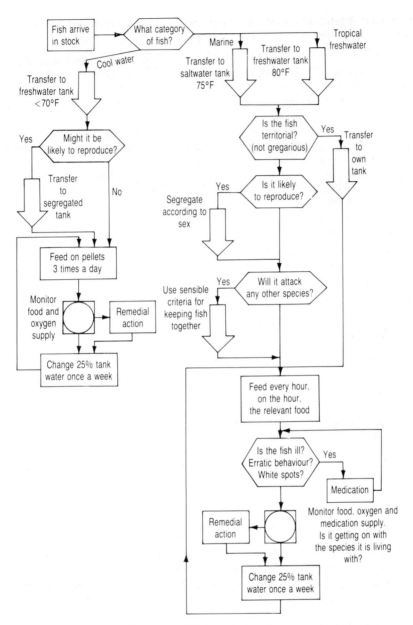

Figure 6.5 Diagram of fish arrival and care system.

freshwater fish, 80°F; pond fish, below 70°F).

2.   Pumps air and ozone through the tanks and filters out impurities.

To run out of any of these resources would be catastrophic, so the shop keeps large stocks of everything and owns its own generator.

▷

Special factors which influence decisions on storing and handling fish
Some peculiar problems arise when handling fish as stock:

1. Some fish are territorial and in the wild would command hundreds of square feet to themselves — they do not mix, even with fish of their own species.
2. Many fish of different species do not mix, so one has to be very careful which species are put together. Sensible criteria such as size, diet, habitat, Latin name and colour are the best guidelines.
3. Some fish are extremely fertile and, left to their own devices, would reproduce in their thousands, causing havoc.
4. Fish can ail and die, making stock bought in totally worthless. Stock turnover in this shop is very high, so this is seldom a problem, but this and other considerations must be taken into account when handling stock.

▲

6.6 An integrated method study approach — the medical operation

There are two key activities that we have not yet brought into our illustrations: inspection and delay. If we add them, we will be using all the standard concepts employed by methods analysts. Figure 6.6 shows all these concepts in use.

6.6.1 *Extensions to analysis*

The basic surgical situation is viewed very differently by the various participants:

The patient
The ward staff
Staff in the operating theatre

For example, to the patient, the anaesthetist's role may appear rather minimal. In fact, after rendering the patient unconscious, the anaesthetist and his or her staff will be involved in a string of major support activities until the patient recovers. The anaesthetist deals with the fluid and blood supply, the ventilating machine, intravenous drug supply, as well as the continual monitoring of the heart rate and blood pressure. At every moment during the operation the surgeon depends on the anaesthetist to know whether the operation can continue. And, after the operation, the anaesthetist continues surveillance until the patient begins to come round in the recovery ward.

There are also many other hospital activities by specialists that the patients might not be aware of. Surgical support staff need to procure instruments and equipment for specific operations several days before and ensure that they are available in a sterile

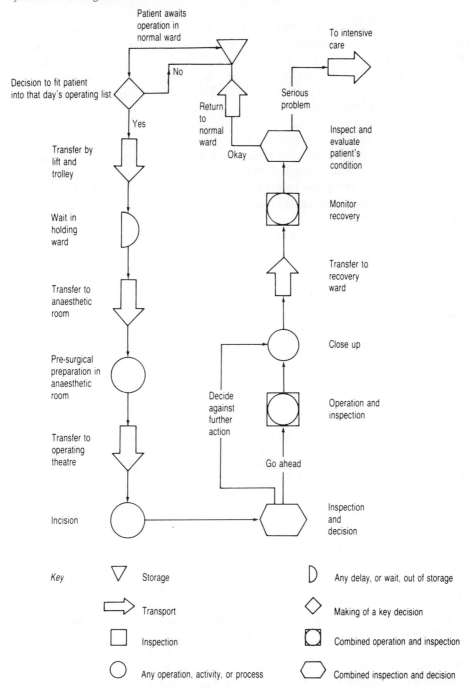

Figure 6.6 Basic procedures associated with hospital surgery.

condition, correctly laid out at the time of the operation. By its very nature, the time taken to complete an operation will be uncertain. Where there is a sequence of operations, it will be difficult to keep to schedule. However, advance schedules need to be prepared because there is at least a four-hour preparation time for the patient, so that last-minute substitutions are impossible. To complicate matters further, surgeons will be travelling between different hospitals, so scheduling their time is also important.

All this reinforces the point that our systems diagram, which illustrates the processes of just one typical surgical operation, is very simple when compared with the workings of a total hospital system. But what would happen if you tried to design *one enormous* systems chart for the whole hospital? (Answer: a nervous breakdown for anyone who attempts it.) Rather, we would recommend separate systems charts for each hospital department and subsystems charts within each of these (a fuller explanation of the philosophy behind this approach is given in the work-breakdown schedule of the project planning chapter (Chapter 9) and in the next example on pottery manufacturing). So, for any large system, there is an art in choosing the scope and detail of any systems chart you design and how many separate systems charts should be done.

Despite all the above difficulties, we would argue strongly that constructing systems charts is an excellent starting point when approaching any complex situation. For example, the NHS is subject to much comment and criticism from politicians and patients, who have only an imperfect understanding of the internal mechanisms, resources and constraints. Setting out hospital procedures in the form of systems diagrams is one way of getting greater understanding and consensus from outsiders.

▼   **Contact exercise**

Check whether what we say about the value of systems diagrams is valid. Contact anyone who works in the NHS and, with their help, construct a small but detailed systems diagram for just that part of the NHS with which they
▲   are most intimately involved.

6.7 Systems exploration — the pottery example

There is a fairly standard method of pottery manufacture, whatever the item being made. Clay is broken up and purified, then mixed with water and additives to get a putty-like base. It is then cast into shape and passed through a firing oven to emerge hardened but pretty fragile. Next it is covered with a sticky glaze and sent through a kiln, after which it emerges with a hard protective cover and is ready for use.

At a large manufacturer's, the above process will involve much labour, space and expensive equipment: storage and mixing vats; mould-shops ovens and kilns serviced by gas, air water and electricity services; and a variety of handling equipment such as conveyors, rail-cars, trucks, trolleys and fork-lifts. So, at a large pottery firm, there

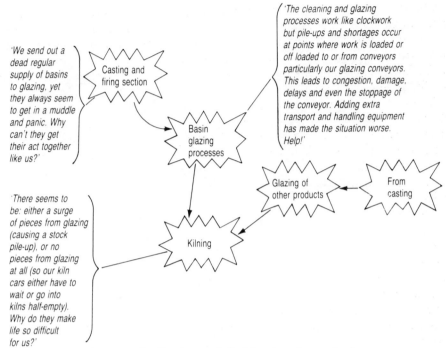

Figure 6.7   Pottery — A first level systems chart.

is a very complex system (or set of systems), prone to a host of difficult co-ordination problems. How should a systems analyst set about understanding what is going on? At first, it helps to take broad-brush approach, identifying just the most prominent problems in the context of a very general systems chart. For example, consider the piggy-in-the-middle position of that section of a pottery factory that glazes washbasins, shown in Figure 6.7.

This crude overview can be used to see which particular part of the system needs to be put under the microscope and set out in more detail. It appears that there is a material handling problem at the conveyor loading/unloading points. On investigation, you find that between conveyors, material is moved around or stored on trolleys — they are a bit like large supermarket trolleys but with an upper and a lower deck. Each trolley usually takes six basins, although this can vary from four (for the largest) to eight (for the smallest). Paying particular attention to the logistics of the trolleys in the glazing section gives this more detailed systems chart, in Figure 6.8.

6.7.1 *Extended discussion on the pottery case*

6.7.1.1 The inefficiency points

The inefficiency points (indicated by ★ in the figure) highlight areas of potential improvement. These concern not merely waste materials or idle labour, they also

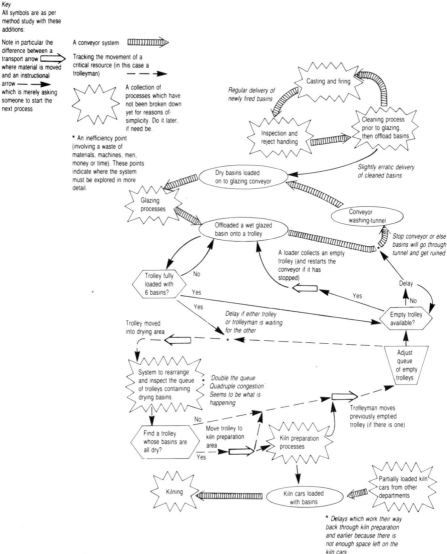

Figure 6.8 Pottery — A second level systems chart.

highlight stoppages, high levels of work-in-progress or deteriorating quality. We can use the inefficiency points to break out of a narrow approach to problem-solving.

From 'optimizing within constraints', e.g.:

• Switching men from loading to transporting duties.
• Changing the inspection interval for trolleys with drying basins.

To 'attacking constraints within a limited system', e.g.:

- Redesigning the trolleys so that they are either more manoeuvrable or pieces can be loaded and unloaded more easily.
- Negotiating with the workforce so that a loader or washer can do a trolleyman's job and vice versa, so allowing for more labour flexibility.

To 'attacking constraints imposed by related systems', e.g.:

- Reversing authority of departments so that the glazing department tells the casting department the type and timing of products to be sent on (a PULL rather than a PUSH system).
- Moving the whole basin-glazing section so that these heavy items are loaded first, instead of last, onto the kiln cars.

6.7.1.2 Systems improvement via shopfloor feedback and the Andon Approach

When developing a systems chart, there comes a point when it is worth showing your preliminary findings to a shopfloor worker and asking for his or her comments. The exercise helps to confirm or refute one's existing understanding of the system and exposes further areas that need attacking. This is the feedback from one shopfloor worker:

'Basins are constantly coming in from the casting department and are pushed through the operation to the kilns. There often need to be stoppages of the conveyor because no trolleys are there in time to take the pieces off before they crash into the washing machine. Also, when there isn't a trolley load of dry basins ready to be loaded on the glazing conveyor, workers are idle at the glazing processor and there are knock-on effects making utilization worse all the way through to kilning.

If you think that is bad, you ought to see the panic at higher throughput rates. Trolleys rush around, we run out of places to store the trolleys full of drying pieces, pieces have to be stored on working space on the factory floor, which makes normal working slower and more difficult, so creating a vicious circle. In such circumstances, if we try to speed up loading, more pieces get damaged, or trolleys crash into each other in the passageways that are blocked and cramped by the excessive stock.

The workers themselves are specialists in one particular process. They just do their jobs; there is little communication. They are not aware of how their operation fits in with others or why the variations in production occur. When the colour of a spray is changed at lunchtime, it just happens: no-one is told in advance. Likewise, no-one knows in advance what type or size of basin is going to come through the system next. Workers would like to know this because of the different skills needed to handle each type. In particular, with the conveyors going at a constant rate, they are expected to load and offload the largest and heaviest basins just as quickly as the rest. This is difficult to do and results in many breakages.'

Comment

Clearly, some immediate gains can be made by changing the work practices, the manning and the layout. But there is the more general issue of how to ensure that in future the workforce will be motivated to identify problems and make improvements themselves without being told to do so by a management specialist or outsider. Such a positive climate flourishes better if workers are not tied down to a special location but have flexible assignments. It is also helped if a group bonus is in operation covering all systems that are interrelated. It would also be helped by a different approach to problem-solving. Wherever any operative experiences an inefficiency point whilst working, he or she should immediately call over everyone associated with it. They should stop their normal work and congregate on-site to discuss what to do about it, and *this should have priority over everything else even if it stops the factory flow.* This is the key feature of the Japanese Andon (traffic-light) approach to systems improvement.

6.7.2 *Pottery: what next beyond systems analysis?*

Suppose you take the second-level chart back to the workplace and show it to the people who have to live with the system. If they say, 'Yes, you are onto something here', what do you do next? With their help, you could expand the systems chart, in particular by looking at decisions associated with the inefficiency points (*), or by breaking down the processes in any fuzzy black box that is causing trouble. Or, you can combine this approach with the diagnostics of Ishikawa's Fishbone Diagram (explained and illustrated in the next chapter). At this finer level of detail, you may find yourself looking at the job elements and cycle times of an individual worker (see Chapter 4 on people) or looking at the downtime and variation in throughput of an individual machine (see Chapter 3 on machines). Whatever the approach, you should now be ready to start work on finding out about numerical data connected with each activity in a system — that means throughput-volume, timings and resources needed. When that information has been collected, you are in a position to achieve greater systems efficiency by applying the numerical technique illustrated in Chapter 10 on scheduling.

▼   **Contact exercise**

Arrange a visit to a production, service, transport or distribution operation and make a systems diagram of its processing and handling sequence.

The operation should be of reasonable size, approximately twenty employees or more. It is recommended that you do not tackle an operation with more than about five hundred employees because of the complexity of the system.

A brief report should accompany your diagram, explaining the nature of the company and system. Discuss the major problems the company has, based
▲   on your interviews with staff and your observations.

6.8 Recommended reading

We recommend that you start with the short, confidence-building exercises in Schmenner, *Production/Operations Management Concepts and Situations*, 4th edn (Macmillan, 1990). These include designing systems diagrams for Beacon Glass (p. 25) and Sunmeadow Dairy (p. 26) with the help of the Androscoggin example that preceded it. Then we would design systems for further short cases, Brown Smith and Jones (p. 82) and Welch's Ice Cream (p. 85), with the aid of the 'Jos. A. Bank Clothiers' illustration that preceded it.

After that, look at Schmenner (*Cases*), 'Carmen Canning', to see if you can distinguish *constraints* from CONSTRAINTS, and at the English Steel case in Nicholson, *Managing Manufacturing Operations* (Macmillan, 1978) to draw a systems diagram and identify potential inefficiency points. Finally, from Sasser *et al.*, *Cases in Operations Management: Analysis and Action* (Irwin, 1982), use National Cranberry Co-operative to identify and resolve bottlenecks in fruit-growing, and Max-Able Medical Clinic to untangle the trivial from important when designing a new system. Then, for an astounding read, pick up Eli Goldratt's *The Goal*, a management classic.

Chapter 7

The quality revolution

7.1 Introduction

Over the past ten years, the quest for quality has become a major management issue in the UK. But what is quality? To the production engineer, quality may imply a reduction in scrap, rework times and inspection, with a resultant reduction in production costs. However, marketing staff may be more concerned with how the customer perceives the quality of a product (see Chapter 2). The first view is inward-looking, with its emphasis on quality control and conformance to quality specification. The second view is outward-looking and involves customer-perceived quality linked to value and satisfaction. But to achieve customer satisfaction, offering the best product at the right time, at the right place and at the right price, all the systems and techniques of the inward-looking view are also needed.

To achieve this goal, we need to adopt the central quality philosophy of continuous improvement, *kaizen* as it is known in Japan. The drive for quality is a never-ending activity, taking very seriously in Japan, and is responsible in large measure for the success of Japanese industry over the past twenty-five years.

Japan has not always been renowned for its quality products, however. In the immediate post-war period, Japanese companies were noted for their cheap and shoddy goods. Ironically, ignored by their native USA, statisticians Drs Deming and Juran introduced their ideas to top Japanese managers. They promulgated the key concepts of quality control and statistical process control. Their Japanese audience listened and adopted these techniques, resulting in Japanese companies being able to compete internationally by supplying reliable products at lower prices. This was the springboard for the whole quality movement which, once started, moved on rapidly in Japan. During the mid-1960s, the drive for quality started to pervade whole companies, and the concept of total quality management (TQM) was born. This philosophy began to be embraced throughout the Pacific Rim, and countries such as Singapore, Korea and Hong Kong applied the Japanese experience to their industries. In the late 1970s, the USA reacted to the erosion of its markets; the famous quote by Florida Power and Light Chief Executive Bud Hunter, after a visit to Japan in the 1970s, illustrates this awakening:

I swaggered to Japan at the time, feeling that the US did it all better anyway, and quite simply staggered out again as a humbled man. (Hunter, B., *Total Quality Management: A Way of Life in Corporate USA and Japan*, PA Consulting Group, Report on International Study Tour, 1988.)

The more perspicacious managers such as Hunter realized that quality could not be quickly bought and installed, like an up-to-date machine. Nor was it simply adopting Japanese techniques willy-nilly. There was an underlying cultural influence in Japan. Other nations had to match their own quality objectives to their own culture or else try to change that culture. Finally, by the early 1980s, Western Europe and the UK realized that quality was a key strategic issue, so that today it is the word that most frequently springs to mind when management seeks factors critical to future success.

7.2 Total quality management: what does it mean?

The term 'total quality management' (TQM) is frequently used, but less frequently defined and understood by the user. It can be defined as an approach or attitude:

TQM is an approach to improving the effectiveness and flexibility of business as a whole. It is essentially a way of organising and involving the whole organisation ... more an attitude of mind. (Oakland, J.S., *Total Quality Management*, Heinemann, 1989.)

Often it is defined by what it is about:

Total quality is about success through people.

Quality is about attitudes, culture and commitment.

Quality management is a systematic way of guaranteeing that all activities in an organisation happen the way they have been planned ... about prevention by attitudes and controls. (Collard, R., *Total Quality: Success through People*, St Clair Press, 1977.)

Companies often define it by what it means as an end-product:

British Telecom's definition, as seen by two facilitators of the program at Sheffield, described TQM through a set of fifteen vision statements summarizing what the organization and people will be like when TQM has been achieved. (BT vision statement provided by Steve McCormick, Facilitator of TQM Program at BT.)

Finally, it can be defined as a system:

A cost-effective system for integrating the continuous quality improvement efforts of people at all levels in an organization to deliver products and services which ensure customer satisfaction. (*Personnel Management*, Factsheet, May 1990.)

The following working definition was designed by Steve Matthews. This definition attempts to capture the spirit of TQM, whilst allowing for differing means to the same end:

> *Total quality management is the empowerment of people through effective organiza-tional design and communication that creates an attitude, culture, and commitment to continually better the strategic position of the company by focusing on quality* [our italics]. (Matthews, Stephen W., 'Total Quality Management — The Royal Mail and the Sheffield Mechanised Letter Office', unpublished MBA dissertation, 1990.)

7.3 Quality improvement via BS5750

How does a company start on the road for TQM? Perhaps the first stage is the recognition that it needs to invest in preventing rather than detecting defects: so a quality system is needed. In 1979, the UK government introduced the National Quality System Standard BS5750 which, despite much publicity and customer clamour, is still, in 1992, not in place in many UK companies. The details of this standard are given in the reference section to this chapter, but the essence can be gleaned from the following report written by the authors after visits to companies trying to get to grips with the standard.

The sales pitch for BS5750 argues that:

1. Getting the procedures right means that companies are more likely to get their products right first time, leading to less reworking and less scrap.
2. More inspectors are not necessary because quality is being built into the product.
3. Managers have more control and can trace problems much more easily and speedily.

In most cases, the impetus to start on the road came from customers. Indications that customers, usually major customers, would eventually expect all suppliers to meet BS5750 left these managing directors with no choice but, at the very least, to think about the standard.

Despite the publicity, some of the MDs initially had surprising misconceptions about the standard. Because it has a BS prefix, one thought it would involve a tighter specification for his product. Another, because it was about quality, that it was primarily an inspection system. This gave these MDs enough cause for concern, but the concept of a quality management system embracing all procedures from supplier vetting to customer delivery proved daunting. Of those who thought they knew what the standard was trying to achieve, the initial perceptions of BS5750's impact on their companies was less than positive: 'We'll be swamped with paperwork'; 'We'll get bogged down in the system and have no time to produce anything'; 'It won't improve our quality, it will just tell us more effectively that we're making rubbish.'

This latter comment came from perhaps the most interesting company. The MD, a new man in the company, took stock of his production processes. He found that customer complaints were almost unknown because good final inspection prevented below-specification products leaving the factory. However, up to 30 per cent of the output needed reworking. During reworking, some products were damaged and required further reworking. To use the MD's words, a 'black hole seemed to exist, into which a certain proportion of products disappeared'. He named it the 'rework roundabout', and wisely decided that until he got better control over his twenty-eight less-than-stable processes and got his 30 per cent down to a more acceptable level, BS5750 — although he thought it attainable — was a pointless exercise. A message which managers in similar situations would do well to heed.

On a typical visit to another MD, the results of twelve days' work by a consultant sat on the table between us, four inches high. The despairing MD asked me, 'What do I do with it? I've read bits of it, but I don't know where to begin.' He expressed concern at the volume and apparent incomprehensibility of the reports received. He felt that the manuals were really meant for ICI rather than for his own small operation. Consultants take note!

The MD said they had insufficient time themselves to tailor the manual, write up the detailed procedures required, then follow this up with an audit. So progress was inevitably slow. Because of the size of the company, he had nobody to delegate this work to, except an overworked production manager or supervisor. 'How can I get off this treadmill and take stock of things?', he said. '5750 has just got pushed to one side in the drive to meet demand.'

This lack of management time was not the only problem. He feared operatives would resist filling in forms and inspecting their own work because it would slow them down and reduce their output. This was of particular concern to the MD, who operated a volume-based bonus system as a major proportion of the operatives' wages. He felt that BS5750 might even cause them to review their payment methods, 'as if we didn't have enough problems'. The companies who were making the fastest progress were those who operated hourly-rate payments systems and who had spent time explaining to operatives why BS5750 was important to the company, and how they, as operatives, could help and benefit. All this, the MDs complained, took that precious commodity, time, even though all said it had been time well spent.

So far, BS5750 seems all doom and gloom; but the problems during the implementation of any new system always seem insurmountable to the main participants, as the MD of the company who made it in less than twelve months was quick to point out. 'Was it worth it?', we asked him.

> From an output point of view, no, I don't think so, yet. Our reject rate has gone down a little so that's good news, but running the system still takes time. You can't put a system in and ignore it. You need to monitor it continuously: via audits, and reject analysis meetings. But it's all coming together. When problems arise now, I can trace the process and the operative from where the problem originated and we can get things put right before we end up with trays full of rejects. I know exactly what's happening on the shop-

floor, and last week we got a really good suggestion from an 18-year-old operative on how to speed up a process. We've never had this sort of involvement before!

I think one of the main plus points is the confidence it's given us. Our customers know what they're getting. We're one step ahead of the competition at the moment, and we want to stay that way.

7.3.1 *Beyond BS5750 — Alloy Fabricators Limited*

Alloy Fabricators Ltd (AFL) specializes in making corrosion-resistant plant for the maritime, chemical and oil industries. In 1989, several of its larger customers demanded that AFL become a BS5750 approved supplier quickly or lose their business to competitors. AFL felt very happy with their quality standards but, when they looked at what BS5750 required them to do, they were appalled at how they had let things slip. At that time, they had a very buoyant order book, but working at capacity had led to disorganization and sloppy practices (see section 7.3.1.1).

AFL therefore embarked on a vigorous campaign to re-establish good housekeeping (see section 7.3.1.2). In a short period of eighteen months, they completely turned their systems upside-down; they gained BS5750 approval, and tighter quality approvals from other organizations.

For a while they sat on their laurels, but a general downturn in trade and a visit to Japan by a director changed all that. What the director saw in Japan was not only higher quality but a completely different approach to achieving it. When AFL had rushed to get BS5750, it had taken a vigorous, hack and thrash approach — very successful for getting the big gains possible in the early stages of quality improvement (what we call the Napoleonic approach). Having visited Japan, the director realized that a more subtle approach was needed to move from good to excellent quality (see section 7.3.1.3). Note in particular that we are *not* saying that one approach is better than the other: each approach is relevant at a particular phase in an organization's development.

7.3.1.1 Diagnosis prior to implementing BS5750

1. AFL does not present a good image to visitors; its boundaries, fencing, workshops and the surrounding area are in a state of disrepair.
2. AFL does not have sufficient shopfloor space for fabrication.
3. AFL does not have sufficient shopfloor space for segregated and secure storage of materials.
4. AFL does not adopt a policy of segregating different materials from one another when in fabrication.
5. AFL does not adopt a clean conditions policy for its fabrication operation.
6. AFL does not attempt to separate its different operations, i.e. cutting, burning, grinding, rolling, pressing and welding are all carried out in a confused manner

next to each other, thus affording an opportunity for frequent cross-contamination and much inefficiency.

7. AFL does not enforce sufficient discipline on its personnel in matters of cleanliness, security, honesty and in all matters of quality assurance.
8. AFL does not have an adequate means of control for care and repair of tooling.
9. AFL does not have adequate storage space for equipment.
10. AFL does not have adequate control on scrap materials, thus affording the opportunity for substitution of wrongly made parts.

7.3.1.2 The successful plan to obtain BS5750

It is proposed that the following outline plan be costed and followed in order to achieve an improvement in efficiency and quality.

1. Erect perimeter fence.
2. Dismantle existing compound and move works Portacabin to compound area.
3. Erect a light fabrication shop to be used solely for storage of plate materials and equipment. Scrap materials to be kept in stores also. No material will be stored outside this area except in extreme cases. A light 'A'-frame-type crane will be required. No admittance will be allowed to unauthorized personnel. Goods-inward storage area to be part of this store. Alternative material controller be appointed to control materials paperwork. The main benefit of creating this purpose-built stores is that all offloading of materials will be possible within the stores area, which is central to all company workshops. Only fully inspected material will be permitted onto the shopfloor, thus for the first time allowing true goods-inwards inspection and control.
4. Existing light fabrication shop to be used for purpose of plate-marking, cutting and grinding. Adequate extraction to be added to this shop to comply with safety legislation. Guillotine to be moved to new position in the shop. Additional cranage will be required for this shop. Large plate edge planer and CNC plasma-cutting machine to be considered at some later date. All carbon steel plating and welding work will be performed in this shop, space permitting. Additional space could be created by the absorption of the corridor in the shops. This would necessitate the purchase of a Portacabin for use as a locker room.
5. All shopfloors to be repaired and painted. All machines to be painted.
6. Main workshops to be used for assembly only, cutting and grinding to be restricted to branch holes, and some rectification and fitting work in these workshops. Additional fume extraction required to comply with safety and health legislation.
7. No. 2 workshops to be used as ultra-clean conditions shops for high-grade alloys and metals.
8. The machine shop to be moved off-site and enlarged. The existing clean-room to be doubled in size by removing the partition wall.
9. Parts racks to be made for each team to use in the designated area; also standardized tool boxes to be provided as far as possible.

7.3.1.3 From the Napoleonic to the Tao-Zen style

Many of the improvements in section 7.3.1.2 may appear to be no more than a vigorous move to a 'good housekeeping' policy. But when enough of these little initiatives are proceeding simultaneously, they help convince everyone of management's commitment to quality. Beyond BS5750, it is not sufficient for management to show its dedication. A fundamental change in attitude, culture and philosophy is needed. This is illustrated by the following comparisons.

Napoleonic Approach   *Tao-Zen Approach*

On progress

Progress depends on central management becoming aware of how things are done better elsewhere. Then, by high-profile evangelistic campaigns, management exhorts workers to adopt radically new practices. Management faces an uphill task because, unless it hammers home the issues of quality continuously, the workers will regress to their old habits.

'The road fashions the walker; the weapon the hunter; the palace the King.'

There is a similarity between the drive for quality in business and biological evolution which is driven by the hidden hand of natural selection and genetic variation within the framework of a changing environment. A subtle management designs a working environment where workers search for better quality without being told to do so. An even subtler management designs a working environment where improvements spread to other departments without having to be pushed by the centre. The foundations of this philosophy are to let proposals to improve quality initiate from front-line workers, followed by patient, lengthy discussions by everyone to reach consensus (akin to the Japanese *ringi* system). The initial delays caused in slowness in reaching a decision are more than compensated for by the organizational goodwill that ensures its success.

On control

Top management must maintain its authority over shopfloor activities. It must be able to make decisions from a quick, comprehensive and accurate

'The King who is always controlling has lost control.'

'Good riders rarely use the whip or spurs.'

information system of what is happening in its operating units. It must ensure that these decisions are implemented by a control system which does not allow the centre's wishes to be diluted, delayed or misinterpreted.

Intelligent management designs a system which runs just as well in its absence. All regular issues of information and control are the exclusive province of the shopfloor: for example, work is scheduled via a *kanban* card system rather than from a central production control department.

On aberrations

Develop specialist staff functions to look out for and to police deviations in quality and systems behaviour. Lay down rigorous procedures which the specialists follow and which can assign the blame for every deviation. Make sure that the person responsible for the fault is strongly discouraged from repeating it. In this way, you will develop a quality system where all faults are eliminated, apart from the freak happenings that no-one could expect or be blamed for.

'A theory that explains 999 events but fails to explain the remaining one, tells a thousand lies.'

Aberrant happenings should be openly discussed and investigated by everyone in the organization. Faults are never a matter of individual blame but a joint responsibility of a network of trainers, supervisors, managers and those both sides of the material chain. If faults recur, fundamental changes must be contemplated in every aspect of the operation — not only the checking procedures but the product design, the material used, machinery and the human behaviour involved.

▼   **Class exercise in TQM diagnostics — restaurant quality 1**

We have seen that TQM emphasizes that quality pervades every aspect of running a business. A good example is to think of all the things that go to make up a good restaurant. Suppose that you had just taken over a restaurant of average quality and would like it to get a more favourable mention in next year's *Good Food Guide*. What standards would you aim for with respect to the following twenty aspects of your restaurant? Before setting out your quality standard for each aspect, it might help to focus your mind by marking each aspect with the following symbols.

Importance of this aspect in TQM of the restaurant:

   (∗)   So important that the aspect needs splitting up into sub-aspects
   ∗   Important
   ?   Minor importance — possibly combine with other minor aspects
   —   Irrelevant — delete

Expense involved in improving quality for this aspect: ▷

£££ (expensive) to £ (not very expensive)

Number of people involved in improving this aspect:

    ⟶ Everyone involved
    ⟶ Just one person involved
    - - - ➔ Hardly anyone involved at all

Time needed to secure a quality improvement:

     ⟶ a long time; — a short time

Customer attitude to 'improving' this aspect:

   + + All strongly in favour, + = most in favour, no real objection
   + − A mix of customers for and against

Twenty aspects contributing to a restaurant's quality:

   Reservation policy
   Convenient location
   Printed detail in menu
   Range of dishes on offer
   Quality of wine list
   Helpfulness of waiters
   Decor and lighting
   Atmosphere (other customers)
   Seating and table comfort
   Hours of opening
   Customer dress requirements
   Vegetarian options
   Special provision for children
   Background music and noise
   Cutlery and crockery quality
   Speed of service
   Quality of cooking
   Time allowed to eat
   Policy towards smokers
▲   Prices

▼ **Contact exercise — restaurant quality 2**

The previous exercise is only a starting point for TQM. That exercise helped
formulate a vision, or a business direction; but what are the practical
obstacles which prevent higher levels of quality being attained? For example,
it seems to be agreed that, in general, French restaurants have an all-round
superiority over their British counterparts. Why is this so? Cannot the British
learn from the French and improve? Put these questions (politely) to a British
▲ restaurateur and take a record of his or her reaction and suggestions.

Another good case in quality diagnosis of restaurants is 'Benhinna's of Tokyo' in Sasser *et al.*, *Cases in Operations Management: Analysis and Action* (Irwin, 1982).

7.4 The detailed design and operation of a quality system

7.4.1 *Introduction*

So far we have discussed quality in a broad context: how TQM should fit into the grand strategy for a firm. But, having completely shaken up your firm to accept the TQM approach, it is still necessary to educate the workforce in the detailed application of quality techniques. We show how quite advanced concepts can be explained by a series of experiments that are simple to set up and to operate.

7.4.2 *The rationale behind inspection procedures*

As a start to exploring detailed quality techniques, let us look at material inspection. In the world at large, material may be inspected for many reasons: for example, to further scientific knowledge. Not so in operations management. Here, inspection must have a direct economic purpose. Inspection of materials is necessary:

1. To decide what to do next with the material.
2. To identify a faulty previous process so that it can be corrected.
3. To achieve the requirements of the ultimate consumer.

'Inspecting material' can be interpreted to cover a wide range of management situations outside its obvious manufacturing sense. For example:

An eye-test prior to purchasing new glasses
Judging defendants at a criminal trial
Selecting students for a place at college
Evaluating bids for a television franchise
Testing the purity of a holiday resort's sea-water

Whatever the application, there are certain fundamental components to an inspection system:

1. How items are measured.
2. How inspection errors are classified.
3. How the consequence of an inspection (or absence of one) is costed.
4. Scientific method in laying out a full inspection process.
5. Diagnostics.

We cover these five topics in order, the middle three via a series of matchbox experiments.

Attribute and measurement techniques

Inspection techniques vary according to whether the material is assessed crudely by attribute or numerically by interval measurement such as length or weight.

Attribute techniques

By this we mean sorting material into just a few major categories often associated with properties relevant to the consumer. For example:

> bananas may be *unripe, saleable* or *over-ripe*
> body tissue may be *cancerous* or *normal*
> cheques may be *transactionable* or *invalid*
> a land journey may be made by *car, train* or *bus*

It may seem that such classifications are crude compared with numerical measurements, but we would argue that, at the end of the day, measurements of a product or service have to be translated back into attribute terms — particularly from the consumer's point of view.

Measurement techniques

These are where interval or ratio scales are used, often in considerable detail. For example:

> weight of packaged food to the nearest hundredth of a gramme
> dimensions of a screw to the nearest thousandth of an inch
> constituents of an alloy in parts per million

These finer aspects of measurement must somehow be linked and translated to the objectives of operations management. We explain this in terms of four criteria, which move from the purely scientific to the economic:

> Resolution
> Precision
> Accuracy
> Relevance

Resolution. This answers the question, 'What is the smallest interval that the measure can perceive?' For example, 'How many dots make up a TV picture?' Can a radar speed trap distinguish individual cars? Can a particular microscope see individual blood corpuscles? Having equipment capable of the finest resolution is not by itself satisfactory, it should also take account of the next criterion.

Precision. This answers the questions, 'Can you repeat an exercise with your measuring equipment and get the same result again and again and again within the context of the finest level of resolution?' 'If you fire several rifle bullets, will they all hit the same spot on the target? Can several examiners mark a student's exam paper without conferring and each award it 48 per cent?' 'Will an autopilot enable a whole series of planes to land in a similar fashion in fog?' Precision, then, is an improvement on resolution alone, but it is still not ideal. It is better if the next criterion is covered.

Accuracy. By itself, precision can be deceptive if two measures rely on each other. For example, the station master says, 'I set the clock to precisely noon when the level-crossing-keeper opens the gates.' And the level-crossing-keeper says, 'I open the gates precisely when the station clock says 12.00.'

Circular arguments such as this can be found in several areas of operations management:

- One police force checking on another when a disciplinary enquiry is needed (and vice versa).
- Universities checking on each other's academic standards.
- All of the many advertisements and assertions about companies' high quality (as seen through their own eyes).

To avoid circularity you need to refer to some outside objective standard — this is the characteristic of *accuracy* used in the scientific sense.

▼   **Quick exercise**

▲   What were the missing outside standards for the three examples given in the precision section?

Measuring equipment should satisfy an outside calibration laboratory. Working practices should satisfy an outside Health and Safety Executive. The quality of food as advertised for sale should meet the requirement of the Weights and Measures Department. In general, as we have seen, a firm's quality procedures should conform to those set by an independent outside body (BS5750). Even so, there is one more criterion to be met.

Relevance. Consider a military exercise to remove a well-camouflaged sniper from a house. You could attempt to kill the sniper with a rifle (precise to within the area of a saucer, say) but unlikely to succeed because you do not know where he is. You could, alternatively, lob in a mortar bomb and destroy the whole house. The bomb achieves its primary objective (killing the sniper) so that it is certainly accurate. But much else is destroyed and innocent people might be harmed. The 'relevance' criterion tries to cost out every consequence of your action not only of your main achievement, but the side-effects as well.

Just as with the mortar bomb, quality management problems can be tackled by an overkill approach — as shown by the enthusiasm and resources devoted to quality. Some people say that this does not matter and that investment in quality is free. This might be true when you are jacking up firms to a reasonable level of competence but, in our view, firms that are already performing to high quality standards have to be discriminating and subtle when seeking further improvements — and that means costing out the side-effects of the alternatives being considered.

With the previous four criteria in mind, we now introduce a series of graded experiments.

7.4.3 *The matchbox experiments*

Equipment: Twenty boxes of matches. One sharp knife. Four coloured pens. A blindfold.

Preparations: You are going to make four types of *bad* match:

Dead: Take two boxes of matches. Light each match and *immediately* blow it out.

Short: Take another two boxes of matches. With the sharp knife, cut off about one-tenth of an inch (or 2 mm) from the non-striking end of each match.

Bent: Take another two boxes of matches. Bend each match carefully until it splinters, but does not break, then straighten the match out again.

Thin: Take another two boxes of matches. With the sharp knife, peel (very thin) shavings from the centre section of each match so that it is more round than square.

In later experiments, all these matches are going to be mixed up and re-sorted. To speed up the identification process, it helps if you use a different colour pen to mark each of the four types of bad match.

Group the matches in piles of 100. In each pile put:

10 dead
10 short
10 bent
} collectively known as *bad* matches
10 thin

+ 60 *good* matches that you have not tampered with.

The proportion of bad to good in this exercise is clearly much higher than would be acceptable in real life. This has been done deliberately to bring out the points we want to make more clearly and to make the exercise less time-consuming. With twenty boxes of matches, you should be able to make at least seven piles of 100. Stir up each pile so that the good and bad are well mixed.

7.4.3.1 Experiment 1 — evaluating a single 'blindfold' inspection system

Many inspection systems are required to be speedy, cheap and to minimize the labour element. As a result, they sacrifice certainty. This experiment simulates such a 'blindfold' inspection system.

Sit in front of a pile of 100 matches and put on a blindfold. You are going to see if you can distinguish the good from the bad matches by feel alone. You may like to adopt your own way of doing this, but here is one suggestion.

Hold a normal, good match in your left hand so that the striking end of the match is near the tip of your index finger and the other end is held by your thumb. With your right hand pick up a match from the pile. Compare the match's length by placing it next to the match held in the left hand. Whilst you are doing this, you will have to rely on the feel of the match to decide whether it is dead, bent or thin. After this inspection, drop the match in *accept* or *reject* piles (making sure these piles can easily be located blindfold). For this first experiment, only have one reject pile (i.e. you don't have to specify which of the four types of bad match you think you are rejecting).

Inspect all 100 matches at a regular fast pace. You should *not* give yourself time to make too close an investigation of an individual match. You should maintain a speed of between 4 and 5 seconds per inspection cycle. Ideally, someone with a watch should monitor you to ensure that you keep to this pace. An example of the pattern of results that you might achieve is shown in Figure 7.1.

Anyone watching the inspector at work is in a position to pick up interesting details, such as:

- Whether the inspector improves or deteriorates over time.
- Whether there is any particular type of match that is giving the inspector trouble.

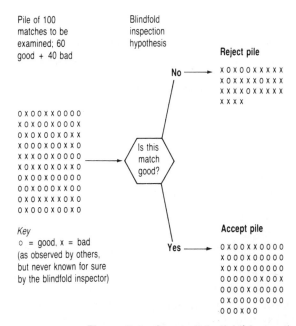

Figure 7.1 Simple 'blindfold' inspection.

Suppose, for the purposes of the experiment, that you do not tell the blindfold inspector everything that you observe about his performance. Suppose you do not give a running commentary on how he is doing, but merely tell him about his average performance when he has finished inspecting a pile. To wit, how many good and bad matches are in his **accept** pile, and how many good and bad are in his **reject** pile. From Figure 7.1, we can see that in our example:

>   54 good matches were found in the **accept** pile
>   12 bad matches were found in the **accept** pile
>   6 good matches were found in the **reject** pile
>   28 bad matches were found in the **reject** pile

Thus, we can see that, of the 60 good matches fed into the system, 90 per cent were accepted and 10 per cent were rejected. Similar calculations can be done for the bad matches. The inspector's performance can be portrayed as coefficients in a matrix.

Inputs

Good		0.9	0.1
Bad		0.3	0.7

Accept Reject
pile   pile

This is known as an *inspection transformation matrix*. The inputs are multiplied by the coefficients and summed vertically to find the accepts or rejects. For example:

60 good	$0.9 \times 60 = 54$	$0.1 \times 60 = 6$
40 bad	$0.3 \times 40 = 12$	$0.7 \times 40 = 28$
	66 accepts	34 rejects

If you feed in any other quantities of good and bad, the coefficients can be applied to work out accepts and rejects.

Two of the above coefficients have special labels:

* The 0.1 (the proportion of good matches sent to rejects) is associated with a *Type I* error, rejecting the true hypothesis 'This match is okay.'
* The 0.3 (the proportion of bad matches sent to accepts) is associated with a *Type II* error, accepting the false hypothesis 'This match is okay.'

To check that you understand the explanation so far, calculate the coefficients from the results of your experiment.

Evaluating the inspection process. No inspection process exists in an economic vacuum:

1. There will be certain costs associated with the process and certain values attached to the stream of material going into and coming out of it.
2. Even in the most elementary situation, an inspection process will not exist on its own, it will be part of a system. For example, if material is rejected, someone has to sort and handle the rejects.

3. Material that has been accepted will be passed on to someone else who may either use it or return it as unsatisfactory. These subsequent handlings will have costs and revenues which it is necessary to know about.

Returning to experiment 1, suppose that the original blindfold inspection process is part of the system shown in Figure 7.2, which includes an infallible visual reinspection of rejects and customer returns. The total costs associated with Figure 7.2 are:

Input	− 400p
Blindfold inspection	− 100p
Consumer returns	− 120p
Visual reinspection	− 230p
	− 850p

The total revenues associated with Figure 7.2 are:

Thin	+ 60p
Bent	+ 20p
Dead	0p
Short	+ 100p
Good	+ 720p
	+ 900p

Net profit is therefore: +50p.

It is possible to obtain a neat shorthand representation of all the costs. Firstly, trace each different type of item through the systems diagram, summing the costs.

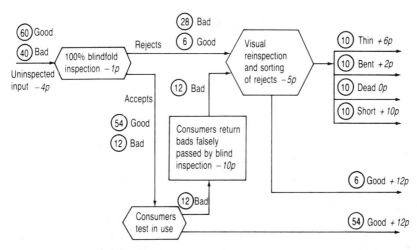

Key   Flow of material is circled
      Money units are costs (−) or revenues (+), in pence per unit.

Figure 7.2   Full evaluation of the inspection process.

1. *Good matches accepted* have costs of:

    Input cost (4p) + blindfold inspection (1p) = 5p

2. *Good matches rejected* have costs of:

    Input cost (4p) + blindfold inspection (1p) + visual reinspection (5p) = 10p

3. *Bad matches accepted* have costs of:

    Input cost (4p) + blindfold inspection (1p) + consumer return (10p) + visual reinspection (5p) = 20p

4. *Bad matches rejected* have costs of:

    Input cost (4p) + blindfold inspection (1p) + visual reinspection (5p) = 10p

Put these costs per item in the right-hand part of each cell in the inspection transformation matrix. Costs (pence per item) inset:

		To	
		Accepts	Rejects
From	Good	5p	10p
	Bad	20p	10p

If you know the numbers going through the system, you can multiply them by these costs to get total costs. Again, using the numbers in Figure 7.2:

		To		
		Accepts	Rejects	
From	Good	54 × 5p	6 × 10p	= 850p
	Bad	12 × 20p	28 × 10p	

If you repeat experiment 1 with different volunteer inspectors, you will find that each produces a different inspection transformation matrix. Using these matrices and the costs given in Figure 7.2, you can see which inspector is achieving the best results. Note that we define 'best' entirely in monetary terms.

7.4.3.2 The design of quality control systems

A quality controller must be able to justify the inspection system that he or she operates and must be able to put a money value on what is being done and the alternatives. This issue should take precedence over *all* other aspects of quality control, and yet is skimpily treated in the literature. In particular, three questions must be answered:

1. What are the economic consequences of removing an inspection process from the system? Are we really much worse off?

2. What is so special about this particular inspection process? Are there not many other alternatives, all giving about the same results?
3. What are the economic consequences of *adding* an inspection process to the existing system?

Let us take these three points and demonstrate what we mean.

1. Removing an inspection process from the system. Refer to Figure 7.2. Suppose we had removed the blindfold inspection process (the cheap and quick inspection) and fed everything into visual reinspection (full infallible testing and sorting of all items), eliminating the need for customer returns. Figure 7.3 shows the new system.

Total revenue is +900p as before, and total cost is −900p, giving a net profit of 0. Any blindfold inspection process must be able to beat this or it is a non-starter.

2. Do other alternatives give similar results? Let us return to the inspection system which included the blindfold process. There is a spectrum of *very different* transformation matrices which give *very similar* economic results. For example, assume we feed 60 good matches and 40 bad matches through two very different inspection systems, each with a different transformation matrix:

Situation A

Feeding in	through this inspection matrix:		gives these flows	
	Accept	Reject	Accept	Reject
60 Good	0.67 × 60	0.33 × 60	40	20
40 Bad	0.25 × 40	0.75 × 40	10	30

Situation B

Feeding in	through this inspection matrix:		gives these flows	
	Accept	Reject	Accept	Reject
60 Good	0.50 × 60	0.50 × 60	30	30
40 Bad	0.125 × 40	0.875 × 40	5	35

Now take the flows of matches in situations A and B and apply the original cost matrix; that was:

	Accept	Reject
Good	5p	10p
Bad	20p	10p

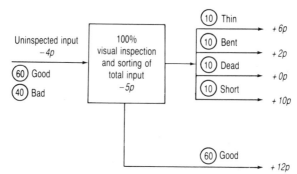

Figure 7.3 'Visual-only' inspection process.

It will be seen that for each situation you get the same net result if you total up costs (total cost 900p, zero net profit).

The above two examples and all other solutions which give zero net profit can be charted as illustrated in Figure 7.4. The straight line formed by these points gives the boundary between worthwhile and unprofitable inspection systems. This clearly shows that an inspection system is worthwhile if the Type I and Type II error coefficients fall in the shaded area.

However, if the range of alternatives merely trades off Type I for Type II errors (i.e. runs parallel to the boundary line), it does not matter which alternative you choose and a sophisticated evaluation of alternatives is a waste of effort.

3. The economic consequence of adding extra inspection processes. This is best illustrated via an exercise. Suppose you add a second blindfold inspection process, as illustrated

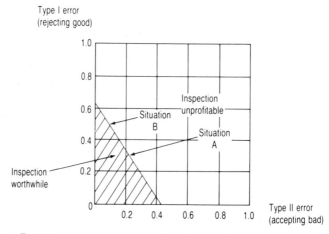

Figure 7.4 Breakeven chart for a blindfold inspection process which tests the hypothesis 'This is good'.

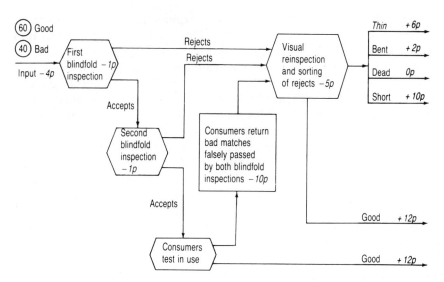

Figure 7.5 Chains of inspection processes.

in Figure 7.5. Do your net profits go up or down if it costs 1p/item to operate? Use the following inspection transformation matrix to do your calculations:

0.9	0.1
0.2	0.8

Note that the second blindfold test could have been positioned to examine the reject stream rather than accept stream. It is left to the reader to check whether this is worthwhile.

In what industrial situations do you get *chains* of inspection process? If you get a chain of blind inspections on the *accepts*, this denotes a cautious but miserly approach. A bit like a hypochondriac seeking a second or third medical opinion from cheap but unconvincing doctors. A chain of blind inspectors on the *rejects* can indicate a quality controller more worried about short-run quantity targets than the longer-term effect of sending bad items to consumers, i.e. following the motto 'Keep on testing and if I'm lucky enough to get an accept I'm in the clear to send it off.'

7.4.3.3 Example — screening for cervical cancer

Sometimes we cannot cost our errors just in monetary terms. The effect of Type II errors in some situations is much more severe. For example, consider tests for cervical cancer. Recently in the UK, it was found that on a second inspection of 45,000 tests (accepted initially as showing no abnormalities), 911 were found to show problems. At this point, further testing took place on those 911 and 424 were cleared. Of the

487 women whose tests were still showing abnormalities, 157 needed to undergo various treatments to deal with cancerous growths. That is, there were 157 Type II errors.

The inspection process is clearly imperfect for several reasons. Firstly, it is difficult to identify abnormal cells. At present, it is a matter of judgement not measurement. Secondly, the slide under inspection contains a sample of the smear taken, which in itself is a sample of the millions of cells in the area in which the cancer can attack. With these problems, it is unlikely that the test will ever be foolproof, but cross-checking is obviously necessary and is being adopted to reduce errors.

We have so far looked only at the Type II errors in this example, but Type I errors also occur. Our best knowledge tells us that if 157 of the 911 needed treatment, then 754 were *probably* wrongly diagnosed and were, in our terms, Type I errors in the second inspection process. The worry caused to the woman thinking she may have cancer whilst she awaits the results of further tests is considerable. Naturally, her faith in medical diagnostics will have been shaken. In equity, the further tests must be of higher standard.

7.4.3.4 The use of sampling in quality control

Our last example introduced the concept of sampling because 100 per cent visual inspection of millions of cells is clearly totally impossible. Sampling is used in many situations where the cost of inspection is high and/or the proportion of defectives is low. On the evidence of defects found in a sample, a decision has to be made on whether to accept or reject the batch from which it was drawn. Before such a decision is made, statisticians find out about the quality standards expected in the specific business situation. There are certain standard definitions used:

- *Acceptance quality level (AQL)*. If you examined output as a whole and found less than a certain percentage of defects, the AQL, the output would be acceptable.
- *Rejectable quality level (RQL)* or *lot tolerance percent defect (LTPD)*. If you examined output as a whole and found more than a certain percentage of defects, the RQL, the output would be rejected.

There may be a gap between the AQL and the RQL, indicating a quality level that you may be unhappy about but do not immediately reject.

7.4.3.5 Experiment 2

Experiment 2 takes up and develops the concepts introduced above. Let us assume an AQL of 11 per cent and an RQL of 28 per cent. Arrange for a blindfold inspector to test matches until he has generated (what he thinks are) 100 'accepts'. These should be placed in a bag so that no-one can see if they are really good or bad. The blindfold inspector passes the bag to another person who accepts or rejects the whole bag after *visual inspection* of a random sample of ten matches that he withdraws from the bag. Suppose this person makes a snap judgement and comes up with these rules-of-thumb:

- *Accept* if there are one or less defects in the sample of ten.
- *Reject* if there are three or more defects in the sample of ten.
- Otherwise, *sample another ten.*

The 1/10 and 3/10 sample decision points roughly correspond to the 11 per cent AQL and 28 per cent RQL. Later, we discuss why this relationship need not be precise.

Exercise break. It would be a good idea to run through the experiment up to this point, getting another blindfold inspector to generate another bag of 100 of his 'accepts' and comparing the sampling results with the first run-through.

If you judged many bags of 100 in the above way, a pattern would emerge. On the whole, justice would be done.

If the sample found 3/10 or more matches to be bad, then this would usually correctly indicate a bad bag, containing 28/100 or more bad matches.

Similarly, if the sample found 1/10 or fewer matches to be bad, then this would usually correctly indicate a good bag, containing in total 11/100 or fewer bad matches.

Occasionally, though, your sample will give you a misleading impression of the whole bag. When this happens, you experience either a Type I error (rejecting a bag you should have taken), or a Type II error (accepting a bag you should have left).

In the particular jargon of acceptance sampling, a Type I error from sampling is known as *producer's risk* and a Type II error from sampling is known as *consumer's risk.*

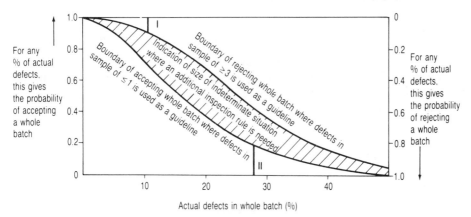

What happens if a whole batch turns up with a (then unknown) percentage of defects just at the AQL level of, say, 11%? **Line I** tells you how frequently such a batch will be immediately rejected.

What happens if a whole batch turns up with a (then unknown) percentage of defects just at the RQL level of, say, 28%? **Line II** tells you how frequently such a batch will be immediately accepted.

I and II can be looked upon as 'what if?' producer and consumer risks. They are not *actual* producer and consumer risks, which depend on the distribution of defects in all the batches that arrive.

Figure 7.6 Operating characteristics curve for a sample of ten items using defect-in-sample levels of 1 and 3 as accept/reject guidelines.

The relationship between these errors, the rule-of-thumb sampling-decision rules, and the AQL and RQL can all be portrayed on an *operating characteristic (OC) curve*, as shown in Figure 7.6.

7.4.3.6 On deriving the operating characteristics curve

For much of this book we have set up experiments without going deeply into the mathematical processes that underlie them. (This reverses the normal teaching method which wants students to have a full grasp of a subject before setting them tasks to do.) We took our approach because we wanted people to achieve a quick end-result, even if they had an imperfect knowledge of the tools they were using. An analogy is this: this book is of the 'how to drive a car' type, and only touches on 'how to repair a car' or 'how to make a car' or 'the theory of the internal combustion engine'.

Continuing the analogy, we felt that when people can drive and get enthusiastic about motoring, they will quite naturally open up the bonnet, tinker with the engine and explore the machine's finer points. In the same way with quality control, we would rather you ran experiments even if you had an imperfect knowledge of the statistical guidelines that you were using. *When* you have run quite a few experiments, it is then and only then that your curiosity is likely to be aroused as to what exactly is going on. For example, suppose you have been using an operating characteristics curve for a bit, and one day ask yourself, 'How and why is the OC curve constructed?', this is what you would discover.

Constructing an operating characteristics curve from the binomial formula

Suppose there is an actual proportion of defects (P) in a large batch. If you take, say, a sample of 10 from that batch, then numbers (F) in Table 7.1 shows how frequently you will find a certain number of defects (E) in your sample. Table 7.1 was constructed from the binomial formula:

$$F = \frac{10!}{E!(10 - E)!} \times P^E (1 - P)^{10 - E}$$

Table 7.1

P, actual proportion of defects in your large batch

		0.05	0.10	0.15	0.20	0.25	0.30	0.35	0.40	0.45	0.50
E, number of defects in your sample of 10:	0	0.60	0.35	0.20	0.11	0.06	0.03	0.01	0.01	—	—
	1	0.31	0.39	0.35	0.27	0.18	0.12	0.07	0.04	0.02	0.01
	2	0.07	0.19	0.27	0.30	0.28	0.23	0.18	0.12	0.08	0.04

Frequencies (*F*) are in the body of the table, showing how often a certain number defined by *E* will occur.

Table 7.2

P, actual proportion of defects in your large batch

	0.05	0.10	0.15	0.20	0.25	0.30	0.35	0.40	0.45	0.50
Accept	0.91	0.74	0.55	0.38	0.25	0.15	0.08	0.05	0.02	0.01
Reject	0.02	0.07	0.18	0.32	0.48	0.62	0.74	0.83	0.90	0.95

Frequencies *F* are in the body of the table.

A second table has been constructed by combining certain *E*-rows in Table 7.1.

Top row   Combine the frequencies of $E = 0$ and $E = 1$ in Table 7.1
Bottom row   Combine the frequencies of $E = 0$, $E = 1$ and $E = 2$ and subtract
               from 1.00

The two new rows in Table 7.2 provide guidelines for what happens if you follow these rules:

Top row   Accept, if you find 1 or less defects in a sample
Bottom row   Reject, if you find 3 or more defects in a sample

Values in this table are the same as those appearing in the operating characteristics curve shown in Figure 7.6.

▼   **Exercise for those who feel comfortable with the maths**

(a) Construct an operating characteristics curve with a sample of 20 instead of
         10 and using the following accept and reject guidelines:

         Accept if you find 2 or fewer defects in a sample.
         Reject if you find 6 or more defects in a sample.

(b) What is the difference in shape between this operating curve and the earlier
         example? Which is the more stringent curve? Should you always prefer to
▲   use the more stringent curve?

A word of warning
The decision-making capability of the OC curve and its constituents is often overstated. For example, it is often said that a supplier and purchaser negotiate to arrive at mutually agreed levels of producer and consumer risks. These risks, together with the known AQL and RQL, can be analysed via OC curves to determine an optimal sampling policy.

In our experience, this conforms neither to business practice nor to logic. Producer and consumer risks, and AQLs and RQLs, fluctuate according to the business environment, and the mix of suppliers and distribution outlets to which they are exposed. For example, it may be necessary to take material from a less reliable supplier because the usual supplier has a strike on his hands. Or when breaking into a new market you may be sending material to first-time consumers who are going to have difficulty using it properly. Both these examples illustrate changes in the risk element. A proper response to such situations, therefore, is to apply a 'what if' approach via the operating characteristics curve, and to find out the consequences of various changes to:

1.   The size of the sample.
2.   The accept/reject guidelines (acceptance numbers) used with the sample.

To repeat, OC curves do *not* provide a comprehensive answer to a quality-control situation.

7.4.3.7 Quality control with irregular quality of inputs

The statistical control methods we have talked about are valid only if the inspection process has just one set of transformation coefficients *whatever the quality of input*. This is clearly not always the case. For example, when a doctor inspects patients, his success rate in diagnosis depends on the types of patient he has dealt with previously. Or, when a bon viveur attends a wine-tasting, his ranking of the wines often depends on the order in which he has drunk them. Or, a teacher marking exam papers from an above-average class may grade them differently depending on whether or not he knows the class is above-average. Even pure machine inspections can be capricious. They can vary in efficiency according to age (spring weighing machine), throughput (volume meters) or type of input (coin phone boxes).

Consider this example which, for a while, baffled quality-control staff in a processed-food factory. Tins were being machine-inspected on a fast-moving conveyor line. If a tin's seal was defective, a mechanical arm (the equivalent of a blind inspector) pushed the tin off the line into a reject basket. The inspection process was so fast and obscured by other machinery that it was difficult to observe what was going on. When baskets of rejects were removed from the conveyor area and examined carefully, the *proportion* of good/bad tins in the reject basket stayed at 50 : 50 regardless of the varying quality of the input, i.e. you got matrices like those shown in Figure 7.7(a) and (b) for the same inspection process.

The answer was found when a video recording was made of the inspection process and played back in slow motion. When the mechanical arm knocked a defective tin off the conveyor, its timing was slightly wrong and it was *knocking off the subsequent tin as well*.

7.4.3.8 Adaptive quality control

A system developed to inspect materials in which approximately 2/100 are defective will be inappropriate if the defect level rises to 10/100. In many processes, such fluctuations can occur and methods to deal with them have been developed. These are known as *adaptive quality-control methods*.

Adaptive quality control tries to walk a tightrope between an expensive 100 per cent

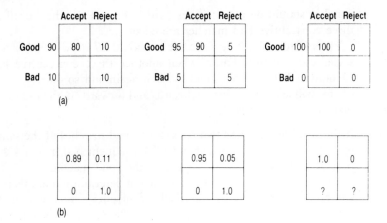

Figure 7.7 Illustration — Constant reject proportions but variable transformation rates. (a) Material flow matrices. (b) Transformation matrices.

inspection (unnecessary if there is a long period of high quality) and limited sampling systems which, by themselves, cannot handle sudden ebbs and flows in the rate of defectives.

The advantage of adaptive quality-control procedures is demonstrated in the following experiments.

7.4.3.9 Experiment 3

Experiment 3 has been designed to:

1. Give the reader a feel for the different intensity of quality control at different levels of alertness.
2. Show the necessary connections in a quality-control system which covers the full range of situations.
3. Illustrate a 'complex' system which is easy to evaluate, adjust and understand.
4. Provide a format suitable for visual interactive modelling on a computer.

Take 500 matches including, as before, 60 per cent good and 10 per cent of each of the four bad types.

Part 1: generating inputs of different quality. Select two volunteers: one to be a sorter, the other a quality controller (or inspector). Mix the matches and feed them in a long line to the sorter. The sorter examines the matches in sequence and puts them 50 to a box following these rules:

> *Rule 1* Initially, put only good matches into the box and put all bad matches aside. Then, when the sorter encounters three consecutive bad matches (of any type), he or she should put these aside. But *all* subsequent bad

matches should be put in boxes (with the good matches) until another three consecutive bad matches are encountered.

These three should be put aside as should *all* subsequent bads, as the sorter did initially. Later, when another three consecutive bads are encountered, the sorter should switch again and so on.

This will lead to a swing backwards and forwards in the number of bad matches in the boxes.

Rule 2   If the sorter encounters two consecutive bad matches of the same type, these two must be discarded and *all* subsequent bad matches with this particular defect put in the box with the good matches.

This procedure will lead to a permanent deterioration in quality which will be corrected only by the quality controller's intervention. His job is explained in part 2 of the experiment. The procedure should continue until the quality controller asks for this procedure to be stopped and asks the sorter to put all bad matches of this type aside as before.

Part 2: inspecting varying quality via an adaptive system. The sorter passes boxes of 50 matches to the quality controller. The quality controller's job is best explained by the decision flowchart shown in Figure 7.8. It is useful if there are spare helpers to keep a record of what is going on and to organize the flow of matches through the sorter and quality controller. Matches which have been finished with can be mixed up and recirculated.

Instructions to quality controller. Enter the system. Pick up the first box of matches you are to inspect. Answer the question in the decision frame (initially frame A). Exit to the next relevant decision frame, decided by the number of rejects (bad matches) you found in your sample. Pick up the next box of matches. Answer the question in the decision frame in which you find yourself. Exit as directed by the number of rejects, and so on, as shown in Figure 7.8.

You can see that, as the level of rejects found in the samples goes up, we move from sampling 10/50 of the matches (the trouble-free system) to 100 per cent inspection. At a certain reject level, the quality controller is in a state of slight alert ready to act should the reject situation deteriorate.

As the situation deteriorates, the controller starts collecting information to try to identify the problem causing the decreasing quality. As further deterioration takes place, he or she begins tinkering with the procedures and, finally, if this does not correct the problem, the whole system may need to be revamped. You can also see that when the situation improves, the inspection *automatically* reverts to a 10/50 sampling system. Thus, the system is adaptive to fluctuations in quality.

Review of the experiment. It is worth considering the following questions: How were the parameters of the quality controller's decision chart determined? Why are samples

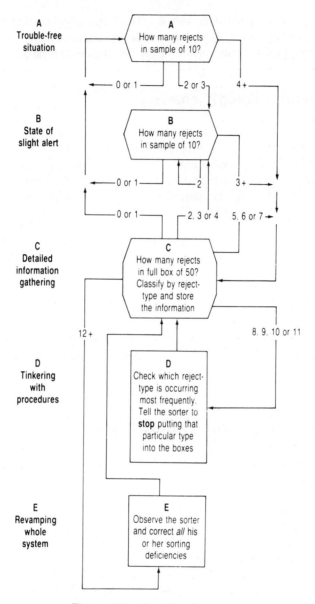

Figure 7.8 Decision flowchart.

of 10 taken rather than 15 or 20? Why are '2 or 3 defects' in a sample rather than some other numbers used to move from a trouble-free situation to a state of slight alert?

When such adaptive systems are set up, the parameters are not determined precisely or mathematically, they are ad hoc, rule-of-thumb guesses. But after the system has been operating for a while, managers can observe whether it is biased towards the costly, high-quality *revamping* mode or towards the cheap, lower-quality *trouble-free sampling* mode. By a system of trial and error, better parameters can be adapted.

7.4.4 'How am I doing?' charts

We saw in our simulation experiment 3 that quality fluctuations are not always random: they are frequently caused by a problem or procedure. If we could identify these problems easily by inspection we could take corrective action, preventing costly rejects being produced. The earlier that problems like this can be spotted the better. Clever measurement inspection may spot potential problems before the products begin to fall outside the tolerance range. Thus we can take corrective action even before rejects are produced.

Let us take the four sets of results A, B, C and D shown in Figure 7.9. Deductions from the *pattern* of inspection measurements help us to identify the cause of problems.

When using patterns of measurement to investigate quality, a key feature is to establish *'how am I doing?' charts*, instantly recorded and visible to the operator and his or her workmates. The statistician is better employed in a background role, establishing which variations are assignable to a cause (and therefore improvable) and which are due to limitations on measurement or machine setting. These latter random variations are known (rather misleadingly) as *process capability*. A full study of this topic takes us too deeply into statistics.

7.5 Cause and effect explorations

The above example illustrates a proper use of statistics in quality control to indicate a worthwhile *direction* for exploration. Suppose that you start your investigation knowing little about the system. There are certain rough-and-ready rules on where to start collecting data:

1. Each side of a 'dodgy', expensive or subcontracted process.
2. Just prior to the blending of inputs or just after the separation of outputs.
3. Halfway between the longest chain of operations where information is missing.
4. Where incomplete or inaccurate data emerge because of faulty recording machinery, or because staff cannot record data or do their job properly, or because it is not in the nature of staff to do what is asked of them.

With this extra information, you will be in a better position to identify inefficiency points (see Chapter 6 for examples). Then you can use an interesting device for extending your analysis: a *cause and effect diagram* (also known as a *fishbone* or *Ishikawa diagram*). The procedure is to start with the effect and work backwards, constructing a branch-like system of causes which could lead to that effect.

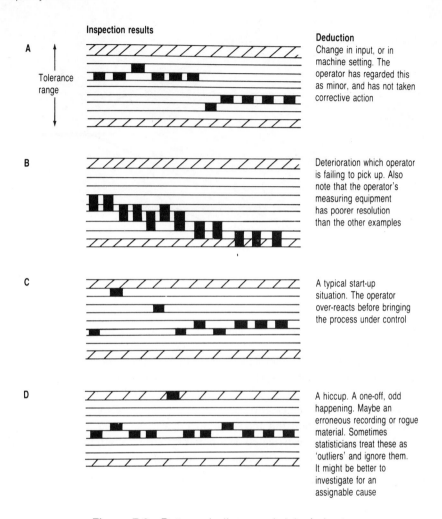

Inspection results

A

Tolerance range

Deduction
Change in input, or in machine setting. The operator has regarded this as minor, and has not taken corrective action

B

Deterioration which operator is failing to pick up. Also note that the operator's measuring equipment has poorer resolution than the other examples

C

A typical start-up situation. The operator over-reacts before bringing the process under control

D

A hiccup. A one-off, odd happening. Maybe an erroneous recording or rogue material. Sometimes statisticians treat these as 'outliers' and ignore them. It might be better to investigate for an assignable cause

Figure 7.9 Patterns in 'how am I doing' charts.

For example, consider excessive breakdown and poor-quality output occurring on an office printer. The initial diagram might start like this:

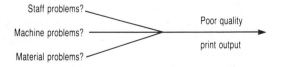

Staff problems?

Machine problems?

Material problems?

Poor quality

print output

On exploring backwards through the question marks, possible major causes are drawn

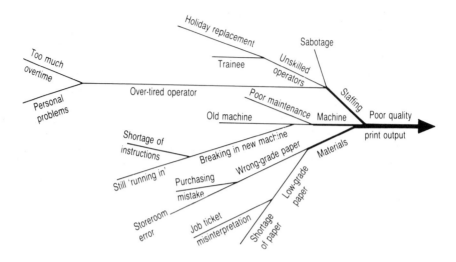

Figure 7.10 Cause and effect diagram.

as branches and minor (or secondary) causes as twigs leading into those branches, as shown in Figure 7.10.

Having constructed quite a complex diagram like Figure 7.10, a most likely chain of cause and effect is investigated working backwards from the trunk towards a twig. As the investigation proceeds, dead ends are encountered, or new information is gathered causing extra branches and twigs to be drawn in. Often, the investigation has to backtrack towards the trunk and set off in a new most-preferred direction. When a promising twig is being investigated as a possible cause, all attention is focused on it until a definite conclusion is reached. This involves:

1. Posing a hypothesis as to the cause of a fault.
2. Designing an experiment which is capable of confirming or rejecting the hypothesis.
3. Acting on the results of the experiment to change operating procedures.
4. Confirming the improvement resulting from the changes.

A Japanese tale

For a long time a large British engineering company had been unhappy about the quality of a high-grade alloy component supplied to it. None of its suppliers was able to meet the RQL of 8 per 1000 that the company wanted. So an order was placed with a Japanese firm, acceptance being subject to the 8 per 1000 defective rate. A few weeks later the first consignment of a thousand units arrived from Japan in two parcels, one big and one small. The big parcel contained 992 units, marked 'perfect'. The small parcel contained 8 units, marked 'defective, as requested'!

7.6 Recommended reading

Start with Sasser *et al.*'s 'Hans Kolb' — a short, controversial case with rich spin-offs, in *Cases in Operations Management: Analysis and Action* (Irwin, 1982). Then try Meier's Ohio case in *Cases in Production and Operations Management* (Prentice Hall, 1982), in particular seeing the beneficial effect of reversing the order of priority of his four discussion questions. Then tackle the Winton Shirt Company in Constable and New, *Operations Management* (Wiley, 1976), meditating on 'Why do doctors need an abundant supply of invalids, policemen criminals, QC inspectors defects, and foxes rabbits?' Does this help if you are designing a radically different TQM approach to Winton's problems? Finally, from Schmenner's *Cases in Production/Operations Management* (SRA, 1986), you may see if your confidence is up to 'The Problem with Kathy' cases A and B. There is a lot of detail to comprehend, but remember what Alexander did to the Gordian Knot.

Other mini case studies and attractive, controversial, readable articles on this subject can be found in the journal *TQM*. For example:

An interview with Joseph Juran (Nov. 1989).

A zippy argumentative article by J. Nicholls, 'Value to the Customer' (April 1990).

A letter on the dangers of quality hype by R.J. Barnes (June 1990).

A discussion on buzz-words by Oakland and Nicholls (Aug. 1990).

Chapter 8

Forecasting — from predictions to plans

8.1 Introduction

8.1.1 *What is a forecast*

'Forecast' can take on a wide range of meanings, for example:

- From *a vague intuition* There will be heavy snowfall next winter
  to *a certainty*   The days will get longer next springtime

- From *a binding commitment* A legal contract to deliver goods on a future date
  to *an informal promise* A shop assistant saying, 'I expect it to be in stock soon' to a customer

- From *an objective stance* A Western economist's assessment of an African famine
  to *an intimate involvement* A besieged army's assessment of its own survival chances

- From *events that the forecaster can control* A manager forecasting staff overtime levels
  to *events beyond the forecaster's control* Exchange rates to an exporter

8.1.2 *What topics should forecasting cover?*

We have mentioned how some subjects in operations management have been hit by a revolution that has changed their emphasis, scope and philosophy. Stock control has been turned upside down by the just-in-time (JIT) methodology, and quality control has been extended to total quality management (TQM). We feel that a similar movement is under way, changing the approach to forecasting and planning. For this reason, this chapter changes the emphasis and broadens the scope of forecasting and planning as traditionally defined in the textbooks. In general, our discussion proceeds within the following framework:

1. Our attitude to the future is strongly coloured by emotions: by hopes, fears, opportunities and threats. Any system of forecasting and planning must recognize and incorporate such feelings; it should not confine itself to a bare exercise in mathematics.
2. There is much important preliminary work to be done before mathematical techniques should be considered.
3. Planning and forecasting are very much intertwined.
4. Planning and forecasting should be placed firmly in the context of large strategic and environmental events that affect them.

8.2 Scenario analysis

In spite of all the effort that goes into predicting the future, there are still major happenings that take everyone by surprise: for example, Chernobyl, the Gulf War, the break-up of the Communist Bloc or the massive defaults on Third World debt. These events cause not only an immediate shake-up in business and social life, but set in motion a ripple of activity for many years afterwards. It is not the purpose of scenario analysis to predict a cataclysmic event; instead, it traces the logical consequences and side-effects of such an event. See how this can be done by working through these exercises.

▼   **Exercise in scenario analysis**

For each of the following scenarios, how would adjustments occur (perhaps over several years and across several countries) in business, political and social life?

(a) A new drink made from seaweed is shown to add five years to an average person's life but needs to be consumed several times a day. It is very addictive. Sales of tea, coffee and beer slump to one-tenth of their current levels.

(b) Ten million people are killed by an earthquake that devastates the Tokyo region. The effect on Japan's industry, transport and infrastructure is worse than the Second World War.

(c) For under £10,000, anyone can purchase a personal helicopter that can carry four people and is safer and cheaper to run than a car. The most efficient fuel for it is sugar.   ▷

(d) A drug is developed which gives all the benefits of eight hours sleep in two hours. It has no side-effects.

(e) An intelligent prawn arrives from outer space and colonizes the oceans. Its military hardware and scientific knowledge is far superior to anything we have got. It is quite happy to leave the human race alone if we do not go fishing and do not use ships.

▲

▼   **Extension exercises**

Set some scenarios of your own and follow through the consequences. When you do this, it is challenging and amusing to split into two groups so that group A can tackle (say) three scenarios invented by group B, and vice versa.

▲

From scenarios to action plans

Scenarios help get people out of a rut. The world is such a dangerous and challenging place that it is worth hammering home the message that big changes are bound to happen (whatever they are). To cope with these changes, you need two main attributes:

1. *Vision* (from scenarios).
2. *Action* (actually doing something when the big change happens).

8.3 The vulnerability and responsibility of the operations manager

The operations manager needs forecasts for several reasons:

1. To decide how to cope with the future volume of customer orders.
2. To react to the price and delivery availability of raw materials.
3. To determine future machine and labour availabilities.
4. To respond to what is happening in his industry and the economy.

In all of these forecasting situations there is no dividing line which says, 'These forecasts concern narrow parochial issues; these others are affected by global matters.' Today we are all members of a global interactive economy. Just as Chernobyl decimated the Norwegian reindeer industry, thousands of miles away, so the Gulf War can save a Canadian shipyard from closure, or the purchase of a Japanese karaoke machine can double the takings at a working men's club.

Furthermore, in operations management, forecasts and plans merge into statements of intent, such as:

'This is how we are going to cope with a doubling of sales this year.'
'We'll earn 25 per cent profit on that contract.'
'We must get three of those new machines.'

These statements put the manager in a head-on-the-block situation. This is quite different from the detached, objective stance adopted by other forecasters, particularly economists and journalists. Unlike them, the operations manager has to act on his or her forecast — to face censure or dismissal if things go badly wrong, and perhaps to receive a little praise if things work out.

How far should an operations manager keep his eyes and ears open for any piece of news that might affect his firm? Any good manager has to strike a balance between:

1. A restless exploration of all news items and letting day-to-day work slip.
2. Regarding all news, gossip and 'soft information' as distractions from the job-in-hand, thus missing out on a few new opportunities.

Certainly, there is no shortage of business information available. Apart from the daily financial press, there are databanks of updated statistics accessible via computer links for 24 hours a day. Also, most managers' in-trays attract mailshots, trade journals, invitations to business seminars, salespeople's brochures and project reports. One sign of a good manager is how well he or she filters, files or handles this stream of incoming data. In particular, when information is received that contains forecasts, how can one pick out dubious logic, irrelevancies and bias? These issues are tackled next.

8.4 A structured approach to forecasting and planning

We would recommend that any operations manager embarking on a forecasting exercise goes through these four exploratory stages:

Exploration 1	The impact of forecasting on the planning process.
Exploration 2	Evaluating the consequences of forecasting error.
Exploration 3	Redesigning the whole operating framework with 'better forecasting' as one of the goals.
Exploration 4	Fine-tuning the forecasting method to improve its accuracy (i.e. the mathematical bit).

8.4.1 *Exploration 1 — the impact of forecasting on the planning process*

Is the forecast part of a process that leads to action being taken? If so, how far do the recommendations implied by the forecast get ignored, watered down, delayed, misinterpreted or reformulated?

In Greek legend, the gods bestowed on Cassandra a blessing and a curse. The blessing was to see into the future and to know exactly what was going to happen. The curse was that no-one would believe her warnings. Expert forecasters must sometimes feel the same way, although it is understandable for the public to be wary of them. The eternal pessimist may say 'I told you so' when one of his dismal predictions comes to pass; but against that, what of his many predictions which were not confirmed? These, he would wish us to forget about.

▼   **Quick exercise**

From a library, look at a back issue of *Old Moore's Almanac* and its predictions for the year that has just gone by. Look at its predictions of those world events which would have the biggest impact on business.

(a) Were the predictions specific and verifiable? Or were they vague and capable of alternative interpretation?

(b) Which were clearly true?

(c) Which were clearly false?

(d) Would you recommend any business to take the predictions of Old Moore
▲   seriously? If not, which organization has a better track-record of predicting world events and why?

Accepting that many of us are in the business of giving and receiving advice or forecasts, what are the general rules covering the credibility of such advice? Often, a decision-maker is faced with conflicting forecasts from competing pressure groups, for example:

- *What will be the effects of giving planning permission for a hypermarket?* (Forecasts from other traders, employment agencies and local residents.)
- *Should cattle receive hormone injections that might or might not affect meat and milk?* (Forecasts from farmers, chemical companies, doctors and consumer groups.)

In the above cases, the forecasts may well be distorted by vested interests. But is such bias absent if it comes from a disinterested expert? What if the expert involved in a feasibility study would also be involved in the investment project if it went ahead? What if the expert comes up with the answer you want (though it is wrong) because he wants you to look at him favourably when other projects need an adviser?

For different reasons, the message in a forecast may be distorted by a client. For example, suppose that the client has asked for a report on the following subjects:

- *How crowded are our prisons? Is the situation going to get worse? What should be done about it?*

- *What are the economics of tidal power stations? Could they replace some nuclear power stations? If so, when, and to what extent?*

Note that in these examples the decision-maker has asked for a complex mix of:

More information + Forecasts + Recommendations

These three elements are often combined (rather than requested separately) so that advisers are made to feel that they are being taken seriously by their clients. This does not mean that the client will accept the advisers' recommendations. He may be working to a different personal agenda (e.g. political survival) from his advisers (e.g. the national good).

Even where an organization has an established role for forecasting it can still be manipulated, reinterpreted or massaged for reasons of internal politics, for example:

- A Borough Treasurer's forecast of percentage of non-payment of poll tax. (Featured prominently according to whether the ruling political party is for or against the tax, and whether the percentage of non-payment is high or low.)
- A meteorologist's forecast of snow conditions and avalanche danger at a ski resort. (The hoteliers may say, 'Let us get the skiers here. If the snow is too dangerous they can stay in the hotel and have a good time anyway.' The mountain rescue services might think the hoteliers have an ulterior motive in saying this.)

These may be rather dramatic illustrations, but organizations require many routine 'forecasts' from its employees which, for tactical reasons, can end up quite biased. For example:

- Request from administration — *Targets* — We want forecasts from you that can be converted into targets which will determine when your bonus payments will start.

  Response from employee — *Muted* — Provide quite a precise figure, to make it look as though you have worked carefully on it, but make it on the low side.

- Request from administration — *Budgets* — We want forecasts for our management by exception system. We will store them away, compare them later against actual results, then come back to you and ask you to explain the discrepancies.

  Response from employee — *Vague* — Round up or down the nearest 100, 1000 or 10,000 (whatever you can get away with). Amalgamate products or materials into broad categories, then there is less chance that you will get involved in a nit-picking inquest.

- Request from administration — *Suspicious* — What reasons can you give for spending all this money on your pet project?

Response from employee	*Dramatic*	Edge towards optimism — especially with respect to distant revenues when everyone will have forgotten this forecast. Highlight also the terrible cost of *not* undertaking this project: exploit admin's paranoia that 'competitors might steal a march on us'.

To recap the main point brought out in this section: your first step in any forecasting exercise should be an examination of the motives of those giving and receiving the forecast. Otherwise, much subsequent work could be wasted.

8.4.2 *Exploration 2 — evaluating the consequences of forecasting error*

If the decision-maker implements a plan based on a forecast, is there any way of evaluating the consequences of making a forecasting error? Are these evaluations accurate and relevant? Do these evaluations take into account spin-offs on other parts of the operating system?

Consider a self-employed taxi-driver who can choose where, when and how long to work. When deciding whether to work, he will have in mind a break-point such as, 'If I can't earn £40 in the next four hours, I'd rather stay at home.' If he sets out, he will soon know whether his sortie was a success by adding up his takings. If he stays at home, he'll never know what he could have earned or, in general:

Opportunities missed are much harder to measure than failures experienced.

This is a common situation in forecast evaluations. For example, imagine your organization decides against:

Launching a pre-emptive attack against a dangerous dictatorship
Marketing a new product
Going for a new export market
Embarking on a collaborative venture
Appointing a promising, dynamic colleague

These opportunities may never crop up again, so you can never calculate what you would have won or lost. But if you had grasped any of the above opportunities and they had failed, the financial or human consequences would be starkly apparent. This introduces a conservative, cautious bias into forecasting and planning.

Conservatism is also apparent in 'successful' firms working at full capacity that are not too interested in the business they may be losing. In a few cases (new Rolls-Royces or places at Eton College), customers may be willing to wait for years, but normally, customers who are turned away go elsewhere. Rarely is a record kept of these customers. Worse still, potential customers often go elsewhere without leaving you much clue of their existence: motorists drive past overcrowded service stations; potential diners do not bother to enter a restaurant or take-away that is too busy; patients go elsewhere if a dentist's waiting list is too long. Such 'ghost business' has major implications for forecasters. If firms do not know what their lost business is (they argue), what is the point of calculating the cost of each unit lost? Without these calculations, it is pretty hard to carry out a valid forecasting exercise.

8.4.2.1 The costs of over- and under-forecasting — the airline example

Are there businesses where it is possible to evaluate the consequences of forecasting error (both plus and minus)? To a certain extent, this is possible in the airline industry. On occasions, an airline will accept more bookings for a flight than the plane can carry. They anticipate that not all passengers will be ready at departure: some will be delayed on the way to the airport or on a connecting flight; and other passengers will make a last minute request for a later flight or they will cancel. If cancellations, etc. happened regularly and consistently, an airline could confidently over-book and get away with it.

But suppose that all of the booked passengers turn up for a flight. Then the airline is faced with the awkward problem of persuading some passengers to postpone their flight. On some US internal flights, persuasion is in the form of a Dutch auction:

> Okay, which of you passengers would like to go on a later flight if we gave you $200? ... $250? ... $300? Tell you what, we will throw in a free off-peak ticket too ...

and so on, until the requisite number of passengers have given up their seats. From a record of such compensation payments, an airline can put a pretty good estimate on the cost of over-booking. As for under-booking, each empty seat on a plane loses the company its net profit per passenger on that particular route.

With costs available for both under- and over-booking, the company is able to evaluate its forecasting error and adjust its policy accordingly. An interesting insight is given in the British Airways case by Armistead in Voss *et al.*, *Operations Management in the Service Industries and the Public Sector* (Wiley, 1985). A fuller exploration of the costing consequences of under- and over-booking can be found in the Schmenner case study, 'Citrus Airlines situation and discussion', in *Production/Operations Management Concepts and Situations*, 4th edn (Macmillan, 1970). The most authoritative detail is in 'Yield management at American Airlines' in the Jan./Feb. 1992 issue of *Interfaces* (voted prizewinner for outstanding achievement in management practice).

8.4.2.2 Calculating the error of a multiple-purpose forecast

Consider the national weather forecast. It is hard to cost out an overall forecasting error because of the many different businesses and recreational activities which have used it. For example, suppose that one April morning, the daily weather forecast says that there is going to be a heavy snowfall. Certain people may well act on this forecast. For example: hill farmers will move their animals to lower ground; builders will postpone concreting, roofing and external decorating jobs; local councils will spend money on gritting; holidays will be terminated, postponed or cancelled.

Now, if the forecast were wrong and no snow falls, certain people will have been inconvenienced. For example:

- On each of 4,000 hill farms, 4 man-days were lost bringing the animals in and taking them up again.
- Fifteen thousand builders have each fallen a day behind on their projects.
- Fifty councils spent an average £27,000 on material, fuel and labour payments for gritting that was not necessary.
- A spokesman for Bournemouth's eight hundred hotels and boarding houses said that bookings were down 20 per cent because of the erroneous weather forecast.

▼   Short exercise

Identify the different and most important categories which will be affected by the weather forecast saying, 'Today it will be clear and sunny', when actually there is an unexpected thick fog. For each major category, put in an approximate estimate of the number of decisions involved and the
▲   consequences.

Having dwelt upon some of the difficulties in costing out forecasting errors, we want to emphasize that it is worthwhile attempting such a costing, however crude and approximate. For some reason, many forecasters completely avoid this most important topic whilst going into enormous detail on more trivial aspects of their work.

8.4.3 Exploration 3 — redesigning the whole operating framework with 'better forecasting' as one of the goals: MBA applications

If the consequences of forecasting error have been evaluated, and they are deemed to be serious, how can the systems of operation, information and control be adapted so that there is a smaller, more appropriate deviation between forecast and actual results?

A common theme of this book has been:

To attack constraints rather than optimize within them.

Forecasting is a fruitful area for this principle. Take a simple example from the institution where we ourselves work. Sheffield's School of Management runs an MBA attracting a large percentage of overseas students.

If we made offers to 200 applicants, about 150 would accept, and we could expect anything from 50 to 100 enrolments. This variability causes considerable last minute difficulties in finding the right size of lecture rooms for the MBAs and the appropriate allocation of lecturing staff to service them. Even after a close inspection of application forms from previous years, it was very hard to identify characteristics telling us which candidates were most likely to turn up. So we changed the system. When we accept a student, usually 3 or 4 months before the start of the course, we ask them to send a £200 deposit against their fees (non-returnable if they do not arrive for the course). Now, we make a greater number of offers (270) but fewer people accept our offer (110) and nearly all of these turn up (between 85 and 95). Thus, changing a problem constraint (imposing an application fee) has greatly changed the accuracy of forecasting.

This discussion on academic planning can be developed to illustrate certain general issues:

> How far ahead to forecast?
> How frequently to forecast?
> When to forecast?

The answer to these questions varies according to who is using the forecast and why. When forecasting MBA numbers, this information may be wanted for three very different purposes:

1. *Within the School of Management.* In this case, the forecasts are used to help juggle around existing resources: for example, to work out a student selection policy which will be feasible in terms of current staff and teaching space. In this context, these are the answers to the three general questions.

    (a) *How far ahead to forecast?* Focus on the coming year with maybe a provisional forecast for the year after that. Further than that is unnecessary because any such forecast would be superseded by a better forecast nearer the time.
    (b) *How frequently to forecast?* Once a year, to match the once-a-year admissions.
    (c) *When to forecast?* The best time is twelve months before the MBA course begins in October of any year. This enables us to plan the scale of our advertising effort in the previous autumn, to receive applications in the winter, and to make offers and process them in the spring and summer before the course starts.

2. *Within the university.* Here, the forecasts of future MBA student-numbers are compared with forecasts for other courses. If an imbalance looks likely to arise, new staff will be authorized for the hardest-pressed areas, or departments will be relocated to make better use of teaching space.

    (a) *How far ahead to forecast?* Sheffield University tries to work with a ten-year horizon both for manpower planning and the shifting of departments. This makes sense in that it can take ten years to assess and disentangle itself from a mistaken decision in these areas.
    (b) *How frequently to forecast?* Forecasts should really be updated yearly, or even less. Even if the university has to live with its decision about a department for many years, it needs a continual stream of information from it to help make decisions about other departments which roll forward one-by-one for review.
    (c) *When to forecast?* This should be found out by working backwards from when a decision is implemented. If new staff are to start work in October, at least six months should be allowed for the advertising and selection process. If departments

are to be relocated, this is best done during vacation time, especially if structural alteration is necessary. This means that the forecast must be ready to allow time for proposals, counter-proposals and committee deliberations.

3. *Within the Higher Education sector.* Here, the forecasts of the School of Management's MBA students are just one extra piece of information that contributes to matters of national interest. For example, the neighbouring Sheffield Business School also runs a popular, prestigious MBA. Civil servants in the Department of Education may well wish to press for the two Sheffield MBAs to combine as part of a grander strategy to rationalize management education.

(a) *How far ahead to forecast?* If two institutions are to be amalgamated, probably involving a new building and a thorough academic and administrative overhaul, we really need a vision for at least twenty years forward.

(b) *How frequently and when to forecast?* These questions are best taken together. Bold initiatives such as an academic amalgamation only crop up at infrequent intervals — often connected with the appointment of a reforming Minister of Education. Ideally, each institution should have a contingency plan with forecasts at their fingertips if the issue of amalgamation suddenly erupts.

Constraints, **Constraints** and CONSTRAINTS

The previous discussion raises an issue of some importance for forecasting and operations management: 'When attacking constraints one needs to be very clear about how tightly they bind you.' Hence the title of this section which implies, 'Examine carefully the severity of your organizational constraints.'

The least binding constraints

When forecasting MBA students in the School of Management, we are subject to certain constraints which are self-imposed and which we ourselves, within the department, have the will to transcend if only we realize it. For example:

• The number of subjects and options making up the course.
• The number of lectures per subject.
• The extent of supervision for any dissertation and its length.

Tougher constraints

With other constraints the School of Management is not free to make decisions, but may find it possible to alter these constraints after negotiation. For example:

• Adjusting the percentage of tuition fees retained by central administration.
• Securing funds for part-time teachers to supplement the full-time staff.
• Ending agreements by which students from other departments join the MBA classes.

ABSOLUTELY BINDING CONSTRAINTS

An absolute CONSTRAINT is one that defies the laws of God and nature (to teach for twenty-five hours a day, or to execute students who fail). Short of these extremes, there are certain situations which would not be contemplated in education:

- Allowing students to cheat openly in exams.
- Allowing an MBA degree to be bought.
- Withdrawing an offer to a student on the day he arrives to start the course.
- Having no library for the students to use.

We have spent some time on the above distinctions because, in operations management, it is all too easy to mistake CONSTRAINT for *constraint* or vice versa. As we have seen in the Japanese approach to management, a key element of success is to attack and overcome a constraint that was thought to be inviolable.

Other educational implications of this discussion

We live in times when there is management turmoil not only in universities but in polytechnics, colleges, secondary and primary education. The forecasting and planning issues that were illustrated with respect to the MBA are relevant throughout the educational system. Indeed, in other educational sectors the issues of forecasting and planning are even more dramatic as they involve immediate decisions on the closure or amalgamation of existing facilities.

8.4.4 *Co-ordinating case study — the post office*

This case illustrates the three explorations that we have just discussed.

On a normal day, Sheffield's Mechanical Letter Office (MLO) will clear over 600,000 letters. On a peak day, just before Christmas, this figure may rise to over 1½ million. Staff working at the mechanized sorting machines are expected to sort letters at the rate of about 1,350 per hour. Consequently, over an average day of 600,000 letters, about 450 hours have to be allocated to the sorting operation alone, and that does not allow for mechanical breakdown, wrong coding or mis-sorts. Allowance has to be made for the labour involved in bringing the mail to the sorters, bagging and tagging it after sorting, and moving mail to the next stage of the delivery process. On top of that, reserves for absentees, and support staff such as cleaners, clerical staff and supervisors are also involved.

Someone has to work out in advance how many staff will be needed for all these operations. This is done by forecasting letter-volumes, then converting these volumes into workers required to handle them. Every Tuesday, a forecast is made of the number of letters that will be handled on each day of the following week. The forecasting is quite a subtle exercise, computer-aided, and taking into account the known forward plans of its major business customers such as government departments, public utilities and mail-order houses. As business letters account for 70 per cent of the volume, there is some scope for collecting advanced information compared with the more unpredictable private mail.

With this information as a starting point, how does this fit into our schedule of explorations?

8.4.4.1 Exploration 1 applied to the post office

The impact of forecasting on the planning process

Some service industries have to respond immediately to a sudden surge of business from their customers. In the post office's case, they have a little bit of leeway in that second class mail, accounting for 70 per cent of its business does not have to be delivered immediately. Nevertheless, the post office takes seriously the requirements of its big customers that use the second class post, especially the mail-order houses. It is for this reason that their forecast is based on information from the mail-order houses themselves who have advance knowledge of their postings. However, these big customers may find it advantageous to overstate their forward postings. In this way, they may manipulate the post office to provide more than enough staff, and thus gain extra insurance against the possibility of a backlog developing (which always hits second class mail most severely).

8.4.4.2 Exploration 2 applied to the post office

Cost of over-forecasting per 1000 letters

Sometimes, because there was over-forecasting, a sorter came in and found he was being paid £8.90 per hour (his scheduled overtime rate) to do nothing. As he could sort 1350 letters an hour this £8.90 was equivalent to *£6.60 per 1000 letters.*

Cost of under-forecasting per 1000 letters

Sometimes, extra workers have to be asked at short notice to do unscheduled overtime at £10.80 per hour. In an emergency you might have to call on trainees, supervisors, part-timers or other grades to do sorting, and efficiency drops from an average of 1350 to 1150 letters per hour. So the £10.80 per hour converts to £9.40 per 1000 letters. This compares to the £6.60 per 1000 that it would have cost if you had made advance plans. The difference between £9.40 and £6.60 gives the cost of under-forecasting, for example *£2.80 per 1000 letters.*

If the costs of over- and under-forecasting are applied to actual errors that occur, one can get some idea of the scale of the problem, at least in so far as the sorting operation is affected. A typical week's results are shown in Table 8.1. If you work out the cost of forecasting error for that week, you should confirm that it comes to £985. This is quite substantial but it is doubtful if improving forecasting technique is the way forward (see next section).

Just out of interest, Table 8.2 shows the forecast for the subsequent week. Is there the same pattern and extent of forecasting error?

Table 8.1 Forecast made on Tuesday, 20 November 1989 for the week 26 November to 2 December ('000 letters)

	Mon	Tue	Wed	Thu	Fri	Sat	Sun
Forecast	748	698	637	663	650	96	—
Actual	727	734	564	629	660	100	—

Table 8.2 Forecast made on Tuesday, 27 November 1989 for the week 3 December to 9 December ('000 letters)

	Mon	Tue	Wed	Thu	Fri	Sat	Sun
Forecast	725	697	683	627	657	98	—
Actual	729	640	603	669	701	126	—

▼   **Exercise — exploration 3 applied to the post office**

Redesigning the whole operating system with 'better forecasting' as one of the goals
This is best explained via an exercise. Below are sixteen brainstorming suggestions which may or may not be positive steps for the post office to take:

A   Persuade the unions to have complete flexible manning arrangements.
B   Why can't post office vans use bus priority lanes?
C   Cut overload by making last posting times earlier in the evening.
D   Standardize envelope size to speed up sorting rates.
E   Any letter without a postal code to go only by second class post.
F   Arrange extra Saturday collections from mail-order houses.
G   Reward big customers who do not leave postings till late afternoon.
H   Install warning lights above sorting stations to warn supervisors of 'go slows'.
I   Avoid 'go slows' by making unscheduled overtime rates less attractive.
J   Arrange for big clients to hold back postings if you are pushed.
K   Encourage magnetic markings/bar coding to speed up sorting.
L   Have small teams of sorters bidding for business against each other.
M   Subcontract out surplus postings to a neighbouring office that is under-capacity.
N   Scrap hourly rates; go back to piece-rates for sorters.
O   Reduce overtime rates but increase bonus rates to compensate.
P   Let backlogs of letters pile up rather than pay excessive overtime.

(a) Regardless of the merit of each suggestion, what would be the effect on the forecasting situation?

▷

          \   forecasting would be more accurate
          X   forecasting would be less accurate
          ?   I don't know, or little change

(b) Mark each of the sixteen suggestions with the constraint category you think is involved.

      o   a *constraint*
      o   a **constraint**
      ●   a CONSTRAINT

(c) Of the sixteen suggestions, choose the three that you think the post office should pursue most actively.

(d) If the post office take up your ideas, is there any need for them to change their weekly Tuesday forecasting system with respect to:

      How far ahead to forecast?
      How frequently to forecast?
      When to forecast?

      The above questions initiate a broad attack on the post office's planning problems. Forecasting is tackled simultaneously with other issues. This is better than focusing on techniques which are concerned exclusively with
▲   reducing forecasting error.

8.4.5 *Exploration 4 — fine-tuning the forecasting method to improve its accuracy*

If forecasting is part of a suitable operating framework, how can the techniques of forecasting be fine-tuned to give further incremental reductions in forecasting error?

As a gentle and structured way in to mathematical forecasting, we address the following topics in this logical order.

1. Checking on the reliability of the forecasting information.
2. When to segment and when to cluster the information.
3. Identifying seasonality and predictable cycles.
4. Moving averages.
5. Trend analysis.
6. The role of regression analysis in forecasting.
7. The analysis and forecasting of erratic time-series.
8. Causal analysis and leading indicators.

Issues which need longer mathematical explanations are left to the appendices to this chapter.

8.4.5.1 Checking on the reliability of forecasting information

This involves bringing in four criteria first mentioned in the chapter on quality (Chapter 7): *precision*, *accuracy*, *resolution* and *relevance*. Let us show their role in forecasting by referring to the weather.

Precision	Precision is often confused with accuracy or resolution (described below) but is really quite different. In science, precision is the ability to repeat an experiment and get the same result if the same experimental constraints operate. If ten weather forecasters all use the same method to predict wind direction, and they are asked (simultaneously without conferring) 'Which way will the wind be blowing at midnight?' and they all reply 'From the north-east', then the forecasting method is *precise*. (It might be wrong, but that is another matter.)
Accuracy	In addition to being precise, an accurate person always forecasts the right outcome (as defined by an objective outsider, not himself). If he says the wind is going to be stronger than force 3 on the Beaufort Scale, it always is.
Resolution	As well as being accurate, this defines the narrowness of the range that the forecaster sets himself. Saying that the wind will be greater than force 3 is not so impressive as saying, 'The wind will be force 7' and always getting it right.
Relevance	This refers to whether the forecast focuses on the things that matter (as discussed in our 'Explorations' section). In weather forecasting it is all very well making a precise, accurate, finely resolute forecast of barometric pressure, but that is pointless if you ignore forecasting what people really want to know: rain, wind and temperature.

The application of these four criteria is crucial when we turn to business forecasting. Very often there is a serious shortcoming with respect to one or more criteria. Consider the mini-cases below, and see how you rate them in respect to our four forecasting criteria.

Mini-case A

My Dear Bank Manager,
I wish to obtain a loan from you to purchase a boat for my Thames pleasure tour business. After thorough market research I have calculated revenues, set out below in Table 8.3. I also include details of the operating and capital costs. The internal rate of return on all these cash flows is 26.37 per cent. At the 19.3 per cent rate of interest that you charge for such a loan, the net present value of this project is £1077.33.

Table 8.3   Cash flows for pleasure boat business

Year from purchase	0	1	2	3	4	5
Revenues		+ £4,500	+ £5,000	+ £6,000	+ £10,000	+ £10,000
Operating costs		− £5,180	− £4,540	− £3,860	− £ 3,540	− £ 3,220
Capital costs (purchase and resale values)	− £6,067					+ £ 2,000

Mini-case B

Dear Sir,
In a separate document I enclose full details of our estimate to build an extension to your hotel. If you accept our offer, there will be no increase in the price we charge you, apart from the usual increments if materials and wages go up. We can give you an absolute guarantee that once we start the work, we will be finished in four months. We will be able to start your job sometime in the New Year, depending on the weather and the completion of our existing jobs.

Mini-case C

In the intensive-care profit-centre, each patient accepted adds £2150 to our revenue. With each patient staying, on average, 18.3 days and costing £84 per day our return is satisfactory, but further progress should be within our grasp. If we work hard at speeding up throughput we should be able to cut patient-stay to 12.6 days, thus improving our value added. This will also increase the turnover of the mortuary profit-centre from which we could reasonably negotiate a transfer payment in our favour.

Mini-case D

Empty shelf-space in pet foods has fallen from 6.33 per cent to 5.15 per cent during the year but the trend should decelerate to 4.29 per cent by 1996. Again, there has been no demand for smoked venison, and this situation is expected to continue. The number of customers wearing spectacles decreased to 8.9 per cent, but this figure is expected to increase to above 10 per cent next year.

Mini-case E

Over most of Britain there will be a continuation of the warm, settled weather we have experienced in the past few days. There is a possibility that isolated thunderstorms may develop over a wide area leading to occasional showers, prolonged at times, and turning to sleet or snow in places. Winds will be light and moderate if the gales which were expected to move in from the Atlantic yesterday do not materialize. The further outlook is very much the same.

An aside — outliers and checking your information sources

One of our postgraduate students was working on a short-term forecasting exercise for a major brewery. His work got held up by a weird result (an outlier) in his data. People in Leeds drank ten times as much cider in April 1986 as they did in April 1985. This particular outlier was much too important to be ignored, but if it was included in his data, his forecasting programme threw up absurd results. We did a bit of brainstorming on why so much cider was drunk and came up with: a spell of warm weather? Easter holidays? a big Pop Festival? rival brewery running short of cider? None of these was the answer. In the end, our student went up to Leeds to talk to the clerk wh·· had sent down the statistics. On checking the manual records with the computer input, a decimal point had been put in the wrong place.

We are now going to move on to ways in which data can be manipulated mathematically to help with forecasting. But we hope that our extended discussion up to this point has reinforced the motto: Garbage in, garbage out. In other words clever mathematical processes cannot do much to clarify foggy, unreliable data.

8.4.5.2 Segmentation and clustering data

In forecasting you have the common problem of how to strike a balance between too much and too little detail. For example, in a large supermarket someone has to keep tabs on every type of item in stock so that there can be day-to-day replenishment of shelves. But suppose that for every such item, a forecast was made not only for tomorrow and the day after that, but also for every succeeding day in the year. Clearly there would be information overload; no-one would have time to make a proper analysis of it, even if it was accurate. Yet advance forecasts are needed for a year or more ahead (so that product lines can be promoted, or amalgamated, so that shelf space can be adjusted, and so that future staffing levels can be assessed). Decisions can be made on these issues if there is a sensible clustering together of individual items. There will be broad categories for long-run yearly strategic forecasts, e.g. 'meats', 'confectionery' or 'tinned food', through narrower categories for monthly seasonal forecasts, e.g. 'salad vegetables', 'potatoes', 'apples', down to the specific items for the day-to-day forecasts, e.g. for potatoes '14 lb washed red', '14 lb washed white', 'loose unwashed old', 'loose washed new'.

Now take an operating situation at the other extreme. Suppose you make just one major product. Does this mean that you should only forecast this one simple category? No — because within it there might be many different market segments, each with its own distinct pattern of consumption. For example, if you supply windows this would be a helpful segmentation.

1. *By type of installer.* Builders have a *derived demand* for windows linked to the houses they are completing, whereas domestic consumers buy more for replacement demand arising from damage.
2. *By purpose.* Thickened windows for security purposes depend on fears of theft. Windows for double-glazing purposes depend on the free availability of finance and subsidies.
3. *By user.* There are large variations in the amounts of capital investment in new shops, offices, factories, schools, hospitals and houses, each of which will have its own special rate of demand for windows.

The segmentation principle is of importance to manufacturers of durable goods, in particular in helping them to distinguish between initial (first-time) buyers and cyclical (replacement) buyers. If they fail to make this distinction, they may be misled into thinking that rapidly expanding demand (unknown to them caused by a rush of first-time buyers) is going to continue. When the market has been fully penetrated and the number of first-time buyers tails off, sales collapse along with the suppliers who have not anticipated this situation (as in colour television sets, video recorders, personal computers and house purchases).

One common segmentation device used in forecasting is ABC analysis. In a multi-product firm suppose you have:

A   The first 10 per cent of items account for 60 per cent of turnover value
B   The next 20 per cent of items account for 30 per cent of turnover value
C   The last 70 per cent of items account for 10 per cent of turnover value

Such categories are often used as a prior sorting device in forecasting and materials management systems. A-items (as the most valuable) are given the closest attention. Any old, cheap, automatic forecasting system can be used for C-items. An in-between system is used for B. ABC analysis crops up in a variety of guises, sometimes with different percentages, sometimes with criteria other than turnover value, and sometimes with a different purpose (e.g. for quality control). We feel that ABC analysis is a useful first stab at tackling problems but should not be used dogmatically. In forecasting, for example, it would be disastrous for a Sheffield alloy firm to put a small turnover metal like molybdenum in the C category. *All* metals which make up their alloy must be treated with equal care. A shortage in any metal, whatever its percentage use, can cause alloy manufacturing to grind to a halt.

8.4.5.3 Identifying seasonality and predictable cycles

We are going to widen the normal definition of seasonality to embrace any significant repeatable variation. For example, for consumer demand there might be a 'seasonal' cycle which is daily (gas demand), weekly (shopping) or yearly (package holidays). For ease of calculation, our examples all involve quarterly data over a year: but the principles are the same for the other cycles.

In approaching data where you suspect there is a seasonal element, it is useful to ask these preliminary questions:

- *How regular is the seasonal cycle?* It may be absolutely fixed (going to church every Sunday), slightly variable (the timing of winter weather) or erratic (the interval between flu epidemics).
- *What is the cause of the seasonal variation?* It might be tied tightly to another predictable variable (electricity for lighting tied to hours of darkness). Or it might be tied to something a bit more unpredictable (ice cream sales tied to average summer temperatures). Or the cyclical pattern may have no obvious explanation (the changing lengths of skirts in fashion).

A warning — the analysis of awkward seasonal cycles

We are going to approach seasonality via some easy examples. But it would be misleading if we left you with the impression that the techniques for handling seasonality are always that simple. A more typical (and important) example would be how to forecast the time series in Figure 8.1. It includes a 'seasonal' cycle which varies both in amplitude and length.

People have written whole books on how to forecast such difficult time series. In this particular case, rather than use the simple analysis that we explain next, you would need to combine several other techniques mentioned in this chapter:

1. Separating out new from replacement purchasers (segmentation).
2. Defining the effect of general economic activity on car sales (causal analysis and leading indicators).
3. Working out the consequences of repurchase depending on the age of the buyer's current car (autoregression: Appendix 3).

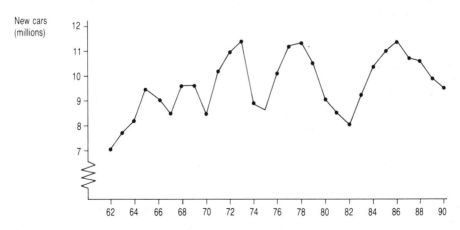

(*Source:* Table S-32, *Survey of Current Business*, US Department of Commerce.)

Figure 8.1   Retail sales of new passenger cars, USA 1962–1990.

Seasonality calculations for a fixed regular cycle

Here, the seasonal effect can be expressed numerically if you have reliable data stretching back over several years. For example, take recent statistics for births in the UK over a ten-year period shown in Table 8.4.

In this case, the seasonal deviations have been calculated in the most elementary manner: as absolute numbers. An alternative method is to express the deviations as a percentage from a norm. Percentage deviations are a better guide when there is a great range in the numbers being analysed (for example, crude oil or share prices). For our data, where the annual quarterly averages fall within quite a narrow range (179–199), it is sufficient to use the simpler absolute deviations.

8.4.5.4 Moving averages

There is another way of handling seasonal variations which has the added advantage of giving an updated record of any trend. This is the moving average method. One such formula for a moving average is shown below. Notice that all four seasons are given equal weighting:

$$M_t = \frac{1}{4}\left(\frac{1}{2}A_{t-2} + A_{t-1} + A_t + A_{t+1} + \frac{1}{2}A_{t+2}\right)$$

where t is the relevant time period, M_t is the moving average at time t, A_t is the actual data for time t.

For example, from the previous births table, the moving average for quarter II of 1987 would be

Table 8.4 UK live births per quarter ('000)

	Jan.–Mar.	April–June	July–Sept.	Oct.–Dec.	Quarterly average for a given year
	I	II	III	IV	
1981	180	185	189	177	**182.75**
1982	176	180	186	176	**179.50**
1983	175	185	187	174	**180.25**
1984	176	181	191	181	**182.25**
1985	183	189	197	182	**187.75**
1986	182	194	194	184	**188.50**
1987	186	199	201	190	**194.00**
1988	197	200	203	187	**186.75**
1989	189	200	199	189	**194.25**
1990	191	202	208	195	**199.00**
1981–90 average	183.5	191.5	195.5	183.5	**188.50**
Deviation from grand quarterly average of 188.50	−5.0	+3.0	+7.0	−5.0	

$$M_{\text{II}'87} = \frac{1}{4}(\frac{1}{2} \cdot 184 + 186 + 199 + 201 + \frac{1}{2} \cdot 190)$$
$$= 193.25$$

If you have worked out a complete set of moving averages, you can then work out a complete set of seasonal deviations $(A_t - M_t)$. From these you can work out average seasonal deviations giving results that are similar (in fact slightly superior) to those shown in the first births table.

These seasonal deviations from a moving average are the ones you frequently hear mentioned on the news, as in: 'Unemployment rose by 40,000 last month but the long-term trend is downwards after seasonal adjustments.' But this raises the issue: how can you be sure that a trend really is a trend?

8.4.5.5 Trend analysis

Discussion question: Are the comments on these graphs a reasonable way to interpret time series?

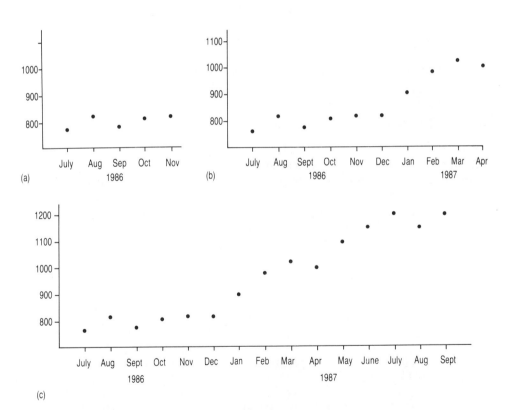

Figure 8.2 Trend-spotting. (a) Little evidence on which to forecast an upward trend. (b) Quite a definite trend is beginning to emerge. (c) Now there is strong evidence of a regular trend from which you can forecast with some confidence.

Answer: The graphs plotted the end-month values of the FT Actuaries' Share Index. Find out what happened in October 1987, and you may agree with Sir Alec Cairncross that:

A trend is a trend is a trend,
But the question is, will it bend?
Will it alter its course
Through some unforeseen force,
and come to a premature end?

▼   **Exercise — graphical interpretation of a time series: the weather**

We give in Table 8.5 temperature data for England and Wales over the past ten years. Plot the moving average on a graph, and then cast a discriminating eye at the results.

(a) Does this evidence convince you that the weather is changing?

(b) Is there a trend to higher values? Or is there just a long-term cycle which will
▲   swing back to a norm? Or do the statistics merely illustrate random
       variations, unconnected to any cycle or trend?

8.4.5.6 The role of regression analysis in forecasting

Every statistics book contains a detailed explanation of simple regression (finding the best fit for drawing a line through a set of points on a graph). For points representing a time series, isn't regression, or some variant of it, the only valid way of making a

Table 8.5   England and Wales: quarterly average temperatures
(°C) with seasonally corrected moving averages in parentheses

	Jan.–Mar.	April–June	July–Sept.	Oct.–Dec.
	I	II	III	IV
1981	5.7 (9.9)	11.2 (9.7)	15.2 (9.5)	6.1 (9.6)
1982	5.2 (9.8)	12.2 (10.1)	16.0 (10.4)	8.0 (10.3)
1983	5.5 (10.2)	10.8 (10.4)	17.0 (10.3)	8.5 (10.1)
1984	4.0 (10.0)	11.1 (10.0)	16.1 (9.9)	9.1 (9.8)
1985	3.0 (9.7)	10.9 (9.4)	15.4 (9.2)	7.6 (9.2)
1986	3.0 (9.0)	10.8 (9.0)	14.0 (9.2)	8.7 (9.3)
1987	3.4 (9.5)	11.2 (9.6)	15.5 (9.8)	7.9 (10.2)
1988	5.9 (10.2)	11.7 (10.2)	14.9 (10.2)	8.3 (10.5)
1989	7.0 (10.7)	11.6 (10.9)	16.8 (11.0)	8.3 (11.2)
1990	7.9 (11.1)	11.8 (11.1)	16.3 (10.7)	8.3 (10.9)

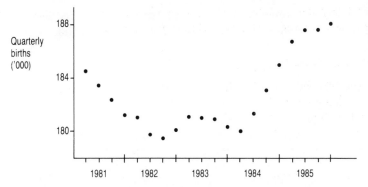

Figure 8.3 Moving average of UK births 1981−85.

forecast? To see why things are not that simple, attempt the following challenge. If you have not got a computer package to do the statistics, do a few freehand drawings (in pencil) of regression lines that attempt to minimize overall deviations from them.

A forecasting challenge

Can you devise a formula which when applied to the 1981−85 figures in Figure 8.3 gives a pretty good forecast of the 1986−90 figures in Figure 8.4? (Note: It is cheating to use the 1986−90 figures when devising this formula.)

A backcasting challenge

Can you devise a formula which when applied to the 1986−90 figures in Figure 8.4

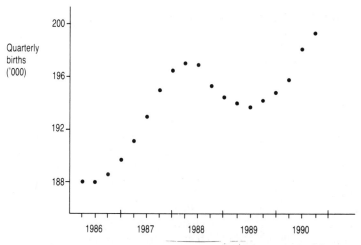

Figure 8.4 Moving average of UK births, 1986−90.

gives a pretty good estimate of the 1981–85 figures which preceded it? (Note: It is cheating to use the 1981–85 figures when devising this formula.)

The moral of tackling these challenges

Most people find the challenges frustrating and difficult: more so if you hope to end up with a common formula that works for both forecasting and backcasting. However, it is possible that you have come up with some new technique that works well — and is superior to the simple regression, exponential smoothing and last-change-scaling techniques described in the appendices to this chapter. If you are quite excited about your special technique, check it against time series quoted in volume 1 of the *Journal of Forecasting* (1982). This is the classic source of data to be used in forecasting competitions between formulae. In general, the moral of this exercise is:

> *If you insist on analysing a time series using only its own data, you have to put in an awful lot of extra intellectual effort to squeeze out only marginal improvements.*

This point is dealt with at more length in Appendix 3 to this chapter.

In spite of the reservations thrown up by the forecasting challenge, regression techniques are very useful *if confined to the search for patterns in existing data prior to a search for causes.* Even here regression has been open to criticisms:

- *Regression cynic's criticism*

  Regression regards recent and ancient data as equally important.

  Regression enthusiast's response

  All you need to do is give us the weightings by which you wish to scale down past data; then we will generate a modified time series and apply regression analysis to that. (Appendix 2 explains a weighting system.)

- *Regression cynic's criticism*

  What is the *economic* justification for minimizing the sum of squared deviations? Why not cubed deviations, or any other formula? Or, more relevantly, surely you should use the *cost* of forecasting errors? (As explained at some length in the Exploration 2 section earlier.)

  Regression enthusiast's response

  Most regression lines are not all that different, whether you aim to minimize absolute, squared or cubed deviations. If costs are important, the original time series should be converted to costs and a regression analysis can be applied to that.

- *Regression cynic's criticism*

  In practice, there are many time series which follow graceful curves (as in the forecasting challenge exercise on birth rates). Surely *linear* regression is never going to represent these situations very well?

Regression enthusiast's response	We can introduce clever polynomial and non-linear methods of regression. If there are not too many points to cover (e.g. the twenty each in the forecasting challenge) we can find an excellent fit for existing data. Mind you, there is no guarantee that we will be able to forecast or backcast very well outside that data; in fact, it is highly unlikely.
• *Regression cynic's criticism*	What about sudden dramatic shifts in a time series, like in 1973 when OPEC put up the price of crude oil from $2 to $10 a barrel? What is the point of trying to get a regression fit for data on each side of this change?
Regression enthusiast's response	A fair enough criticism. The best we can do is to carry out separate regressions on each side of the big shift. But this is not entirely satisfactory.

8.4.5.7 The analysis and forecasting of erratic time series

Most internationally traded commodities exhibit an erratic pattern of price movements — and the most important commodity is one of the worst.

You are not going to go very far by applying regression, or any other statistical technique, to oil prices. It is better to review all news events associated with oil. From this rich picture, can any inferences be drawn? Take, for example, the major happenings over any recent year. We illustrate the happenings in 1986, but any other year would be equally traumatic.

Major world events affecting the oil situations, 1986

January/February	Brent crude oil price falls by some $10 a barrel to $16 a barrel, following the decision by OPEC countries to secure and defend a 'fair share' of the world oil market at the meeting in December 1985 in Vienna.
March	OPEC Geneva meeting cannot secure co-operation on production constraints.
April/May	Oil prices fall to less than £10 a barrel. Norwegian strike results in 0.7 million barrels per day (b/d) of oil production being shut-in; the strike ends on the 26 April. Ten OPEC countries, led by Saudi Arabia, agree to aim for an average 1986 crude oil production of 16.7 million

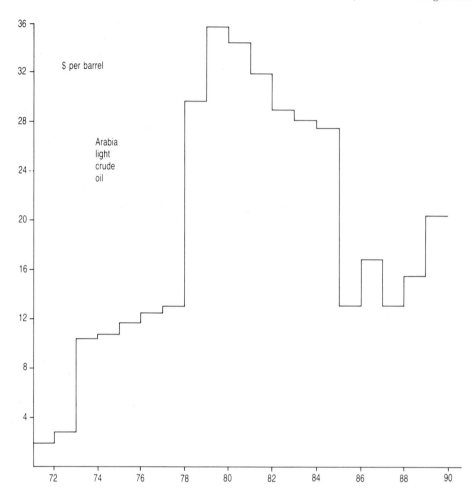

Figure 8.5 Erratic movements in the price of oil, 1971–90.

b/d, with third and fourth quarter levels of 16.3 and 17.3 million b/d respectively. Iran, Libya and Algeria request more drastic production cuts.

Chernobyl nuclear accident in the USSR.

Continued air attacks by Iraq on Iranian targets, including Tehran refinery.

June

Iran opens new oil terminal at Larak near Hormuz.

OPEC meeting in Brioni cannot reach conclusive agreement about new targets or quotas.

Five American oil companies cease operations in Libya at the request of the United States' administration.

July/September	OPEC meeting in Geneva agrees to limit output of all members (except Iraq) for September/October to the 1984 OPEC ceiling of 16 million b/d. In response to this agreement, Brent Crude spot price rises to $15 a barrel from a low point of around $8 a barrel in July.
October/November	Following an OPEC meeting in Geneva in October, agreement is reached to limit output to 15 million b/d for November/December period. Iraq is again excluded from these quotas. Sheikh Yamani is replaced as Saudi Oil Minister by Hisham Nazer. King Fahd announces Saudi Arabia's intention to pursue a price of $18 a barrel.
December	At the OPEC meeting in Geneva a new production quota is agreed for the first half of 1987 of 15.8 million b/d, for the third quarter of 16.6 and 18.3 million b/d for the fourth.

Interpretation of the 1986 events

The world's oil market is at the mercy of a few dominant producers. If they have a mind to, they can flood the market causing the price to halve or withhold supplies causing the price to double. Whether they do so or not depends on political and psychological factors. Although there are enormous gains to be made if major producers form an alliance, any such alliance is unstable because of the suspicion, paranoia and hatred that they have for one another. (See the final chapter of this book for a more detailed discussion of alliances.)

▼   **Exercise**

Take any recent year other than 1985 and from library sources build up a picture of the major events affecting oil supplies. Which of these events could have been predicted? Can you imagine any dramatic political scenario affecting Saudi Arabia which would completely transform the oil supply

▲   situation?

Forecasting prices etc. for other major commodities

Even if oil is the classic example of power-politics in action, other commodities have some equally dramatic events associated with them.

Rice. Shortage or glut depends on the monsoon, war and rural population levels.
Wheat. Through bad weather or mismanagement, countries like the Soviet Union

(that was) have to make massive purchases from the West.

Steel. Painful shakeout in USA and European surplus capacity as these countries are undercut by Asian and South American competitors.

Sugar, coffee, cocoa, copra, cotton, palm oil. Many underdeveloped countries have only one or two cash crops which they must exploit mercilessly because they need foreign exchange to pay debts, however depressed the price for their products.

Dairy produce, meats, cereals. Food mountains caused by governmental farm subsidies.

Tin, copper, bauxite, zinc, nickel, lead. World surplus capacity caused by technical progress and economies of scale in mining, processing and transport. Sometimes there is a complex interaction between these events. For example, the Soviet Union (that was) dumped large quantities of aluminium on an already-depressed world market to pay for the wheat it needed to import. Or, when the twenty-year tin price agreement collapsed in 1985 major ten producers like Malaysia had to earn extra foreign currency by stepping up rubber production.

▼   **Exercise**

Choose any major commodity traded internationally. Find a source-book of statistics which gives you its price history over the past twenty years. What changes have there been in the percentage share of the major producers during this period? What are the most important events that have affected this commodity? Is there a simple explanation for all these events, and could
▲   they happen again?

8.4.5.8 Causal analysis and leading indicators

Earlier in this chapter we analysed the time series of birth rates to see how far the identification of seasonal patterns or trends could act as a forecasting guide. Such an approach is of limited use. It is better to investigate parallel data to see how they might influence birth rates, for example:

- Changes in the number of women in various child-bearing ages.
- Changes in effectiveness and availability of contraception.
- Changes in the laws regarding abortion.
- Many other changes in employment, income-support and migration.

Some of these influences may be very good *leading indicators* — they change maybe years in advance of the change in the birth rate that they cause. Identifying and quantifying leading indicators is a prime skill of a good forecaster. Hence, the next exercise.

▼   **Exercises in causal analysis and leading indicators — road deaths**

Over the past few years there has been a welcome reduction in road deaths in the UK. Why has this been so? See if you can throw any light on this matter by undertaking exercises (a), (b) and (c).

Table 8.6   UK road deaths per quarter

	I	II	III	IV
1980			1556	1606
1981	1311	1331	1593	1611
1982	1310	1382	1596	1644
1983	1227	1287	1377	1513
1984	1144	1312	1519	1624
1985	1071	1207	1373	1514
1986	1161	1232	1391	1598
1987	1050	1243	1409	1423
1988	1104	1177	1296	1475
1989	1232	1186	1422	1533
1990	1278	1254	1267	1418
1991	939	1031		

(a) Look at the road deaths time series in Table 8.6; calculate moving averages and deseasonalize it. What patterns of trends and sudden shifts do you think you can identify?

(b) Search for leading indicators. Can you find information on other factors that might have influenced the road deaths time series (e.g. number of vehicles; changes in legislation affecting seat belts and breathalysers; congestion levels; population; business activity)? Is there an identifiable delay or lag between changes in the leading indicator and road deaths?

(c) If you have identified leading indicators that you think are important, how does your explanation fit into a more detailed analysis of road accidents (e.g. deaths to pedestrians, cyclists, children, young drivers or the non-fatal accident statistics)?

▲   Recommended extra sources of information: *Transport Statistics Great Britain* (see Table 8.7) and *Monthly Digest of Statistics*.

Table 8.7 Further information to help you with the exercises

UK road deaths

	Pedestrians		Cyclists		Motor cycle		Car		Goods vehicle drivers and pass'rs	Bus drivers and pass'rs
	Child	Adult	Child	Adult	Riders	Pass'rs	Drivers	Passr's		
1980	298	1640	86	216	1018	145	1339	939	210	29
1990	229	1447	49	207	591	68	1432	939	194	19

Tests

	'000 breath tests taken ('000 breath tests failed)		'000 MOT tests taken ('000 MOT tests failed)	
	Car drivers	Motor cyclists	Cars and light goods vehicles	Motor cycles
1980	33	5.7	12,900	633
	(11)	(1.7)	(5,300)	(177)
1990	92	7.6	18,200	1087
	(8)	(0.8)	(6,900)	(316)

8.5 Conclusion

As this has been a long chapter, we can put this briefly. Look at forecasting as a pyramid.

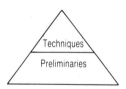

If you do not get the base of the pyramid right, all your fancy forecasting techniques will fall down.

8.6 Recommended reading

Start with the 'Young Forever Boutique' in Schmenner, *Production/Operations Management Concepts and Situations*, 4th edn (Macmillan, 1990, p. 395). Instead of forecasting via statistical techniques, were there better ways of tackling Kathy Wilkerson's problem? Then look at 'Adams Ice Cream' in Nicholson, *Managing Manufacturing Operations* (Macmillan, 1978). As they say it is vitally important, how much reliance can be put on their forecasts? Next look at Arnold's case also in Nicholson and carry out a seasonal analysis for spring sales 1968–73 in Illustration 13.5. What incentive is there for the firm to cut its manufacturing lead time? Now try 'Sea Pines Racket Club' in Sasser *et al.*, *Cases in Operations Management: Strategy and Structure* (Irwin, 1982), and make a rough stab at the cost consequences of under- and over-forecasting tennis court capacity. Finally, look at 'New Orleans Hilton' in D. Collier's *Service Management* (Prentice Hall, 1987). Note the interdependence of forecasting and sales planning.

If you want to know more about forecasting, a useful first book is by J.S. Armstrong, *Long Range Forecasting* (Wiley, 1978).

Appendix 1 *Hindsight evaluation of forecasts*

This appendix should be read as a simple follow-up using the costing and logic described in Exploration 2.

How can you check whether one forecasting technique is better than another? It all depends on how you evaluate the deviations, or errors, between forecast and actual. We will follow the normal practice of letting 'errors' and 'deviation' mean the same thing in this context.

The three most common ways of summarizing deviations are:

BIAS (arithmetic average of deviations)
MAD (mean of absolute deviations)
MSE (mean of squared errors)

Example — *daily bread demand*

At the end of each day, a bread shop has to forecast next day's demand so that the central bakery knows how much to deliver to the shop next morning. Table 8.8 shows the forecast, the actual demand and the calculation of the three basic audit devices.

Table 8.8   Loaves forecasted and demanded per day

		Week 1						Week 2					Sum	$\frac{\text{Sum}}{12}$	Averages
	M	T	W	T	F	S	M	T	W	T	F	S			
Forecast	75	64	67	65	66	93	76	54	70	61	64	85	840	70	= Average forecast
Actual demand	75	60	73	64	71	97	79	53	66	59	72	95	864	72	= Average demand
Error ±	0	+4	−6	+1	−5	−4	−3	+1	+4	+2	−8	−10	−24	−2	= BIAS
Absolute deviation	0	4	6	1	5	4	3	1	4	2	8	10	48	4	= MAD
(Error)^2	0	16	36	1	25	16	9	1	16	4	64	100	288	24	= MSE

Tracking signals. Tracking signals check whether there is any significant change in the forecasting error. They lie at the heart of advanced forecasting methods and can be accumulations, weights, ratios or statistical distributions. Table 8.9 gives a popular procedure for calculating a simple tracking signal from the bread shop data.

The way this particular tracking signal is constructed, it could swing from -3 to $+3$ depending on the level of under-forecasting or over-forecasting. The main value of tracking signals is in automatic techniques handled by a computer without human intervention. (See also the ROQ/ROL example in Chapter 10.)

Any forecasting should seek a balance between the cost of making an over-forecast and the, perhaps very different, cost of making an under-forecast. It is rare for any exposition of BIAS, MAD, MSE or tracking signal to consider this issue.

For example, a supermarket selling bread taken from a freezer has trivial costs from over-stocking (electricity and freezer-space charges). But bread is often used as a loss leader to attract people into a store to do all their weekend shopping. If the supermarket is seen to run out of bread by (say) lunchtime Saturday, people will go elsewhere for all their purchases, and they might be deterred from shopping at that supermarket the following week. So we could have something like: cost of over-stocking 2p, cost of under-stocking £2.00 per loaf.

A village store selling fresh bread has bigger costs from over-stocking. Any bread unsold at the end of the day will go stale and be near-worthless. But if the village store is the only one, and has captive customers, it will not lose their goodwill for other purchases if it under-stocks: all it will lose is the profit margin on the loaf. So, for the village store the cost of over-stocking is more likely to be 30p, the cost of under-stocking 10p, per loaf.

Suppose we take these village store over-stocking/under-stocking costs and apply them to the errors occurring in the previous bread shop example, as shown in Table 8.10.

Look at the most serious individual forecasting errors on a cost basis (e.g. the 120). These do not tie up with the most serious individual 'errors' as identified by the BIAS, MAD and (especially) MSE components.

Look at the total cost of under- and over-forecasting (each 360). That is a nice balance. Compare that with the supposed BIAS in the mathematical audits.

Table 8.9   Bread demand — deviations of forecast from actual

	W	T	F	S	M	T	W	T	F	S
Total of last three errors ± = X	−2	−1	−10	−8	−12	−6	+2	+7	−2	−16
Total of last three absolute deviations = Y	10	11	12	10	12	8	8	7	14	20
Tracking signal = 3X/Y	−0.6	−0.3	−2.5	−2.4	−3.0	−2.3	0.75	3.0	−0.4	−2.4

Table 8.10 Evaluating the cost of over- and under-forecasting bread demand

	M	T	W	T	F	S	M	T	W	T	F	S	Total
Forecasting error	0	+4	−6	+1	−5	−4	−3	+1	+4	+2	−8	−10	
Cost of over-forecast at 30p/unit		120		30				30	120	60			360
Cost of under-forecast at 10p/unit			60		50	40	30				80	100	360

What general conclusions can be drawn up from this example? MSE is only remotely connected with cost effects and should never be used by an operations manager. If costs are not available and there is no obvious 'under and over' distortion, it is fairly safe to use BIAS and MAD.

Appendix 2 *Internally-generated forecasting*

Using only the past data of a time series, what is the best formula for predicting its future value? This has been extensively discussed by statisticians. In short, they found that 'it all depends on the time series'. If we had to select three formulae which we thought were best, this would be our choice:

1. *Last period's actual:*

   $$F_{t+1} = A_t$$

   This very simple formula can beat all-comers when there is a continuous trade-off between current and future values (e.g. for Stock Exchange share prices).

2. *Last-change scaling:*

   $$F_{t+1} = A_t + k(A_t - A_{t-1})$$

   This formula copes well with elementary trends and oscillations.

3. *Double exponential smoothing:*

   $$F_{t+1} = S_t + T_t$$

   where $S_t = \alpha A_t + (1 - \alpha)F_t$, and
   $T_t = \beta(S_t - S_{t-1}) + (1 - \beta)T_{t-1}.$

   This formula frequently beats more sophisticated rivals in forecasting competitions.

Symbols used in the three forecasting formulae are: t = time period, A_t = actual value, F_t = forecasted value, k = scaling coefficient of last change, α = exponential smoothing coefficient of 'actuals', β = exponential smoothing coefficient of the trend.

When applying these formulae to a time series, there are two ways of finding the best k, α and β to use:

1. Take a set of past data and experiment, using whatever coefficient(s) gives the lowest MAD (mean absolute deviation) for the whole test series.
2. Start by giving the coefficients arbitrary values. Calculate cumulative MADs both for the coefficient values you have chosen and for some nearby coefficient values. If any of them has a better cumulative MAD, switch to this better coefficient. Continue, switching further if necessary. Eventually you will settle down to the same values as in (1).

Note that once this system of *adaptive forecasting* has been set up, it can modify its forecasting coefficients without human intervention. However, it is a fine art to set up an adaptive forecasting system which is neither too nervous (continually changing its coefficients) or too phlegmatic (rarely changing the coefficients even when necessary).

A general note on forecasting by formula

There are certain strengths and weaknesses to the formula approach. It is obsessively neutral. It is not concerned about whether the time interval is days, months or years. Nor is it influenced by the thing being forecast; it could equally well be apples, earthquakes or polar bears. It analyses a single stream of numbers divorced from any discussion about what they mean, how they were generated, or how accurate they are. There is no search for leading indicators, associations or causes other than within the time series itself.

In a way, formula forecasting could be rechristened 'Count of Monte Cristo forecasting'. Imagine you had been imprisoned for years in solitary confinement. Suppose you were fed streams of unidentified (but not random) numbers by your gaoler, who, for your torment or pleasure, asks 'Guess the next number?'

Mathematicians have developed advanced techniques for handling this very special situation. Some of these have been a little helpful in untangling special situations (e.g. the Box–Jenkins technique for identifying the complex cycle of events that determine sun-spot activity). These special techniques need an awful lot of data over a long time series before they show any gains over the simpler methods that we have illustrated. Therefore, we would argue that 'Monte Cristo' forecasting should be tried only as a last resort when nothing can be found out about causation.

Appendix 3 'What if?' modelling by autoregression equations

Consider things that last a long time — ships, houses, cars, TV sets. Decisions to replace them depend on how worn out they are. This in turn depends on how long ago they were purchased. So the level of purchases a long time ago can affect replacement decisions and purchases today. This is one area where the technique of autoregression can be helpful. A good example of a 'thing' getting older and being replaced is 'people'. Suppose we are at time t in history. Divide the current population into twenty-year cohorts depending on their age: $(0-20)$, $(20-40)$, $(40-60)$, $(60-80)$, $(80-100)$. Label these cohorts A_t, B_t, C_t, D_t and E_t, where t stands for a particular year in time.

As birth, survival and death rates are strongly related to age, we could apply coefficients to these cohorts to forecast the population twenty years hence. For example:

Births in next 20 years

> related to the number of mothers in A_t, B_t and C_t
> $$A_{t-20} = 0.1A_t + 0.9B_t + 0.1C_t$$

Survival chances

> Of $(0-20)$s living 20 years more: $B_{t+20} = 0.95A_t$
> Of $(20-40)$s living 20 years more: $C_{t+20} = 0.9B_t$
> Of $(40-60)$s living 20 years more: $D_{t+20} = 0.8C_t$
> Of $(60-80)$s living 20 years more: $E_{t+20} = 0.3D_t$

And, if you wanted to know the total population twenty years hence (P_t), this could be found by summing the right-hand side of the above equations:

$$P_{t+20} = 1.05A_t + 1.8B_t + 0.9C_t + 0.3D_t$$

This is a typical autoregression equation. Starting from (say) 1990 statistics, you could apply the equation to get population estimates for the year 2010. And you could apply the equation again (this time to the 2010 results) to get a forecast for 2030, and so on. Table 8.11 shows a numerical example using our estimating equation above.

In this example, although total population stays fairly steady, there can be some dramatic changes in a particular age group — look at the 60–80 year olds. In this particular case, this forecast would have been of great help for those planning health-care facilities. If you are reading this book in an overcrowded college or university,

Table 8.11 Population estimates using autoregression

t	Total popn (m) P_t	Ages				
		0–20 A_t	20–40 B_t	40–60 C_t	60–80 D_t	80–100 E_t
1990	60	16.0	18.0	12.0	10.0	4.0
2010	62.8	18.8	15.2	16.2	9.6	3.0
2030	64.7	17.2	17.9	13.7	13.0	2.9
2050	66.5	19.2	16.3	16.1	11.0	3.9
2070	66.3	17.2	18.2	14.7	12.9	3.3

it may interest you to know that autoregression forecasters identified that a boom in higher education would occur in the early 1990s even before the students causing it were born.

▼   **Short exercise**

Starting from the 1990 population figures in the top row of Table 8.11, forecast population up to fifty years ahead by substituting some or all of the following equations which show the conditions that hold in other parts of the world:

Higher birth rate	$A_{t+20} = 0.3A_t + 1.4B_t + 0.2C_t$
Greater infant mortality	$B_{t+20} = 0.75A_t$
An AIDS epidemic	$B_{t+20} = 0.85A_t, \quad C_{t+20} = 0.8B_t$
A cure for cancer	$D_{t+20} = 0.85C_t \quad E_{t+20} = 0.4D_t$
Campaign to postpone and limit pregnancies	$A_{t+20} = 0.75B_t + 0.15C_t$

▲

Note on autoregression

The example and the exercises show that it is quite easy to understand and apply autoregression forecasting. It is even easier if you have recourse to a computer spreadsheet which can flash through all the calculations and recalculations. Autoregression also appears to be more subtle, logical and relevant than simply extending a trend. However, the strength of autoregression hinges on the reliability of the coefficients that it uses, and deriving these coefficients is quite a difficult statistical exercise.

Chapter 9

Projects — planning and implementation

9.1 Introduction — building projects

Any project, whether it be installing a new computer in a building society's offices or organizing the London Marathon, requires planning. Connected with any such projects will be several interested parties. For example, if we consider the construction of a building we have:

The client:	'I want this sort of building, at this cost, by this date.'
The architect:	'I will provide you with a design, structure and materials to be used.'
The quantity surveyor:	'I can procure the right amount of materials.'
The building inspector:	'Does this plan meet our safety, services and sightline regulations?'
The builder:	'How can I get this building up in view of the help (and hindrance) of the above professionals?'

Enter the *project planner:* 'How can I help the builder by devising a properly ordered schedule of jobs to be done?'

Depending on the size of the project and the managerial skill of the builder, different methods of planning and control are needed. For a small building contract using only two or three workers, an experienced builder can sketch out a rough plan in his head. For example, if he is building a single house, his train of thought might be:

'I'll get a little digger to do the foundations — no trouble hiring at this time of year, and it will save a week over doing it manually. Last time, we got held up waiting for the building inspector to turn up, so this time we try to pin down when he's going to come. For concrete, the job's really too small for a readymix delivery. Instead, I'll mix on-site and bring over a small mixer from our other site for a couple of days ...'

Mentally, the builder is drawing up a project plan. Of particular interest to us is how he makes use of important concepts of the heart of project planning known as *precedence relationships*. These are the relationships established in response to a question like:

> 'Before any task or job is allowed to start, what work must have been completed?'

Before a builder can give a customer a feasible completion date for the whole project, he should have checked out the precedence relationships connected with every job in that project, and ascertained which jobs can be done simultaneously and which have to be done sequentially. If his customer is happy with the quoted completion date, the builder then has to make sure he sticks to schedule. If he falls behind, he will try to employ extra workers or change his building methods to save time.

As projects get bigger — for example, building a block of flats — things cannot be left to chance and memory. If there were no written system, there would be a chaotic muddle of half-finished work, late deliveries of material, idle equipment and workers whose jobs swing from hassle to idleness. So, on a complex building site, it helps the foreman if he can be told:

1. The conditions necessary before the work can start.
2. The resources necessary to do the job.
3. How the job should be done.
4. How often reports should be made, and to whom, on how the job is progressing.

The art of good project planning is in telling a building site foreman all the above points clearly and accurately, but without involving him in too much bureaucracy, jargon or irrelevant detail. The project planner can help the foreman by scanning in advance all specialist paperwork of the architects, planning officers, subcontractors and building suppliers, and extracting just that information relevant to the site-worker's task. A convenient approach is to compress this information into a *bar chart*. (Note, project-planning bar charts are commonly known as *Gantt charts* after Henry Gantt who first used them with great success when building ships for the US Navy during the First World War.)

Example

Figure 9.1 is a *master-chart* which describes only major activities. There will be other charts which go into more detail. For example, the summary chart mentions a single major activity, 'brickwork'. A *work-breakdown schedule* will split up 'brickwork' into, for example:

> Below damp-proof course brickwork
> Above damp-proof course brickwork
> First-storey brickwork
> Brickwork for internal non-load-bearing walls

Also, if you modify your more detailed Gantt chart so that you can vary the depth of the activity boxes according to the number of men working on an activity, it is quite

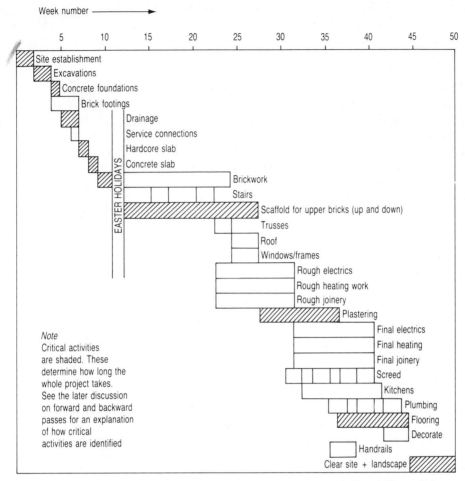

Figure 9.1 Master Gantt chart for the construction of Welbeck Road Flats, Bolsover.

easy to visualize your total labour requirements, or alternatively to formulate it as a *manpower histogram*, as shown in Figure 9.2. Note that a master activity (e.g. 'brickwork') is really just like a little separate project of subactivities. Before you investigate the detail of the subactivities, you tend to think of 'bricklaying' as a block of work with the maximum number of men (14) being fully employed between start and finish (8 weeks). But really every activity, at whatever level, on closer inspection usually has gaps.

For example, in the Gantt chart (Figure 9.2), the subactivity 'inner walls' is shown as lasting 3 weeks and needing 6 men. But, if it were split into height sections, or split according to which interior room it referred to, it too would reveal an uneven manpower histogram and an incomplete jigsaw of subsubactivities. At this level of detail,

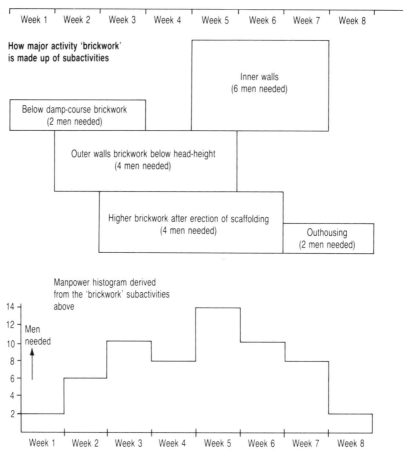

Figure 9.2   Designing a Gantt chart where the depth of a box is proportional to the number of workers.

the work can be represented on a Gantt chart specifying individual days. (See the manpower scheduling Gantt charts later in this chapter.)

9.2 **Precedence relationships and precedence networks**

So far we have talked about the general nature of projects, about how they are broken down into major and minor activities, and why it is good to represent a project by a Gantt chart. At a crude level, a Gantt chart is just putting a list of jobs to be done on a timetable: something that anyone can do. In order to design a really good Gantt chart, though, with full interplay between all the precedence relationships in a project, it helps if you construct and analyse a *precedence network*.

9.2.1 *Designing a precedence network — a small worked example*

Consider a fairly routine hospital operation such as the pinning of a leg broken in a traffic accident. The following would be a summary of the activities involved:

Code	Description of activity
A	Fetch patient from ward
B	Clear and prepare the operating theatre
C	Prepare instruments and equipment needed for operation
D	Anaesthetize patient
E	Assemble and brief the surgical team
F	Anaesthetist monitors patient during operation
G	Bring patient round after the operation
H	Incision of leg and inspect broken bone
I	Reposition and pin the bone
J	Seal incision; sew up leg
K	Collect, sterilize and replace all instruments and equipment
L	Remove patient to recovery ward
M	Return patient from recovery to normal ward

These activities need to be sequenced. See if you can do this by drawing in arrows between the activity boxes in Figure 9.3. Note that F, H, I and J have been combined into one major activity box (just so that this first exercise can be kept simple).

Comment

Quite a few things deserve a further explanation, and in fact have quite profound spin-offs even though the example is simple.

1. *The standardized size of the activity boxes* (apart from the large, major one). In a Gantt chart (such as the earlier example in Figure 9.2), the length of a box is in direct proportion to its duration (e.g. 5 centimetres if it lasts 5 weeks). Precedence networks dispense with this requirement because there is much shuffling and redrawing in the design stage. If you choose a small box as standard, you can get more boxes onto a page or other workspace.
2. *Putting resource-related boxes on the same line.* Activities using the same resource are more likely to be in sequence, so putting them on the same line improves the chance of a tidy and more understandable network.
3. *The left-to-right direction of precedence arrows.* The activity boxes are placed so that all the precedence arrows can point from left to right. The left-to-right direction of precedence arrows is a normal convention for the *final draft* of a precedence network. But it is quite acceptable to design a first-draft network with arrows snaking all over the place.
4. *Justifying the logic in the 'model answer'.* Sometimes, more than one pattern of arrows between boxes will give an equally feasible result. For example, if the hospital operation was straightforward, the instruments could be prepared and laid out

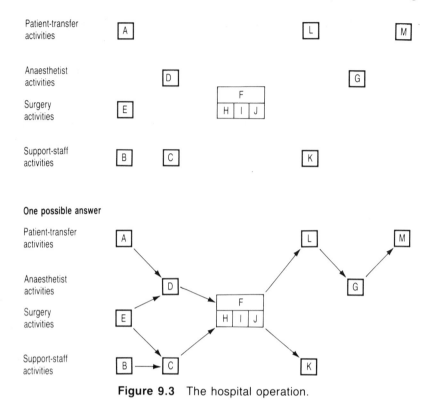

Figure 9.3 The hospital operation.

before the surgical team had their briefing meeting (e.g. C before E). Also, some answers may have allowed the anaesthetist to begin his work before the briefing meeting (e.g. D before E). Which alternative is best depends on the severity of the operation and the robustness of the patient.

5. *Excluding redundant relationships.* When the patient is removed from the operating theatre (L), he is brought round in a recovery ward (G) before being returned to a general ward (M). The logic for these activities *could* appear as:

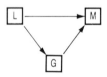

But note that the L to M arrow can be excluded as redundant (because with G coming between L and M, arrows to and from G ensure that L must come before M anyway). Excluding redundant relationships helps keep networks tidy and simple to interpret.

6. *Does this project have a single objective?* In elementary project planning, a lot of mathematical analysis assumes that there is a single completion date which dominates everything else. Some examples spring to mind, like the completion of the Channel Tunnel or getting facilities ready for the Olympic Games. But these examples are not typical. Most projects dovetail into parallel projects and, very often, special equipment, labour and subcontractors have their own strong ideas about when they want to come and go independent of the project's completion date. In our surgical example, the patient feels the project is completed when he gets back to the general ward; the anaesthetist, when the patient returns to consciousness; and the surgeon, when the patient is sewn up. You find that activities may be scheduled differently according to whose objective you think is most important. This re-emphasizes a point that we highlighted at the start of this chapter and that we will return to at the end. Normally, many different parties are involved in a project and it is difficult to resolve their conflicting interests.

7. *What about specifying the time each activity takes?* This hasn't been done yet. It is next step in project planning. Before going into this in full detail (next section), it is worth pointing out that the duration of only a few activities can be assessed accurately (how long it takes to move the patient to the recovery ward). Quite a few durations might be uncertain (how long the operation will take). Some project planning techniques use a statistical technique (beta distributions) to find a 'certain' estimate for an uncertain activity duration. This practice is dubious. We would prefer to use alternative 'what if?' scenarios for the different estimates. Rapid recalculations via computer make it possible to generate many comparative solutions quickly.

8. *What about the arrow-network method of project planning?* In many of the older textbooks you will see networks where activities are represented by arrows and precedence relationships by circled events or dummy arrows. The arrow-network method is falling out of fashion among practitioners, slows up network design, is a more erroneous teaching device, and cannot handle important extensions to the basic method.

9.2.2 *Designing precedence networks (continued)*

The ideas developed during the previous section can now be tested by doing a slightly larger exercise.

▼   **House-completion exercise**

A single-storey house has been half-completed. All the basic structure, brickwork for walls, roofing and concreting have been done. There remain fifteen activities (listed below) which fall within six major resource areas. (Each resource area appears as one line of boxes.) Assume that you cannot have two or more activities in the same resource area proceeding simultaneously.

▷

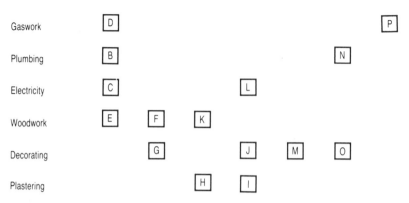

Figure 9.4 House-completion exercise — suggested layout.

With this information, can you draw precedence arrows between the boxes in Figure 9.4.

Major resource area	Code	Description
Plumbing	B	Rough plumbing connections to/from sewage and water mains
Electrics	C	Rough wiring, laying down internal circuit
Gaswork	D	Gas pipelaying from mains to fireplace and boiler points
Woodwork	E	Fitting the window frames and glazing
Woodwork	F	Laying floorboards
Decorating	G	External painting
Plastering	H	Plastering ceilings
Plastering	I	Plastering walls
Decorating	J	Paint ceilings
Woodwork	K	Fit internal doors, shelves, cupboards, boards
Electrics	L	Complete all power points, lights, switches
Decorating	M	Paint internal woodwork
Plumbing	N	Final plumbing of kitchen and bathroom
Decorating	O	Wallpapering
Gaswork	P	Install gas fires and central heating

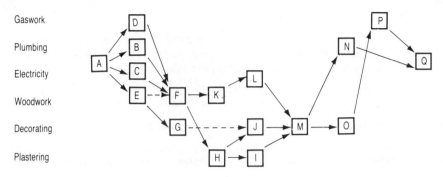

Figure 9.5   One answer to the house-completion exercise.

Comment — on including a source and sink activity

In the network, we have added:

- A, a *source activity*. Arrows have been drawn out of A so that A precedes every activity in the network.
- B, a *sink activity*. Arrows have been drawn in to B so that B follows every activity in the network.

A and B involve no resources and have zero duration. The sole purpose of introducing them is for computational reasons. Having a single source and sink simplifies the *forward and backward pass* process (explained later — though note that there is an easy extension to critical path analysis that can handle many sources and sinks).

Comments — on weak and strong precedence relationships

Figure 9.5 contains two sorts of arrow: an ordinary arrow which indicates that there are strong technical advantages for a particular precedence (e.g. E comes before G because it is pretty essential to have floorboards on which ladders and platforms can be placed for the ceiling plastering), and a dotted arrow which indicates that there is nothing wrong in adopting that precedence order, although it is not essential (e.g. G, external decorating, could be put back after the other decorating jobs; it has been put early in the sequence hoping for good weather for painting. If the weather is bad, then you have the option of rescheduling G).

Strong and weak precedences are also known as *functional* and *resource* precedences. Use of these concepts is growing amongst practitioners but is rarely referred to in textbooks. This is a pity, as the distinction enables more and better alternative solutions to be generated. (For example, see the discussion to the answer to the exercise below — but do the exercise first.)

There is a third, very strong *immediate* precedence relationship (e.g. 'concrete setting' follows immediately after 'concrete laying'), but the implications, though important, are too advanced for this chapter.

▼   **Exercise**

Don't do this exercise immediately. Read the next section on how to do critical path calculations and floats. Then return to apply these calculations to the house-completion exercise using the following data:

Activity	A B C D E F G H I J K L M N O P Q
Duration (days)	0 3 4 3 2 3 3 4 5 2 5 2 2 5 4 6 0

▲   An answer, with comments, can be found later in the chapter.

▼   **Further exercise in precedence networks — the wheel-change problem**

Consider this well-known problem facing a motorist. He has a puncture whilst driving and pulls in to the side of the road to fit the spare wheel.

(a) List all the activities involved. Choose a level of detail so that there are between ten and fifteen activities between stopping the car and driving off with the new wheel in place.

(b) Draw up a precedence network of the activities. Assume that tasks can be done simultaneously because he has passengers to help him.

(c) For each activity, give an upper and lower estimate of how long it will take. Express your estimates to the nearest minute.

Important suggestion: If this exercise is being done in a class adjacent to a car park, go out and change someone's wheel, preferably with their permission. Set observers to split up and time all your activities. If possible, put the observers into two teams that do not communicate until the wheel has been changed. Then ask them to compare notes and justify any
▲   differences.

Suggested answer to the wheel-change problem

Answers will vary according to the tools available, the make of car, the dexterity of the driver, and the traffic and weather conditions. Also, the number of activities you choose to identify depends on the level of detail. Here is one possible answer, listing twelve activities.

Code	Range of duration (minutes)	Description	Comment
A	2–5	Stop car. Find and get out tools	You need to stop on level ground out of traffic danger. Some cars have the tools hidden away, and some only give you the minimum

B	3–6	Remove hub-cap. Loosen, but leave on the wheel nuts	Some hub-caps are wedged tight and need a heavy screwdriver to lever them off. Some nuts can only be loosened if you attach an extension rod to give extra leverage to your brace-spanner
C	2–6	Release spare wheel	Sometimes this may be buried under luggage in the boot. Often, the spare wheel is suspended on a carrier beneath the back of the car, which takes some time to unscrew and lower (often needing a special spanner)
D	1–3	Place chocks to stabilize car	Not all toolkits provide chocks. If not, you can use bricks or something like them
E	2–4	Position jack prior to raising it	Most cars have specific jacking points. The positioning takes longer in the dark or wet
F	2–4	Raise jack	Tedious, but easy if you have the handle-tool which goes with the jack
G	2–3	Take off old wheel. Put on new wheel and screw on nuts loosely with the fingers	Routine, note that you save tightening the nuts really hard until the wheel has been lowered to the ground
H	1–3	Lower jack	Routine
I	1	Remove chocks	Routine
J	1–3	Stow punctured wheel	Again, it might have to be put under luggage or manoeuvred into a carrier under the car
K	2–4	Tighten nuts. Replace hub-cap	An extension rod on the spanner gives extra power to tightening. The hub-cap might need bashing on
L	1	Stow tools. Go	You can take longer packing away things neatly, but at this stage, most people don't bother

9.2.2.1 The forward pass

If the driver has help, so that more than one activity can be done at once, what is the shortest time to complete the project (that means completing the last activity L)? We

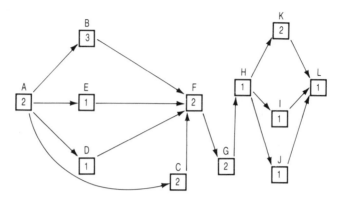

The number in each box gives the minutes duration for each activity using in each case the quickest estimate. These durations are used to illustrate the critical calculations.

Figure 9.6 Suggested precedence network for the wheel-change problem.

find this out by working our way through the network, from left to right for each box, finding out the following:

EST   The earliest start time for an activity, on the understanding that all activities preceding it have been completed.

EFT   The earliest finish time, which is simply the activity's (EST + duration).

▼   **Exercise**

Let the EST of the source box (A) be 0. Can you fill in the remaining ESTs and EFTs in the network?

Hint 1:   It helps to work through the boxes in alphabetical order.
Hint 2:   If there is just one arrow leading into a box, its EST is the same as the previous box's EFT.
Hint 3:   When you get to a box like F, with several arrows leading into it, F's EST will be the greatest EFT of the boxes leading into it (e.g. F's EST will be B's EFT).

▲

Answer

If you completed the previous exercise, you have done what is known in project planning jargon as a *forward pass*. The result is shown in Figure 9.7.

This network gives times where every activity starts as early as possible. What would this look like on a Gantt chart? This is illustrated in Figure 9.8. In this small example, we can show all the precedence arrows, ESTs and EFTs on the Gantt chart too (this would not be advisable for larger examples because there would be too much clutter).

The boxes with thick lines identify the *critical activities*: those activities that cause

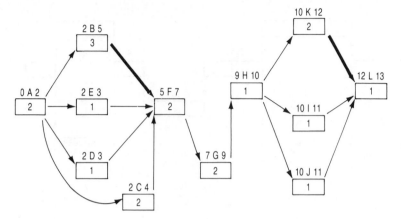

The ESTs are top left. The EFTs are top right. The heavier arrows shows from where an EST was calculated when there was a choice of several arrows going in to a box.

Figure 9.7 Forward pass calculations.

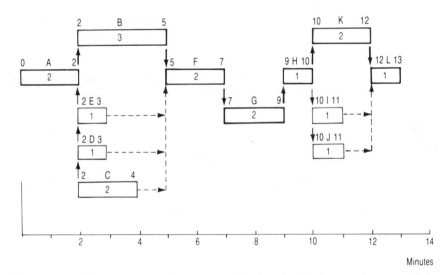

Figure 9.8 Wheel-change where everything is scheduled as early as possible.

the whole project to take thirteen minutes. If any critical activity were just a bit longer, the whole project would take longer too. The remaining boxes are *non-critical activities*. The horizontal dotted arrows show by how much their duration could be extended without causing the whole project to go over thirteen minutes.

9.2.2.2 The backward pass

If you wish to change the wheel in thirteen minutes, you must stick exactly to the indicated start and finish times for the critical activities; but you have some leeway

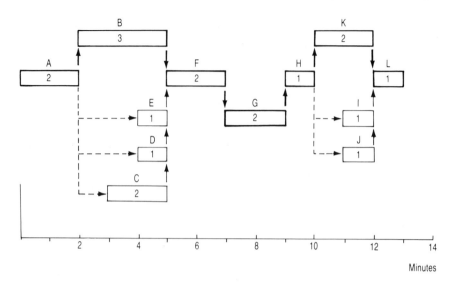

Figure 9.9 Wheel-change Gantt chart where everything is scheduled as late as possible but where the project is still completed in thirteen minutes.

with the non-criticals, depending on the length of the dotted arrows. This would be the schedule if all non-critical started as late as possible but the project still finished in thirteen minutes.

The critical activities are in the same position as in the previous Gantt chart but the non-critical activities have been scheduled later. The position of the boxes in this schedule illustrate two more network definitions.

LFT   The latest finish time for any activity if the whole project is to finish as early as possible (i.e. after 13 minutes in this case).

LST   Simply (LFT − duration).

Rather than shuffling boxes on a Gantt chart, there is another mathematical way of finding LFTs and LSTs by using the precedence network. It is called making a *backward pass*.

Rules for making a backward pass

Hint 1:   Start by setting the LFT of the sink activity at the minimum completion time for the whole project (e.g. put the LFT of L at 13).

Hint 2:   Whenever you have found the LFT of a box, its LST always equals LFT minus duration (e.g. the LST of L = 12).

Hint 3:   Find out the LFTs and LSTs by working through the boxes in reverse alphabetical order; L, K, J, etc.

Hint 4:   When working out LFTs and LSTs, *do not* refer to ESTs and EFTs.

Hint 5: If there is just one arrow leading out of a box, its LFT will be the same as the following box's LST.

Hint 6: If there is more than one arrow leading out of a box, its LFT will be the *smallest* of the LSTs in the boxes that follow it.

▼ **A little exercise**

The backward pass is always a bit more difficult to grasp than the forward pass. If you are puzzled by it, mark LFTs and LSTs on the previous Gantt chart, following the suggested hints. Your numbers should coincide with the marked positions on that Gantt chart. The answer is also given in the next
▲ network shown in Figure 9.10.

Comment on floats

The non-critical activities in Figure 9.10 have a float (in square brackets) attached to them. This shows how much they can be shifted about or their duration expanded, without affecting the project's completion time of thirteen minutes. For any activity, a float's size corresponds to the length of the horizontal dotted arrows in the previous Gantt charts. Mathematically, an activity's float is defined as (LFT − EST − DURATION). As can be seen, *critical activities have zero floats* and that is one way of identifying them. In bigger networks, floats are a bit more tricky to interpret. See our extended discussion on this topic, starting on p. 333.

Comment on the critical path

In Figure 9.10, there is a simple critical path of arrows and boxes. In complex networks, things might not be so easy as there might be parallel critical paths, or the planner

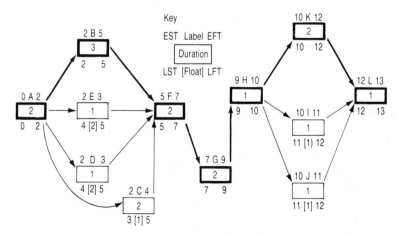

Figure 9.10 The wheel-change network with all critical path calculations illustrated.

might want to highlight a *subcritical path* between activities which share a pretty small float.

Comment — how many numbers should clutter up a network?

The answer to this depends on who is using the network. In our last example, we put on a lot of numbers for teaching purposes. Even more might be added by a planner in his office when he is testing various alternatives. If a network is to be read by a site-worker, though, then all he wants to know is:

Is this activity critical?
If it isn't critical, how much float has it got?

So, if a network is being sent to a site, we would score heavily in the critical path, indicate the floats, but delete ESTs, EFTs, LFTs and LSTs. With the extra space we would give as full description of each activity as possible to supplement the label or abbreviated code.

Comment — how many arrows should clutter up a Gantt chart?

If you transfer too many arrows from a network to a Gantt chart this will certainly confuse a site-worker. We would confine arrows to a few dotted horizontal ones between imposed dates (see Figure 9.12 for an explanation and illustration).

Comment — on labelling algorithms

When doing a forward or backward pass, it was suggested that boxes should be chosen in a certain order, based on the alphabet. We had carefully arranged the labelling of the activity boxes so that you were not stuck for information when doing your calculations. We came to this arrangement by the following process. After assigning the source box as 'A', we continued through the alphabet using this rule:

Only label a box if all boxes leading into it have already been labelled.

This little algorithm is easy to apply if you have a completed network in front of you. Usually, though, you want to put labels on activities as soon as you start doing a first draft of your project network. At this early stage of project planning, it is near impossible to label everything in the correct order. Having given boxes their labels, you might be reluctant to change their labels later. If this is so, when doing a forward or backward pass, you can still survive by employing a *backtracking algorithm*. Work through the network using your inferior alphabetic, etc. order, but:

If you are short of information, move to the box that causes it and work out its EST, etc., then move back.

Backtracking algorithms make critical path calculations a bit more tedious, but that is irrelevant with modern computer power. Moreover, backtracking enables you to take a more relaxed attitude to labelling if many drafts and redesigns of a network are necessary.

Extending the discussion on floats

In the previous network, it was mentioned that each non-critical activity has a float. In that very simple situation, we illustrated what is known as *total float*. In more complex networks, you might find it difficult to schedule an activity, even though it has a big total float because this total float is shared by other non-critical activities. For this reason, it is useful to split total float into *shared* and *independent* floats, as illustrated in Figure 9.11. We use as an example the model answer to the earlier house-completion exercise.

In Figure 9.11, we have erased EFTs and LSTs to avoid clutter. Actually, we only need to refer to ESTs and LFTs when discussing floats below. In the network there are two new concepts:

1. *Independent float* is within square brackets. A simple example is N's float of [5]. This is free from interference from any other non-critical activity.
2. *Shared float* is within round brackets. For example, K and L share a float of (2). If you schedule K as late as possible, it will swallow up L's float. If you schedule L as early as possible, it will swallow up K's float.

Sometimes an activity has a mixture of shared and independent floats: for example, take G's floats. If E is scheduled as late as possible, finishing on day 4, it can knock

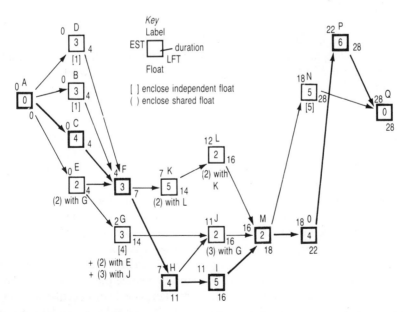

Figure 9.11 Critical path and float calculations for the house-completion problem.

two days off G's potential float. If J is scheduled as early as possible, starting on day 11, it knocks a further three days off G's potential float. There remains an independent float of 4 for G which neither E nor J can affect. For most purposes, it is sufficient to distinguish shared from independent floats: then you can do some quite subtle scheduling on a Gantt chart (see Figure 9.12).

Other float definitions sometimes used are:

1. *Negative float* — how much the duration of an activity *must* be reduced if you have fallen behind schedule.
2. *Free float* — total float minus the biggest shared float with a succeeding activity.

These last two terms are really for network specialists and tend to confuse the general reader. In particular, although 'free' and 'independent' have the same meaning in English, they have, perversely, quite different meanings in the jargon of network analysis.

9.3 Gantt charts and manpower scheduling — example from the house-completion project

Having found a critical path and floats on a precedence network, you still have a fair amount of discretion (for example, in scheduling non-critical activities) before scheduling the activities on a Gantt chart. When doing this, these are some of the most important factors to bear in mind:

1. *Weekends.* A Gantt chart has to allow for breaks in work at weekends, or to specify what jobs are done at weekends attracting overtime rates. It is good to avoid weekend working that involves expensive labour or equipment. Also, if you arrange jobs like painting and plastering to finish on a Friday, the weekend gives extra drying time. Naturally, if there is weekend working, you would expect this to be on critical activities, although there can be exceptions (see K's schedule in the Gantt chart in Figure 9.12).
2. *Flexible and inflexible attitudes to overtime and rescheduling.* Sometimes you have to 'like it or lump it' when calling on the services of a big monopolistic company such as the gas, water and electricity companies. You cannot negotiate with them to work overtime hours, and *they* might tell *you* when they can come, and then an emergency or another customer might delay them. For this reason, activities like B, C and D should be scheduled as early as possible. You can take a different attitude to the people who do the final electrical/plumbing/gas-heating work (L, N and P). These people are usually small subcontractors who are more flexible in their arrangements and, in an emergency, an alternative contractor can be found.
3. *Offering continuity of employment.* If you employ people one day on, one day off, you do not get the best quality of work, or worker. Good workers like some degree of continuity. In the house-completion example, it is a good idea to offer a plastering

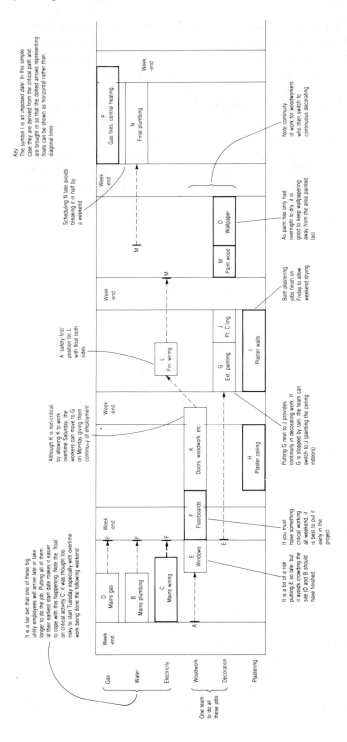

Figure 9.12 Gantt chart for the house completion exercise.

team two weeks' consecutive work. Also, if one team of workers were flexible enough to do all the woodwork and decorating jobs, it would be possible to design a schedule giving them just over three weeks' work consecutively and yet they are never required to work on two activities simultaneously. Figure 9.12 shows how this is done.

4. *Too many cooks* . . . . If there are too many workers on-site at the same time, they could get in each other's way. Subtle scheduling of non-critical activities should aim to minimize overcrowding. For example, if you look at Figure 9.12, E has been scheduled to avoid B and D in the early stages. Overcrowding is more serious, and a bit more difficult to identify, in large, complex projects where *manpower histograms* are useful monitoring devices (as described earlier in the brickwork example).

With all the above points in mind, Figure 9.12 shows a Gantt chart for the house-completion exercise, along with reasons for the precise scheduling of every activity.

9.4 Special techniques for drawing complex networks

If a network and its accompanying Gantt chart are too complicated, they will be ignored by the foreman or whoever else puts their recommendations into practice. In our experience, networks should be limited to fifty (or fewer) activities. If they get bigger than this, then the planner is not making proper use of master networks and work breakdown schedules which we described earlier. If you are forced, though, to draw a big network, here are some hints.

9.4.1 *Labelling*

In large networks, especially computer-based ones, each activity may be labelled in three ways:

1. A full description of what the activity does — perhaps a sentence or more.
2. A shortened description which can be squeezed into a box when the network is drawn.
3. A sequential code (e.g. 01 to 85, or A, B, C) which appears on each box on the network and which is essential to operate the forward and backward passes.

The first two labels are permanent, but the third label, the sequential code, may be changed frequently as new activities are added to the project or old activities are finished or dropped. In most project management software (and databases), relabelling can be performed at a stroke. But if you relabel, you have to beware of old networks and activity lists floating around whose labels conflict with the latest version. This is why we earlier argued for being rather conservative towards relabelling, especially if you can operate the backtracking algorithm for your forward and backward passes.

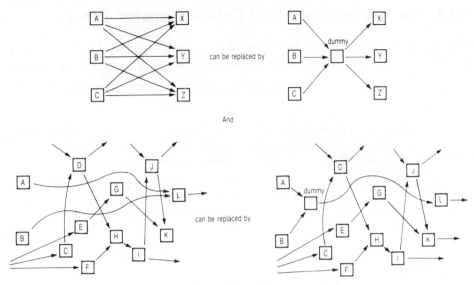

Figure 9.13   Examples of dummy activities.

9.4.2 *Dummy (or relay) activities*

These artificial activities, with zero duration, are introduced to tidy up the drawing of arrows whilst preserving the logic. Two examples are shown in Figure 9.13.

9.4.3 *Black holes*

Sometimes, however you jiggle the boxes around, you get stuck with an arrow which has to snake its way at great length through the network. This can be avoided by having the arrow vanish down a labelled black hole just after it starts, to pop out of another black hole (same label) near its destination. An example is shown in Figure 9.14.

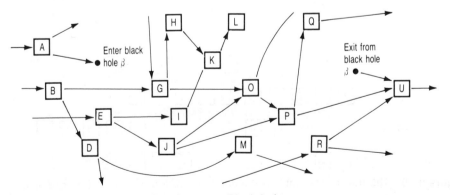

Figure 9.14   Black holes.

9.4.4 *The new biology lab. at Caister Grammar School*

This case study enables you to practise all the techniques described in this chapter. It concerns the conversion of a room into a laboratory using data supplied by the planner.

▼   **Exercise**

(a) Using the recommended layout of activity boxes (see Figure 9.15), and referring to the table of precedence logic (given after the activity descriptions), insert arrows between the boxes to design a precedence network.

> *Hint 1:*   Put your first arrows on in pencil, so that you can erase and improve.
> *Hint 2:*   Remember that you can erase redundant arrows.
> *Hint 3:*   Use black holes to connect M to Y and N to Z.

(b) Carry out a forwards and backwards pass. Determine the critical path and all floats.

(c) Use the calculations on your precedence network to design a Gantt chart where the following extra considerations must be borne in mind:

1.   No more than two plumbers, two joiners, two technicians and one electrician can be employed at any one time.
2.   Try to avoid weekend working and evening overtime.
3.   Avoid giving any team half-a-week's work which does not start on Monday or finish on Friday.

> *Hint 1:*   On your Gantt chart, draw double-depth boxes for those activities that require two men.
> *Hint 2:*   Remember that activities M and N can appear anywhere along their row: they do not have to stick to the left-hand side.
> *Hint 3:*   Break into and extend the critical path if this gives a more efficient manpower schedule. This hint applies particularly to joiners.

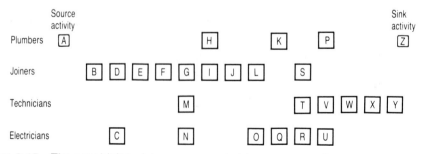

Figure 9.15   The new biology lab: recommended layout to pencil in a precedence network.

Code	Description (workers needed)	Duration (days)
A	The artificial source activity, preceding everything	0
B	Prepare wooden tops for benches and shelves (1 joiner)	2
C	Design and build a switchboard (1 electrician)	5
D	Cut, assemble, Dexion for side benches (2 joiners)	3
E	Cut, assemble, Dexion for shelves (2 joiners)	2
F	Cut, assemble, Dexion for aquaria and sink stands (2 joiners)	2
G	Cut, assemble, Dexion for centre benches (2 joiners)	3
H	Fit aquaria and sink units (2 plumbers)	1
I	Build Dexion ladder over stands (1 joiner)	2
J	Fit wooden top to shelves and benches (2 joiners)	3
K	Fit and connect the water supply (2 plumbers)	2
L	Fit curtain rails and pelmets (2 joiners)	3
M	Procure seawater, filters, accessories for aquaria (1 technician)	2
N	Fit new lights (1 electrician)	3
O	Fit and connect the switchboard (1 electrician)	1
P	Finish aquaria and sink surrounds (2 plumbers)	2
Q	Fit electricity supply to benches (1 electrician)	2
R	Fit electrical connections to aquaria and cages (1 electrician)	2
S	Fit shelves above sink units (2 joiners)	2
T	Paint pelmets (and a wall for a film-screen) (1 technician)	1
U	Connect and test the electricity (1 electrician)	2
V	Fit the curtains (1 technician)	1
W	Move in oven, microscope, filing cabinets (1 technician)	1
X	Move locusts, fruit flies into cages (1 technician)	1
Y	Procure, collect and stock fish, etc. for aquaria (2 technicians)	2
Z	The artificial sink activity, following everything	0

Precedence logic (where '/' means that all activities before the slash must be completed before any activity after the slash can start).

DEF/G	HIJ/K	L/T	U/WXY
FD/H	CJ/O	QR/U	M/Y
G/I	K/PRSX	T/V	A/Everything else
BFGI/J	O/QRU	S/W	Everything else/Z

▲

9.4.5 *Model answer to Caister Grammar School exercise*

First, we show the completed network with all the critical path calculations in Figure 9.16. The we show a model answer Gantt chart in Figure 9.17.

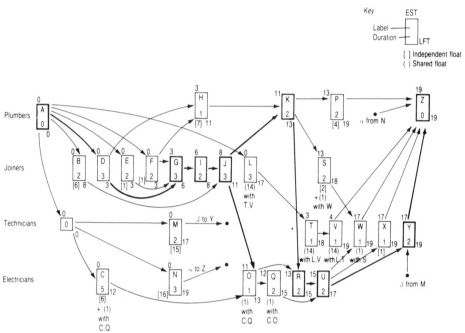

Figure 9.16 The biology lab: precedence network, ESTs, LFTs, critical path and floats.

9.5 Implementation

So far we have dealt with the planning of the project; but planning is only the beginning. Many a seemingly perfect plan has faltered in the implementation stage.

Two British companies joined forces in 1982 to take on a prestigious £25 million contract to build a new zoo in Saudi Arabia. Right at the start, the contractors hit their first problem: the animals. The contract involved demolishing the old zoo before starting work on the new one. However, when the contractors arrived to start work, they found that not only were the buildings and cages still there, but so were the zoo staff and the animals. Obviously there were delays while these hindrances were dealt with.

Water was the next problem. Initially, one supply was required in the contract from

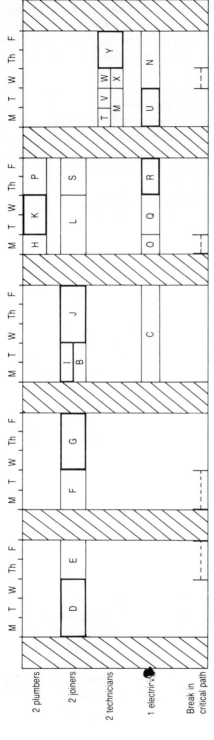

The previous precedence network gives a minimum completion time for this project of 19 days
The Gantt chart schedule takes 33 days. The extra time arises because:
No work is done over weekends (8 days added to minimum schedule)
The critical path is broken at various times during the week to achieve continuity of employment (6 days added to minimum schedule)

Figure 9.17 The biology lab: a Gantt chart schedule with no overtime, no weekend work, no idle time Monday to Friday, and no breaks for a team from the time they are hired until they have finished.

an underground reservoir. This was changed to two supplies, one for drinking and one for irrigation. Because of the risk of animals drinking the impure irrigation water, the client asked for a water-purification plant to be installed. Fifteen months after the start of the project, the client had another change of heart and decided that maybe one supply was best after all.

Changes were then requested to the electricity supply; and so it went on. The problems were compounded by the local company which was supervising the project. It was not in a position to give definite yes or no answers to questions. Such questions had to be referred 'higher up', causing more delays. The project was planned to take two years. Even with a five-month extension and a £2.5 million increase in costs, it was still impossible to meet the deadline. The company decided to cut its losses and pull out, having learnt some valuable lessons.

The chief executive of a large, experienced contracting firm believes that there are two basic secrets to successful project implementation:

1. Finding the right partners.
2. Not being so hungry for work that you go in, full of enthusiasm, to secure a project at all costs.

Even getting this right, companies have found to their cost that you need to 'understand the local mentality' and develop skills in working with local contractors and consultants.

Many contractors do get it right. For example, Esso's £400 million ethylene plant at Mossmorran in Fife, Scotland, was completed five months ahead of schedule and 5 per cent below budget. The contractors put their success down to achieving 20 per cent better productivity than budgeted and the fact that industrial disputes took up only 1.2 per cent of the total man-hours. This is one-third of the level generally experienced on such projects. Industrial relations problems were at the forefront of the contractor's mind before starting on the project, and a site industrial relations manager was appointed well before any earth was moved. Although both unions and management badly needed success after the construction fiascos of the 1970s, particularly involving nuclear power stations, that success had to be planned for. Typical of the planning was the care taken during the rundown period. Workers see redundancy looming and go-slows become familiar. A job information service was set up on-site, which placed some 60 per cent of workers in new jobs.

9.5.1 *Computer packages*

Calculations by hand can be tedious. Many microcomputer and mainframe packages are now available which can produce project plans faster than by hand and do reallocation calculations much faster. Calendars are built into many programs: so weekends and holidays are automatically accounted for in project duration calculations (as in the next case study).

Sophisticated printers allow bar charts to be produced, colour-coded, straight off the computer for easy understanding by groups of workers who just look for their assigned colour. Sophisticated packages are now beginning to change the emphasis of the planning by looking at the people concerned rather than the tasks to be done. This is not important if we are trying to build a house: any competent bricklayer will do, and if one is ill or leaves, the project will not be affected. However, the same cannot be said of skilled professional personnel. A replacement cannot just pick up the threads and carry on from where another person left off. If this were possible, the temporary employment agencies would long since have been in this business.

9.5.1.1 Case study — problems in introducing a new computer system

A retailing organization wanted to upgrade its computer system. Around the United Kingdom, the company had almost a hundred branches. No computer link existed between these branches and head office. All data were sent from the branches to head office in printed form through the post. The company required:

1. A branch system primarily to deal with inventory management, sales-order processing, purchase-order processing and back orders, including a facility to send information between head office and the branches down a telephone line.
2. A new sales ledger system.

Head office was also about to be moved to a new building, so it was decided to undertake both projects — the installation of the computer system and the move — simultaneously.

Several systems were investigated. Alternative hardware and software was considered. One system seemed to satisfy all requirements with minimal modification, except in one respect: branch managers would have to send tapes to head office — the information could not be transmitted down the telephone lines. This option was, therefore, rejected.

During this search, a senior manager happened to be in America. Whilst there, he was shown a software package in operation which seemed to satisfy all his needs. The decision was made to purchase the package and the project was underway. Time estimates were made for various tasks and a project plan was drawn up, using a computer package. This incorporated the move to new premises and the introduction of a new computer system. The plan is shown in Figure 9.18.

All tasks have been abbreviated to fit into the boxes. Some will be meaningful to you and some will not. (But they give you a flavour of large projects.)

The plan was built up from three major separate groups of tasks:

1. The move to new premises.
2. The sales ledger system.
3. The branch system.

You will notice that there is not one single starting point for the network. Jobs 009, 024, 035 and 043 all have an earliest start time of 3.6.1987. This is therefore the start date of the project. However, jobs 012, 018, 025, 026, 027, 028, 029, 030 and 031 have been *allocated* ESTs later than 3.6.1987, although none of these jobs requires

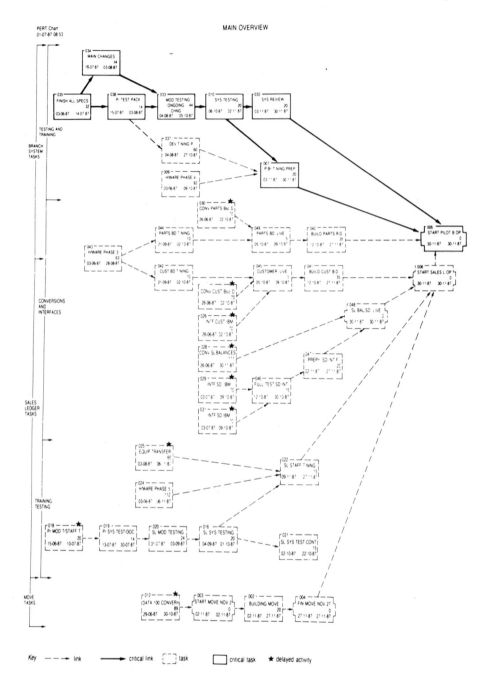

Figure 9.18   Original plan.

the completion of any other job before it can begin. These jobs have been marked with an asterisk and labelled 'delayed' activities in Figure 9.18.

Such jobs have been allocated these later dates using common sense. It did not seem sensible to start on conversion tasks until the project was well under way. Hence jobs 029 and 031, for example, were allocated ESTs of 3.7.1987, one month into the project, although in principle they could have started on 3.6.87. This multiple-start idea is common in large projects.

Work started on the project. The systems team prepared the specifications for the branch software package (task 035) falling one week behind schedule, then sent them to the American software house for the necessary modifications to the package to be made (task 034). Here further problems started. The work started one week late because of the late specifications. The modifications were extensive and the software house had problems tailoring the package. The project fell four weeks behind schedule. Communications flew back and forth over the Atlantic. This meant that the project could not be completed by the scheduled date since these tasks were on the critical path.

It was clear that, although the first revised modules had been received (task 034), there were many other modifications necessary to make the package work successfully for the company. Extra time had to be allowed for this work. Taking into account other problems encountered, particularly on interfacing, the project schedule was extensively revised on 18 September 1987 with a new completion date, some four months later than the original planned date. The revised plan is shown as a bar (Gantt) chart in Figure 9.19.

You will see that total floats and free floats have been shown on the bar (Gantt) chart. These are to tell you how much you can overrun certain tasks and still keep the total project on schedule. Also included are 'milestones'. These are exactly what they say — milestones (or 'deadlines') in the project, e.g.:

004 Finish move
057 Go live with conversion of customer data onto new sales ledger system

Comment

The problems encountered are typical of those in any project. When several subprojects need to be co-ordinated, delay in any one causes delays in completion of the overall project. Over-optimism is a frequent problem in computer systems installations, and buying software from a distant source is generally unadvisable unless you are totally sure it will work on the planned hardware without modification and do exactly what you want it to — a situation almost unheard of in computer systems work.

9.6 Recommended reading

The user's guides to software packages are a good source of information for precedence-network

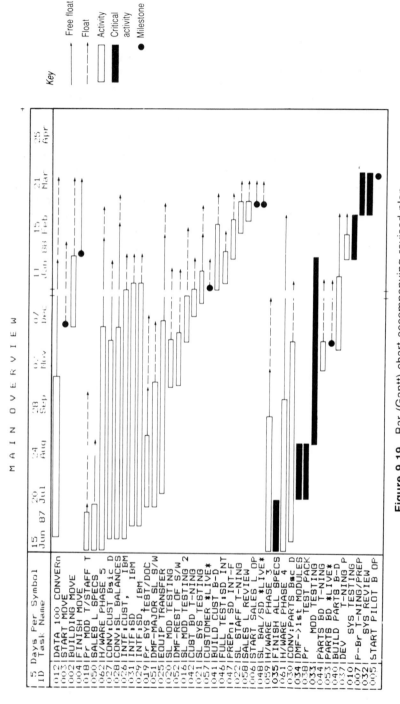

Figure 9.19 Bar (Gantt) chart accompanying revised plan.

methods, but textbooks have been woefully slow at catching up with them. Exceptions are:

Burman, P.J., *Precedence Networks for Project Planning and Control* (McGraw-Hill, 1972). A big, definitive work.

Mulvaney, J.E., *ABC Analysis Bar Charting* (Mantec, 1975). The author who first emphasized that practitioners prefer precedence networks.

Lockyer, K., *Critical Path Analysis*, 4th edn (Pitman, 1984). Thoroughly revamped to incorporate the precedence network approach.

Cases

An easy start is in R. Schmenner, *Production/Operations Management Concepts and Situations*, 4th edn (Macmillan, 1990, pp. 434–45). If you want something as tough as our Caister Grammar School example, try 'Peterson General Contractors' in R.C. Meier, *Cases in Production and Operations Management* (Prentice Hall, 1982). Another difficult, challenging exercise is Sasser *et al.*'s 'Arrow Diagraming Exercise' in *Cases in Operations Management: Analysis and Action* (Irwin, 1982), but use our precedence method, which you should find far less clumsy than their arrow-as-activity technique.

Chapter 10

Scheduling — the nitty gritty

10.1 Introduction

Schedulers take rough-cut plans and put them into practice. In manufacturing, working schedules determine answers to these questions:

What to do?
Who is to do it?
Where to get materials from?
How many to make?
How long will it take?

The same types of question, with one or two substitutions, arise in service industries. 'Materials' (manufacturing) may be people (hospitals), money (financial services) or ideas (education). 'Making' (manufacturing) may be moving (transport), repairing (maintenance) or encoding (communications).

In answering these questions, the scheduler's problem is made more difficult by the dynamic nature of his or her job. That is, 'this week's problem' cannot be treated in isolation. This week's schedule is always squeezed by others, before and after, in both time and place, as shown in Figure 10.1.

There are special problems of *information handling* which make scheduling difficult:

1. Scheduling instructions have to be combined with other documents serving different purposes: for example, inspection or payment records.
2. Schedulers have to calculate and communicate via numbers and writing. But many operatives only really respond to verbal communications and also tend to memorize information rather than file documents.
3. The scheduler rarely gets free access or perfect feedback from the workplace. The schedule may get altered by on-the-spot foremen, or operatives may be careless in filling in a record of work completed.

That is only part of the scheduler's nightmare. He or she also has to meet the following criteria:

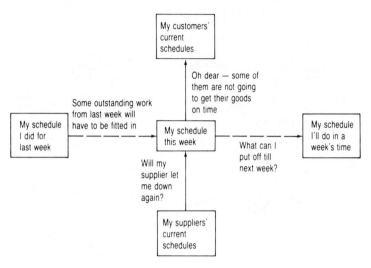

Figure 10.1 The scheduler's problem.

1. *Speed*. He only gets information at the last moment and operatives want instructions *now*.
2. *Size*. His problem can involve hundreds of products, customers or processes and there is rarely a computer program that can provide an optimal or even a feasible solution.
3. *Inter-relatedness*. Whatever solution the scheduler comes up with, it will have knock-on effects on other departments, as well as quality management and personnel, customers and suppliers. Often they will not like his schedule and will try to get it altered.

In all these problems, the scheduler finds that he or she, personally, is dominated by *time*:

When will it come?
Why is it late?

In such circumstances, sophistication is out and the scheduler needs to build error-proof methods into the system (the Japanese *poka-yoke* principle). Any scheduling technique must be *quick, robust, simple* and directed to the scheduler's main concern, *time*. We are going to work through a series of techniques which meet these criteria.

10.2 Route scheduling

One classic area of scheduling is in the routing of delivery vehicles. We have given a general picture of this situation in Chapter 5, section 5.4; now it is time to tackle

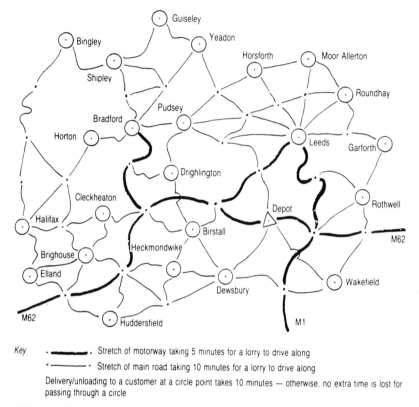

Figure 10.2 Network of trunk roads in the West Yorkshire conurbation.

some specific examples. These are all going to be related to a simplified map of the West Yorkshire conurbation shown in Figure 10.2.

This simplified framework enables you to solve exercises much larger than normally found in textbooks. Also, it serves as an easy introduction to some quite subtle techniques. Without further ado, have a go at the following exercise.

▼   **Exercise 1 — one-man travelling salesman problem (TSP)**

In the map in Figure 10.2, each of the twenty-three circles represents a customer, and the triangle represents a transport depot that services them. Suppose the requirements of all twenty-three customers can be loaded onto one vehicle (i.e. as in a parcels service). Using the timings given in the key to Figure 10.2 above, what is the route that takes the minimum time to set off, deliver to everyone and return to the depot? (*Hint:* 9½ hours would be
▲   quite a good result.) Try to get an answer before reading the next section.

A structured technique for tackling exercise 1

Figure 10.3 shows a doctored map which makes it easier to discover a good solution. These were the stages used to get from the original to this doctored map:

1. Pay particular attention to all customer-connections that are equal to or less than a certain time that you specify. Score these connections in with double lines and call them *prime connections*. In our example, we have used ten minutes as the prime connecting time.
2. With reference solely to double-line links, identify *clusters* and *strings* (with end connectors). The definitions of these terms should be self-explanatory if you look at Figure 10.3. An *isolate* is any *circle* not on a double-line string.
3. Eliminate all roads which are not on the shortest route between any end connector, cluster member or isolate. Sometimes there is an obvious link-up between strings (as in the north and east of our map). In this case, you can confine yourself to an end connector's nearest links, and further eliminations can be made. But be

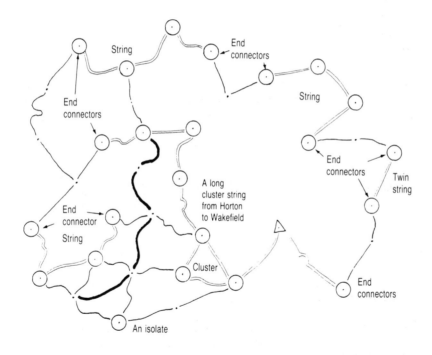

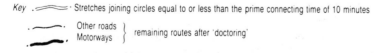

Figure 10.3 Simplified map for parcel delivery type problems.

sure you maintain all shortest links between other *end connectors*, *isolates* and *cluster members* (i.e. those of the map's labels in italics).

4. You are now in a much better position to find a good solution to the TSP. The worth of this method depends on the judgemental skill in choosing the prime connecting time at stage 1. If it is set too high, you will get too many 'double links'. If it is set too low, you will get too many 'isolates'. In either case, the task of finding a good solution is harder.

Answer to exercise 1

This is the best anti-clockwise route (arrival times are bracketed in minutes after starting):

Wakefield (10), Rothwell (40), Garforth (60), Leeds (90), Roundhay (110), Moor Allerton (130), Horsforth (150), Yeadon (180), Guiseley (200), Shipley (220), Bingley (240), Bradford (280), Horton (300), Halifax (330), Elland (350), Brighouse (370), Cleckheaton (390), Pudsey (430), Drighlington (450), Birstall (470), Heckmondwike (490), Huddersfield (520), Dewsbury (550), Depot (570).

▼   ### Exercise 2 — two-man TSP

Suppose that the requirements of the twenty-three customers cannot be fitted into one vehicle so that a second vehicle has to be used. The weights of the orders are such that no more than twelve customer orders must be taken by any one vehicle. Can you find a schedule so that both lorries complete their
▲   deliveries and return to the depot in five hours or less?

A structured technique for tackling exercise 2

Using a doctored map from exercise 1 helps, but apart from that you are on your own. In our experience, pencil and rubber are just as effective tools as the latest route-planning computer software. Just out of interest, we give the optimal solution (which was found quickly by hand).

Answer to exercise 2

Lorry A: Dewsbury, Huddersfield, Heckmondwike, Birstall, Drighlington, Pudsey, Bradford, Horton, Halifax, Elland, Brighouse, Cleckheaton, Depot.
(290 minutes)   ▷

Lorry B: Wakefield, Rothwell, Garforth, Leeds, Roundhay, Moor Allerton, Horsforth, Yeadon, Guiseley, Shipley, Bingley, Depot. (300 minutes)

▼   **Exercise 3 — the many-vehicle bulk delivery problem**

Use the same travel times as in exercises 1 and 2, but instead of a parcels-type service we are now concerned with the delivery of a bulk commodity like oil, sand or cement. Now, *each* of the twenty-three customers wants a full lorry load of this commodity delivered. If you start the day with four lorries, fully loaded, how can they be scheduled to make their drops, come back for reloading and go out again, etc. so that all twenty-three customers have received their orders and the lorries are back at the depot? Two extra constraints are:

1. Reloading a lorry at the depot takes ten minutes.
2. Only one lorry can be reloaded at a time.

▲   (*Hint:* If you read on, you will see how the optimal answer of 7 hours was found, but any answer under $7\frac{1}{2}$ hours would be pretty good.)

A structured approach to exercise 3

1. In this problem there is no need to consider 'between customer' routes as drivers spend all their time going either from depot to a customer or from customer back to depot. So work out shortest distance from depot to each customer and eliminate every other route not used.
2. For each customer, calculate the time for an out-and-back trip, including the ten-minute unloading at the customer and the ten-minute loading at the depot. These round-trip times are put above each customer circle in Figure 10.4.
3. Add up all the out-and-back times (= 1720). Divide by four to get 430 minutes which, if you can give it to each lorry, is the most even result.

    Group customers under each lorry so the out-and-back timings sum to 430 as, for example, in Table 10.1. On the final return to the depot there is no need to include the ten-minute 'loading time for next customer', so all drivers can finish by 420 minutes rather than 430.
4. Whilst the lorries are ferrying backwards and forwards between customers, you have to ensure that the depot is not asked to load two lorries at the same time. If lorries make deliveries in the order listed above, you can work out the time when a lorry leaves the depot (just after being loaded) by accumulating the individual route times. By inspecting these times you can see that there will be no overlap during loading at the depot, and a good schedule has been found.

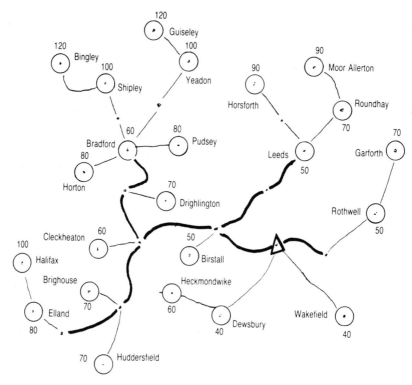

Figure 10.4 Simplified map for bulk-delivery type problems.

Table 10.1 Answer to exercise 3 — out-and-back timings (minutes)

Lorry A		Lorry B		Lorry C		Lorry D	
1. Moor A	90	1. Shipley	100	1. Elland	80	1. Guiseley	120
2. Wakefield	40	2. Dewsbury	40	2. Huddersfield	70	2. Bradford	60
3. Halifax	100	3. Birstall	50	3. Brighouse	70	3. Dewsbury	70
4. Pudsey	80	4. Leeds	50	4. Cleckheaton	60	4. Rothwell	50
5. Bingley	120	5. Horsforth	90	5. Roundhay	70	5. Garforth	70
		6. Yeadon	100	6. Horton	80	6. Heckmondwike	60
	430		430		430		430

Table 10.2 Answer to exercise 3 — departure times after completing a drop and being reloaded (minutes after start)

Lorry A		Lorry B		Lorry C		Lorry D	
1. Moor A	90	1. Shipley	100	1. Elland	80	1. Guiseley	120
2. Wakefield	130	2. Dewsbury	140	2. Huddersfield	150	2. Bradford	180
3. Halifax	230	3. Birstall	190	3. Brighouse	220	3. Dewsbury	250
4. Pudsey	310	4. Leeds	240	4. Cleckheaton	280	4. Rothwell	300
5. Bingley	(Finish)	5. Horsforth	330	5. Roundhay	350	5. Garforth	370
		6. Yeadon	(Finish)	6. Horton	(Finish)	6. Heckmondwike	(Finish)

▼   **Extension to exercise 1**

(a) If you could omit deliveries to three of your twenty-three customers, what route between any remaining twenty would minimize time on a complete circuit of deliveries?

(b) What is the circuit that can cover the maximum number of deliveries in under two hours? Under three hours? (*Hint:* You can cover ten and thirteen
▲   deliveries for these two cases.)

▼   **Extension to exercise 2 — depot location**

(a) In exercise 2, from the existing depot it is just possible for two lorries to cover all customers and return to base in five hours. Is there another motorway junction that would be a better site for a depot, in the sense that two lorries could cover all customers in less than five hours?

(b) If instead of the existing depot you could locate two depots at different junction points, with one vehicle operating from each, where would these depots be to minimize total circuit time? (Only use junction points which are
▲   not within customer circles for depots.)

▼   **Extension to exercise 3 — multiple vehicle utilization***

Suppose, instead of four lorries only three were available to make full drops to all your twenty-three customers. What is the minimum time in which all the
▲   work could now be done?

10.2.1 *General comments on route scheduling*

These route scheduling exercises are only part of the larger problem of transport scheduling (discussed earlier in the book). There are scheduling problems of equal complexity in transport which we can only mention in passing:

Balancing loads (see the 'bundling' section of this chapter)
Handling customer priorities
When to use subcontractors
Taking on return loads

A numerical exercise which took all these factors into account would require a whole

---

*This exercise acts as a bridge between the individual machine analysis of Chapter 3 and the overall capacity analysis of a haulier described in Chapter 11.

book to itself. In general, the mathematical nature of these problems is such that *decisions* are best made by human skill and judgement, reserving computers to provide the *decision-support system* (listing and filing data, and doing the 'what if?' calculations for alternative solutions proposed by humans). Now that we have touched on the stresses and complexity facing the transport scheduler, you should be in a better position to appreciate the Harry Britton case.

10.3 Inventory scheduling 1 — reorder quantity/ reorder level stocking policies (ROQ/ROL)

10.3.1 *From simple to advanced ROQ/ROL scheduling methods*

ROQ/ROL is inventory control with minimum human intervention. Once management has set rules about when to reorder and how much, the system pretty well runs itself. It has developed from the *two-bin* or *place-card* method of inventory control, i.e. the method where, if you drew stock from the top of a box downwards, at a certain point near the bottom you would find a reply-paid card from your supplier saying 'Stocks are running low. Post this off to us today and we will send you another box.' In its more sophisticated form, big retailers have bar coded all their items. Every time an item is sold, a message is sent to a central computer which keeps a running total of how many items the store has left. When the running total drops below a certain level, alarm bells in the computer cause it to send off an automatic message to a central warehouse or a manufacturer saying 'Make another delivery of so much of this item to this store.' *If* subtle rules can be fed into the computer, much clerical effort can be saved.

However, great care is needed in designing even the simplest automatic system. As a minimum requirement, an ROQ/ROL system should be able to cope with:

1. Variable demand.
2. Variable lead times.
3. Handling stockouts.
4. Uncertainty about future orders.

Figures 10.5, 10.6 and 10.7 demonstrate how to handle these situations.

Explanation of the ROQ/ROL tables

The table in Figure 10.5 is mostly blank. It shows all the information coming into the system from outside (i.e. demand, lead time and first period's opening stock). After you have made up rules about ROL (when to reorder) and ROQ (how much to reorder), every remaining number in the table can be filled in, from period 1 to period 20. Then you can evaluate your solution to see how good it is.

Using simple rules, a filled-in schedule is illustrated in Figure 10.6. We now give

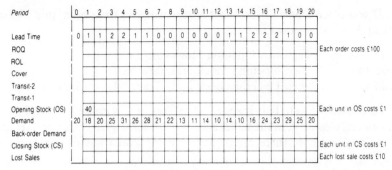

Figure 10.5 ROQ/ROL table.

Period	0	1	2	3	4	5	6	7	8	9	10	11	12	13	14	15	16	17	18	19	20	
Lead Time	0	1	1	2	2	1	1	0	0	0	0	0	0	1	1	2	2	2	1	0	0	
ROQ = 30		30	30		30	30	30	30			30		30			30	30		30			11 orders @ £100 = £1,100
ROL = 60		60	60	60	60	60	60	60	60	60	60	60	60	60	60	60	60	X	X	X		
Cover		40*	52*	62	37*	6*	60*	60*	99	77	64	53*	69	59*	75	65	49*	55*	X	x	x	
Transit-2						30											30	30				
Transit-1			30	30			60	30						30				30	30			
Opening Stock		40	22	32	37	6	0	60	99	77	64	53	69	59	45	65	49	25	2	30	60	894 units @ £1 = £894
Demand	20	18	20	25	31	26	28	21	22	13	11	14	10	14	10	16	24	23	29	25	20	
B/O Demand						10													13			
Closing Stock		22	2	7	6	0	0	39	77	64	53	39	59	45	35	49	25	2	0	0	40	564 units @ £1 = £564
Lost Sales						10	38												14	8		70 units @ £10 = £700

Total stock-associated costs = £3,258

Figure 10.6 Simple ROQ/ROL worked example.

a detailed explanation of what each row in our ROQ/ROL table means, and how numbers in it are calculated.

Lead time tells you how long you have to wait before an order is delivered. In the completed tables, the link lines show how 'goods on their way' shift from period to period according to the lead time. A lead time of 0 means goods ordered at the end of (say) period 7 are delivered at the beginning of period 8. A lead time of 1 means that goods ordered at the end of (say) period 7 and delivered at the beginning of period 9, etc.

Although we have set out all the lead times from period 0 to 20 for completeness, the ROQ/ROL calculations only know and use the current lead time (i.e. when you do the calculations you should not cheat by looking at lead times that apply in the future).

ROQ is the reorder quantity. You specify what this shall be. It might be the same number throughout (e.g. 30 in Figure 10.6) or it could vary according to the latest information you have on demand and capacity (as in a more complicated illustration later, or via the EOQ formula of the next section).

Cover. If you place a new order, what stocks will you have been able to draw on the moment *before* that new order arrives?

If lead time = 0, then just Opening Stock
If lead time = 1, then Opening Stock and (Transit-1)
If lead time = 2, then Opening Stock and (Transit-1) + (Transit-2)

ROL is the reorder level. This is specified by you. If it is greater or equal to Cover, an alarm bell rings (asterisk in the table) and you reorder. Again, it can be a set number (e.g. 60 in Figure 10.6) or there can be a more complicated way of calculating it (see later).

The alarm bell is suspended from periods 18 onwards, and you choose orders of any size so that your closing stock is 40 at period 20 (i.e. you end the exercise with the stock you started with). To remind you that the normal ROQ/ROL rules are suspended, crosses are put in the ROL and Cover rows from period 18 onwards.

Transit-2. When there is a lead time of 2 this is where an ROQ goes to in the period after it is ordered (see wavy lines in the worked tables). After another period passes (Transit-2) becomes (Transit-1).

Transit-1. When there is a lead time of 1 this is where ROQ goes to in the period after it is ordered (again see the wavy lines). After another period passes (Transit-1) is added to Opening Stock.

Opening Stock. This is a summation of those items from the previous period:

Closing Stock + (Transit-1) + (ROQ where lead time = 0)

Demand. This has been generated externally. Although, for ease of presentation, we have printed demand figures right up to period 20, the ROQ/ROL calculation cannot take advantage of this future knowledge. The calculations must work only from knowledge of past and current demand.

Closing Stock. This is zero if Demand exceeds Opening Stock. Otherwise it is: (Opening Stock − Demand − B/O Demand), where B/O Demand is back-order demand. Closing Stock is added to next period's Opening Stock.

B/O Demand (back-order demand) and Lost Sales. If Demand is greater than Opening Stock, you have a stockout. Customers will either go to someone else or come back next period. Depending on the industry and the reputation of the firm, there could be various depletion rates for customers who are unsatisfied. If an ice cream seller runs out, few will wait; if a transplant surgeon is short of organs, those patients that survive will wait. We have used a special rule in our example which may well need to be changed for other situations: 'If you had a stockout in the previous period as well, you can assume all your customers will go to another supplier. In this situation all your stockout is put in the Lost Sales row. If you did not have a stockout in the last period, some customers will wait and some will go elsewhere. Assume half of the stockout is put into Lost Sales and half into next period's B/O Demand.'

Figure 10.6 shows a completed numerical example. Starting with an opening stock of forty in period 1, it was possible to work through the table, period by period, calculating everything else.

Figure 10.7 (overleaf) shows a more sophisticated way of calculating ROQ and ROL. Because Figure 10.7 used more sophisticated rules for calculating ROQ and ROL, total stock costs are substantially lower than in Figure 10.6.

▼   **Exercise**

Can you find an answer which is even better than that shown in Figure 10.7, but still finishing with a closing stock of 40 in period 20?

Hints: The efficiency of your answer depends on how you calculate F, ROQ and ROL. You will not find much improvement, however much effort and intelligence you put into forecasting F.* How you calculate the other variables does make a critical difference (see the notes to Figure 10.7). If you want suggestions, these formulae give good results:

▲
$$ROQ = 10\sqrt{F}$$
$$ROL = 25L$$

10.3.2 *ROQ/ROL — additional comments*

There has been a growing interest in ROQ/ROL approaches because:

1. They fit in well with such technical developments as electronic data interchange (for automatic systems) and interactive spreadsheets (for planning and simulation).
2. They focus on measurements and definitions which tie in closely with just-in-time (JIT) approaches.

It is interesting to trace the history of a firm's approach to ROQ/ROL and to see how greater control imposed on some parameters has led to helpful changes in other parts of the system. In particular, a JIT system imposes tighter discipline in some areas (changing *constraints* to CONSTRAINTS):

*   Smaller, more frequent ROQs.
*   More advanced warning of customers' demand.
*   Insisting that suppliers cut their lead times.

This has meant that less worry is needed in other parts of the system (changing CONSTRAINTS into *constraints*):

*   No special emergency system needed for stockouts.
*   No reserve warehouse needed for buffer stocks.
*   No great variation needed in transport vehicles now that deliveries are standardized.

---

*Reasons for this were given in the section on Monte Cristo Forecasting in Chapter 8.

	0	1	2	3	4	5	6	7	8	9	10	11	12	13	14	15	16	17	18	19	20	
*Let Forecast (F) = Previous Demand		20	18	20	25	31	26	28	21	22	13	0	0	14	10	14	10	16	24	23	29	25	
Lead Time (L)	0	1	1	2	2	1	1	0	0	0	0	0	0	1	1	2	2	2	1	0	0	
*ROQ (see Note below)		40		60	25	0			10	20		5	20	20	15	15	35	50	35	35	60	12 orders @ £100 = £1,200
*Let ROL = F × (L + 1)	60	80	100	77*	60	93	78	56	42	44	26	22	28	30	42	40	64	96	X	X	X	
Cover	40*	62	42*	77*	60	85	57	36*	24*	31	20*	11*	21*	27*	35*	33*	50*	50*	X	X	X	
Transit-2				60	25										20	15	15	35	50			
Transit-1		40			60	25	60	57	24	31		21	11	20		15		18	0	15	35	536 @ £1 = £ 536
Opening Stock	20	40	22	42	17	0	60	57	36	24	31	20	11	21	7	20	18	0	15	35	60	
Demand		18	20	25	31	26	28	21	22	13	11	14	10	14	10	16	24	23	29	25	20	
B/O Demand						7									1	1		3				
Closing Stock (CS)	22	17	17	0	0	0	32	36	14	20	6	1	7	0	0	3	0	0	0	10	40	221 @ £1 = £ 221
Lost Sales		7			7	33									2		3	26	14			85 @ £10 = £ 850

Total stock-associated costs = £2807

* F is only slightly more sophisticated as 'Last Period's Actual'. See Chapter 8 for other ways of forecasting.
* ROQ: Suppose that because of delivery constraints, the precise roq has to be rounded up to a ROQ that is the next multiple of 5.
   Then, if lead time has stayed unchanged, let roq = ROL − Cover.
   Add F to this figure if lead time has just increased. Subtract F from this figure if lead time has just decreased.
   See the EOQ section for a better way of calculation ROQ.
* ROL: This again is a very simple rule-of-thumb elaboration. We are sure you can do better than this.

Figure 10.7 More advanced ROQ/ROL example. The asterisk shows where a procedure has become more sophisticated.

10.4 Inventory scheduling 2 — economic order quantity (EOQ)

Under certain restrictive assumptions it is possible to solve inventory problems by calculus. The commonest example is the EOQ formula in purchasing (economic order quantity). This has the same format as the EBQ formula in manufacturing (economic batch quantity):

$$\text{EOQ (or EBQ)} = \sqrt{\frac{2FD}{H}}$$

where F is fixed ordering or set-up cost independent of batch size, D is constant demand-rate per period, and H is holding cost per item per period.

Many texts explain the quite elementary derivation of this formula in great detail. We are not going to do this because we are going to argue later that EOQ should be abandoned or reformulated. However, here are some brief examples of EOQ being applied. As you read them, think about whether the application makes sense.

10.4.1 *Example 1 — a chip shop*

A busy chip shop has a steady demand for three packets of chips per minute. When chips have been cooked, there is a holding cost of 0.5p per minute per packet. When a batch is made, certain heating and oil costs are incurred, independent of the size of the batch. These costs come to 75p.

$$\text{EBQ} = \sqrt{\frac{2 \times 75 \times 3}{0.5}} = 30 \text{ packets of chips}$$

Critique of example 1

Managing a chip shop is not that easy, and critical decisions have to be made in the following areas:

1. How many counter staff to employ?
2. What are the best hours of opening?
3. Can some food preparation be done in advance?
4. How closely can demand be anticipated?
5. How can operations be speeded up when a queue lengthens?
6. What is an attractive selection of fish and other foods that can be offered with chips?

All of these decisions will swamp and distort the decision, 'What batch size of chips to make?' Quite apart from that, the data on chips given in example 1 are unlikely to be accurate for the following reasons:

1. Have you ever known a chip shop with steady demand?

2. There is mention of a holding cost of 0.5p per packet per minute. This can't be the heating cost as this will be independent of chips stored. It could refer to the loss of goodwill if overcooked chips are sold, but in practice this would be hard to estimate.

10.4.2 *Example 2 — a chicken farm supply problem*

A chicken farmer needs to purchase 200 kg of millet per month. He is some distance from the nearest grain store and the cost of driving there and picking up a bag of millet is £20 irrespective of the size of the load. When the millet is stored on the farmer's premises, damp and vermin cause it to deteriorate at a rate equivalent to 5p/kg per month.

$$EOQ = \sqrt{\frac{2 \times 20 \times 200}{0.05}} = 400 \text{ kg of millet}$$

Critique of example 2

People who live in isolated rural areas do have to order large batches and expect fewer deliveries or collections, and the general principles of EOQ can act as a useful guideline. The simplest situation is where the batch delivered is so large that there is no space for any other goods on the delivery vehicle (e.g. the bulk delivery situation of the route scheduling section). In this case it is fairly easy to put breakpoints into EOQ analysis and see whether 1, 2, 3, etc. whole loads should be delivered. Where the item to be delivered does not take up the whole of the vehicle (as with the millet in our example), the farmer may take the opportunity to pick up other small loads. This too can be incorporated into EOQ analysis.

10.4.3 *Example 3 — a car showroom*

A car showroom sells three new cars per week. To place an order for a new batch of cars to be delivered costs £30. There is a holding cost of £5 per week for any unsold cars kept in the showroom, made up of insurance, security costs, upkeep and obsolescence:

$$EOQ = \sqrt{\frac{2 \times 30 \times 3}{5}} = 6 \text{ cars}$$

Critique of example 3

We found that the firm should order from the manufacturers a batch of six cars to be delivered over two weeks. Suppose each car costs £10,000 and sells for £11,000. If the buying and selling costs are paid on delivery, the cash-flow situation of the firm would be as shown in Table 10.3.

Table 10.3 Cash-flow situation of car showroom (£)

	0	2	4	6	8	10	12	14 etc.
				Days (excluding Sundays)				
Purchase	−60,000						−60,000	etc.
Sales		+11,000	+11,000	+11,000	+11,000	+11,000	+11,000	
Order costs	−30						−30	
Holding costs	−30			−15			−30	

In this case, as in many others, especially high-volume wholesaling and retailing businesses, the purchase/sales cash flows completely swamp the costs that EOQ focuses on. In such circumstances it is better to set out cash flows per period, as above, and analyse via a DCF (discounted cash flow) approach. This can cover many variants difficult to incorporate in EOQ, in particular those associated with varying lags between deliveries in payment.

In general, the (more correct) DCF approach recommends significantly smaller optimal-batch sizes than the more widely known crude EOQ approaches. The difference becomes more noticeable the higher the interest rate. As many businesses have to operate with high costs of capital, often in excess of 20 per cent p.a., this is an important factor to bear in mind when devising an optimal-batch policy.

10.4.4 *Further discussion on economic batch/order quantity*

EBQ/EOQ is probably the most durable and popular formula found in management textbooks and for that reason alone deserves some attention. If the practitioner wishes to make use of it, he should expect difficulties in deriving accurate parameters, and he should beware applying it to the wrong problem. If he does go ahead, he should keep in mind that EBQ/EOQ is rather simplistic in assuming:

- Stable demand.
- A decision about one product is made independently of others.
- That the 'fixed order' and 'variable holding' costs are the dominant costs for batch decisions and that these costs can be estimated accurately.
- That choice is made over a continuum of alternatives.
- That there are no leads and lags between decisions, deliveries and payments.
- That minimizing cost is equivalent to maximizing profit.
- That there are no financial or physical constraints to the solution proposed.
- That it is important to find a point-answer rather than a fuzzier range or approximate answer.

It is difficult to find a situation where all these conditions hold. To a certain extent, expressions and variables can be added to the basic EOQ equation and an answer still found via calculus. This has been done where:

1. There is a period of time over which a manufactured batch is built up.
2. The fixed batch or order cost applies to more than one product, each with their own demand rates and holding costs.
3. There are various penalties for running out of stock before a new batch is made.

We will not dwell on these models because there are growing doubts about whether they are pointing inventory managers in the right direction. One reason is the dubious way in which costs are assembled for EOQ models. Another reason is that, using the same information, there is a better way of laying out and analysing these sorts of problems.

Nevertheless, EBQ/EOQ does highlight a general point of some importance: the operating consequences of having some cash flows which vary according to throughput and some which are fixed whatever the size of the 'batch'. This is a critical feature of business in such widespread applications as the following:

- *Personal activities.* How frequently should I wash up, cut the lawn, go to the bank? What stocks should I get of milk, baked beans or toilet rolls?
- *Leisure management.* What is the best size of concert hall, ice rink, football ground or swimming pool?
- *Transport.* What is the best size of fishing boat, super-tanker, container lorry, airliner, train or ferry?

▼   **Exercise**

Consider the potential EBQ/EOQ applications mentioned under 'personal activities' in the list above:

(a) How far can you go towards finding accurate values for the parameters F, D and H? (Take particular care over H, making sure it is a cost per item per period.)

(b) What is the recommended EBQ/EOQ?

▲ (c) Is the result a useful guideline to you? Why or why not?

10.5 Work cycles

10.5.1 *Machine interference*

In the previous sections we have explored how set-up considerations influence scheduling, and particularly how set-up costs affect batching policy. Set-up situations have another major effect on scheduling: how to co-ordinate the activities of the workers responsible for set-ups. In the past, where machine set-ups were the responsibility of workers in a strong craft union, effective scheduling was limited by the threat of demarcation disputes, but now it is becoming rarer to find a worker setting up a machine, then twiddling his thumbs whilst the machine runs automatically. More often he is expected to accept flexible assignments or to be responsible for a group of machines (the Japanese *nagara* approach). If the latter is the case, good scheduling aims to phase operations so that no two machines need to be set up at the same time.

One industrial example is where one man tends two (or sometimes more) injection moulding machines in a plastics factory. Take the simplest case where an operator is switching his attention between two machines: one machine making product A, the other machine product B. The products have these characteristics:

	Time in minutes	
	A	*B*
Loading time when the man is needed at the machine	2	1
Running time when the machine works automatically	3	3

Figure 10.8 shows two schedules that the man can follow, and you should use this as a guide in the exercise below.

▼   **Exercise — machine interference**

Refer to Table 10.4 and choose any combination of two products A, B, C, D, E, F (but do not take A and B which we have just done).

Design a priority schedule, first for one of these products, then for the other. Use the same layout and symbols as in the worked example of Figure 10.8. Also work out production rates per hour for the two products and idle time per hour for the man and the two machines.

Hint: The exercise is fairly straightforward if you start by ensuring 100 per cent loading for the product with priority. Then fit in the other product as best you can. When both products have been scheduled, can you identify a regular repeating pattern? (See the worked example where this regular pattern or *operating cycle* is marked between heavy black lines.) If you find the operating cycle, it is quite a simple matter to find production rates and

▲   idle time per hour.

Table 10.4 Machine set-up and running times (minutes)

	Products					
	A	B	C	D	E	F
Loading time when the man is needed at the machine	2	1	2	2	1	3
Running time when the machine works automatically	3	3	4	6	5	3

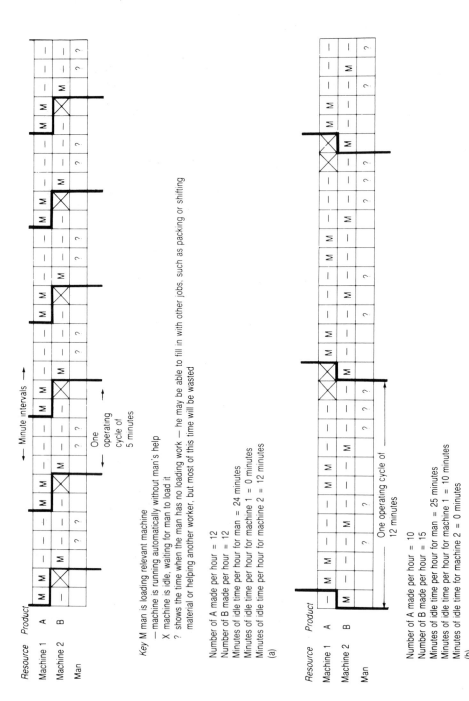

Key M man is loading relevant machine
  — machine is running automatically without man's help
  X machine is idle, waiting for man to load it
  ? shows the time when the man has no loading work — he may be able to fill in with other jobs, such as packing or shifting
      material or helping another worker, but most of this time will be wasted

Number of A made per hour = 12
Number of B made per hour = 12
Minutes of idle time per hour for man = 24 minutes
Minutes of idle time per hour for machine 1 = 0 minutes
Minutes of idle time per hour for machine 2 = 12 minutes
(a)

Number of A made per hour = 10
Number of B made per hour = 15
Minutes of idle time per hour for man = 25 minutes
Minutes of idle time per hour for machine 1 = 10 minutes
Minutes of idle time for machine 2 = 0 minutes
(b)

Figure 10.8 Machine interference and operating cycles. (a) Schedule giving priority to product A. (b) Schedule giving priority to product B.

▼   **More difficult, optional exercise**

Using the information from the previous exercise, suppose instead of one
man choosing two of six products to run on two machines, you have three
men (each man in charge of two machines). Each man is given two of the six
products, A to F.

How would you allocate the products so that you get high production rates

▲   for all six products?

▼   **Even more difficult exercise for scheduling whizz-kids**

Use the same information as before. Now you have two men (each in charge
of three machines). Can you allocate the six products, three to each man, so
that pretty good production rates are maintained?

Hint: For this last exercise, decide on a priority order for your three
products (e.g. D, B, F). Schedule D first, giving it 100 per cent loading.
Schedule B next, as best you can. Lastly, fit F into any remaining gaps.
Sometimes you will find that when you get to F it is impossible to make any
schedule for it at all. If so, that suggests that your D, B, F priority was a
pretty bad one, so try another order (say, F, D, B).

Further hint: There is no mathematical method for finding the 'best' answer
to these problems. However, using a spreadsheet enables you to generate

▲   many answers quickly — from which you can make a best choice.

10.5.2 *Major set-ups and run lengths*

So far, we have investigated how to co-ordinate machines to avoid simultaneous loading,
each loading taking only a few minutes. A more substantial delay to production occurs
when a product is first assigned to a machine. Often, special jigs, dies or moulds have
to be installed or the machine might have to be partially stripped and reassembled.
This *set-up time* can take hours. With such a delay, once a product is on a machine
it is good for it to stay there until a complete customer order is met.

Consider this problem. Eight products have the loading and automatic running times
shown in Table 10.5.

Using our previous analysis, we could match each product against every other product
to see the production rates for any pairing (see Figure 10.9). These production rates
per hour provide a source of quick numerical estimates for the problem that follows.

Suppose you have to meet these rush orders for customer requirements.

A	B	C	D	E	F	G	H
60	60	100	60	60	120	120	120

Table 10.5 Machine set-up and running times (minutes)

	Products							
	A	B	C	D	E	F	G	H
Loading times	2	1	2	2	1	3	1	2
Automatic running	3	3	4	6	5	3	4	2

If these are the rates for the first-priority products ↓

Then these are the rates possible for second-priority product ↓

Second-priority products

First-priority products:

			Second-priority products							
			A	B	C	D	E	F	G	H
A	12	A		12	8	6	9	6	12	12
B	15	B	10		7.5	7.5	10	7.5	11.3	15
C	10	C	10	10		6.7	10	10	10	10
D	7.5	D	7.5	15	7.5		7.5	7.5	11.3	15
E	10	E	10	15	10	6.7		10	10	10
F	10	F	10	10	10	5	10		10	10
G	12	G	12	12	9	6	9.6	8		12
H	15	H	7.5	15	7.5	7.5	7.5	0	10	

(First-priority products label in the first grid)

Figure 10.9 Production rates pairing products for priority.

Two operators each have a pair of machines to help meet this order. When each product is put on a machine there is a two-hour delay whilst the machine is set up. A third man, a skilled craftsman, has to do this. As he is the only person available, two machines cannot be set up simultaneously. Figure 10.10 shows an answer that takes 28 hours.

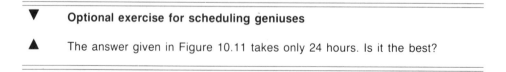

▼ **Optional exercise for scheduling geniuses**

▲ The answer given in Figure 10.11 takes only 24 hours. Is it the best?

10.5.3 *Work cycles — discussion and extensions*

This is a classic area where people can attack constraints rather than optimize within them. Rather than taking the set-up as a CONSTRAINT, suppose extra resources and intelligence are applied to reduce this time. We all know the time difference between

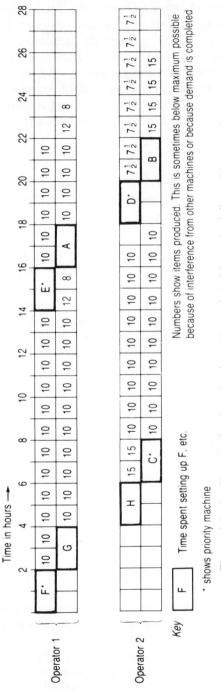

Time in hours →

Key: $\boxed{F}$ Time spent setting up F. etc.

* shows priority machine

Figure 10.10 Illustrated sub-optimal answer to 'machine-scheduling with set-up' problems.

Numbers show items produced. This is sometimes below maximum possible because of interference from other machines or because demand is completed

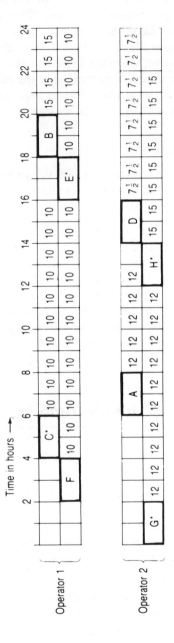

Time in hours →

Figure 10.11 Optional exercise for scheduling geniuses. Best answer?

unscrewing a car wheel-nut manually and using a power tool to remove it in seconds. In the West, we have shown how far this approach can succeed for rapid wheel-changes at motor-racing pit-stops. What we do in our leisure pursuits, the Japanese do in manufacturing, especially via the single-minute exchange of dies (SMED) initiated by Shigeo Shingo at Toyota. Now that set-up times are being reduced in a widespread fashion, there are more situations where a worker (or a small team of workers) is servicing a large number of machines which, most of the time are running automatically. Incidentally, this changes the status of the worker from a semi-skilled routine operator to a skilled maintenance man and innovator.

Illustration

The interaction between the set-ups and automatic running of machines is a common problem in the food industry. Figure 10.12 shows a small part of a schedule for a manufacturer of frozen desserts. Note two things:

1. Each activity distinguishes between where staff attention is needed (shaded) and where the operation is automatic. This helps with the most detailed aspect of manpower scheduling — the actual assignment of workers to jobs on the shopfloor.
2. In the schedule, the activities appear in a similar format to activities in Chapter 9 on project planning — in fact, here they have all been set to a latest finish time. This ensures that there is no break in processing as it would be bad practice to have semi-finished food hanging around. Where it is desirable to have continuous production like this, we are getting very close to a major characteristic of JIT scheduling: soon to be explained in detail.

10.6 Just-in-time scheduling

In the manufacture of cutlery, all spoons and forks are made via the following sequence of operations:

1. Blanking (stamping out flat shapes from thin sheets of metal).
2. Pressing (bending the shapes).
3. Edging (trimming, rounding and pointing the shapes).
4. Cleaning (abrading and polishing).
5. Finishing (trademark etching and packing).

Although the *order* of operations is the same, whatever the item of cutlery, each type of cutlery may have its own special timings (for example, it takes longer to put a good edge on a knife than on a spoon). A further feature of cutlery manufacturing is that it does not have to meet the precise deadlines and quantities of material required by a big retailer buying from a food manufacturer. In cutlery, for example, if a customer has agreed to have 12,000 items delivered during the next year, the supplier has some

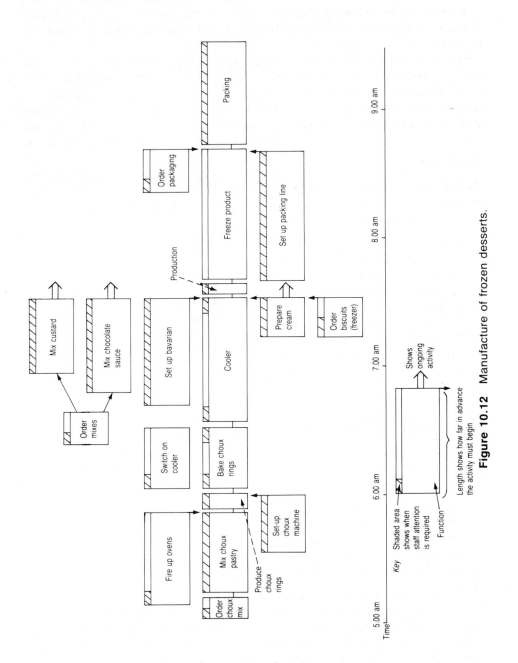

Figure 10.12 Manufacture of frozen desserts.

discretion as to whether this is 1,000 a month or 3,000 a quarter. Nevertheless, in such circumstances it is still worth adopting the food manufacturer's just-in-time maxim: 'When a job starts at the first operation, there must be no break in work until it is finished.'

This maxim is illustrated in the two schedules in Figure 10.13 (two different ways of looking at the same situation). The dual schedule (Figure 10.13(b)) allocates jobs to manufacturing operations exactly as in the primary schedule, but in the dual schedule, any particular row highlights material going through one particular department, labelled according to which customer it is for. If you look at the primary schedule, you will see that there are no gaps where material would be lying around waiting to be processed. The only work in progress is on machines.

Against this efficiency gain is the potentially idle machine time revealed in the dual schedule. As we are dealing with steady arrival and take-off of work, the spaces in the bottom left and top right can be filled up with earlier and later orders. But the spaces in the centre, between the thick lines, are harder to fill in. Some of this could be subcontract work for other manufacturers, non-urgent items, or making for stock. But, on the whole, such gaps in the schedule are not likely to be regarded kindly by the operatives, if they are on piece-work. It is no good telling them that the organization as a whole benefits if they are sometimes idle. Piece-workers much prefer to see a permanent queue of work waiting to be done whether they are low-paid sewing machinists or highly paid hospital consultants. So a prime requirement for establishing a just-in-time (JIT) scheduling system is the abandonment of *individual* piece-work payment systems.

Customer's job J	1	1	2	2	2	3	4	5	5									
Customer's job K					1	2	2	3	3	4	4	4	5					
Customer's job L							1	1	2	2	3	4	5	5	5			
Customer's job M										1	2	3	3	4	4	5		
Customer's job N											1	2	2	2	3	4	4	5

Note: Numbers 1,2, etc. in the primary schedule refer to blanking, pressing, etc.
(a)

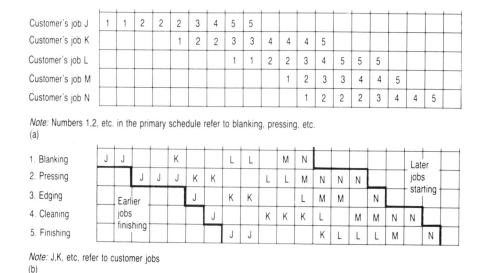

Note: J,K, etc, refer to customer jobs
(b)

Figure 10.13 Primary and dual Just-in-time schedules. (a) Primary, customer-layered schedule. (b) Dual resource layered-schedule.

Apart from reducing material inventories there are other advantages of a JIT system. If you do not send material non-stop through a set of processes, it tends to get put on one side and 'squirreled away', stolen, misrouted or forgotten about.

Also, without the JIT discipline there is a temptation to attack the scheduling problem by *input overloading* or a *just-in-case* system. More material than necessary is pushed through the earlier processes with the vague intention of ensuring that the remaining processes are kept busy, even allowing for material getting lost and muddled up. Such a system gets even more muddled and encourages workers to do their own thing, rather than take note of the schedule.

A further investigation in JIT implementation is via 'Kumera OY' in Schmenner's *Cases in Production/Operations Management* (SRA, 1986).

▼　　**Exercise**

In the previous illustration there were eighteen spaces between the thick lines of the dual resource schedule. Suppose you take the present sequence of customers (J, K, L, M, N) and change it, e.g. to N, M, L, K, J, amongst other possibilities. Can you find a solution where there are only sixteen spaces between the heavy lines? (In fact, there is a solution with just fifteen

▲　　spaces.)

10.7　Job shop scheduling

Job shops make work to order, one customer's job needing to call on many processes and machines. (Note, in this context, 'job' is always a customer order, never a task.) Often, management specifies a manufacturing route, i.e. a sequence of operations, that the customer's job must pass through. This sequence is usually a technical necessity: sometimes, by having a sequence, you help ensure that no task is overlooked. Occasionally there is some flexibility in the sequence of operations that can be followed.

Although we usually think of job shop scheduling in a manufacturing context, there are various applications elsewhere in operations management, e.g. surgical operations, repair work, education modules or catering arrangements. The distinguishing features of the job shop situation are:

1.　Every new time period brings a new, unique set of jobs to handle.
2.　The jobs have to be sequenced through a complex set of processes.

10.7.1　*Job shop scheduling in a service context — car servicing*

Car repair garages are classic examples of job shops, especially garages with specialist mechanics. For example, suppose mechanics specialize within one of these functions:

A   Auto-electrical work
B   Bodywork and passenger interiors
C   Chassis and suspension
D   Drive units: clutch, gearing, crankshafts
E   Engine and ancillaries
F   Fixed replacements: exhaust, brakes, tyres

To keep the illustration simple, we assume that a department can work on only one car at a time.

Figure 10.14 shows all major jobs booked in for repair on a particular day. Along any row is the sequence of operations that a particular customer job must go through. Each box section represents an hour's work.

Suppose S has to be finished by 4 pm, Q by 5 pm and the rest by 6 pm. Figure 10.15 gives a schedule that never loads a department with more than one car simultaneously.

In Figure 10.15(b), a 'dual schedule', jobs are allocated to departments exactly as before, but now all of a department's work appears along the same row, labelled this time as its customer job. This format highlights manpower scheduling. For example, looking at work done between 12 noon and 2 pm, you can see that three departments take a lunch break from 12 to 1 pm, the other three departments from 1 to 2 pm, giving reasonable cover for emergencies.

Because of gaps in the schedule, this might appear to be a pretty slack system. Not so. (Could you get all work finished by 5 pm, even by getting the mechanics to forgo their lunch hour?) Also, in this example, a gap does not mean that a mechanic is idle. Good scheduling provides a bank of other work which can be done at leisure (e.g. cars owned by the repair shop can be stripped, cannibalized or prepared for secondhand sale). Also, 'idle' mechanics can help busy departments by driving to spares shops to get parts that are needed.

The dual also helps identify where there is a potential for flexible work assignments. Note that men in department A have no work in the afternoon, and men in department E have no work in the morning. You could pay men in each team for only half

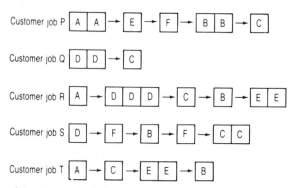

Figure 10.14   Job shop scheduling — summary of sequences for the car repair illustration.

	9am	10	11	12	1	2	3	4	5	6pm
Customer job P			A	A	E	F	B	B	C	
Customer job Q						D	D	C		
Customer job R	A	D	D	D	C	B		E	E	
Customer job S	D		F	B	F	C	C			
Customer job T		A	C			E	E		B	

(a)

Exactly the same schedule can be drawn up in another way:

	9am	10	11	12	1	2	3	4	5	6pm
Repair Dept A	R	T	P	P						
Repair Dept B				S		R	P	P	T	
Repair Dept C			T		R	S	S	Q	P	
Repair Dept D	S	R	R	R		Q	Q			
Repair Dept E					P	T	T	R	R	
Repair Dept F			S		S	P				

(b)

Figure 10.15 Job shop scheduling, for the car repair illustration. (a) Primary schedule highlighting job sequences over hours of work, 9 am to 6 pm. (b) Dual schedule highlighting the loading of departments from 9 am to 6 pm.

a shift. Or, if men expect a full day's work and were willing to switch department, just one team could do all A's work in the morning and all E's work in the afternoon.

Slotting in extra jobs

The original schedule considered only major jobs requiring the attention of several departments. There is room to slot in a few minor jobs, especially those dealt with by only one department (e.g. along the F row, fitting a new exhaust or replacing brake pads). But trouble can occur if a late, minor job turns up and is given priority. For example, what would happen if you fitted a minor job (e.g. a clutch adjustment) into D's morning schedule arguing, 'It'll only take us an hour to do, and we'll have plenty of spare time to finish our work in the afternoon'?

Department D may have spare time, but other departments dependent on D will have all their work put back. So, one little addition can cause havoc elsewhere.

The effect of crude priority rules on an overall schedule

Good scheduling pays careful attention to *interdependencies*. Sometimes such a schedule is overruled on the shopfloor by expediters, who want to get more work through a particular point or for a particular customer. Also, when there is a queue of work waiting at a process, items are sometimes taken from the queue according to certain *priority rules*, and these rules can ruin a good tight schedule.

Priority rules commonly used involve giving priority to the job:

1. That has been waiting longest.
2. With shortest time to completion.
3. With longest time to completion.
4. Needed earliest.
5. With the least slack time left.
6. With the most remaining different types of operation.
7. With the lowest critical ratio (where critical ratio = time to completion/periods of work left to do).

If any of these rules were applied to the example in Figure 10.15, they would make matters worse. For example:

Rules 1, 2 and 4 would get D working on Q at 10 am.
Rules 3, 5, 6 and 7 would get A working on P at 10 am.

For either of these happenings, the garage cannot get its work done, even cutting into the mechanics' lunch breaks. So this is a good example of where priority rules do not work very well because each rule is too crude and too narrowly focused.

▼   **Exercise**

A different list of customer jobs for a garage is given in Figure 10.16. As in the previous example, each block represents an hour's work in the named departments, A to F. Using primary and dual schedules, tackle questions (a) to (d). Assume a starting time of 9 am.

(a) Can you find a suitable schedule that finishes by 7 pm and which gives everyone apart from department A staff a one hour lunch break?

(b) Why is it impossible to give department A an hour off for lunch and finish at 7 pm?

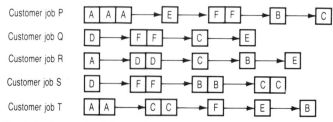

Figure 10.16   Job shop scheduling — summary of sequences for the 'new' car repair exercise.

▷

(c) Can you find a schedule that meets the conditions in (a) and also ensures that there is no more than an eight-hour gap between a department starting and finishing work?

(d) Suppose that you want to save on labour by getting a flexible rostering agreement so that the same team of men does all of department A's work first, then switches to do all of department E's work. And another team does all of department D's work, then switches to department B's work. Can you still finish by 7 pm? (Note that these busy teams will miss lunch and have to be paid for working more than an eight-hour shift.)

▲

10.8 Combinatorial problems

10.8.1 *Introduction*

Many of the scheduling problems we have investigated have required a *sequence* to be imposed (e.g. food processing, car repairs, cutlery manufacturing). There are circumstances where no strict sequence needs to be followed, but nevertheless it is still difficult to co-ordinate a jumble of activities. For example:

- Examination and class timetables in education.
- Bundling or packing items into a vehicle or container.
- Assigning salespeople territories or customers.
- Devising compatible work-teams for military or emergency services.

All these applications pose *loose—tight* problems for the scheduler:

Loose ... in that he or she can dispense with the sequencing constraint to consider a wider range of options.

Tight ... in that people other than the scheduler think that combinatorial scheduling is easy — and they throw in all sorts of complications and conditions which sometimes mean that *any* solution is impossible (and there is no way of finding that out until an awful lot of time has been wasted).

These points should become clearer after our illustrations.

10.8.2 *Timetabling*

We focus on a timetable for college courses, although the general principles have a wider application both within education (examination timetables) and out of it (theme-park activities, out-patient appointments, security schedules).

Consider the weekly timetable that needs to be drawn up for an MBA course. Wednesday has already been accounted for (compulsory Policy for everyone in the morning, sport or private study in the afternoon). There remains eight sessions (one in the morning, one in the afternoon for Monday, Tuesday, Thursday and Friday) into which twelve subjects must be squeezed. Some subjects will have to be run simultaneously but that is not a fatal flaw as any student takes no more than four of the twelve subjects. However, because students are allowed to take options, some care must be taken in the timetabling to make sure that no-one has a clash.

In this particular case, MBA students *must* take all three subjects which fall within their specialist area. They then opt for one more subject outside their specialist area. All student choices are shown in Table 10.6.

The class registration data act as the starting point for designing a good timetable. We are looking for an answer within a dominant CONSTRAINT: two classes should not be held at the same time if a student has put down to do both of them. We should also bear in mind other desirable but not essential *constraints* such as: overall, it would be nice to give students an even spread of work (either a morning or afternoon session, but not both). The first important CONSTRAINT can be tackled via what is called a *clash matrix*.

10.8.2.1 The clash matrix

If there is a timetable clash for any two subjects, 'disappointed' students can only go to their compulsory class (shown by the arrow direction in Figure 10.17).

Everything in the clash matrix has been derived from the registration table. For

Table 10.6 Class registration numbers

Students registered for specialist areas:	18	14	28	24	Total class size
Specialist areas:	Quantitative	Human resources	Accounting	Marketing	
Course name (code)					
Operations Management (OM)	(18)	4	8	7	37
Operations Research (OR)	(18)		2		20
Statistics (ST)	(18)		5		23
Industrial Relations (IR)		(14)		1	15
Personnel Management (PM)	5	(14)	8	12	39
Organizational Theory (OT)		(14)		4	18
Financial Management (FM)			(28)		28
Mgmt Control Systems (MC)			(28)		28
Mgmt Info. Systems (MI)	2		(28)		30
Market Research (MR)	7		5	(24)	36
Retailing (RE)	2	4		(24)	30
Advertising (AD)	2	6		(24)	32

Numbers in parentheses are compulsory registrations for students specializing in an area. The remaining numbers show options.

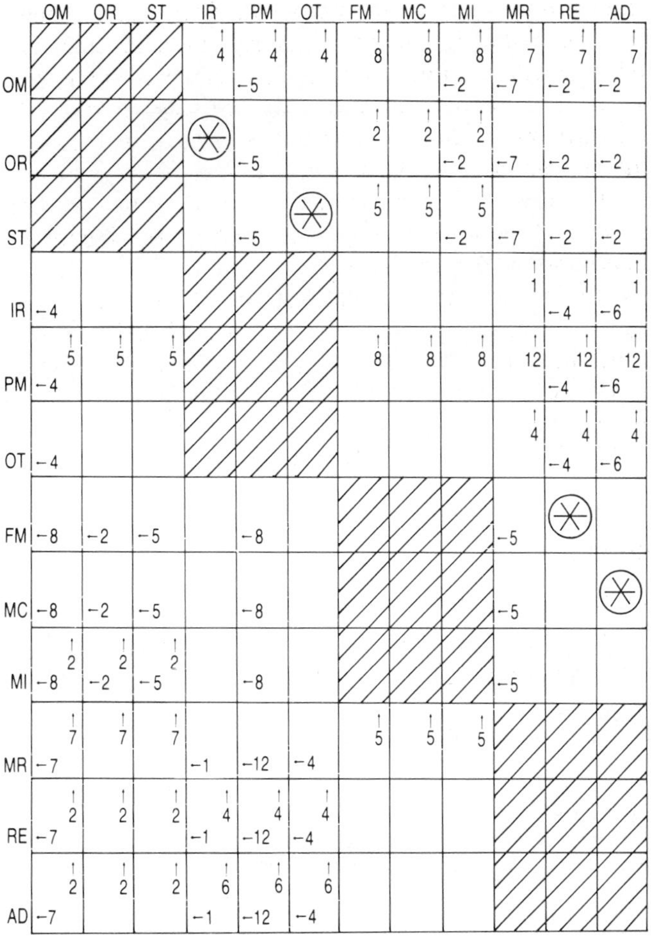

	OM	OR	ST	IR	PM	OT	FM	MC	MI	MR	RE	AD
OM	▨	▨	▨	↑4	↑4 / −5	↑4	↑8	↑8	↑8 / −2	↑7 / −7	↑7 / −2	↑7 / −2
OR	▨	▨	▨	⊗	−5		↑2	↑2	↑2 / −2	−7	−2	−2
ST	▨	▨	▨		−5	⊗	↑5	↑5	↑5 / −2	−7	−2	−2
IR	−4			▨	▨	▨				↑1	↑1 / −4	↑1 / −6
PM	↑5 / −4	↑5	↑5	▨	▨	▨	↑8	↑8	↑8	↑12	↑12 / −4	↑12 / −6
OT	−4			▨	▨	▨				↑4	↑4 / −4	↑4 / −6
FM	−8	−2	−5		−8		▨	▨	▨	−5	⊗	
MC	−8	−2	−5		−8		▨	▨	▨	−5		⊗
MI	−8	↑2 / −2	↑2 / −5	↑2	−8		▨	▨	▨	−5		
MR	↑7 / −7	↑7	↑7	−1	−12	−4	↑5	↑5	↑5	▨	▨	▨
RE	↑2 / −7	↑2	↑2	↑4 / −1	↑4 / −12	↑4 / −4				▨	▨	▨
AD	↑2 / −7	↑2	↑2	↑6 / −1	↑6 / −12	↑6 / −4				▨	▨	▨

Figure 10.17 The clash matrix.

example, the top row (fifth column) shows the effect of OM and PM clashing. Five Quantitative students have to give up PM. Four Human Resources students have to give up OM. The 5 and 4 can be found from the options in the previous registration table, as can all remaining figures in the clash matrix. Actually, this matrix is symmetric, and we could have excluded the information either above or below the diagonal. We have kept it in for a purpose (constructing the next matrix).

Any two subjects within a specialist area must not be allowed to clash: hence the shaded areas running down the diagonals. The clash matrix shows that for some combination of subjects there will be no disappointed students forced to give up their option. These preferable combinations are shown by empty boxes, and from these the circled stars show which combinations have been actually chosen when constructing the timetable.

The clash matrix solves the timetabling problem within the major CONSTRAINT: how to ensure that no student has to give up an option because of a timetable clash.

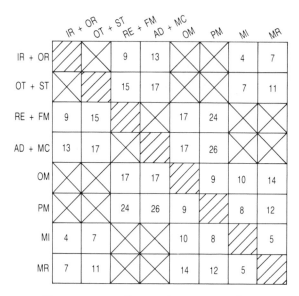

Figure 10.18 The assignment matrix.

There remains the lesser problem of trying to give as many students as possible an even load (e.g. avoiding both morning and afternoon sessions). This can be tackled via an assignment matrix.

The assignment matrix shown in Figure 10.18 uses eight labels for its rows and columns: the four pairings suggested by the clash matrix plus the remaining four subjects. Now, we want to split these eight labels into morning and afternoon sessions for four days of the week — and on any day have morning and afternoon sessions that are most convenient to the students. By 'convenient' we mean:

1. Students do not have two subjects within a special area on the same day (in the matrix, the crosses exclude this possibility).
2. A timetable is generated so that as few students as possible have both a morning and an afternoon session.

If subjects are bracketed together for the same day, the number of students with a full day's work can be found from the cells in the matrix. The numbers in these cells were in their turn derived from the clash matrix. For example, the 17 found at the intersection of the OT and ST row and the AD and MC column was found by totalling these intersections in the clash matrix, i.e.:

	MC	AD
ST	5	
		2
OT		4
		6

Like the clash matrix, the assignment matrix is symmetrical. If you want to find a good solution by eye, this can be done by inspecting just half of the matrix and circle four pairings which involve a low number of students doing two sessions a day. The best answer is set out below.

	am	pm	Students with am and pm classes
Monday	IR + OR	RE + FM	9
Tuesday	OT + ST	AD + MC	17
Thursday	OM	PM	9
Friday	MR	MI	5
		Total	40

Alternatively, a best answer to the problem in the assignment matrix can be found mathematically. The solution method is known as the Hungarian Method (or the Konig Kuhn algorithm). It is explained in detail in many textbooks on operational research and being a relatively easy technique to computerize it underlies most software packages which offer solutions to the timetabling problem.

▼ **Exercise**

▲ Solve the timetabling problem in Table 10.7, which uses the same definitions as the problem we have just worked through.

Table 10.7 Class registration numbers for the exercise

Students registered:	23	24	19	21
Specialist areas:	Quantitative	Human resources	Accounting	Marketing
Course code				
OM	(23)	7	5	6
OR	(23)		3	3
ST	(23)		2	3
IR		(24)		
PM	3	(24)		
OT		(24)	4	4
FM	10		(19)	
MC		4	(19)	
MI		8	(19)	5
MR	10		5	(21)
RE				(21)
AD		5		(21)

10.8.2.2 General comments on timetabling-type problems

Trying to resolve timetable clashes is a common feature of academic life. Even quite a small institution may have twenty or more subjects to handle, over two hundred students, and a horrendous array of options which have been allowed. In one sense, it is good that the consumer has been given the freedom of choice leaving those in charge with a challenging intellectual problem. We have only touched on this problem as its difficulty is compounded by having to allocate classes to rooms of varying sizes and (with many institutions being on split sites) making sure that students do not have to travel excessive distances in short times.

For class timetabling, there are opportunities to relax some of the constraints. For example, large classes may be split into two, lunchtime or evening sessions may be arranged or, if the worse comes to the worst, some subjects can be postponed for a year if they are part of a three-year course.

However, for other timetabling problems there is not so much scope for changing the rules. In particular, the constraints have to be tighter for examination timetabling: you cannot have examinees sitting the same exam at the two different times because of the danger of cheating. And, of course, you must not under-estimate numbers because every examinee must be guaranteed a desk. At Sheffield University, scheduling exams is so complex that a highly skilled mathematician works full-time, twelve months a year, just to obtain a feasible result — and it is touch and go whether he succeeds.

10.9 Bundling problems

10.9.1 *Overview*

There are many different situations where a variety of items are bundled into a confined space. More details of this were given in the *road transport* case examples in Chapter 5. Specifically, these were having to balance loads to keep within axle weights, having to avoid 'snaking' problems, and having to minimize repacking after every intermediate delivery. Similar care has to be taken when bundling loads for other forms of transport:

In shipping: Balancing cargo-weights amongst fore, aft and middle holds.
In aircraft: Balancing not only fore and aft, but also between left- and right-hand sides of the plane.

Equally important bundling problems apply not only to other transport containers (buses, railway wagons, pallets, hoppers), but also crop up in service industries where the 'bundle' and the 'container' might appear in unusual guises.

Health care: Finding compatible bundles of patients for each ward?
Education: How to split up mixed-ability students into classes/tutorials?
Tourism: How to devise suitable groups for Himalayan trekking expeditions?
Retailing: What is the best loading strategy for a supermarket trolley?

Although every bundling problem has its own special flavour, there is a general method of attack which acts as a useful starting point: the combinatorial approach. We illustrate this with an example of bundling moulds into a foundry hopper.

10.9.2 *Illustration — scheduling foundry operations*

Consider a foundry which, on one particular day, must meet the orders of six customers. Each customer requires a different casting type, and has a different size of order, as follows:

Type of casting	A	B	C	D	E	F
Individual weight of each casting (kg)	280	250	190	180	110	90
Number of castings required	6	18	12	2	9	6

Castings are made by filling a ladle with molten metal from a furnace and then pouring the metal into a hopper containing up to three moulds. Because of certain constraints on ladling operations, the total weight of castings in any hopper must lie between 450 and 550 kg. After being filled, the hopper moves off along a conveyor and is left alone until the metal has cooled and solidified. The moulds are then broken and the castings removed from the hopper. The hopper is recycled to receive new moulds.

It is quite a tricky business to prepare new moulds in a hopper. It requires a team of highly-trained men to work with speed and precision. Firstly, they put a hopper on a turntable on which up to three 'replicas' have been placed (these replicas having the shape of the final castings). The replicas are positioned in the hopper, then the spaces round the replicas are packed with a special mixture of sand and resin. When this mixture hardens, the replicas are removed leaving a space into which the molten metal will pour to make the castings. After the replicas are removed from the hopper, the hopper is taken off the turntable and a new, empty hopper takes its place. If this hopper is to take the same three moulds as previously, this work can start immediately. Otherwise one or more replicas must be removed from the turntable and replaced. It takes three minutes to remove and three minutes to replace any replica. This process is shown in Figure 10.19.

There are several complex scheduling problems involved in this example, but let us focus on just one of them:

The turntable operators will want to know which replicas to fit on their turn-

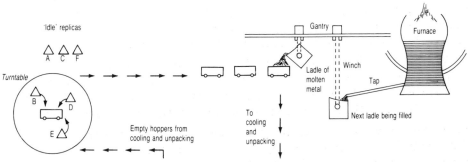

Figure 10.19 Foundry moulding

Table 10.8 Feasible combinations of replicas

Type of casting	Weight of associated castings (kg)	g	h	i	j	k	l	m	n	o	p	q	r	s	t	u	v	w	x	y	z	α	Number of castings required
A	(280)	1	1	1	1									1	1								6
B	(250)	1													2	1							18
C	(190)		1	1		1	1	1	1	1	1	1					2	2	1				12
D	(180)				1				1	1	1	1						2	2	2	2	3	2
E	(110)				1								2	2		1	1		2	2	1		9
F	(90)									1	1	1		1		1		1	1		1	1	6
Amount by which a particular combination is beneath 550 kg		20	80	0	70	0	20	10	30	100	70	90	50	90	50	80	60	80	0	80	100	10	

Any column shows a combination of castings which can be packed into one hopper because the combination lies between 450 and 550 kg table and, once they have got this particular combination on, how many hoppers to pack before switching to a new set of replicas. For example, in our illustration, replicas B, D and E are on the turntable. The first thing to check is whether the three replicas together will take a weight of molten metal from the ladle that is feasible (i.e. lies between 450 and 550 kg). In this case, summing the three individual weights comes to 540 kg. This is quite desirable because 540 is only 10 kg underneath the maximum allowed, and so does not waste much of the ladle's capacity of 550 kg.

Before considering a full answer to this scheduling problem, it helps to set out every feasible combination of replicas that the turntable operators could use. (Having a set of either two or three replicas on the turntable and each with a total weight between 450 and 550 kilos.) This is set out in Table 10.8 (opposite).

Table 10.8 is quite a useful scheduling aid: it sets out all the options available, and the bottom row gives you a rough idea of their efficiency (low numbers in this row are good as they show that nearly all of the ladle's capacity is being exploited).

The numbers in Table 10.8 can also be used to make a quick evaluation of how good any particular schedule is. For example, suppose that the whole day's orders are met by the turntable using only:

combination g, (A + B)	6 times
combination k, (B + C + E)	9 times
combination l, (B + C + F)	3 times
combination n, (B + D + F)	3 times

Extracting these four combinations from Table 10.8 and evaluating the molten metal 'wasted', we get the results shown in Table 10.9.

Table 10.9 Evaluation of the efficiency of selected combinations

Combinations g to n made	6	9	3	3	Items A to F required	Items made surplus to requirements	Total weight of surplus items (kg)
Weight of item (kg)	g	k	l	n			
280 A	1				6		
250 B	1	1	1	1	18	3	750
190 C		1	1		12		
180 D				1	2	1	180
110 E		1			9		
90 F			1	1	6		
							930
One combination's short-weight	20	0	20	30			
Total short-weight	120 +	0 +	60 +	90 =	270		1200

▼ **Exercise**

▲ In our Table 10.9 example, total waste = 270 + 930 = 1200. Find a
different set of feasible combinations which gives less waste.

▼ **Expanded foundry exercise for scheduling geniuses**

Basically, the technical terms and the layout are the same as in the previous
'elementary' exercise. However, there are a few changes in the problem
parameters.

1. Now the turntable must have a set of replicas which will give castings
   whose total weight lies between 1050 and 1150 kg.

2. There are customer orders for fifteen different types of castings (labelled
   A to O in Table 10.10).

3. Instead of three there are five positions on the turntable.

4. When choosing combinations of replicas, any combination must take
   account of these extra contraints. Any combination must contain:

   No more than one of A, C or G
   No more than one of H or I
   No more than one of K or L
   No more than one of D, E or F
   No more than one of M or N
   No more than one of C or O

Table 10.10 Foundry exercise data (expanded problem)

Replica	A	B	C	D	E	F	G	H	I	J	K	L	M	N	O
Casting weight (kg)	450	390	330	310	290	270	250	230	220	210	190	180	170	150	110
Number of castings needed	33	55	14	52	36	23	58	93	21	68	47	20	59	93	88

▲

Comment on these exercises

Finding and selecting combinations is a common scheduling problem in a wide variety
of situations. Previously, much of the 'finding' part of this exercise had to be done
by hand, but now there are computerized database techniques which can give quicker
solutions for some of the simpler situations. As for the 'selecting' part, there are certain

circumstances where linear programming (LP) can give an optimal answer. We give some hints on how you could formulate a set of equations for doing this for our illustrated exercises. We leave a full explanation of how LP works to special books on this subject or to the particular LP software package that you use.

Hint 1: Refer to the section in LP textbooks called 'trim loss problems'.

Hint 2: The LP constraint equations take a format close to that given in our previous tables. For example, in the first elementary problem:

> The basic variables will be: g, h, i, ..., α
> The constraint will be: A, B, C, etc.
> Each constraint equation will be $\geq$ a RHS
> (e.g. constraint A: $g + h + i + j + r + s \geq 6$)

We leave it to the LP textbooks' explanations of trim loss to describe the surprisingly simple format for the objective function.

Hint 3: If your optimal LP answer gives fractional amounts, you will have to round up or use integer programming instead.

Hint 4: If you had to work a lot with this sort of problem, you should use special programming techniques which exploit the fact that the coefficients contain a lot of noughts (and the rest are whole numbers).

A further aside

Having found out *which* combinations to make, the scheduler still has to find the *order* in which the combinations are to be scheduled. To do this, he or she wants to minimize the time taken to remove and replace replicas on the turntable. For example, consider these two changes:

Change 1

Old combination (i)	A			D	F
New combination (k)		B	C		E

Change 2

Old combination (j)	A		E	F
New combination (o)		B	E	F

Change 2 wastes less time as just one combination is removed from the turntable and just one combination replaces it.

If you want to find a schedule which minimizes these changeover times, you are tackling (perversely) a travelling salesman problem (TSP), identical in intellectual content to that facing delivery drivers.

10.10 Conclusion and review

When you become proficient at all the scheduling techniques we have covered, there are certain general issues worth remembering when looking for ways to exploit your skills.

1. *Diversity*. All of the techniques have wider applications than the obvious ones that we illustrate.
2. *Mess management*. These techniques can be of great help if you are trying to split a complex problem into separate parts.

We now look at each of these in a bit more detail.

Diversity of application of the scheduling techniques described

All of our techniques have applications over a wide spectrum: public or private sectors, manufacturing or services, military or civilian, front line or general management. This point can be reinforced by considering the following potential applications:

1. *Route scheduling*. There are obvious extensions to all delivery services (postal and milk rounds) and sport (motor rallying and orienteering). But, as we showed in the 'bundling' section, travelling salesman problems (TSP) also pop up when loading foundry hoppers. TSP has many other surprising applications (sequencing programs through a mainframe computer or minimizing changeover operations in advanced manufacturing technology).
2. *ROQ/ROL*. Monitoring the extent of famine in a Third World country and co-ordinating relief supplies, allowing for delivery lead times. Monitoring overdraft levels for a bank's clients, and in automatically setting off the initial procedures for a refinancing package.
3. *EOQ/EBQ*. How much money should you withdraw from a cash dispenser? When designing a skyscraper, should there be a few big twenty-passenger lifts or more, smaller, ten-passenger lifts?
4. *Machine interference cycles*. How should security guards rotate their visits? What is the best routine maintenance cycle for a large firm's plant, machinery or vehicles?
5. *Set-ups and run lengths*. How should a chain of theatres co-ordinate the set-ups and run lengths for its plays, concerts and operas? How should a large quarry or mine co-ordinate development and extraction from its several adjacent workings?
6. *JIT schedules*. How should a slaughterhouse handle animals of different types and batch sizes? How should estate agents, solicitors, mortgage lenders and surveyors co-ordinate their activities to have JIT-type operations for house-buying?
7. *Job shop scheduling*. How should a health club spread and sequence its clients through its facilities? How should work be co-ordinated for clients of a gardening/landscaping agency?

8. *Combinatorial/timetabling problems.* Co-ordinating a political party's election campaign. Scheduling television programmes (to minimize clashes if you are the Independent TV Watchdog representing the public; to maximize clashes if you are a television company trying to annoy its competitors).

Scheduling techniques and their contribution to mess management

When you are confronted with a big messy problem, it is not enough to have energy and enthusiasm. A big mess has to be approached with a method, and this involves knowing how to split up activities in such a way that when you untangle one activity, you do not cause too many extra problems elsewhere.

We all have some proficiency in mess management from the procedures that we intuitively use to tackle a big jigsaw: edge pieces are sorted out first and these are further colour sorted for the earth, trees and sky sections. Then, and only then, is an attempt made to construct the outer frame of the jigsaw. If you think about it, there are quite a few other intuitive rules that you employ: switching between sorting and fitting in a regular way; deciding on what is a reasonable size cluster of similar pieces; exhaustive matching of combinations of a group of similar colour and shape pieces when all other methods fail. All of these mental activities are very similar to certain scheduling techniques that we have just discussed.

Similarly, without perhaps realizing it, many of us are skilled schedulers in our leisure and non-business pursuits. Consider all the scheduling problems associated with jumble sales. Here we have:

1. *Route scheduling* for the dealers who have to zip between as many jumble sales as possible on a Saturday.
2. *ROQ/ROL* for restocking tables with reserve items.
3. *EOQ/EBQ* for deciding whether to have many collectors responsible for small areas, or a few, who will need bigger intermediate storage space.
4. *Set-ups and run lengths.* How frequently should a church or other organization hold a jumble sale and, if they do, how much old unsold stuff should be recycled?
5. *JIT scheduling.* How can you locate stalls so that people pass through in a logical way, without zigzags, or queue too much?
6. *Job shop scheduling.* How should the pile of stuff to be sold be inspected, sorted, priced and stacked?
7. *Timetabling.* What is the best roster for collectors and on-the-day helpers?
8. *Bundling.* What is the best way of getting rid of all unsold items by piling them together in a few vehicles and taking them to appropriate waste-disposal points?

We have discussed this example at some length because it reinforces our belief that many individuals (and nations) have an inferiority complex about their time management and scheduling skills in business, when all the time they demonstrate skills of the highest kind in their leisure activities:

The Americans are pretty good at sports spectaculars
The Italians at staging opera
The French at banquets
The British at State Funerals
The Australian aborigines are superb at search and rescue operations.

The important point is for people to be able to recognize their inherent abilities in handling messes — to recognize that there is a common foundation of similar scheduling techniques that are transferrable over a wide range of operations management situations.

10.11 Recommended reading

We have already given cases for some specific techniques but a classic integrative case suitable for a hard end-of-year assignment is 'Medina' in T.A.J. Nicholson, *Managing Manufacturing Operations* (Macmillan, 1978). Also, see what you make of the deceptively simple OPT quiz on pp. 520–21 of J.R. Evans's *Applied Production and Operations Management*, 2nd edn (West Publishing Co., 1987).

Chapter 11

Scheduling — the grand plan

11.1 Introduction

The previous chapter showed how complex situations could be broken up and their scheduling problems dealt with separately. An alternative approach is to try to cover everything. If so, you must either stick to a very simple scheduling mechanism which can operate for large problems or else you must lump together items into a few broad categories.

The latter approach was illustrated in Chapter 9 on project planning, where the broad-category approach was introduced via work breakdown schedules. Critical path analysis is also a good example of a 'simple mechanism that can handle large problems'. As it only involves elementary logic and mathematics, there are no special computational problems in handling a network of five hundred activities rather than fifty. The same principles apply to the three total scheduling techniques of this chapter:

Capacity planning
MRP
Linear programming

Although our examples must be kept small because of the limited area of a textbook page, these techniques can be applied to problems that are ten times greater.

11.2 Capacity planning

11.2.1 *Simple rough-cut capacity planning*

In the simplest case, the capacity of a firm depends on the capability of just one machine, vehicle, person or property. Thus, in small business:

- The capacity of the ice-cream vendor depends on his serving rate.

- The capacity of a dentist depends on the hours she wishes to work.
- The capacity of a football club depends on its spectator space.
- The capacity of a one-man transport operator depends on the size of his vehicle.

Take the last situation, that of a one-man transport operator. Firstly, suppose he has answered, 'What business am I in?' (e.g. courier, parcels, long distance, local, bulk). Suppose he decides to concentrate within a fifty-mile area on bulk deliveries of aggregate; gravel, sand, topsoil, stone and the like. For this work he will be using a tipper lorry. It helps if he sketches out the operating characteristics of his tipper — and its costs — as part of an overall capacity planning strategy. Data for one size of tipper is given in Table 11.1.

Using the total annual costs as a baseline to be covered, one can work out how much a customer should be charged for each kilometre tonne. At the maximum feasible capacity of 184,300 km tonnes, a charge of £0.15 per kilometre tonne will bring in pretty well exactly the revenue required (184,300 × £0.15 = £27,645).

Suppose that business is slack and, instead of covering 43,200 kilometres in a year, only 80 per cent of that distance is covered. As a consequence the haulier will:

Lose 20% of revenue:	−£5530
Save 20% of running costs	+£1120
Net effect	−£4410

This brings the haulier's income to just below £8000.

▼   **Exercise in judgement**

The recession has meant that many hauliers have had to ask themselves whether they should quit. What advice would you give to the haulier in the situation above? (What do you think are the lowest work-rate levels he can survive on, and for how long?)

▲

▼   **More cheerful exercise**

Suppose that the haulier is thinking about using a bigger vehicle (a 24 tonne GVW tipper). If he can still get £0.15 revenue for each kilometre tonne, would he be better off? That depends on the level of his capacity. Using the relevant data given in Table 11.2 (p.278), follow through the same work-rate calculations as for the 17 tonne GVW tipper:

(a) For a maximum feasible work rate.

(b) For only 80 per cent of that rate.

▲   Assume the owner-driver would still like to earn £12,000 + and that he is currently charging £0.15 per kilometre tonne to do this.

Table 11.1   Capacity calculations for a tipper, 17 tonnes gross vehicle weight (GVW)

Annual work-rate calculations

Maximum load it can carry	10.6 tonnes
Normal load carried, allowing for incomplete loads	90% × 10.6 = 9.5 tonnes
Effective working weeks per year	48 weeks
Days worked per year	240 days
Driving hours per day	6 hours
Driving hours per year	1440 hours
Average driving speed	30 kph
Distance driven per year	1440 × 30 = 43,200 km
Percentage of time driven unloaded	55%
Distance p.a. driven loaded	45% × 43,200 = 19,400 km
Maximum feasible work rate p.a.	19,400 km × 9.5 tonnes = 184,300 km-tonnes

Annual cost calculations (£)

Capital charges p.a.	£8370[a]
Tax and insurance p.a.	£1830
Variable running costs scaled up to 43,200 km:	
Fuel	3650
Tyres	680
Maintenance	1260
	£5590
Owner's desired remuneration to himself or driver, etc.	£12,000 +
Total	£27,790

[a]The annual capital charge is derived from a purchase price of £31,000, a resale price after 4 years of £7000 and interest charges of 15%. The formula for deriving it was found by subtracting £7000 from £31,000 and dividing the result by A (where A is the 4 year annuity value at 15% = 2.87). Refer to finance textbooks to see how and why annuity values are calculated.

11.2.1.1 Extension to the haulier's capacity problem

Many haulage businesses possess a fleet of vehicles, thus making decisions on capacity planning much more difficult and critical. The one-man haulier will stick to the same vehicle for quite a wide range of business situations (as long as he is making *some* money, he will just slacken or tighten his belt accordingly), but a haulier employing other drivers has not the option to make great variations in their wages: he is expected to pay the going rate.

Table 11.2   Relevant data for the 24-tonne tipper

Maximum load it can carry	16 tonnes
Normal load carried, allowing for incomplete loads	Use your own technical and business judgement as to whether the 17-tonner's 90% scaling should be applied
Driving hours per year	1440 (as for the 17-tonner)
Average driving speed	Somewhat less than the 17-tonner's 30 kph, especially in urban areas because of poorer acceleration and manoeuvrability. Use your judgement
Distance driven per year	1440 × average driving speed
Percentage of time driven unloaded	55% (as with the 17-tonner)
Distance p.a. driven loaded	45% × distance driven p.a.

Annual cost calculations

Capital charges	£11,860[a]
Tax and insurance	£2780
Scale-up these running costs which are for 10,000 km to whatever distance is driven p.a.:	
Fuel	£923
Tyres	£250
Maintenance	£446

---

[a]The capital charges were derived in a similar fashion to the 17-tonner, with the same interest rate of 15%. For your information, the purchase price was £42,850 and the trade-in value after 4 years was £9384.

In that case, how can such a haulier cope with all the ups and downs in trade? Can he hire and fire people at will? Up to a point, as many drivers expect their work to be seasonal or on a short contract. But if this hire-and-fire policy is adopted too vigorously, the firm will not get the most desirable employees (and the drivers themselves may leave the firm without warning when better jobs arise). It is better to float between the little crests and troughs of business with a reasonably stable list of workers and assets. This can be demonstrated on a modified Gantt chart (Figure 11.1).

Each asterisk in the figure shows a unit of surplus capacity indicating that new business must be found, or the truck and driver sidelined. The asterisk in July shows that there is a case for retiring a truck earlier than August as planned. From this chart, quite satisfactory schedules can be generated by referring to a mixture of priority rules, such as:

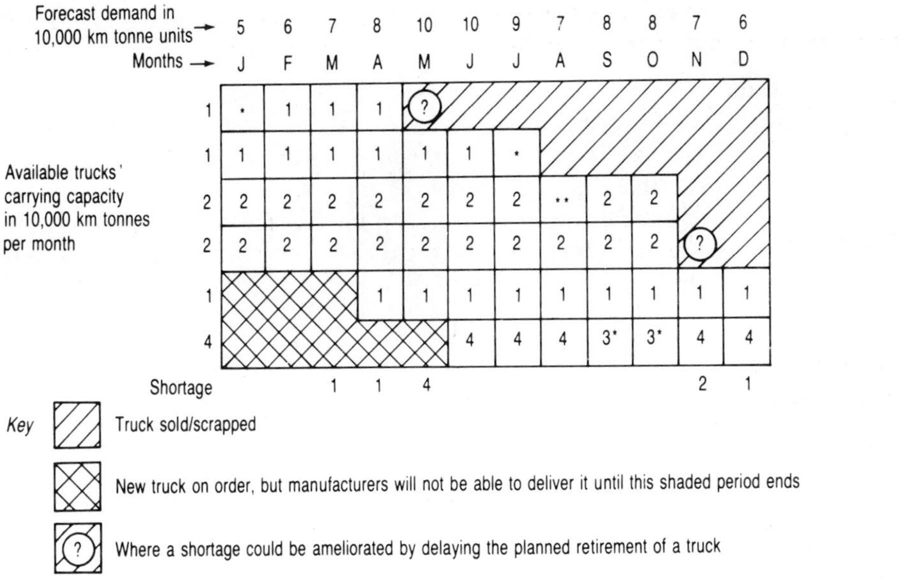
Forecast demand in 10,000 km tonne units → 5 6 7 8 10 10 9 7 8 8 7 6
Months → J F M A M J J A S O N D
Available trucks' carrying capacity in 10,000 km tonnes per month
1 • 1 1 1 ?
1 1 1 1 1 1 1 •
2 2 2 2 2 2 2 2 •• 2 2
2 2 2 2 2 2 2 2 2 2 2 ?
1 1 1 1 1 1 1 1 1 1
4 4 4 4 3* 3* 4 4
Shortage 1 1 4 2 1
Key
Truck sold/scrapped
New truck on order, but manufacturers will not be able to deliver it until this shaded period ends
Where a shortage could be ameliorated by delaying the planned retirement of a truck

The 'shortage' row shows when total available capacity cannot meet demand. Work will have to be turned away or subcontracted to others.

Figure 11.1 Simple rough-cut capacity plan for a freight haulier.

Retire an old vehicle before a new vehicle.
Don't plan to retire an old vehicle until two months after its replacement has been delivered.
Never subcontract out work for a new, important customer.
Even though bigger lorries have cheaper unit costs, keep a reasonable mixture of sizes to help the scheduler when he later has to do his daily juggling act.

11.2.2 *Capacity planning in manufacturing*

Service industries find it very hard to adapt to certain shocks, whether from customers or the environment. To some extent, manufacturers can introduce tactics that can handle these shocks, for example:

1. Making for stock as well as supplying to order.
2. Holding over spare capacity for urgent new orders.
3. Anticipating future orders.
4. Handling plant shutdowns.

5. Distinguishing different operating conditions (introducing a new shift, or setting a general limit on overtime working).

Capacity planning can incorporate all of these features by exploiting a matrix with time on both axes, as shown in Figure 11.2.

After the blank table has been designed, rough-cut estimates of capacities and forward orders are set down (those numbers shown to the left and above the central cells in the table). Finally, allocations are made to cells within the table so that rows and columns 'balance'. Note that the bottom two rows and the final column can act as sumps to mop up any imbalances.

11.2.2.1 Capacity planning and product variety

The examples we have used so far were drawn from firms with an unusually simple product range. The freight haulier shifting bulk commodities can use kilometre tonnes

Figure 11.2   Capacity plan for a sleeping bag manufacturer (all items in units of ten sleeping bags).

as a good indication of his efficiency and profit, even if he is transporting many different products. Likewise a sleeping bag is a fairly uniform item and if this was all that was manufactured, a plan would be easy to construct. In fact, sleeping bags accounted for only 60 per cent of the turnover of this particular firm as tents and outdoor clothing were also manufactured.

Under these circumstances, the table has to be expanded and the units of measurement changed. Now we will have:

1. Customer orders for each product per period in unit quantities.
2. Shift hours worked.
3. In the body of the table, conversion factors showing how many hours are needed to make each product.

Figure 11.3 shows how this works for just part of the previous table. This chart shows

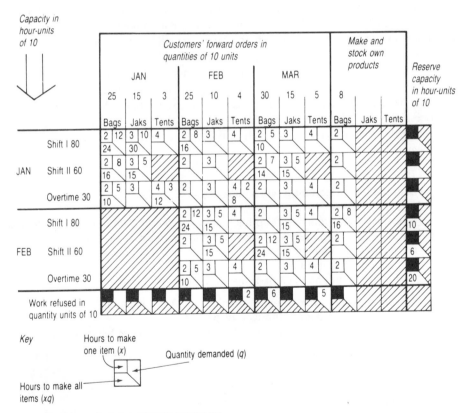

Figure 11.3 Capacity plan for sleeping bag manufacturer including other product varieties.

that, even for a small business, the presence of product variety makes capacity calculations quite complex. This is because you *have* to convert Marketing's revenue or quantity figures to Production's utilization criteria such as hours worked. Without such a conversion, capacity planning does not make sense. Our matrix is one simple illustration of this message although it is reinforced in both the materials requirement planning (MRP) and linear programming (LP) sections that follow.

Both this matrix and the earlier simple one could be 'optimized' by assigning cost or revenue per unit to each cell and using an OR technique known as the transportation method. However, we would advise caution before using an optimization process because we are dealing with key strategic decisions such as:

- How much work to give subcontractors.
- What levels of overtime to aim for.
- How many own-products to make.

Management will make these decisions according to 'business feel' and are likely to be put off by sophisticated techniques. For example, management will take on business in a depression so long as it feels that the business will cover marginal costs and/or lead to future business. And it will reject quite profitable work in a boom if it thinks that even more profitable work is around the corner. When difficult issues such as these arise it is best to analyse them via a simple communicative framework.

See the William T. Gamble D.D.S. case in D.A. Collier's *Service Management* (Prentice Hall, 1987) for a thorough presentation of the records of a dental practice, challenging the reader to design a better appointment system, and thus to overcome certain capacity constraints.

▼   **Exercise for scheduling whizz-kids**

A hospital management group has under its control sixteen units: six general wards, six nursing homes and four intensive care units. It divides its patients into four classifications: geriatrics, incurably ill, victims of serious accidents and short-term patients.

The figures in each cell of Table 11.3 show:

- The cost (in £ per week) of running a unit at full capacity, that cost varying according to the type of patient.
- How many patients can be taken by a unit if it is at full capacity.

The average number of patients that require to be in hospital at any point of time is:

Geriatrics	800
Incurably ill	300
Serious accident victims	400
Short-term patients	400

It may not be possible to admit all patients, and a cost has been imputed on those who cannot be taken, based on the cost of medical services needed for them to survive at home (per week). These are: ▷

Table 11.3 Resource allocation in health care

	Geriatric patients	Incurably ill patients	Serious accident patients	Short-term patients
General ward	£18,000 150	£18,000 120	£20,000 100	£16,000 200
Nursing home	£14,000 100	£20,000 120	£18,000 80	£12,000 150
Intensive care unit	£20,000 40	£20,000 50	£24,000 60	Inadmissible allocation

Geriatrics	£200 per person
Incurably ill	£150 per person
Serious accident victims	£400 per person
Short-term patients	£ 70 per person

Find an allocation of patients that minimizes overall costs. Note that a unit may take a mixture of patients but should apply linear scaling when working out its capacity limits (e.g. a nursing home would be at full capacity with fifty geriatrics and forty serious accident patients).

Hint: For those who are really into this sort of thing, refer to the 'Aircraft Routing Problem' in G.B. Dantzig's *Extensions to Linear Programming* (Princeton University Press, 1963).

▲

11.3 MRP

MRP is an acronym whose meaning has changed over the years. MRP-1 (materials requirement planning) analyses the timing and quantity of materials passing through a network of processes. It has formalized and improved the work of estimators, purchasing officers, quantity surveyors and production planners by providing a framework in which the whole of a complex operating system can be monitored. A wide range of industries have benefited from the application of MRP: heavy industry (car plants), light industry (electronic assemblies), furniture, food processing, distribution and construction industries: almost anywhere where work-in-progress exists between the raw material and the finished product.

MRP was developed in the USA during the 1970s under the auspices of a professional society (the American Production and Inventory Control Society, APICS). MRP pioneers (Plossl, Orlicky and Wight) were closely associated with IBM. Under the guidance of APICS and IBM an accepted terminology evolved.

Then, the MRP proponents became ambitious and MRP-1 (materials requirement planning) was enhanced by MRP-2 (manufacturing resources planning) which goes beyond immediate scheduling to cover the complete operating strategy, information and control system of a company.

To a certain extent, MRP has been replaced as the fashionable technique by JIT (just-in-time). Where JIT is a management philosophy which can be introduced piecemeal, MRP demands a heavy all-or-nothing financial commitment by management to invest in an integrated computer package, to collect special information that is needed by that package, and to have that package's instructions obeyed. This was possible in the well-organized, high-tech firms like IBM which pioneered the technique, but firms with little experience of formalized planning had great difficulty in understanding, installing and implementing expensive MRP systems. This is a pity. There are some very simple, very convenient little subprocedures in MRP that operating managers should be aware of even if they do not want to install an all-singing, all-dancing MRP computer package. So we are going to explain some bits and pieces of elementary MRP rather than investigating the full-blown advanced system.

The product structure tree

This adds certain numerical data to the Gozinto chart (see Chapter 5). An augmented Gozinto chart for a cake manufacturer is shown in Figure 11.4.

The coefficients placed against the arrows enable you to find out the quantities of ingredients to make any product. For example, if you want to make 80 units of Christmas pudding you will need 0.35×80 of pudding mix and 0.65×80 of fruit mix. But MRP is concerned not only with the quantities of raw materials but also with the time when they should be prepared and passed on. For this reason, every operation has a lead time affixed to it.

Levelling

There is a certain principle of dynamic programming which greatly helps untangle complex situations: 'work backwards from where you want to be, rather than work forwards from where you are at the moment'.

Levelling is a preliminary to this dynamic programming principle. In the confectionery example, finished products (by definition) have arrows only going into them. Put all these at level 0. Of the remaining boxes, put those at level 1 that have arrows going only to level 0. Of the remaining boxes, put those at level 2 that have arrows going only to level 1 or less. The general rule should be for a many levelled system.

The purpose of levelling is to disentangle the element of derived demand. Many businesses are making things not directly for their customers but for other departments in their organization, or for a subassembly that is going to be embodied in a final product. By working backwards from levels 0, 1, 2, etc., you avoid your calculations of derived demand going round in circles.

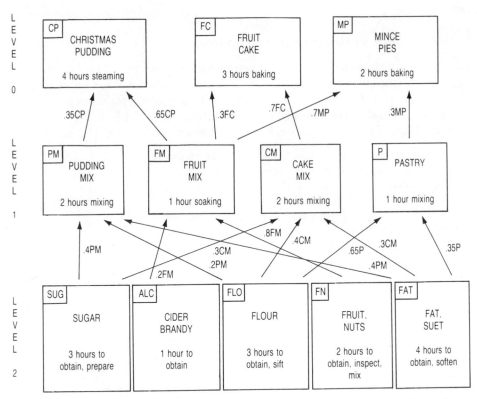

Figure 11.4 Augmented Gozinto chart for some of a cake manufacturer's products.

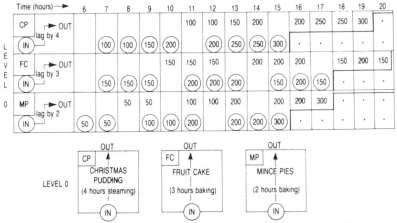

The figure starts with the known outputs from a process, applies the lag (the time the process takes) and so, is able to fill in an input time. For example, on the first row you are told that 100 units of Christmas Pudding (CP) are needed to be outputted at time 11. You also are told that Christmas Pudding making takes 4 hours. Therefore you need to input 100 units into the Christmas Pudding making process at time 7, and this is shown by the ringed number.

Figure 11.5 The 'lagging' part of the backwards explosion from level zero.

Exploding backwards (lagging and sourcing)

Starting with the known demand, at a known time for level 0 products, the lead times (lags) and coefficients in the product structure tree are used to work out how much of, and when, level 1 products should be made. This is then replaced to find level 2, etc. This is explained via a worked example getting from level 0 to level 1 (Figures 11.5 and 11.6). Then, try exercise 1 to see if you can get from level 1 to level 2.

Key The ringed outputs at level 1 have been newly found from the unringed inputs at level 0

The asterisks in the later periods show where you await information

Time (hours) →	5	6	7	8	9	10	11	12	13	14	15	16	17	18
LEVEL 0														
CP														
IN			100	100	150	200		200	250	250	300	·	·	·
FC														
IN			150	150	150		200	200	200		150	200	150	·
MP														
IN		50	50		100	100	200		200	200	300	·	·	·
LEVEL 1														
PM (OUT) = 0.35 CP			(35)	(35)	(53)	(70)		(70)	(88)	(88)	(105)	·	·	·
FM (OUT) = 0.65 CP			(65)	(65)	(98)	(130)		(130)	(163)	(163)	(195)	·	·	·
+0.3 FC			(45)	(45)	(45)		(60)	(60)	(60)		(45)	(60)	(45)	·
+0.7 MP		(35)	(35)		(70)	(70)	(140)		(140)	(140)	(210)	·	·	·
CM (OUT) = 0.7 FC			(105)	(105)	(105)		(140)	(140)	(140)		(105)	(140)	(105)	·
P (OUT) = 0.3 MP		(15)	(15)		(30)	(30)	(60)		(60)	(60)	(90)	·	·	·

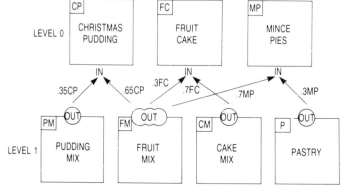

Figure 11.6 The 'sourcing' part of the backwards explosion illustration from level zero to level one.

▼ **Exercise 1**

Use Figure 11.7 to complete a backwards explosion from level 1 to level 2. Do this in three stages.

(a) Complete the sourcing part. Refer to the previous augmented Gozinto chart in Figure 11.4 to find how you can work out level 2 outputs by taking proportions of level 1 inputs.

(b) Complete the lagging part. Again, refer to the augmented Gozinto chart to find the relevant lags between level 2 outputs and level 2 inputs.

▲ **(c)** Be careful to identify the figures in the later time-periods which might have to be increased when information, at present unavailable, is released.

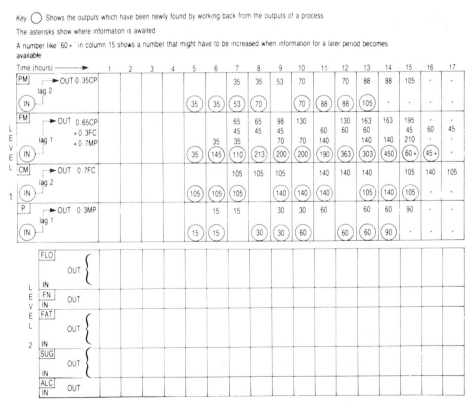

Key ○ Shows the outputs which have been newly found by working back from the outputs of a process

The asterisks show where information is awaited

A number like '60 +' in column 15 shows a number that might have to be increased when information for a later period becomes available

Figure 11.7 The 'lagging' part of the backwards explosion illustration at level one and a blank level two figure for Exercise 1.

▼ **Exercise 2**

(a) Design an MRP table which represents the Gozinto chart in Figure 11.8, providing column spaces from 0 to 12 hours.

▲ (b) Using the information given for level 0 output in Table 11.4, explode backwards to find the material requirements at levels 1 and 2.

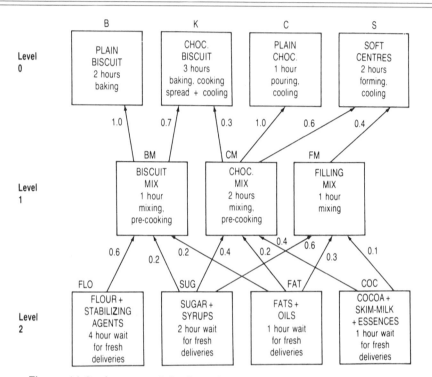

Figure 11.8 Augmented Gozinto chart for confectionery manufacturer.

Table 11.4 Level 0 output for the chocolate manufacturer

Code			Time (hours)				
		7	8	9	10	11	12
B	Plain biscuits	150	150	100	50		
K	Choc. biscuits			60	100	120	120
C	Plain chocolate	50	100	100	50		
S	Soft centres			40	80	100	100

Quantities are shown in 10 kg units.

11.3.1 *Converting MRP to a simplified JIT schedule*

In Chapter 10 we showed a JIT schedule that had the distinguishing feature: once a job has started, there is no interruption in processing it until it has been finished. This is a good condition to maintain in certain MRP situations. In our example there is better hygiene and quality of food if you avoid having half-cooked ingredients hanging around. From the Gozinto chart or the MRP table you can work out the minimum processing time for any product by adding up the relevant lead times. Then you can put these products in a cascading production schedule — a logical order in which products must be initiated if all of the output times are to be achieved. Such a schedule is demonstrated in Figure 11.9 for the previous (chocolate manufacturer's) exercise, with some extra information on it which is explained afterwards. For example, row 1 shows the first batch of products to be initiated: 60 units of plain chocolate biscuits. This takes 8 hours (the minimum possible) using times 1 to 7 inclusive.

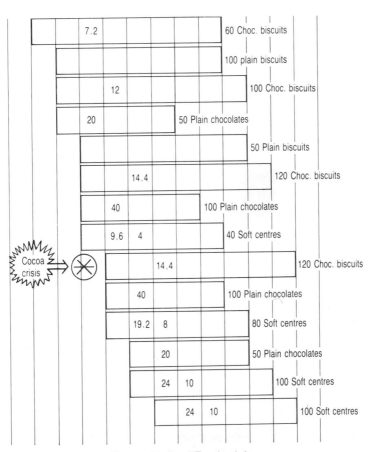

Figure 11.9 JIT schedule.

11.3.2 *How MRP copes with disruptions*

One big advantage of an MRP system is the speed with which it can compute alternative schedules if there is a last minute upset. Even better, these alterations can be displayed graphically in an interactive software package. For example, suppose you are happily operating to schedule in period 3 of our chocolate example when you are told that there has been a hitch in cocoa deliveries — you are going to be 10 units short in both periods 4 and 5. You make immediate plans to ensure an extra 10 units be delivered in periods 6 and 7 but, in the meantime, you have to juggle about with your schedule. What information can MRP give you to help?

It is possible to get an immediate printout of how much cocoa is being used for each product-line period-by-period in the current schedule. The numbers in the boxes in the previous JIT schedule show this relevant information. Summing these numbers column-by-column, you can get a histogram of cocoa usage (see Figure 11.10). You can then use this histogram, the JIT schedule numbers and the Gozinto chart to help attack the cocoa shortage crisis.

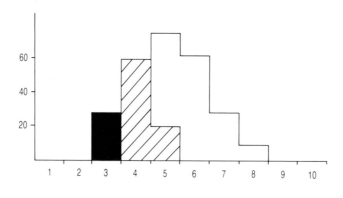

Key

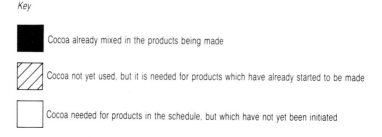

Figure 11.10 Review of cocoa requirements to cope with a disruption in supplies threatened for period 4 onwards.

▼   **Exercise for scheduling whizz-kids**

What would *you* do, assuming that some plain chocolate production can be delayed and some soft centre production can be brought forward?

Hint: What is the best alternative route for the sugars being prepared for the plain chocolate order in the 9th row of the JIT schedule?

Further hint: If you can overcome the immediate crisis (the subject of the first hint), you then need to think of rescheduling production that has not yet started (the last six rows of the JIT schedule). It helps if these six orders are expressed as cards which you can shuffle around like beads on an abacus. The layout for these cards is shown in Figure 11.11. Shuffling these cards is called doing a 'pegging exercise', as in the old days before computers this

▲   was always done on a pegboard.

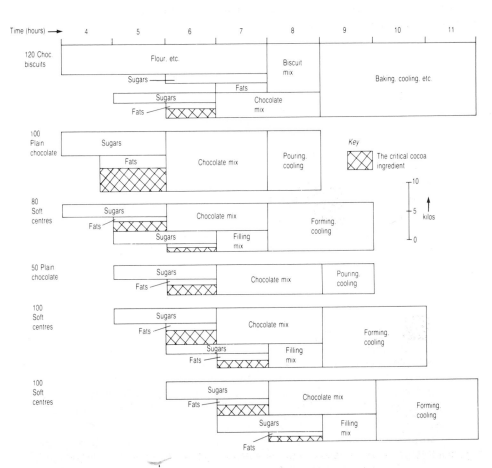

Figure 11.11 Pegging exercise for the last six product lines to be made.

11.3.3 *Comment on MRP*

We hope that you can see how complicated scheduling can get, even for our grossly simplified examples. MRP comes into its own because it can calculate and illustrate schedules far quicker than by hand. But this is only a start to MRP's advantages: it can incorporate many of the little scheduling techniques which we have explained in this chapter (variable lead times, batching, set-ups and production smoothing). Also, as a consequence of greater computer power and user friendliness there has been a movement from *regenerative MRP* (where a new MRP is only recalculated at weekly or monthly intervals) to *net change MRP* where the schedule is continually updated.

Where management have become proficient at MRP scheduling there is also a move to superior practices. Consider our 'cocoa crisis' example. In the old days, management were not just able to visualize all the spin-offs and interconnections arising from such a crisis. Therefore there was a temptation:

1. To hold excessive safety stocks.
2. To end up with an unbalanced schedule with half-finished stock hanging around.
3. To be really late with customer deliveries.
4. To skimp on quality (e.g. lower the correct proportions of the material in short supply).

For all these reasons there are potential benefits for firms with relevant problems to move towards MRP-type approaches. However, there is a proviso. Many firms underestimate the management effort, the systems reorganization and the time involved. This problem is getting worse as we move from MRP-1 to the more extensive MRP-2 (no doubt with MRP-3 and 4 to follow). We would prefer people to explore more thoroughly the foundations of MRP. If you like, the following are the sorts of phase you should pass through before you even consider an MRP computer package:

- *MRP-Minus Five* — Monitoring, Recording, Plotting. There should be a culture of intellectual freedom and detachment to collect information needed for new purposes. The information should not be a rehash of information already collected for existing accounting or engineering functions.
- *MRP-Minus Four* — Modelling Real Processes. This should follow the precepts laid down in Chapter 6 on systems, with special attention paid to the decision points.
- *MRP-Minus Three* — Mastering Reorder Problems. The firm should have experience of structured rather than judgemental approaches to ordering. (The ROQ/ROL section of Chapter 10 is an example of a structured approach.)
- *MRP-Minus Two* — Maintaining Realizable Production. Production schedules should be more than guesswork. A scheduling system should be employed which passes the verifiability test (as explained in Chapter 8 on forecasting) and which has an understandable layout, however crude (as explained in Chapter 10).
- *MRP-Minus One* — Maximizing Resource Potential. You should be able to identify

over- and under-capacity and identify a bottleneck and the knock-on effects that it causes (see the capacity planning section of this chapter).

- *MRP-Zero* — Making Reforms Pay. This is the knock-out punch. Even where firms have geared themselves up for a new system, they fail at the last hurdle. There is nothing wrong with their intelligence or commitment; rather, they just do not keep financial tabs on the development. In the excitement of the new activity, people are fooled into thinking that expense is no object.

11.4 Linear programming

11.4.1 *Introduction*

In our previous section on MRP, you were taking customer requirements for finished products, then, aided by a Gozinto chart you worked backwards through a series of processes to see what raw materials needed to be input. This was a classic *pull system*.

Suppose you do things the opposite way round. Suppose you take whatever materials are given to you, feed them through various processes and see what output you end up with (whether you can sell the result is a different matter). This is a classic *push system* and it uses a different scheduling structure based on Kumzaatov charts.

11.4.1.1 An aside

Bitzat Kumzaatov was an eminent Russian engineer. He was an arch rival of the Italian designer Zepartzat Gozinto, inventor of the Gozinto chart. The Kumzaatov approach was strongly preferred in Communist bloc countries and partially accounts for some of their economic difficulties. Nevertheless, Kumzaatov charts are a useful addition to the operations manager's toolkit if combined with some pull-system constraints. (We develop this point later by adding customer constraints and revenues into a Kumzaatov system. You also need to introduce government constraints to stop Kumzaatov-based organizations polluting the environment — we also examine this issue in more detail later.)

11.4.2 *A simple Kumzaatov illustration*

Consider a gross simplification of an oil refinery, either as an input–output diagram or as an associated table.

If you feed in the crude oils on the left through a refinery, what outputs result as a proportion of the respective inputs?

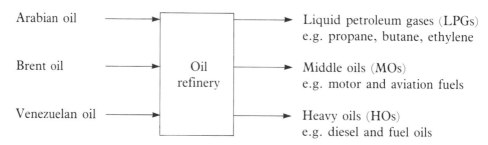

Answer: according to the input—outut coefficients, you get out the following units:

	LPGs	*MOs*	*HOs*
If you feed in 1000 units of Arabian oil	90	480	610
If you feed in 1000 units of Brent oil	150	530	450
If you feed in 1000 units of Venezuelan oil	70	290	440

You could use the above input—output tables for broad-brush planning purposes (such tables were used by economists when they first tried to model the national economy) but, assuming the coefficients are accurate, an observant reader would immediately raise one or two questions about the numbers that have been given:

1. Both Arabian and Brent oils seem to defy the laws of matter. Take the 1000 units of Arabian oil that are fed through the refinery: how on earth can you get out $(90 + 480 + 610) = 1180$?
2. Conversely, look at Venezuelan oil. You find that feeding in 1000 units results in an output of $(70 + 290 + 440) = 800$. What happened? Did it vanish down a plughole or go up in smoke?

We will provide you with an answer to these questions by exploring the black box called 'oil refinery' and describing processes in more detail. As we do this, remember that we are going to keep to the Kumzaatov approach: everything is structured around the idea of 'outputs as proportions of an input'.

11.4.3 *A detailed Kumzaatov illustration*

Crude oil is fed into distillation on the left-hand side of Figure 11.12. After passing through various pipelines (arrows), tanks (circles) and processing plant (boxes), it emerges as finished products on the right-hand side of the diagram. The scheduler is free to choose which of ten crude oils to feed into distillation and can take either a single crude oil or a mixture. Table 11.5 shows what happens when one unit of each type of crude oil is fed through distillation.

Apart from distillation, every other plant has only one input feeding into it (a gross

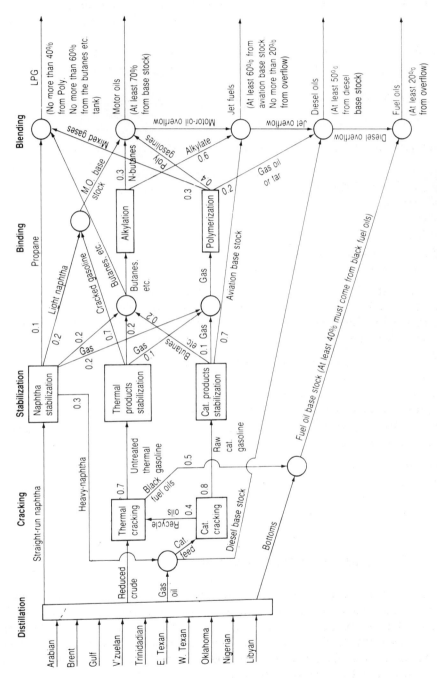

Figure 11.12 Simplified flows and processes in an oil refinery.

Table 11.5   How 1 unit of crude oil input splits up after distillation

	Straight-run naphtha	Reduced crude	Gas oil	Bottoms
Arabian	0.1	0.4	0.3	0.2
Brent (N. Sea)	0.3	0.4	0.2	0.1
Gulf	0.3	0.2	0.2	0.3
Venezuelan	0.1	0.2	0.2	0.5
Trinidadian	0.2	0.3	0	0.5
East Texan	0.2	0.3	0.2	0.3
West Texan	0.3	0.3	0.2	0.2
Oklahoma	0.3	0.3	0.1	0.3
Nigerian	0.4	0.1	0.1	0.4
Libyan	0.2	0.3	0.4	0.1

simplification which can easily be overcome in more detailed models). Output from any of these plants is expressed as a decimal fraction of the relevant input. These decimal fractions are placed against the output pipelines in Figure 11.12. Total yields from various chemical processes do not always sum to 1.0: e.g. thermal cracking converts 1 unit of reduced crude into 0.7 units of untreated thermal gasoline and 0.5 units of black fuel oils. This is because as oil is flowing continuously through pipes, it is impossible to weigh, therefore measurements have to be of volume via flow-meters. It is for this reason that outputs from a plant can be 'greater' than inputs (when liquids are changed to gases or their molecules broken up, their density usually lessens, i.e. the same weight takes up more space). This is why, in the earlier input–output table, 1000 units of Arabian oil gave 1180 units of output.

Usually, total tank input and total tank output should balance. If it is impossible to meet a blending requirement, oil can be drained to waste, either at a tank or anywhere else in the system. This is not very friendly to the environment, and we deal with that point later.

▼   **Exercise**

Choose one of the ten crude oils on the left-hand side of Figure 11.12. Feed 1000 units of your chosen oil into distillation and, using the yields at distillation and subsequent plants, work out the quantities of finished products. Try to meet all the blending requirements without having to send too much oil to waste. Keep things simple by rounding down rather than dealing in fractions of a unit.

If you have chosen Venezuelan oil, it is soon obvious that you cannot meet fuel oil base stock blending requirements without wastage. This was why, in the earlier input–output table, 1000 units of Venezuelan input gave only 800

▲
units of output. This does not mean that Venezuelan oil is useless. It might
give excellent results when combined with another oil, or its cheapness might
overcome the wastage incurred.

▼ **Exercise**

Charge yourself for the 1000 units of crude oil that you have just used and
total up the revenues that you collect from the finished products, using the
costs and revenues in Table 11.6.

By subtracting total costs from total revenue, you get a rough idea of the
profit that your schedule would earn. It is an overestimate because in
practice one also subtracts other refinery charges, notably materials (e.g.
catalyst and lead additives), utilities (e.g. water and electricity charges),
storage, repair, labour costs and rates. Nevertheless, the cost and revenue of
▲ oil products completely dominate these other expenses.

▼ **Exercise for scheduling whizz-kids**

Can you find a legitimate schedule that earns the refinery a profit if the
following extra constraints must be met? As well as using less than or equal
to 1000 units of crude:

1. No more than 100 units of LPG must be produced.
2. Input into the polymerization plant must be no greater than 100.
3. Input into the alkylation plant must be no greater than 100.

This time, rather than feeding in just a single type of crude oil, explore the
▲ effect of taking a combination. Why is the result often better?

Table 11.6 Costs and revenues for the oil refinery (exercise 2)

Crude oil costs ($/unit)		Sales revenues ($/unit)	
Arabian	16.0	Liquid petroleum gases (LPGs)	20
Brent	18.0	Motor oils	24
Gulf	14.0	Jet fuels	17
Venezuelan	9.0	Diesel oils	10
Trinidadian	9.5	Fuel oils	6
East Texan	14.0		
West Texan	15.5		
Oklahoma	14.0		
Nigerian	12.0		
Libyan	17.0		

11.4.4 *Further analysis of refinery scheduling*

If you have access to a computer package, this particular problem is amenable to an LP solution. However, it will take quite a time to write in the data, as it involves forty-nine basic variables and forty-six constraints. The forty-nine basic variables are the ten crude inputs and the thirty-nine arrowed pipelines. The forty-six constraints are made up of three plant capacities, one demand limit, eight blending constraints, ten tank balances and twenty-four constraints for each yield coming out of a plant. (An example of a yield constraint would be 'propane ≤ 0.1 straight-run naphtha'.)

We think it is important to practise hand-solutions *before* solving via an LP package. People who go straight to the package rarely have a feel for the problem and find it difficult to spot formulation errors.

Having introduced what seems like quite a detailed problem, it is now necessary to sound a word of warning. This model, with about fifty constraints and about fifty variables is still a gross approximation. At any normal-sized refinery or chemical plant there will be at least twenty major groups of finished product, at least twenty major processing plants and, between them, hundreds of pipelines. Also, we have brought in only a few simple constraints. In reality, there are an enormous number of other constraints concerning a product's volatility, viscosity, octane rating, sulphur content, gravity and purity.

To schedule a refinery properly you need to move to another level of detail. Within just one of the plant boxes (for example, cat cracking) there will be another Kumzaatov chart just as complicated as Figure 11.12. At this level, not all constraints can be expressed as linear equations of an LP. Chemical and control engineers find that they are optimizing within their own local area, rather than taking account of all the interrelationships with other plant.

11.4.4.1 An aside on taxation and pollution control

Left to their own devices, oil companies, and others, often find that a certain amount of pollution or oil spillage gives them the best results, even if that has a bad effect on the environment. Spillages are difficult to identify, measure and monitor, so what should a socially-conscious government do about it? One answer is, paradoxically, to give the oil companies more money. Suppose they are given a subsidy for the total weight of their outputs and an equal tax is imposed on their input weights, you get something like this:

Situation before a tax/subsidy is imposed for a company which wastes 10 per cent on its input

Output quantity	× Revenue/unit	= Total revenue
90	$11	$990
Input quantity	× Cost/unit	= Total cost
100	$9	$900
	⇒ Profit	
	+$90	

Situation after a $10 tax/subsidy for the same company

Output quantity × Revenue/unit = Total revenue
90               $21 $1890

Input quantity × Cost/unit = Total cost
100             $19 $1900

⇒ Profit
− $10

Ideally, the tax/subsidies should apply to weights, but the system still works quite well in a volume-based system like the exercise you have just done. For example, if your best answer to this exercise involved wasting products, try reworking it when all the crude oil costs are increased by $10/unit and all sales are also increased by $10/unit. In the new system, there is a strong incentive to avoid waste.

11.5 Conclusion

In the introduction to this chapter we mentioned a similarity between total scheduling techniques and the critical path method of the project planning chapter (Chapter 9). In particular we mentioned these two similarities:

1. The ability to switch from broad-brush to fine detail (as in the work breakdown schedule of project planning).
2. The operation of a simple scheduling mechanism which can be applied to large problems (e.g. the forwards and backwards passes in the critical path method).

These same advantages are at work in our total scheduling techniques.

In *capacity planning*, the monthly time-buckets can be replaced by quarter-years (less detail) or weeks (more detail) and the product lines expanded from three (in Figure 11.3) to twenty or more.

If there is a move to more detail, it is easy to calculate answers to the expanded formulation. If it is only required to balance columns and rows, this can be done heuristically on a spreadsheet. If it is required to find a cost-effective answer, this can be done by using the well-known transportation LP algorithm (for which there are many software programs).

In *MRP* (materials requirement planning) we have taken a broad-brush illustration so that all the calculations can be fitted onto one page of a textbook. An even broader brush would replace our time units of an hour by eight-hour shifts or days. With respect to other constraints, it is more normal to find that business applications go into much more detail than our illustration. We have dealt with only a dozen variables (raw materials mixes and finished products) over only three levels. Most firms need MRP to cope with fifty or more variables over five levels: and it is MRP's strength that the simple method of calculation is not upset by this extra complexity.

In *continuous (linear) processing (LP)*, we compared the broad-brush to the more detailed approach in our two examples. As to the simplicity of the method, you can use PC software to solve the 'extended exercise for scheduling whizz-kids'. When you become proficient at LP formulation, this should take you no more than an hour (fifty minutes to submit the computer input, five minutes for the computer time, five minutes for the printout).

Looking to the future, we feel that if there is a new technique of total scheduling, it will still have to keep its central method of calculations very simple. There are other total systems approaches (for example, industrial dynamics and simulation) which use more advanced mathematics and which provide useful 'what if?' insights. However, these methods are, in our opinion, of limited use in scheduling, which needs techniques which are robust, communicable, quick and certain.

11.6 Recommended reading

Voss *et al.*'s 'Ranmoor Car Hire' in *Operations Management in the Service Industries and Public Sector* (Wiley, 1985) is an easy extension of our vehicle capacity analysis.

If you want to tackle a large scale integrative planning case in trucking, try 'Commonwealth Transport' in Collier, *Service Management* (Prentice Hall, 1987).

'Canning Glass Works' in Sasser, *Cases in Operations Management: Analysis and Action* (Irwin, 1982), is good practice at distinguishing CONSTRAINTS from *constraints*.

For detailed manpower planning implications, developed from an aggregate planning context, see 'Swift River Box Co.' in Sasser, *op. cit.* 'Macphersons', in Schmenner's *Cases in Production/ Operations Management* (SRA, 1986), poses capacity planning/forecasting trade-offs. Also 'Jones Meter' in the same book really gets you to question whether a proposed MRP installation will improve on a crude ROQ/ROL system.

Chapter 12

The strategic manager

12.1 Introduction

The general manager has to juggle and balance all the resources, functions and vested interests within his or her organization, as well as handling a possibly hostile external environment. In doing so, many aspects of operations management have to be combined. At this level, management involves a vision, a philosophy, a shrewdness that involves elements of *diplomacy* and *grand strategy*. We are going to explain what we mean via a lengthy case study which also involves tackling a series of exercises, each dealing with different levels of decision-making. In this way, we hope that you will be able to understand the difference between tactics and strategy, and how apparently insular operations management decisions have considerable knock-on effects on other aspects of the business.

12.2 Jackson Interiors

First of all, read the case study quickly, just to familiarize yourself with the names and situation. Then look at the questions that follow the case before rereading it and giving your evaluations.

12.2.1 *The interviewees*

Unnamed person	A competitor of Jackson's
Sheila Jackson	Current owner, widow of Ernest Jackson
Maisie Bowerstock	Office Manager
Norman Shields	Shop Foreman
Jeff Smith	Salesman

Simon Wilson	Quality Manager
Lucy Todd	Designer
Desmond Tang	Ex-MBA student
John Fletcher	Service Engineer
Margaret Ball	Shopfloor Machinist
Gerry Richards	Financial Adviser
John Edwards	Fitter

12.2.2 *Introduction to Jackson Interiors*

Jackson Interiors is a Manchester firm that supplies and installs furnishings for a wide range of customers: private homes, hotels, flats, nursing homes, student halls of residence, schools, hospitals, offices, pubs, cafes, nightclubs, shops. The firm's main product lines are soft furnishings, e.g. curtains, carpets, blinds, wall and light fittings, bedspreads, shower curtains. The firm has twenty-five full-time employees: eight office staff, seven machinists and a mixture of blue-collar and craft workers. In addition, there is a floating working population of part-timers, trainees and casuals who can be called upon to cover a temporary surge in business.

The firm is located about two miles from the centre of Manchester in an area that is a warren of other small and medium-sized businesses. It occupies a converted Methodist meeting-house dating from Victorian times, a solid two-storey stone building. The upper floor is mostly devoted to storage. On the lower floor are the cutting and sewing rooms where most of the manufacturing operations take place.

Jackson Interiors is a family firm. Recently, the sole owner and managing director, Ernest Jackson, died of a heart attack. His widow Sheila took over and is running the business today. The following notes are summaries of conversations that were held with various parties with an interest in the future of Jackson Interiors.

12.2.3 *Interview reports*

A competitor's appraisal of Jackson Interiors

'Under Ernest Jackson they grew from half a dozen employees to the largest specialist furnisher in the district. They've got a good reputation and a wide customer-base, from millionaire penthouses to Salvation Army hostels. Recently, they've come in with some very competitive tenders which have won them a lot of business, but I can't see them making much profit out of them. I think the recession is going to force the new management to have a complete rethink about what they should do. They could make a big profit by selling that Gothic horror they call a factory; some developer would snap it up. Then they could move to smaller premises in an Enterprise Zone and use all the money to buy up-to-date machinery. Or they could stay where they are and buy up the order book and equipment of one of the several furnishing firms going bankrupt.'

Sheila Jackson — Owner-Manager

'Eleven months ago my husband died suddenly of a heart attack. It was completely unexpected. Although he was in his sixties, he worked from dawn to dusk for the business and was as happy as a sandboy. After the funeral, I talked to the family and his colleagues and decided to try running the business myself. It was what he would have wanted me to do. It wasn't a completely new experience because I had been going into the office two or three times a week to help tidy up accounts and chase up bills, etc. Also, very fortunately, I had just finished an evening management diploma at the Poly and felt ready to put theory into practice. I started off getting by with a lot of sympathy and support from colleagues and clients, but that soon passed. In the long run, I've got to survive on merit. Now, I'm going to take some hard decisions that are going to surprise a few people. Some people think of me as a dithering softie, but I wanted to know the business inside-out before making any big changes.'

Maisie Bowerstock — Office Manager

'As you can see, it is a bit hectic in this office. There is just me and Jill [her secretary] to handle the telephones, do the paperwork, and keep in touch with the letters, diaries, schedules and plans of everyone else. I don't mind people treating this office like a railway station if they keep me informed of what is going on. Really, we desperately need more clerical help, but we lost Simon, as I'll explain. Next to us is the office for Lucy [the designer] which she shares with the two salesmen.

'There is the bigger, manager's office upstairs which none of us used to go into much when Mr Jackson was alive. Sheila lets it be used for all sorts of meetings now. She'll knock on my door and say, "I've been kicked out of my office again by the Workers Design-Skills Circle. Do you mind if I come and help you out for half an hour?" I think she lets herself be pushed around too much. They exploit her good nature. Look at young Simon Wilson who used to work for me. Because he was pushy and ambitious, Sheila made him Quality Manager. Now he is hardly in the place, always visiting customers and suppliers. You should see his travel expenses, it's a disgrace. I mean, you expect it with the salesmen, but someone should keep an eye on young Simon or there'll be trouble, mark my words. To be honest, I was more than a bit miffed when Sheila took Simon away from me. I've worked for the Jacksons for twenty-five years and Mr Jackson always used to consult me about staff changes.'

Norman Shields — Shop Foreman

'I was brought in as a stop-gap measure the day after Mr Jackson died, and expected to stay no more than two or three weeks until they got a proper replacement. I'm long in the tooth (in my sixties), had been unemployed for six months and had no experience of furnishings. I'd spent my life as a machinist, foreman and progress chaser in the engineering industry. I was a friend of Mr Richards, their accountant, and he persuaded me to help him out. The first week was hell ... correction, the first *month* was hell. Mr Jackson had tried to be the manager, foreman, salesman, the lot. No wonder it killed him. A lot of the customers' orders were all in his head and he left a lot of shorthand notes around about processing instructions which were double-Dutch to me. The phone never stopped ringing with customers complaining about their delayed orders. Eventually we got it sorted out because the girls worked several evenings to clear the backlog . . . and wouldn't take overtime rates. And I couldn't have got better help from the office staff. Maisie took over the production scheduling — she still does it now. And Lucy Todd [the designer] was a marvellous calming influence on the girls when the salesmen and fitters were bullying them to hurry up. Eleven months later, things are ticking over nicely — I like the atmosphere, the challenges, the teamwork. They can't pay me much but, if they want me, I'm happy to stay here until I retire.'

Jeff Smith — Salesman

'When Sheila Jackson took over, I really worked my butt off to keep this firm going. I won lots of business by offering good discounts. I hassled the shopfloor continuously to make sure the big orders came out on the dates I had promised. I really got this firm moving. Then, the other day, she calls me into her office and says she cannot afford me. Crazy! Last year I got £12,000 basic, plus £16,000 commission plus usual car and promotion expenses. I earned every penny of it. Now she says I'm not going to have commission, only share the same bonus with other staff. She thought that if she upped my basic salary, that would make it all right. No way! She can't threaten me like that. Everyone in the furnishing trade knows me as *the* champion salesman. I've got more contacts than she's dreamed of. They know I can get results for them and I've proved it. Just see how many customers she loses if I leave.'

Simon Wilson — Quality Manager

'I worked as a draughtsman for GEC, but the engineering slump left me unemployed — aged twenty-three, with two kids and a mortgage. At the time, the only job going was this dead-end accounts work in Jackson's office. I stuck it for two years, all the time sending off applications for something better, but no luck. I got on shortlists, even had several interviews, but I always had the bad luck to be interviewed by stupid thickheads who weren't on my intellectual wavelength. One day, completely unexpected, Sheila pulled me out of Maisie's office to do something different. She said, "If you want, you can be the firm's Quality Manager. You won't get any more money because I can't afford it. You won't even have an office because you wouldn't be doing your job if you were sitting in it." Straight away I went to a few seminars, read a few books and got stuck in.

'Now I make sure we get the best stuff from the suppliers — Maisie used to take offcuts as a favour to them but I won't. I'm also on the backs of the fitters if they don't do their jobs properly. I'm also doing a deal to lease some up-to-date, more reliable machines: so you can see I'm really shaking up this place. I don't care who gets offended. If I'm not happy with anything I'll say so. If Sheila's too timid to call a spade a spade, I don't mind doing the dirty work for her. I've sorted out that designer Lucy Todd a few times. Everyone else is scared of her temper, but not me.'

Lucy Todd — Designer

'I've worked for ten years with the Jacksons and they were a lovely couple. Basically, my job is to provide a furnishing and decorating service for the 20 per cent of our business which comes from wealthy private customers. I win business by personal contacts and by word of mouth. I control everything from the first enquiry to the final installation. My reputation is too much on the line to let anyone else at Jackson's interfere. What my clients want is something unique — a work of art, a celebration of their lifestyle. So I have to ensure that the highest levels of craftsmanship are involved. When girls on the shopfloor work on my designs, it is under my constant supervision — they love it — such a change from their other boring, routine work. Poor Mr Shields wrings his hands when I'm around because, he says, the place grinds to a halt because of me ... But poof ... I just wave him back to his little rabbit hutch and tell him not to bother us. That makes the girls giggle. Mr Jackson always used to say I was the firm's invisible salesman. Look at all the businesses my clients run: and those businesses need furnishings too. Now Sheila's in charge I'm not sure how much support I've got. I know she listens too much to Mr Richards who thinks I'm a luxury. Apart from the girls, my only real supporter is young Simon, the Quality whizz-kid. He often asks my advice about this and that. I tell him quality is all about style. "No, it isn't", he says. "It is all about systems." We have some great arguments which are a right laugh.'

Desmond Tang, MBA — previous industrial placement (now in Hong Kong)

'I was sorry to hear of Mr Jackson's death. One reason I did my three-month project at Jacksons was to try to find ways of reducing his very heavy workload. I didn't see much of him because I worked mostly under Mrs Jackson's direction. She was interested in whether more uses could be made of the computer beyond basic packages that did payroll, invoices and monthly accounts. First, I looked at production scheduling, but things like MRP were not suitable and were too expensive — and Maisie and Mr Jackson had a magic way of doing everything in their heads anyway. So, instead, I did a market research survey. This gave some interesting results. I clustered all the customers into segments so that, within each segment, demand was driven by the same trends and leading indicators. Then I suggested the allocation of extra resources so that different marketing campaigns could be directed at each of these segments. I gather Mr Jackson liked my idea in principle and appointed an additional salesman, and was starting to revamp the marketing approach when he died. I have also been told that things have not worked out the way I suggested because Lucy Todd and Jeff Smith have carved up all the best accounts between them and won't let anyone else interfere.'

John Fletcher — Service Engineer

'I come in on a service contract to maintain and repair their sewing machines. My overall impressions of them? Everyone is very friendly. Lots of chit-chat on the shopfloor. The machinists know what they are doing: Lucy Todd trains them to do everything. They are probably the fastest, most skilful, most versatile machinists I've come across. But the firm's got problems. Their equipment is getting obsolescent and they can't afford to buy new ones. I'd just persuaded Mr Jackson to lease some electronic machines when he died. Mrs Jackson put the idea on ice, but I've got young Simon, the Quality man, to speak to her about it. Simon's really on the ball when it comes to installing the latest gadgetry.'

Margaret Ball — Shopfloor Machinist

'What do I think of working here? At its worst it is boring, cold, draughty and doesn't pay well. But it's convenient — I live just round the corner — and friendly. Some firms don't let you have Walkmans, and have supervisors breathing down your neck all the time. Here, we can make the workbench just like home, with pot plants and decorations. If it's anyone's birthday, we all go to the pub at lunchtime. Mr Shields the foreman is a real old-fashioned gentleman. Very conscientious, very polite, very considerate if any of us are not very well or have got trouble at home.

'Usually, they let you get on with work at your own rate, but if you make a mistake, you're expected to correct it out of hours. Sometimes the salesmen get in a panic and come here tearing their hair out, telling us to get a move on, but we just ignore them. Lucy screams at us too: but she's different, she screams at everyone. She's not really a dragon, she's got a heart of gold. She helps us to set up the machines and teaches us to do difficult embroidery. She's brilliant. Not like Simon in Quality. He thinks he's brilliant but we all call him Simple Simon behind his back. He doesn't know the first thing about cutting and sewing, and it makes me sick when he comes up with all these schemes to improve the place just to impress Mrs Jackson. We think Simon is dead jealous of Lucy and makes life difficult for her. Mrs Jackson should stop treating him as her blue-eyed boy. It is about time she started managing this place properly instead of locking herself away.'

Gerry Richards — Financial Adviser

'I've been a friend of the Jacksons for years. I audit their accounts and give them advice, though Ernest Jackson was a law unto himself. Sheila has done very well to keep the firm going but she's got some tough decisions to make in the coming year. As far as I can judge, they are in the black (just), but really, they should be making more profit considering the volume of business they are doing. Something is wrong, but I won't be able to pin it down until I see the year-end accounts. In the meantime, I've told Sheila to hold back on any plant investment and to sort out her paperwork. The office is in a mess, and really, Maisie needs to be retired and replaced by someone with a proper accountancy qualification. I also told Sheila to look into staff overheads and expenses. You've got to give the salesmen good expense accounts or you will lose them, but some of the other staff could be taking liberties. For example, I've heard rumours from the fitters that Lucy Todd is siphoning off business on her own account. If I had my way, I'd get rid of high-and-mighty Miss Todd like a shot.'

John Edwards — Fitter

'There are six fitters with three vans, so we can be doiong three jobs at once — but if there is a big job we'll all be working together. Unlike the rest of Jacksons, we are on piece-rates, so we try to get our act together and finish quickly. I'd say we are so experienced we can finish work in half the time it would take someone else. Quite often, we work so hard early in the week that we can take Thursday or Friday off, or do jobs for another company. Why shouldn't we if we work hard? Jeff Smith, the salesman, has plenty of contacts whenever we want to do work on the side. Not like Lucy Todd: she has her own fitters for her wealthy clients. Jeff reckons she is getting quite a few backhanders which she doesn't tell Jacksons about.

'The other thing that really bugs us is when the factory gives us a delivery date and when we go to get it, it isn't ready. There we are, twiddling our thumbs with nothing we can do at short notice, and a customer who shouts at us, not them, when it's late. I've told Sheila Jackson it is not fair. Norman Shields, the foreman, is useless. She should get rid of him and put in someone who can get things done on time. Then there is that idiot Quality man, Simon Wilson. He goes on and on at the customer, asking if we've done the job perfectly — and if you keep on like that of course they'll mention some trivial fault and we'll have to go back and put it right. It's all right for him, he's on travel expenses for customer visits. We're on piece-work and don't get a penny for the extra trouble he causes. So, you can see, Jacksons isn't the easiest firm to work for.'

▼   **Exercise 1**

How would you evaluate the seven options listed below if you are endeavouring to secure an immediate improvement in Jackson's cash-flow situation? Use this marking scheme:

`\` a good idea;	X a bad idea;	? neither good nor bad
`\\` very good;	XX very bad;	?? could be very good or very bad

Options

1. Have an all-round increase in prices and stop offering discounts.
2. Manage with two less office staff than at present.
3. Cut back on staff expenses, bonuses and commissions.
4. Have a blitz on making customers pay up quicker, even if it annoys them.
5. Urge the salesmen to win more business quickly, giving them more office support to do so.
6. Increase the time before you pay your creditors by three or four weeks.
7. Cut out some of your product range, enabling you to sell off some material stock which will then be surplus to requirements.

▲

▼   **Exercise 2**

Consider in turn each person on the list below, and say how much of a
disaster it would be if Jacksons lost their services. Use this marking scheme:

> ??? Catastrophic   ?? Serious   ? A nuisance, but no more
>   0 No effect   ! It would actually be beneficial

1. Maisie Bowerstock
2. Simon Wilson
3. Jeff Smith
▲ 4. Lucy Todd

▼   **Exercise 3**

Consider certain areas of operations management at Jacksons, listed below.
How important is it necessary to carry out investigations in these areas? Use
this marking scheme:

> * * *   *Vital*   The whole management team should throw
>   themselves into *tackling* this problem now. (Of
>   everything marked vital, rank areas 1, 2, 3, etc. in
>   order of importance.)
>   * *   *Important*   This must be *investigated*, but it does not need
>   everyone in management to get involved.
>   *   *Relevant*   These issues should be *borne in mind* but no
>   specific investigations made into them at the
>   moment.
>   —   *A diversion* Management would be *wasting their time* to think
>   about them.

1. Carry out a value analysis on current and potential products.
2. Should any equipment be modernized or replaced?
3. Change the payment schemes for the shopfloor and the fitters.
4. Reshuffle the duties of the office staff, possibly involving new
   appointments or retirements/dismissals.
5. Relocating the firm on a new site.
6. Consider ways in which you can reduce the time from placing an order
   to installation (currently this averages eight weeks).
7. Aim for a quality standard conforming to BS5750.
8. Develop a better forecasting and market information system.
9. Devise a scheduling system that everyone can operate and understand,
   not just Maisie.
10. Install a production scheduling software package.
11. Switch to a JIT system so that hardly any raw material stocks are kept
    on the premises.

▼   **Exercise 4**

How frequently and how intensely should *Sheila Jackson* interface with certain parties who are listed below? Use this marking scheme:

* * *   Establish an intense relationship, see frequently, giving them unlimited time to explore issues with her if they want it.

* *   Establish regular contact and a comprehensive working relationship but do not make meetings too lengthy.

*   Occasionally give time for them when special situations arise, but usually see them only briefly or delegate someone else to see them.

—   Keep at arm's length. Evade, avoid and minimize time with these people.

Local rivals
Material suppliers
Industrial customers
Software salesmen
Management consultants
Trade associations and trade fairs
Lucy Todd
Simon Wilson
Maisie Bowerstock
Norman Shields
Jeff Smith
▲   Alex Humphries (the other salesman)

12.2.4 *General issues raised by the Jackson exercises*

12.2.4.1 Handling imperfect information

1. Inadequate details

How would the decisions you were asked to make have been improved if you were confronted with 20, 40, 60 or 80 pages of description? One would expect some improvement so long as relevant issues were expanded, and that you were not fed red herrings and trivia. But that begs the question as to what is regarded as 'relevant'. An accountant would have liked financial statements; an economist, an industry analysis; an industrial engineer, an exploration of materials technology. For the purposes of general management, we have summarized the confused and contradictory positions taken by key stakeholders in Jacksons. Like the Duke of Wellington at the Battle of Waterloo, decisions *have* to be taken even if you cannot see because of the fog, not many messengers are getting back from the front line, and the messages that you do get are garbled and unreliable.

2. Personal bias in communications

In conversation, there is a common tendency to exaggerate, to gossip and to win the sympathy of the listener. Run-of-the-mill disagreements between employees are often magnified by those wishing to observe or to participate in a live soap opera of their own making. Nor is the general manager, as a receiver of information free from personal bias. Employees intent on flattering Sheila Jackson will be tempted to tell her what she *wants* to hear not what she *needs* to hear. Or Sheila may have received such good advice from a specialist in the past that she accepts bad advice from him without independent corroboration. Or Sheila may be persuaded to act impulsively by the last person to win her ear. From her comments, Sheila seems to be aware of these dangers and is giving herself time to absorb and evaluate information before making strategic decisions.

3. Chinese whispers

Unlike the front-line manager, the general manager may be one, two or more steps removed from where the action is happening. If your information is transmitted via a chain of intermediaries, it is more likely to get corrupted. For example, Sheila Jackson will be advised by Jerry Richards to get rid of Lucy Todd. His advice will have been influenced by what the fitters have told him about Lucy's backhanders. The fitters have been told this by Jeff Smith, the salesman. Jeff, the original source, may or may not have had good grounds for his opinion, but the intermediaries have *wanted* what he said to be true and so have embellished the rumour before passing it on.

4. Distinguishing soft from hard information

There is a temptation to say to the general manager, 'Act only on hard information; statistics, accounts or historical facts.' On closer inspection, such sources are not so reliable as they seem. (For example, see our earlier discussion on F.W. Taylor and his 47½ tons per day ingot loading rate.) Valuations too, can be unreliable. A balance sheet may record the value of property or raw material as that at the time of purchase, or scaled down by an inappropriate depreciation factor or set at an over-optimistic 'current market price'. Such false valuations may seriously mislead a general manager when he/she decides to re-equip, relocate or expand.

On the other hand, a general manager may have strong confidence in certain soft information. In Sheila Jackson's case, for example:

The strong loyalty of her production workforce
The excellent goodwill of her customers
The absence of a serious local rival

A good general manager will be in touch with these aspects and have a 'gut feeling' about them, rather than converting them to quantifiable evaluations. This is not to argue that everything should be decided by intuition. Rather that good decisions are based on a shrewd reinterpretation of all the hard and soft information that is available.

12.2.4.2 Notes on exercise 1 — from tactics to strategy

The difference between tactics and strategy is clearly appreciated by anyone who plays chess. A fork, a pin or a discovered check are all simple tactical devices usually demanding an immediate response from your opponent. For beginners, springing a simple tactic often secures victory. This is rarely the case for professionals. Grandmaster chess is determined much more by long-term positional strategy and a build-up of subtle parallel threats, not all of which can be answered.

Similar principles operate in business. Tactical skills are demonstrated by quick, co-ordinated action, by hustle, by expediency; the seizing of a one-off opportunity or the successful response to an unexpected emergency. This is all very well, but an obsession with tactics leads to 'seat of the pants' or 'ad hoc' or 'fire fighting' management style. Just like a chess grandmaster, the general manager should be proficient at tactical skills but only because they are elements in a greater strategy. This can be illustrated by re-examining the tactical options 1–7 that you were asked to evaluate in exercise 1.

Option 1 was to 'have an all-round increase in prices and stop offering discounts'. To be successfully implemented this tactic needs:

* Maisie to work on new price lists and brochures.
* Sheila to give new guidelines on price negotiations to Lucy and the salesmen.

But before option 1 is adopted, Sheila should work through the knock-on effects that will follow after the tactic has been completed. For example:

* Certain segments of the market (schools, colleges and hospitals) are working to very tight budgets and will be put off by Jackson's price increases.
* If higher prices lead to a loss of turnover, it may be necessary to reduce the size of the labour force.
* If the salesman can no longer offer discounts to win business, their commissions and bonuses could be affected. They might become demotivated or even leave Jacksons.

Suppose we carry out a similar analysis for option 2: 'manage with two less office staff than at present'. As before, first spell out the steps necessary to implement such an option. Of the several possibilities, suppose the following is decided: Jill (Maisie's assistant) and Alex Humphries (second salesman) leave. To stop Maisie being over-burdened, production scheduling is shifted back to Norman Shields. Jeff Smith takes over Alex's customers.

Again, before this tactic is adopted, Sheila should meditate on the following knock-on effects:

* Maisie will be very upset by having 'her' staff reduced yet again.
* Jeff could be picking up commissions from Alex's old customers, and that might make him happier.
* But Jacksons are now far too dependent on Jeff.
* Norman might make a mess of the production scheduling.

So far, we have looked at the consequences if Jacksons adopt *either* tactical option 1 *or* tactical option 2. By comparing consequences, we can assess whether it is incompatible to adopt both simultaneously. In this particular case there must be reservations about this. Maisie will certainly be demotivated and overworked, and the fundamental disagreement between Jeff and Sheila has been left unresolved.

▼   **Follow-up to exercise 1**

For each of the remaining tactical options 3–7:

(a) Spell out what must be done for the tactic to succeed.

(b) Anticipate the knock-on effects.

▲ (c) Check whether it is unwise to implement a tactic simultaneously with any other tactics.

The follow-up exercise has moved from the operation of one tactic to an investigation of what happens if several tactics are co-ordinated. This is the beginning of strategic management which will be explored further in the next section.

12.2.4.3 Notes on exercise 2 — working towards a functional strategy

A *functional strategy* concerns a long-term co-ordinated approach within a business department. For example:

- A *marketing strategy* will seek to co-ordinate such things as promotions, pricing policy, salesforce deployment, packaging and advertising.
- A *financial strategy* will seek to co-ordinate such things as profit distribution, borrowings, cash management, acquisitions and disposals.

There are several other functional strategies and one of these, the *human resources strategy*, can be illustrated by expanding exercise 2. Sheila is faced with a fair degree of uncertainty in evaluating the effectiveness of the four key members of staff mentioned in the question. This can be illustrated on a matrix, shown in Figure 12.1.

Each of the circled positions in Figure 12.1 expresses Sheila's rough evaluation of her staff's effectiveness. Simon, for example, in the top left has shown his willingness to take on a new role (high change-potential), but is still making quite a nuisance of himself (low current contribution). Maisie, in the bottom right is a loyal, long-serving employee holding the firm together with her scheduling skills (high current contribution), but is probably incapable of enhancing her existing role or skill (low change-potential).

Each circle has arrows projecting from it, and the length of an arrow indicates the degree of uncertainty Sheila possesses when making her assessment. For example, the

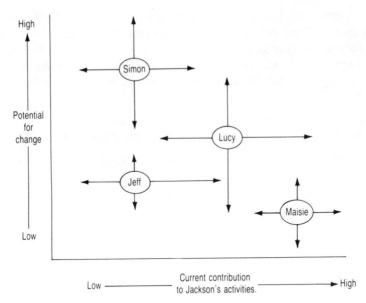

Figure 12.1 Human resource portfolio mix.

long horizontal arrows associated with Lucy highlight the fact that people are either very much for her or very much against her. The short vertical arrows associated with Jeff indicate his uncompromising attitude to Sheila over his reward system.

▼   **Quick exercise**

Put in circles and arrows for:

    Norman Shields
    Gerry Richards
▲   John Edwards

The tactics of staff negotiations

Sheila can use the previous matrix for both tactical and strategic purposes. Tactically, in one-to-one negotiations she needs to adopt a different style according to where that person is on the matrix, where that person wants to be, and where that person will be if nothing is done. Thus, she saw Simon trying to get out of a dead-end position by trying to escape from the firm, so she gave him the opportunity for greater potential which he seized with alacrity. With Jeff, Sheila's approach should be different. Rather than waste time on someone who is stubborn, she should see if the other salesman (Alex) is more amenable to persuasion. If he is, she can re-approach Jeff with more power to her elbow. Sheila is providing moral and social support for Maisie (but needs to back it up with more secretarial help) because Maisie's expertise has been a critical factor in keeping the firm going after Mr Jackson's death. Sheila has delayed taking action on Lucy until she has resolved some of the large uncertainty surrounding Lucy. These are examples of the one-to-one tactical approaches which can be defined with the help of the matrix.

A portfolio strategy for human resources management

Now look at the wider issue. How should Sheila Jackson develop a balanced human resources strategy for all her workers?

1.   Via a crude reward and punishment strategy?
2.   Via a more subtle nudging of staff along a positive management development cycle?

The previous matrix (Figure 12.1) can be used to illustrate these approaches (see Figure 12.2).

The four symbols that appear in Figure 12.2 are the same ones that are used by the well-known Boston Consulting Group approach for a holding company to evaluate a portfolio of its subsidiaries. We show how it can be used to manage a portfolio of human beings.

Suppose that everyone has been given a position on the matrix. This would be how the 'reward and punishment' strategy would proceed:

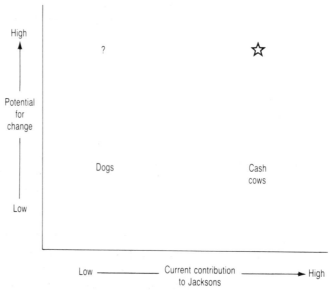

Figure 12.2   Human resource portfolio using Boston Consultancy Group symbols.

1. *Management attitude to '?' staff.* Put them under extreme threats and promises. If they move towards a dog, make it clear they will be sacked. If they move towards a star, then promise that they will be a step nearer promotion.
2. *Management attitude to star staff.* Reward them lavishly to stop them leaving and as an inducement to '?' to join them. Try to recruit outsiders who are rated as 'star' quality.
3. *Management attitude to cash cows.* They are stuck in a rut within your organization so that you do not have to worry about them leaving. Make things comfortable and secure for them so that they are happy working at a high capacity. But do not subject them to drastic changes or extreme rewards as this might drive them to deviancy.
4. *Management attitude to dogs.* Ruthlessly dismiss them as soon as they are identified.

Such an approach at least has the virtues of efficiency, consistency and every employee knowing the 'rules of the game'. Disadvantages are that it can lead to neurosis, envy and selfishness. This crude human strategy is likely to be as ineffective as the equivalent corporate stratey where dog subsidiaries are sold off and new star subsidiaries acquired. To the BCG strategist's chagrin, many of the supposed stars floundered because they were managed badly, and some of the dogs he sold off flourished under better management.

The alternative management development approach

In contrast to reward and punishment, a management development strategy searches for an employee's hidden potential which is waiting to be released. But this is not trying to push everyone to the star category. It is recognized that one person may shift between quadrants for many reasons:

- A brilliant researcher who drives himself to nervous exhaustion may swing backwards and forwards between star and dog.
- Very few people pick up all their techniques before joining a firm. The revolution in IT, for example, has meant that every few years we have had to go through a major relearning process. Therefore it is quite acceptable to fulfil the roles of say 'cash cow for three years,? for one year' in a repetitive cycle.
- For teamwork, you do not always get the best results from a group of stars: there would be too much bitchiness and manic running round in circles (for example, we have always been impressed by the activities of student committees when compared to their professors).

Overall, the management development approach has a more tolerant attitude to variations in an individual's current contribution. However, it does try to manipulate people into work situations where their 'potential for change' is stretched, even if people want to stay in a rut. In the Jackson case, Sheila has indicated that this is the strategy she intends to follow by 'firing shots across the bows' at both Jeff and Maisie.

12.2.2.4 Notes on exercise 3 — strategic choice

Previously, we mentioned how Sheila Jackson wished to absorb information, to gain a feel for the business, before launching certain strategies. However, she cannot go on considering alternatives endlessly without making *any* decision. This is a real danger, even for a small company like Jacksons. For example, exercise 3 lists eleven strategic options in the area of operations management. If you add options in other areas, such as marketing and finance, at least thirty strategic options will be competing for Sheila's attention. Without any support staff to carry out prior investigations, Sheila must find her own way through the strategic option maze. There is no shortage of advice from academics, many books being devoted exclusively to this subject. We are most impressed by the empirical work carried out by William Glueck, who reckoned that there was a unique, simple characteristic shared by successful US managers.

> They tackled their most important problem and didn't look at anything else until it was resolved.

This begs the question, 'how did they know it was their most important problem?' We return to this tricky question in a minute. In the meantime, look again at your answers to exercise 3. How many options did you rank as vital? According to Glueck, no more than one option should have this tag. In our opinion, there is even a case for severely restricting the number listed as important.

▼   **Quick recap exercise**

▲   We think that only three of the eleven options warrant classifying as vital or important. What do you think the three were?

In visual terms, we wish to devise an effective filtering process (see Figure 12.3).

In Jackson's case, various people will try to impose their will on the filtering process and, unless Sheila is assertive, this could lead to the wrong strategy popping out of the filter. Unless she is careful, each option will be mangled on one or more of these grounds.

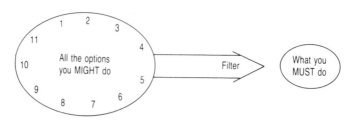

Figure 12.3   The Options Filter.

'It can't be done.'
'Thou shouldst not do it.'
'We don't want to do it.'

We will give illustrations of these arguments as they apply to the exercise 3 options.

'It can't be done' (capability test)

Against option 2	We haven't got the money to buy new machines.
Against option 5	Our current workers will be unable to travel to a new factory on an Enterprise Zone site.
Against option 9	Even if we could afford the software, we can't afford the consultants to install the system and train us.

'Thou shouldst not do it' (suitability test)

Against option 3	Why go through the turmoil of changing a payments system which is running smoothly?
Against option 4	Isn't it immoral to upset office staff who have been so loyal to Jacksons through difficult times?
Against option 7	Our customers don't care about BS5750 so long as the end product is good.

'We don't want to do it' (acceptability test)

Against option 4	Jeff Smith and Lucy Todd will resist strongly any interference with 'their' clients.
Against option 6	The machinists will ignore any attempt to make them change their way of doing things.
Against option 9	Maisie will be very miffed and won't co-operate helping to tell others how to do 'her' job.

If you look through the list of options, the only one likely to pass these filters is option 8. (In practice, a second MBA student did a three-month project following up on the work of Desmond Tang. The project was cheap (under £2000, 1990 values), no-one at Jacksons felt that the temporary assignment of a student encroached on their territory, and everyone benefited from the recommendations.) Although this option was successfully implemented, there is no guarantee that the three-fold filter method will work well in other cases. In particular, there is another principle which we think is universal to general management.

You can't be nice to everyone all the time: decisions have to be taken that will hurt some people

Some managers try to avoid giving pain by postponing a critical decision — but they cannot escape responsibility so easily. Postponement (or the making of no decision) is a decision in itself and often not a very satisfactory one. (Would the Allies have won so easily if they had delayed the war against Saddam Hussein?)

Postponement does, however, introduce the element of time and it is possible to construct a synchronized strategy, a sequence of options which dovetailed into each other over time. If this is done we would lay down some fairly perverse guidelines as to which options should have precedence.

Don't put the easy-to-implement options first

If Sheila Jackson goes for the easy options, she is announcing to the world that she is scared of grasping nettles. There is also a tendency to dwell for an excessive period on these options in order to delay the day when more unpleasant tasks have to be undertaken (psychologists call this displacement activity).

Don't necessarily tackle the most urgent options first

What is so bad about a general manager giving priority to urgent problems? Well, look at the urgent problems which Sheila Jackson, or anyone in a similar position, *could* get involved in. Customers wishing to make urgent last minute changes to their orders; suppliers asking if she minded if a delivery was delayed; an employee in urgent need of a shoulder to cry on; an equipment salesman with an 'urgent offer that expires next week'. Now, it is true that there are certain general managers who glory in such activity (and they attract even more supplicants as an open jampot attracts wasps). In our view, these managers are in the wrong job. Much of this ad hoc activity should be delegated. How much attention should the British Prime Minister pay to the three sacks of mail that arrives at Downing Street every day, demanding his/her immediate personal intervention? Only by freeing him/herself from urgencies can the general manager assimilate, meditate, anticipate and plan. See 'Too Short the Day' case in the introductory chapter to Terry Hill's *Production/Operations Management*, 2nd edition (Prentice Hall, 1991) for a good example of a manager who cannot free himself from urgent problems to get round to strategy.

Avoid the push-down pop-up approach to problem solving

In matters of health, medicines solely aimed to relieve symptoms often cause the disease to pop up with a vengeance elsewhere. The same is true if a business organization's problems are tackled by a symptoms-only approach. The following are examples of push-down pop-up approaches which could foul up Jacksons:

- *Push-down*   Simon Wilson plays 'Mr Nasty' when suppliers try to unload offcut material on Jacksons.
  Pop-up   Suppliers will not do Jacksons any favours when they next have a delivery problem.

- *Push-down*   Jeff Smith is given the authority to let a favoured customer jump the queue.

| *Pop-up* | The altered production schedule means several other customers miss their delivery dates and they complain. |

- *Push-down*   Jacksons dismisses girls who refuse to do voluntary overtime and hire some new machinists who welcome it.

    Pop-up   Jacksons get an overtime-greedy workforce who hold up work during normal hours.

If you are in a push-down pop-up cycle of problems, this indicates that you have failed to tackle an underlying primary problem. If you succeed in finding it, and give it priority, it is easier to tackle a group or sequence of secondary problems afterwards. So, finding and prioritizing a primary problem is a key element towards an effective grand strategy of linked action.

For example, in the Jackson case, we would try to give priority to option 9, as we believe this tackles a primary issue. (Option 9 aims to free the firm of its dependence on Maisie for scheduling.) This is partly for reasons of contingency: if Maisie were to fall under a beer-lorry, the firm would be in a real mess. But just as importantly, option 9 is a gateway for staff development and education. Knowledge of scheduling spreads to more people in the workforce, enabling dialogue, feedback and teamwork to become possible when the following secondary issues are tackled in this order:

Option 6	Reducing manufacturing lead times
Option 11	Installing a JIT system
Option 10	Installing a software scheduling package

▼   **Quick exercise**

▲   Of the remaining options in exercise 3, can you find any other primary and secondary relationships?

Recommendations as to where Sheila Jackson should concentrate her effort

1. *Option 9:*   Establishing a social rapport with Maisie and reassuring her as to her future value and role in the firm before persuading her to explain to others how she schedules so well. Create a social reward system for Maisie so that she *wants* to evangelize, delegate and get everyone involved.

2. *Option 4:*   Break up the territories that have been carved out in 'sales', 'fitting', 'shopfloor', 'office' and 'design'. This will stretch Sheila's negotiating skills to the limit and will require intense human interaction with everyone involved. It could take a year before everyone settles down and Sheila should be prepared to face blackmail, sabotage and people

resigning, possibly setting up in opposition. If Sheila does not establish her authority, she will be 'the managed' and not 'the manager'.

All the other options can be delegated, sequenced or slotted around these two. But note this is our preferred solution for *this particular firm at this particular time for its own special situation*. If another, similar firm were faced with the same options there could be a different answer. This emphasizes that general management requires skill in discriminating between options as well as proficiency in carrying out an option.

12.2.4.5 Notes on exercise 4 — implementation via alliances

Put at its crudest, management can be summed up as:

What to do?   (choice), and
How to do it?   (implementation)

For *management tactics*, choice and implementation are hard to separate. Things are very different for *strategy*. Here, there is often a long, agonizing process of choice, followed by an equally long process of implementation (but requiring very different management skills from those required for choice). Some of the difficulties in implementation can be appreciated if we consider two different approaches:

1. *Implementation by dynamic intervention.* The general manager personally supervises, commands and controls what he or she wants done. This is commonly observed in a small business and appears to have been the style of the late Ernest Jackson. It could be a feasible style for a large business, but it is high-risk because it depends on the general manager maintaining his or her nervous energy and mental stability: this is not easy where he or she is expected to be frenetic, macho, domineering and impulsive. Such a manager also tends to have a bad effect on the psychological make-up of the employees: they tend to split into two camps with nobody in between.
    Camp (a). Those who are subdued and overwhelmed by fear, who will do anything they are told to do, but as unthinking robots.
    Camp (b). Those who react to pressure from their boss by a countervailing greater resistance (psychologists' force-field theory). Their resistance may not be open-defiance but is nevertheless effective via go-slows, sabotage and diversions.
2. *Implementations via subtle manipulation.* This approach does not try to subdue the 'prima donna' instinct that all of us possess (aggression fuelled by the search for personal power and independence). It allows people to build up territories and the authority to make decisions. Of course, such a system may lead to corruption, abuse of power and interdepartmental conflict. These bad effects are controlled not so much by direct intervention but by indirect manipulation of the shifting web of *alliances* which make up such organizations (in other words by diplomacy). This can be illustrated by an analysis of the principal alliances that currently exist at Jacksons.

Sheila Jackson and Gerry Richards

This is a loose-knit alliance maintained more for historical and personal reasons than for strong mutual benefits. Either could pack in the alliance without losing out too much. As such, the relationship is mature, neither party being upset if they are not supported by the other.

Simon Wilson and John Fletcher

A typical short-term expedient alliance to secure new machinery (for their own different reasons), after which the alliance will weaken. The alliance is only of moderate strength as both have other irons in the fire.

Sheila Jackson and Simon Wilson

A protective alliance (Sheila nurturing Simon, hoping for long-term benefits to the firm). However, others have misperceptions (Maisie, Margaret) and view the alliance as pushy Simon dominating weak Sheila.

Lucy Todd and Simon Wilson

A delusionary alliance. Lucy thinks she's in an alliance; Simon doesn't. This could mislead Lucy in her stance against her enemies. However, Lucy and Simon have a good no-holds-barred *working relationship*.

Jeff Smith and his customer contacts

An alliance dangerous to Sheila because if Jeff leaves, he claims many customers will leave too. Sheila could investigate legal remedies to stop this happening but the law is slow, expensive and uncertain. It could be that Jeff has no intention of leaving but is blustering to stop Sheila messing him around. If this is so, an empathetic Sheila will propose deals that will save Jeff's face but reduce his stranglehold on the firm. Whether Jeff is going to leave or not, Sheila needs to negotiate with Alex (the other salesman) and commission agents whom she might employ.

Lucy Todd and her customer contacts

This alliance is, potentially, even more dangerous to Sheila because Lucy has reached a stage in her life where she is wondering whether to set up on her own — she has the customers, she has the technical knowledge, she could build up a devoted workforce of machinists, and she has the drive. The only thing that is stopping her is, probably, finding premises, borrowing the money to start and the uncertain business climate. If Sheila wants Lucy, she'll need to offer her some big incentives (not necessarily cash) to stay.

The six fitters

This is a tightly bonded defensive alliance: not surprising as the men work together off the firm's premises gaining the same rewards. Although Sheila may wish to break up this alliance, it would be a mistake to do this precipitatively. The men appear to be doing quite a good job and it would be difficult immediately to find subcontractors to reach the necessary quality. If what they really want is more work, Sheila needs to persuade Lucy to give the fitters some of her contract work (a difficult extended diplomatic task).

Norman Shields and the machinists

This is an alliance that has not really got off the ground. The machinists like him and he likes them but you need more than friendship to operate a successful alliance. When Lucy tells Norman to get lost, the girls take Lucy's side.

What can we conclude from these thumbnail pictures? If Sheila Jackson is to be a successful manipulative manager, she should aim to create an atmosphere in which positive alliances flourish and negative alliances decay. Briefly, what we mean by such alliances is as follows:

Positive alliances
- Benefit Jacksons without being told to do so.
- Give an incentive for key staff members to stay with the firm.
- Provide informal support for training, communication and motivation.

Negative alliances
- Filch business and resources away from Jacksons.
- Undermine good employees, protect bad employees.
- Encourages jealousy and 'dog in the manger' behaviour.

In general, Sheila needs to encourage interdepartmental alliances. It may be that she is already doing this via her design-skill workshops in the manager's office (note that she does not take part herself: a subtle aspect of good manipulation). Another innovation would be to have a mixed team of machinists, fitters and clerical staff having the authority to deal with all stages of a big contract order, rather than it being left in the hands of a single salesman or progress chaser.

Alliances with external forces

As well as fostering good alliances internal to the firm, a general manager has the prime duty of establishing alliances with a variety of external stakeholders.

External diplomatic activity can be neatly summarized via the well-known model of competitive strategy developed by Michael Porter. The same model can be viewed in three different ways, depending on the general manager's state of mind (see Figures 12.4, 12.5 and 12.6).

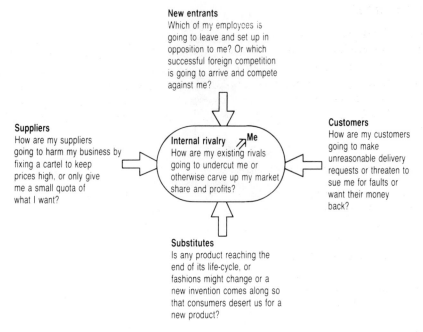

Figure 12.4 'Paranoic' Porter analysis.

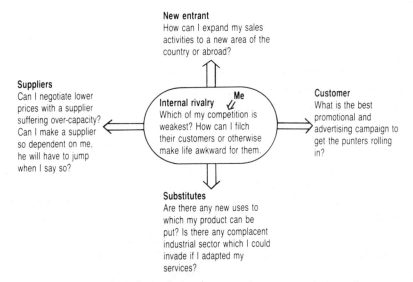

Figure 12.5 'Predatory' Porter analysis.

Of the three illustrations we would recommend Sheila to adopt the 'progressive' mindset. This implies embarking on major diplomatic initiatives. Accepting the challenge, she must be prepared for times when she will be locked into intense negotiations, leaving little time for other management duties. If this is so, she must

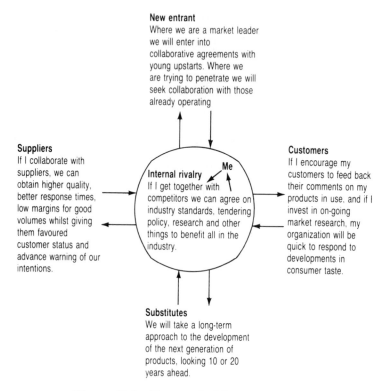

New entrant
Where we are a market leader
we will enter into
collaborative agreements with
young upstarts. Where we
are trying to penetrate we will
seek collaboration with those
already operating

Suppliers
If I collaborate with
suppliers, we can
obtain higher quality,
better response times,
low margins for good
volumes whilst giving
them favoured
customer status and
advance warning of our
intentions.

Internal rivalry　　**Me**
If I get together with
competitors we can agree on
industry standards, tendering
policy, research and other
things to benefit all in the
industry.

Customers
If I encourage my
customers to feed back
their comments on my
products in use, and if I
invest in on-going
market research, my
organization will be
quick to respond to
developments in
consumer taste.

Substitutes
We will take a long-term
approach to the development
of the next generation of
products, looking 10 or 20
years ahead.

Figure 12.6　'Progressive' Porter analysis.

anticipate her workload carefully, bearing in mind Glueck's maxim: 'only do one important thing at a time'. Also, it helps if diplomatic activity is undertaken by a team, for two reasons:

1. Where employees are 'turned around', spending more time negotiating with outsiders, less time is spent on internal bickering and more team spirit results.
2. Some outsiders can be softened up better for a deal if they are hit by different people with different attitudes from different directions (somewhat analogous to the criminal who is interrogated in turn by PC Nasty and PC Nice). Thus, if Simon (quite rightly) is being nasty to suppliers in refusing offcuts, it helps if simultaneously, Sheila approaches the suppliers offering to give more forward, more regular orders. Sheila should adopt a reverse position with some of the individual customers. Here, Jeff Smith has been playing Mr Nice, offering too-favourable discounts. Sheila somehow has to indicate to the customers that these discounts are not repeatable unless the customer in its turn can make some concessions (so in this case, Sheila plays Mrs Tough).

Concluding comments on implementing via alliances

Implementing via alliances has been a neglected area of operations management, but we feel it has central and widespread relevance. Of course, it was uppermost in the mind of military strategists (the outcome of nearly all great wars has depended on who joins the alliance rather than on fighting skills). Alliances are also an implicit foundation for many of the 'conclusions' in classic management theory. For example:

- Frederick Taylor developed his ingot-loading experiments in an attempt to demolish the alliance of lazy Hungarian immigrants (his view) whom, he felt, had a stranglehold on loading operations. He later gained fame as a result of his experiments, but in practical terms his work was a disaster as he had no friends amongst either the managers or the workers (apart from Schmidt).
- Elton Mayo's Hawthorne experiments highlighted supervisor–employee alliances but came to disputable (probably erroneous) conclusions, still echoed in most management textbooks. (In the small group put under intensive study, two 'troublemakers' were excluded halfway through the experiments.)

Nowadays, the issue of progressive alliances is becoming more prominent because this is a key feature of Japanese management practices, as we have indicated at various points in this book.

Follow-up exercises

So far in this chapter we have strung together rather a lengthy argument because we wanted to show how tactics, strategy and diplomacy all contribute in a rather complex way to general management. Now it is time to have a break and to see whether observation and experiment confirm or refute the general drift of our argument. Exercises 5–8 attempt to put in a broader perspective the problems tackled earlier in exercises 1–4.

▼ **Exercise 5 — tactical skills and how they can be linked to form a strategy**

We mentioned chess as an example of where tactical skills are distinct from strategic skills. Make this distinction for one of these sports: football; cricket; rugby; hockey; basketball. How do tactical elements combine to make up a
▲ strategy?

▼ **Exercise 5 — alternative**

(This is for historians and armchair military experts) Refer to a biography of Hernando Cortes or Napoleon Bonaparte or Adolf Hitler. How were their (and their opponents') successes and failures affected by strengths and
▲ weaknesses in tactics, strategy and diplomacy?

▼   **Exercise 6 — designing an overall management development strategy**

Look at the members of a major political party in your country. How would
you position them on our human resources BCG matrix (including the arrows
indicating the degree of uncertainty about your judgement)? Looking at the
complete pattern of placements, what implications does the pattern have for
▲   that party's management development and teamwork potential?

▼   **Exercise 7 — deriving a successful strategy by focusing on a primary
      problem**

Set out the variety of options that have been tried (or have been proposed) to
tackle the long-standing problems listed below. Why are these problems still
with us? Within each problem, what do you think are symptoms and what do
you think are root causes?

       Football hooliganism
       Holiday traffic jams
       High levels of crime
▲   Inadequate railway services

▼   **Exercise 8 — alliances: how they act as barriers or breakthroughs for
      implementation**

Choose one of the following of which you have good knowledge:

       A university or college
       A hospital
       A local authority
       A religious society

Look at your chosen organization's attitude to external stakeholders and give
your opinion as to whether it is paranoic, predatory or progressive (as defined
by our Porter analysis). Back up your opinion by describing your organization's attitude to suppliers, customers, new entrants, substitutes and rivals
(just a few sentences for each of these five categories). Comment on the
likelihood of your organization being able to change its attitude and what
▲   diplomatic activity this will involve.

12.3 World-class manufacturing strategies

As we have indicated throughout this book, managers in the US and Europe have been
working hard to determine the key factors which led to the success of Japanese
companies. Over the past twenty years the Japanese competitive advantage has been
quality, dependability and productivity in a mass-production environment. Japanese

manufacturers have unashamedly emphasized manufacturing and engineering in their corporate strategies, whilst in the West, both manufacturing and engineering have found themselves the poor relations of the boardroom. The Japanese have committed themselves to continuous improvement in quality, technology and, especially since the 1973 oil crisis, to the elimination of waste in respect of all resources, not merely the physical ones. The list of companies following this road seems endless: Toyota, Toshiba, Canon, Mitsui Bank, Richol and Nissan are just a few companies that have adopted the *kaizen* (continuous improvement) philosophy, with perfection or zero defects as the ultimate goal.

Furthermore, the Japanese have made major capital investment to boost workforce productivity, employing the focused factory concept widely. The objective of flexibility with low cost has been brought about by many small steps introduced company-wide. To an outside observer, the nature of improvement can be obscured by a thick alphabet-soup of acronyms: TQC, JIT, TPM, MRP, CAD, FMS, CAM. Let us take just the most prominent of these, the JIT (just-in-time) approach.

Originally, JIT was visualized as quite a narrow subject, implemented by one person (Taiichi Ohno), in one profession (industrial engineering), in one area (reducing work-in-progress), at one firm (Toyota), in one country (Japan). Now, though, the ramifications of JIT are enormous: it would be more appropriate to rename JIT 'Japan's industrial transformation' (and not just Japan, the net is so wide). What was originally regarded as a technique applicable to quite a boring, dead-end subject (stock control) is now seen as central to topics of business culture, strategy and philosophy.

The ramifications of JIT can be seen from the increasing space given to it in operations management textbooks. Our book is no exception, and its influence has pervaded every chapter:

Chapter 2 (product)	On product performance taking priority over product specification
Chapter 3 (machines)	On attacking what were thought of as inviolable constraints, particularly set-up times
Chapter 4 (people)	On all aspects relating to culture and teamwork
Chapter 5 (materials)	On the much greater, intimate relationship with suppliers
Chapter 6 (systems)	On the identification of waste in a push-type system and how to reform it
Chapter 7 (quality)	On the parallel and overlapping aspects of total quality management (TQM) with JIT
Chapter 8 (forecasting)	On how arranging schedules further into the future can improve the current operating system
Chapter 9 (project planning)	On the 'keep it simple' philosophy implicit in both JIT and work breakdown schedules

| Chapters 10 and 11 (scheduling) | Convey many of the finer numerical techniques associated with JIT |
| Chapter 12 (general management) | On how JIT philosophy has a profound effect on long-term business development and carrying through change |

Many of the techniques associated with JIT are deceptively simple and (with hindsight) blatantly obvious: but it must be emphasized that any organization introducing JIT principles cannot expect overnight success. If there are lessons to be had from Japan's experience, it is that intelligence must be allied to patience, and that the social culture of the organization and of a nation is a critical factor as to whether JIT succeeds or fails.

A stable political situation with a supportive government has certainly contributed to the success of Japanese industry. Education has been geared to promoting industry and particular emphasis has been placed on engineering education. However, the competitive environment is changing as the globalization of business activity continues unabated and the newly industrialized countries (NICs) become forces to be reckoned with.

Changes are also taking place within Japan. The Japanese home market is now mature and the country is predicting relatively low economic growth. Much has been made in the past of the in-built Japanese work ethic and the influence of 'jobs for life' on the motivation of the workforce, but now attitudes are changing. The present generation of Japanese students are becoming more like their Western counterparts than their parents; they are individuals with their own ideas. The homogeneity of these people, long regarded as a major factor in developing corporate commitment is disappearing. Will this increase creativity? If so, how can Japan maintain its competitive advantage?

Certainly, 'catch-up' is no longer a possible strategy. That has been achieved. The Japanese are now on the receiving end of the NIC's catch-up strategies. This is neatly illustrated by an article in the *Malnichi Daily News*, which reported that:

> Taiwanese cast-aluminium garden chairs thought to be imitations of those developed by a Saltama [Japanese] based foundry were sold recently at a special sale sponsored by a major supermarket featuring products from NICs.

The Japanese foundry, Jusco, had invested some 30 million yen developing the chair, which formed some 40 per cent of annual turnover. Such unwelcome and, as Jusco claimed, unfair competition new to Japanese companies, illustrates the changing environment in which those companies are now operating.

So what should Japanese industry do in the face of these changes? Four options have emerged. A first option is to 'stick to the knitting' — to develop automated manufacturing systems based on existing know-how. To achieve competitive advantage here, low prices would need to be the selling point, and this would almost inevitably involve moving to offshore manufacturing.

We have already seen that flexibility has contributed to Japanese success. A second option is to take advantage of this flexibility know-how to develop a reactive strategy, to handle volume changes and product-mix changes, and to adopt new technologies rapidly and efficiently.

Thirdly, and more adventurously, Japanese manufacturers could shift to become innovators of new products or technologies, products which do not compete on price, relying on the freer-thinking, younger generation to provide the necessary creative drive.

A fourth, more worrying option has emerged from a research project carried out at Waseda University, Tokyo, the aim of which is to design a new manufacturing strategy for Japan for the twenty-first century. Professor Nakane has suggested the possibility of developing 'a new multinational management system to cope with the globalization of business'. Quite what this would entail is a little unclear, but such phrases as 'leadership by aggressive innovators' and a 'breakdown of corporate bureaucracy' are being used by Professor Nakane. Whatever the route chosen, it is clear that Western companies will soon be fighting a new battle, with new rules. We believe that the following will be the critical attributes which will give companies a competitive edge:

1. A positive attitude to problems.
2. A flexible organization.
3. An ability to respond quickly to challenges.

Postscript. Just as the West has found difficulty in adopting Japanese approaches, it is evident that in all those newly-free countries of the former Soviet bloc, there will be more to economic success than adopting Western machinery, Western techniques and Western finance. Old practices, perceptions, habits and laws cannot be killed stone dead by a management or any other type of revolution. You must expect the old culture to co-exist and struggle with the new culture for perhaps a generation or more.

12.4 In conclusion

Having moved onto issues of grand strategy and world-class manufacturing in this chapter, we hope we have not turned you into yet another armchair strategist. The whole philosophy of this book has been to go out, find out, and try things. We hope you will pursue your interest in operations management not only by reading but by direct contact with managers. Theory and practice go hand-in-hand.

12.5 Recommended reading

Cases
Start with Nicholson's 'Micronair' in *Managing Manufacturing Operations* (Macmillan, 1978) to identify why an apparently strong manager is losing control. Then try Sasser's 'Sunshine

Builders' in *Cases in Operations Management: Analysis and Action* (Irwin, 1982), which integrates quality, people and project planning and is an excellent test to give people at the end of an operations management course. Sasser's 'Kalamazoo' and 'Sedalia' cases in the same book bring out the strategy/alliances issues. Voss *et al.*'s 'Chicago Pizza Pie Factory' case in *Operations Management in the Service Industries and the Public Sector* (Wiley, 1985) highlights the interaction between strategy, tactics and management style.

Books

On strategy and alliances, and for sheer unalloyed pleasure, read *The Carpetmakers* by R. Jones and C. Lakin (McGraw-Hill, 1978). On strategy, a book with many excellent short cases and illustrations with fully backed-up explanations is G. Johnson and K. Scholes, *Exploring Corporate Strategy: Text and Cases* (Prentice Hall, 1989).

Index